Life On the Mississippi

A Vivid Memoir of Adventure, Culture & the Changing Tides of the American River

A Modern Translation
Adapted for the Contemporary Reader

MARK TWAIN

Translated by Tim Zengerink

Table of Contents

Preface
Message to the Reader

Rebuilding the Greatest Library in Human History

Thousands of years ago, the Library of Alexandria was the heart of global knowledge — a sanctuary where the wisdom of every known civilization was gathered and shared freely.

And then, it was lost.

Now, we're rebuilding it — and you are invited to join us.

At the Library of Alexandria, we've set out to make every book available to every person on Earth — not just in print, but in every language, every format, and for every reader.

Here's how we do it:

- **Deluxe Print Editions at True Printing Cost** - Order any book as a high-quality paperback, elegant hardcover, or stunning boxset — and only pay what it costs to print. No markups. No middlemen.
- **Unlimited Access to the Greatest Works** - Enjoy thousands of timeless classics — from Plato to Shakespeare to Tolstoy — in beautiful, modern eBook and audiobook editions. Read and listen without limits — for every reader, everywhere.
- **Modern Translations for Every Language & Dialect** - We're reimagining the classics in clear, accessible language — and translating them into every dialect imaginable. Everyone deserves to understand humanity's greatest ideas.

When you visit **LibraryofAlexandria.com**, you're not just accessing books — you're joining a global movement to restore, preserve, and share the wisdom of civilization.

Join us today at LibraryofAlexandria.com

Together, we'll ensure the light of human wisdom never fades again.

With gratitude,

The Modern Library of Alexandria Team

Visit:
www.libraryofalexandria.com
Or scan the code below:

Introduction to *Life on the Mississippi*

The River That Shaped a Nation and a Writer

Life on the Mississippi is more than a memoir, more than travel writing, and more than a love letter to the American South—it is one of Mark Twain's most ambitious and enduring works, a sprawling narrative that fuses autobiography, satire, history, and cultural commentary into a vibrant portrait of a rapidly changing America. First published in 1883, the book chronicles Twain's youthful experiences as a steamboat pilot on the Mississippi River before the Civil War, his return to the river decades later, and his reflections on what had been lost, gained, and forever altered along the way.

At its surface, the book is a journey—both literal and symbolic. Twain first guides the reader back to his teenage years in the 1850s when he became apprenticed to a riverboat pilot and learned the intricate, life-or-death art of navigating the twisting waters of the Mississippi. With vivid prose and humor, he recounts the rituals, rivalries, and personalities of the steamboat culture: the fierce pride of pilots, the omnipresent dangers of submerged logs and shifting currents, the unspoken codes that governed the river. This portion of the narrative offers some of the richest firsthand accounts we have of life before the Civil War in the river towns of Missouri, Illinois, Louisiana, and Mississippi.

But *Life on the Mississippi* is far from a nostalgic ode. Twain is too sharp, too self-aware, and too honest to allow sentimentality to cloud his judgment. In the second half of the book, he recounts a return journey down the river, now as a successful and famous author revisiting the haunts of his youth. What he finds is a world transformed. The steamboat era has faded, replaced by railroads and modern commerce. The frontier spirit has given way to industrial pragmatism. The towns have changed, the river has changed—and Twain has changed, too.

This structure—half youthful memoir, half mature reflection—gives *Life on the Mississippi* its profound power. Twain invites us to see the river not just as a physical place but as a metaphor for America itself: ever-flowing, unpredictable, sometimes violent, sometimes serene. His genius lies in capturing both the romance and the reality of river life, the exhilaration of youth and the melancholy of time's passing, the comedy of human folly and the tragedy of historical blindness.

Indeed, Life on the Mississippi is not merely personal. It is a cultural artifact that captures the tensions of a nation in transition. Twain writes with wit and irony about slavery, race, politics, class, and the myths Americans tell themselves about progress. His prose dances between reverence and ridicule, documentary precision and tall-tale exaggeration. Through it all, the Mississippi River becomes a character in its own right—an ancient, restless force shaping the land, the people, and the writer who loved it.

Apprenticeship, Memory, and the Invention of an American Voice

Much of *Life on the Mississippi* revolves around Twain's training to become a river pilot—a process he renders with astonishing detail and drama. In no other book do we see so clearly Twain's fascination with craft, skill, and the complexities of real-world knowledge. Being a pilot wasn't just a job—it was a discipline that required memory, intuition, courage, and a near-spiritual understanding of the river's moods. Every bend, bar, and bluff had to be memorized. A mistake could mean disaster. It was, Twain says, a profession that demanded nothing less than total mastery of an ever-changing environment.

These passages do more than educate—they reveal the making

of a writer. The young Samuel Clemens (Twain's real name) absorbed not only the physical landscape but also the social, linguistic, and emotional textures of river life. He developed an ear for dialects, an eye for hypocrisy, and a nose for absurdity. The river taught him how to observe. It also taught him humility, patience, and the limits of knowledge—lessons that would later shape his fiction.

It's important to recognize how deeply *Life on the Mississippi* informs Twain's most famous works. Without this book, there would be no Adventures of Huckleberry Finn—or at least not the same one. The river, as both symbol and setting, plays a central role in Huck's story, just as it does in Twain's own. The theme of travel as moral education, the contrast between appearance and reality, the voices of the marginalized and the misunderstood—all find their roots in this memoir.

Yet Twain is not interested in heroic self-presentation. He consistently undermines his younger self with irony and humor. He admits his arrogance, his ignorance, his many mistakes. He mocks his own illusions. This self-deprecating honesty gives the book its charm and credibility. Twain invites us not just to admire his story, but to laugh at it—and with him.

But this laughter is never simple. As he looks back, Twain also mourns what has been lost: a way of life, a sense of wonder, a landscape unscarred by industry and greed. His memory is both affectionate and critical, warm and unsparing. This duality—nostalgia tempered by realism—is one of the book's great achievements. It reminds us that growth often comes with cost, and that memory is never free from the weight of history.

Empire of the River:
Industry, Irony, and the Myth of Progress

In the second half of *Life on the Mississippi*, Twain becomes a traveler and observer, moving through cities and towns along the river's length. Here, the tone shifts. The magic of his boyhood river gives way to the ironies of modernization. Steamboats have lost their dominance. The once-bustling river towns have become tourist stops or waypoints for commerce. Twain visits old friends, revisits old landscapes, and offers commentary on the changing face of American life.

He remains deeply entertaining throughout—telling jokes, recounting odd characters, and describing strange events. But beneath the humor is a sharp critique of American self-congratulation. Twain is deeply skeptical of the national myth of progress. He sees the destruction of natural beauty, the exploitation of workers, and the persistence of social inequalities masked by patriotic rhetoric and technological advancement.

Twain also reflects on the legacy of slavery and the ongoing racial dynamics of the postbellum South. Though he never offers a systematic analysis, his observations are pointed and often devastating. He mocks the romanticism of the "Old South," challenges the assumptions of white superiority, and highlights the contradictions of a nation that claims freedom while practicing exclusion. His irony becomes a moral tool, exposing the gap between ideals and reality.

And yet, for all his criticism, Twain never turns bitter. He remains curious, engaged, and attentive. He sees America with all its contradictions—not to condemn it entirely, but to understand it more fully. In doing so, he expands the possibilities of American literature. *Life on the Mississippi* blends genres, tones, and perspectives in ways that prefigure modern narrative nonfiction. It is personal and political, comic and tragic, descriptive and philosophical.

By the book's end, the river remains—as it always has—indifferent, immense, and awe-inspiring. It outlasts the steamboats, the towns, the people. It flows through history, memory, and imagination. Twain does not try to tame it or define it. Instead, he honors its mystery.

In *Life on the Mississippi*, Twain gives us more than a memoir. He gives us an origin story—for himself, for his fiction, and for a vision of America that remains as vital, conflicted, and compelling as the river itself. This book is a journey, a reckoning, a eulogy, and a celebration. It teaches us to look closely, listen carefully, and never mistake the surface for the whole. And as Twain reminds us again and again, the current never stops. The river flows on.

The 'Body of The Nation'

The Mississippi basin represents the heart of our nation. All other regions serve as vital parts, significant on their own but even more crucial in how they connect to this central area. Not counting the Lake basin and the 300,000 square miles in Texas and New Mexico that in many ways belong to it, this basin covers approximately 1,250,000 square miles. In size, it ranks as the world's second largest valley, surpassed only by the Amazon. The valley of the frozen Ob River comes close to matching its size; the La Plata valley follows in area and likely in livable space, containing about eight-ninths of its territory; next comes the Yenisei valley with roughly seven-ninths; the Lena, Amur, Yellow River, Yangtze River, and Nile each cover about five-ninths; the Ganges spans less than half; the Indus covers less than one-third; the Euphrates occupies one-fifth; the Rhine takes up one-fifteenth. It surpasses the entire area of Europe, excluding Russia, Norway, and Sweden. It could hold Austria four times over, Germany or Spain five times, France six times, the British Isles or Italy ten times. Ideas we form based on the river basins of Western Europe get completely overwhelmed when we examine the scope of the Mississippi valley; nor do concepts drawn from the barren basins of Siberia's great rivers, the high plateaus of Central Asia, or the vast expanse of the swampy Amazon prove any more suitable for comparison. Climate, altitude, and precipitation all work together to make every section of the Mississippi Valley able to sustain a large population. As a home for civilized people, it stands unmatched anywhere on Earth.

EDITOR'S TABLE, HARPER'S MAGAZINE,
FEBRUARY 1863

Chapter 1: The River and Its History

The Mississippi River deserves serious attention and study. This is no ordinary waterway, but rather an extraordinary river in every possible way. When we consider the Missouri River as its primary tributary, the Mississippi becomes the longest river on Earth, stretching four thousand three hundred miles. We can confidently claim it's also the most winding river anywhere, given that along one section of its course, it meanders through one thousand three hundred miles to traverse territory that a crow could cross in just six hundred and seventy-five miles of direct flight. The river releases three times the volume of water that flows through the St. Lawrence, twenty-five times more than the Rhine, and an astounding three hundred and thirty-eight times more than the Thames. No other river system commands such an enormous drainage area: it collects water from twenty-eight states and territories, stretching from Delaware on the Atlantic coast all the way to Idaho on the Pacific side—spanning forty-five degrees of longitude. The Mississippi gathers and transports to the Gulf waters from fifty-four smaller rivers that can accommodate steamboat traffic, plus hundreds more that support flat-bottomed boats and keelboats. Its drainage basin covers an area equal to England, Wales, Scotland, Ireland, France, Spain, Portugal, Germany, Austria, Italy, and Turkey combined; nearly this entire vast region consists of fertile land, with the Mississippi valley itself being particularly rich and productive.

This river stands out for an unusual characteristic: rather than becoming wider as it approaches its mouth, it actually becomes narrower while growing deeper. From where the Ohio River joins it to a point halfway to the sea, the river averages about a mile wide during high water periods. From that point to the sea, the width continuously decreases until it reaches the 'Passes' above the mouth, where it measures just slightly more than half a mile across. Where the Ohio River meets the Mississippi, the depth measures eighty-seven feet, and this depth gradually increases, reaching one hundred and twenty-nine feet just above the mouth.

The variation in water levels between high and low periods is also striking—not in the upper section, but in the lower portion of the river. The water level increase remains fairly consistent all the way down to Natchez (three hundred and sixty miles upstream from the mouth)—approximately fifty feet. However, at Bayou La Fourche the river rises only twenty-four feet; at New Orleans it rises merely fifteen feet, and just upstream from the mouth it rises only two and one half feet.

An article in the New Orleans 'Times-Democrat,' drawing from reports by skilled engineers, reveals that the river dumps four hundred and six million tons of mud into the Gulf of Mexico each year—which recalls Captain Marryat's crude nickname for the Mississippi—'the Great Sewer.' If this mud were compressed into solid form, it would create a mass measuring one mile square and two hundred and forty-one feet in height.

The mud deposits slowly expand the land—but the process is gradual; the river has extended it by less than a third of a mile during the two hundred years that have passed since it became part of recorded history. Scientists believe that the river's mouth was once located at Baton Rouge, where the hills end, and that the river created the two hundred miles of land stretching from there to the Gulf. This allows us to determine the age of that region quite easily—one hundred and twenty thousand years. Even so, it represents the youngest section of land in that entire area.

The Mississippi River is extraordinary in yet another way—its tendency to make enormous leaps by cutting through narrow strips of land, thereby straightening and shortening its course. On multiple occasions, it has reduced its length by thirty miles in a single leap! These shortcuts have produced fascinating consequences: they have left several river towns stranded in rural areas, while creating sandbars and forests in front of them. The town of Delta was once located three miles downstream from Vicksburg: a recent shortcut has dramatically altered the geography, and Delta now sits two miles upstream from Vicksburg.

Both of these river towns have been forced into rural isolation because of that cut-off. A cut-off wreaks havoc on boundary lines and legal jurisdictions: for example, a man lives in the State of Mississippi today, a cut-off happens tonight, and tomorrow the man discovers himself and his property on the opposite side of the river, now within the boundaries and under the authority of Louisiana state law! Such an event, occurring in the upper river during earlier times, could have moved a slave from Missouri to Illinois and transformed him into a free man.

The Mississippi River doesn't change its location through cut-offs alone: it constantly shifts its entire course—always moving its whole body sideways. At Hard Times, Louisiana, the river now flows two miles west of where it used to run. Because of this shift, the original location of that settlement is no longer in Louisiana at all, but sits on the opposite side of the river, in Mississippi. Almost all of those one thousand three hundred miles of the old Mississippi River that La Salle navigated in his canoes two hundred years ago is now solid, dry land. The river flows to the right of it in some places, and to the left of it in others.

Although the Mississippi River's mud builds land slowly down at its mouth, where the Gulf's waves interfere with its work, it builds much faster in better protected areas upstream: for example, Prophet's Island contained fifteen hundred acres of land thirty years ago, and since then the river has added seven hundred acres to it.

But I've shared enough examples of the great river's peculiar behaviors for now—I'll provide several more of them later in the book.

Let us set aside the Mississippi's physical history and discuss its historical development instead. We can take a quick look at its sleepy early period in a few short chapters; examine its second, more active era in a couple more; explore its most vibrant and bustling period in many following chapters; and then discuss its relatively peaceful current era in the remaining portion of the book.

The world and books have become so used to applying, and overusing, the word 'new' when describing our country that we develop and keep the lasting belief that nothing about it is old. We certainly understand that American history contains several relatively old dates, but the numbers alone don't give our minds a proper understanding or clear sense of the actual time span they represent. When we say that De Soto, the first white person to see the Mississippi River, witnessed it in 1542, we're making a statement that presents a fact without explaining its meaning: this resembles describing a sunset's size through astronomical measurements and listing its colors by their scientific names—the outcome is that you obtain the basic fact of the sunset, but you don't actually experience the sunset. Creating a painting of it would have been more effective.

The year 1542, by itself, doesn't mean much to us; but when we group some related historical dates and facts around it, we gain perspective and depth, and then we understand that this is one of the American dates that is quite impressive in terms of age.

For instance, when a white man first laid eyes on the Mississippi, less than twenty-five years had passed since Francis I suffered defeat at Pavia; since Raphael died; since the death of Bayard, Sans Peur Et Sans Reproche; since the Turks expelled the Knights-Hospitallers from Rhodes; and since the posting of the Ninety-Five Propositions the action that launched the Reformation. When De Soto caught his first sight of the river, Ignatius Loyola remained an unknown figure; the Jesuit order hadn't yet reached its first anniversary; Michelangelo's paint was still fresh on the Last Judgment in the Sistine Chapel; Mary Queen of Scots hadn't been born yet, though she would arrive before the year ended. Catherine de Medici was still a child; Elizabeth of England hadn't yet entered her teenage years; Calvin, Benvenuto Cellini, and Emperor Charles V had reached the height of their renown, each shaping history in his own distinctive way; Margaret of Navarre was composing the 'Heptameron' and several religious works—the first endures while the others have been forgotten, since wit and impropriety sometimes preserve literature better than piety; loose court morals and the ridiculous chivalry tradition flourished in full glory, and jousts and tournaments provided regular entertainment for noble gentlemen who fought more skillfully than they could write, while religion consumed their wives' devotion, and categorizing their children into those of legitimate status and those recognized by favor occupied their leisure time.

In fact, everywhere around them, religion was experiencing an unusually flourishing period: the Council of Trent was being convened; the Spanish Inquisition was torturing, stretching on the rack, and burning people with complete freedom; across other parts of the continent, nations were being convinced to live holy lives through the sword and fire; in England, Henry VIII had shut down the monasteries, burned Fisher and a couple of other bishops, and was successfully launching both his English reformation and his collection of wives. When De Soto stood on the shores of the Mississippi, Luther still had two years left to live; eleven years would pass before Servetus would be burned at the stake; thirty years would go by before the St. Bartholomew's Day massacre; Rabelais had not yet been published; 'Don Quixote' had not yet been written; Shakespeare had not yet been born; a full hundred years would still need to pass before Englishmen would first hear the name of Oliver Cromwell.

Without a doubt, the discovery of the Mississippi River is a documented historical event that significantly softens and tempers the gleaming freshness of our nation, lending it a highly respectable outward appearance of age and ancient heritage.

De Soto only caught a brief glimpse of the river before he died and was buried in its waters by his priests and soldiers. You would expect the priests and soldiers to exaggerate the river's size by ten times—which was the Spanish habit of that era—and thereby inspire other adventurers to immediately go and explore it. Instead, their accounts when they returned home failed to generate that level of interest. The Mississippi remained unvisited by white people for a period of time that seems unbelievable by today's standards of energy and enterprise. You can get a sense of this time span by breaking it down this way: After De Soto glimpsed the river, just under twenty-five years passed, and then Shakespeare was born; he lived slightly more than fifty years, then died; and when he had been dead for well over fifty years, the second white man laid eyes on the Mississippi. In our time we wouldn't let one hundred and thirty years pass between sightings of such a wonder. If someone were to discover a creek in the county next to where the North Pole is located, Europe and America would launch fifteen expensive expeditions there: one to explore the creek, and the other fourteen to search for each other.

For more than one hundred and fifty years, white settlements had existed along our Atlantic coastlines. These settlers maintained close contact with the Native Americans: in the southern regions, the Spanish were stealing from them, killing them, enslaving them, and forcing them to convert to Christianity; further north, the English were exchanging beads and blankets with them for various goods, while also providing civilization and whiskey as extras; and in Canada, the French were giving them basic education, sending missionaries to work among them, and bringing entire groups of them to Quebec, and later to Montreal, to purchase furs from them. It was inevitable, therefore, that these different groups of white settlers would have learned about the great river of the far west; and they did indeed hear about it in a vague way—so unclear and imprecise that its path, size, and location could barely be guessed. The sheer mystery surrounding this matter should have sparked curiosity and driven exploration; but this didn't happen. It seems that no one particularly wanted such a river, no one had a use for it, and no one felt curious enough to investigate it; so, for a century and a half, the Mississippi stayed off the radar and remained untouched. When De Soto discovered it, he wasn't searching for a river and had no immediate need for one; as a result, he didn't consider it valuable or pay much attention to it.

But eventually La Salle the Frenchman came up with the idea of finding that river and exploring it. It always occurs that when someone takes hold of an overlooked yet significant idea, people fired up with the same concept appear everywhere around them. This is exactly what happened in this case.

Naturally, the question arises: Why did these people suddenly want the river when no one had shown interest in it during the previous five generations? The answer seems to be that they finally believed they had found a way to make it valuable. People had come to think that the Mississippi River flowed into the Gulf of California, which would provide a direct route from Canada to China. Before this, everyone had assumed the river emptied into the Atlantic Ocean, also known as the Sea of Virginia.

Chapter 2: The River and Its Explorers

LA SALLE personally petitioned for certain important privileges, and Louis XIV graciously granted them to him. The most significant of these was the right to explore extensively, construct forts, claim entire continents, and transfer ownership to the king, while covering all expenses from his own pocket. In exchange, he would receive various small benefits, including exclusive rights to trade buffalo hides. He invested several years and nearly all his wealth making dangerous and grueling journeys between Montreal and a fort he had established on the Illinois River, before finally managing to organize his expedition well enough to head toward the Mississippi.

Meanwhile, other groups had enjoyed greater success. In 1673, Joliet the merchant and Marquette the priest traveled across the territory and arrived at the shores of the Mississippi River. They journeyed through the Great Lakes, and from Green Bay they paddled in canoes along the Fox River and the Wisconsin River. Marquette had made a sacred promise on the feast of the Immaculate Conception that if the Virgin Mary would allow him to find the great river, he would call it Conception in her honor. He honored his commitment. During that era, all explorers brought priests along on their journeys. De Soto traveled with twenty-four priests accompanying him. La Salle also brought several priests with him. The expeditions frequently ran short of food and lacked adequate clothing, but they always carried the ceremonial items and other necessities required for celebrating mass; they were always ready, as one of the colorful historians of that period expressed it, to 'explain hell to the savages.'

On June 17, 1673, the canoes carrying Joliet and Marquette along with their five companions arrived at the point where the Wisconsin River meets the Mississippi. Mr. Parkman describes the scene: 'Before them a wide and rapid current coursed athwart their way, by the foot of lofty heights wrapped thick in forests.' He goes on to say: 'Turning southward, they paddled down the stream, through a solitude unrelieved by the faintest trace of man.'

A large catfish crashed into Marquette's canoe and frightened him, which was understandable since the Indians had warned him that he was embarking on a reckless journey that could even prove deadly, as the river housed a demon "whose roar could be heard from a great distance, and who would swallow them into the depths where he lived." I have witnessed a Mississippi catfish that measured more than six feet in length and weighed two hundred and fifty pounds, and if Marquette's fish was similar to that one, he had good reason to believe that the river's roaring demon had appeared.

At last, buffalo started to show up, feeding in groups across the vast grasslands that lined the river at that time; and Marquette describes how the old bulls looked fierce and dull-witted as they gazed at the strangers through their matted hair that almost covered their eyes.

The travelers proceeded with great care: 'They came ashore after dark and built a fire to prepare their dinner; then put it out, got back in their boats, paddled further downstream, and dropped anchor in the current, posting a guard to keep watch until dawn.'

They continued this routine day after day and night after night; after two weeks had passed, they hadn't encountered a single person. The river was a terrible wilderness back then. And it remains so today, along most of its length.

But at the end of two weeks, they discovered human footprints in the mud along the western riverbank one day—a Robinson Crusoe moment that still sends an electric thrill through readers when they encounter it on the page. They had received warnings that the river Indians were as savage and merciless as the river demon itself, killing all visitors without provocation; nevertheless, Joliet and Marquette ventured into the wilderness to track down whoever had made those prints. Eventually they located the tribe and received a hospitable welcome and generous treatment— assuming one considers it hospitable to be greeted by an Indian chief who has removed his final piece of clothing to present himself in his finest form; and assuming one considers it generous treatment to be fed abundantly with fish, porridge, and various game meats, including dog, with these foods being placed directly into one's mouth by the bare fingers of the Indians. The following morning, the chief along with six hundred of his tribal members accompanied the Frenchmen back to the river and gave them a warm farewell.

On the rocks above what is now the city of Alton, they discovered some crude and strange Indian paintings, which they described in detail. A short distance downstream, 'a torrent of yellow mud rushed furiously across the calm blue current of the Mississippi, boiling and surging and sweeping logs, branches, and uprooted trees along in its path.' This was the mouth of the Missouri, 'that wild river,' which 'coming down from its frenzied journey through a vast unknown wilderness, poured its muddy waters into the embrace of its peaceful sister.'

Eventually they reached the mouth of the Ohio River; they passed through cane-brakes; they battled mosquitoes; they drifted along, day after day, through the profound silence and isolation of the river, dozing in the limited shade of improvised awnings, and sweltering in the heat; they met and exchanged pleasantries with another group of Indians; and finally they arrived at the mouth of the Arkansas River (approximately a month after departing from their starting point), where a tribe of war-crying natives rushed out to meet and kill them; but they prayed to the Virgin for assistance; so instead of a battle there was a celebration, and plenty of enjoyable conversation and festivities.

They had confirmed to their complete satisfaction that the Mississippi River did not flow into the Gulf of California or into the Atlantic Ocean. They were convinced it emptied into the Gulf of Mexico. They turned around at this point and brought their momentous discovery back to Canada.

But belief is not proof. It was left to La Salle to provide the evidence. He was frustratingly delayed by one misfortune after another, but finally got his expedition moving at the end of 1681.

In the depths of winter, he and Henri de Tonty, son of Lorenzo Tonty who created the tontine, his second-in-command, began their journey down the Illinois River with a group of eighteen Indians brought from New England and twenty-three Frenchmen. They traveled in formation across the frozen river's surface on foot, pulling their canoes behind them on sleds.

At Peoria Lake they encountered open water, and paddled from there to the Mississippi River, turning their boats southward. They pushed through the fields of floating ice, passing the mouth of the Missouri River and later the mouth of the Ohio River. Gliding past the expanses of bordering swampland, they landed on February 24th near the Third Chickasaw Bluffs, where they stopped and constructed Fort Prudhomme.

"Once again," Mr. Parkman explains, "they set sail; and with each phase of their daring journey, the secrets of this enormous new world became increasingly revealed. Step by step, they moved deeper into the domain of spring. The soft, misty sunlight, the gentle and sleepy atmosphere, the delicate leaves, and the blooming flowers all signaled nature's awakening life."

Day by day they drifted down the great river bends, traveling in the shadow of thick forests, and eventually reached the mouth of the Arkansas River. At first, the local natives greeted them just as they had previously welcomed Marquette—with the thundering of war drums and displays of weapons. The Virgin Mary had resolved the conflict in Marquette's situation; the peace pipe served the same purpose for La Salle. The white man and the red man shook hands and hosted each other for three days. Then, to the amazement of the natives, La Salle erected a cross bearing the French coat of arms and claimed the entire territory for the king— the casual custom of that era—while the priest solemnly blessed this theft with a hymn. The priest explained the mysteries of the faith through gestures to save the souls of the natives, thereby offering them potential rewards in Heaven to make up for the definite earthly possessions they had just been stripped of. And also through gestures, La Salle obtained from these innocent children of the wilderness pledges of loyalty to Louis the Putrid across the ocean. No one found these enormous contradictions amusing.

These performances occurred at the location where the future town of Napoleon, Arkansas would be established, and it was there that the first confiscation-cross was erected along the banks of the great river. Marquette's and Joliet's journey of exploration concluded at this very same location—the site of what would become the town of Napoleon. When De Soto caught his brief glimpse of the river, far back in those distant early times, he viewed it from that identical spot—the site of the future town of Napoleon, Arkansas. Consequently, three of the four significant events related to the discovery and exploration of the mighty river happened, by chance, in one and the same location. This represents a most remarkable distinction when one examines it and reflects upon it. France claimed that enormous territory at that spot, the future Napoleon; and eventually Napoleon himself would return the country once again!—making restitution, not to the original owners, but to their white American descendants.

The travelers continued their journey, stopping at various locations along the way. They passed through areas that would later become the historic sites of Vicksburg and Grand Gulf, and they visited a powerful Indian ruler in the Teche region. His capital city was built solidly using sun-dried bricks mixed with straw, creating structures that were actually superior to many buildings found in that area today. The chief's residence featured a reception hall that measured forty feet on each side, and it was here that he welcomed Tonty with full ceremonial honors, surrounded by sixty elderly men dressed in white robes. The town also had a temple, which was enclosed by a mud wall decorated with the skulls of enemies who had been sacrificed to the sun god.

The travelers visited the Natchez Indians near where the modern city of that name now stands, and there they discovered a "religious and political despotism, a privileged class descended from the sun, a temple and a sacred fire." It must have felt like returning home again; it was actually home with a benefit, since it didn't have Louis XIV.

A few more days passed quickly, and La Salle found himself standing in the shadow of his claiming cross, where the waters from Delaware, from Itaska, and from the mountain ranges near the Pacific merged with the waters of the Gulf of Mexico, his mission complete, his remarkable feat accomplished. Mr. Parkman, in concluding his captivating narrative, summarizes it this way:

On that day, France officially gained an enormous territory on paper. The rich flatlands of Texas; the immense Mississippi River valley, stretching from its icy northern headwaters to the sweltering shores of the Gulf; from the forested slopes of the Appalachian Mountains to the barren summits of the Rocky Mountains—a land of grasslands and woodlands, sun-baked deserts and rolling prairies, crossed by countless rivers, roamed by countless warrior tribes, came under the rule of the King of Versailles; and all because of a weak human voice that couldn't be heard from half a mile away.

Chapter 3: Frescoes from the Past

The river seemed ready for commerce now. However, the settlement of people along its shores proved to be just as calm, methodical, and time-consuming a process as the original discovery and exploration had been.

Seventy years passed after the exploration before the river's shores had a white population worth mentioning, and nearly fifty more years went by before the river developed any real commerce.

From the time La Salle opened up the river until it could truly be called a route for regular and active trade, seven different monarchs had sat on England's throne, America had gained its independence, Louis XIV and Louis XV had decayed and died, the French monarchy had collapsed in the bloody chaos of revolution, and Napoleon had become a name people were starting to discuss. Without a doubt, progress moved at a snail's pace in those times.

The river's earliest trade relied on large barges—keelboats and broadhorns. These vessels drifted and sailed from the upper waterways down to New Orleans, where they exchanged their cargo, then were laboriously pulled and pushed back upstream by hand. A single round trip could take as long as nine months. Over time, this trade expanded until it provided work for countless rough and resilient men; crude, unschooled, courageous individuals who endured terrible hardships with sailor-like endurance; heavy drinkers who engaged in coarse revelry in immoral districts like the notorious Natchez-under-the-hill of that era, fierce brawlers, reckless characters all, enormously cheerful, crude-minded, and profane; wasteful with their earnings, broke by journey's end, attracted to gaudy ornaments, tremendous boasters; yet fundamentally honest, dependable, true to their word and obligations, and often remarkably generous in striking ways.

Eventually, the steamboat arrived on the scene. For the next fifteen to twenty years, these men kept operating their keelboats downstream, while the steamboats handled all the upstream traffic. The keelboat operators would sell their boats in New Orleans and make the journey home as deck passengers aboard the steamers.

But eventually, steamboats grew so numerous and fast that they captured all the commercial trade, causing keelboating to disappear forever. The keelboatmen found work as deck hands, mates, or pilots on steamers, and when no steamer positions were available, they took jobs on Pittsburgh coal barges or pine rafts built in the forests near the headwaters of the Mississippi.

During the golden age of steamboat prosperity, the entire river was dotted with coal fleets and timber rafts, all operated by hand and employing large numbers of the rough characters I have been attempting to describe. I recall the yearly processions of enormous rafts that would drift past Hannibal when I was a child—each raft containing an acre or so of white, fragrant boards, a crew of twenty-four men or more, and three or four makeshift shelters scattered across the raft's enormous flat surface for protection during storms—and I remember the crude manners and boisterous conversation of their large crews, the former keelboat workers and their admiringly imitative followers; we would often swim out a quarter or third of a mile to climb aboard these rafts and take a ride.

To illustrate keelboat conversation and customs, along with that vanished and barely remembered raft life, I'll include here a chapter from a book I've been working on intermittently over the past five or six years, and might actually complete within another five or six. The book tells a story that describes certain episodes in the life of an uneducated village boy, Huck Finn, son of the town drunk from my time out west. He has escaped from his tormenting father and from a well-meaning widow who wants to transform him into a polite, honest, respectable young man; a slave belonging to the widow has also fled with him. They have discovered a piece of a lumber raft (the water is high and it's the dead of summer), and they drift down the river at night while hiding among the willows during the day—heading toward Cairo—from where the slave plans to seek freedom in the heart of the free states. However, in a fog, they float past Cairo without realizing it. Eventually they start to suspect what has happened, and Huck Finn is convinced to put an end to their troubling uncertainty by swimming down to a massive raft they've spotted in the distance ahead of them, sneaking aboard under the cover of darkness, and obtaining the information they need by listening in:—

But you know a young person can't wait very well when he's eager to find something out. We discussed it, and eventually Jim said it was such a dark night that it wouldn't be any risk to swim down to the large raft and climb aboard to listen—they would talk about Cairo, because they would be planning to go ashore there for some fun, maybe, or at least they would send boats ashore to buy whiskey or fresh meat or something. Jim had a wonderful clear head, for a Black man: he could almost always come up with a good plan when you needed one.

I stood up and shook the dirt off my clothes and jumped into the river, then swam toward the raft's light. When I got close to it, I slowed down and moved carefully and quietly. But everything seemed fine—no one was at the oars. So I swam along the side of the raft until I was almost even with the campfire in the middle, then I climbed aboard and crept along until I hid among some bundles of wooden shingles on the far side of the fire from the wind. There were thirteen men there—they were the night watch on deck, of course. And they were a really rough-looking bunch, too. They had a jug of liquor and tin cups, and they kept passing the jug around. One man was singing—bellowing, you could say; and it wasn't a decent song—not for polite company anyway. He bellowed through his nose and drew out the last word of every line really long. When he finished they all let out a kind of Indian war cry, and then another man started singing. It began:—

> 'There was a woman in our town,
> In our town did dwell,
> She loved her husband dearly,
> But another man twice as well.'
> Singing too, riloo, riloo, riloo,
> Ri-too, riloo, rilay—
> She loved her husband dearly,
> But another man twice as well.

And so on—fourteen verses. It was pretty bad, and when he was about to start the next verse, one of them said it was the tune the old cow died to; and another one said, "Oh, give us a break." And another one told him to take a hike. They mocked him until he got angry and jumped up and started cursing the crowd, and said he could beat any thief in the bunch.

They were all about to rush toward him, but the biggest man there jumped up and said—

"Stay where you are, gentlemen. Leave him to me; he's mine to deal with."

Then he leaped into the air three times, clicking his heels together each time. He threw off a fringed buckskin coat and said, 'You stay there until the beating is finished,' then flung down his ribbon-covered hat and declared, 'You stay there until his suffering ends.'

Then he leaped into the air and clicked his heels together once more, shouting—

'Whoo-oop! I'm the original iron-jawed, brass-mounted, copper-bellied corpse-maker from the wilds of Arkansas!—Look at me! I'm the man they call Sudden Death and General Desolation! Fathered by a hurricane, mothered by an earthquake, half-brother to cholera, closely related to smallpox on my mother's side! Look at me! I eat nineteen alligators and a barrel of whiskey for breakfast when I'm feeling strong, and a bushel of rattlesnakes and a dead body when I'm sick! I split eternal rocks with my stare, and I silence thunder when I speak! Whoo-oop! Step back and give me space to match my strength! Blood is my natural drink, and the cries of the dying are music to my ears! Set your eyes on me, gentlemen!—and stay low and hold your breath, because I'm about to let myself loose!'

Throughout this entire speech, he kept shaking his head and looking menacing, while pacing around in a small circle, adjusting his cuffs, and occasionally standing tall and pounding his chest with his fist, declaring, 'Look at me, gentlemen!' When he finished speaking, he leaped up and clicked his heels together three times, then let out a thunderous 'Whoo-oop! I'm the fiercest son of a wildcat alive!'

Then the man who had started the fight pulled his old slouch hat down over his right eye; then he bent forward in a crouch, with his back curved and his rear end sticking out, and his fists pushing out and pulling back in front of him, and moved around in a small circle about three times, puffing himself up and breathing heavily. Then he straightened up, jumped into the air and clicked his heels together three times before he landed again (which made the crowd cheer), and he began to shout like this—

"Whoo-oop! bow your neck and spread, for the kingdom of sorrow's coming! Hold me down to the earth, for I feel my powers working! whoo-oop! I'm a child of sin, don't let me get started! Smoked glass, here, for everyone! Don't try to look at me with the naked eye, gentlemen! When I'm playful I use the meridians of longitude and parallels of latitude for a net, and drag the Atlantic Ocean for whales! I scratch my head with the lightning, and purr myself to sleep with the thunder! When I'm cold, I boil the Gulf of Mexico and bathe in it; when I'm hot I fan myself with an equinoctial storm; when I'm thirsty I reach up and suck a cloud dry like a sponge; when I roam the earth hungry, famine follows in my tracks! Whoo-oop! Bow your neck and spread! I put my hand on the sun's face and make it night on the earth; I bite a piece out of the moon and hurry the seasons; I shake myself and crumble the mountains! Look at me through leather—don't use the naked eye! I'm the man with a petrified heart and cast-iron bowels! The massacre of isolated communities is the pastime of my idle moments, the destruction of nationalities the serious business of my life! The boundless vastness of the great American desert is my enclosed property, and I bury my dead on my own premises!" He jumped up and cracked his heels together three times before he landed (they cheered him again), and as he came down he shouted out: "Whoo-oop! bow your neck and spread, for the pet child of calamity's coming!"

Then the other one started getting all worked up and boastful again—the first one—the one they called Bob; next, the Child of Calamity jumped back in, even more aggressively than before; then they both went at it simultaneously, puffing themselves up and circling each other while throwing punches that nearly connected with each other's faces, whooping and yelling like Indians; then Bob started calling the Child names, and the Child fired back with his own insults; next, Bob hurled even harsher names at him and the Child responded with the most vicious language possible; next, Bob knocked the Child's hat clean off, and the Child picked it up and kicked Bob's fancy hat about six feet away; Bob went and retrieved it and said never mind, this wasn't going to be the end of this matter, because he was a man who never forgot and never forgave, and so the Child had better watch out, for there was a reckoning coming, just as sure as he was breathing, when he would have to answer to him with the best blood in his body. The Child said no man was more eager than he was for that time to arrive, and he would give Bob fair warning right now never to cross his path again, for he could never rest until he had waded through his blood, for such was his nature, though he was sparing him now on account of his family, if he had one.

Both of them were backing away in opposite directions, growling and shaking their heads while talking about what they were going to do; but a small man with black whiskers jumped forward and said—

"Come back here, you pair of cowardly chickens, and I'll beat both of you!"

And he did it, too. He grabbed them, he yanked them this way and that, he kicked them around, he knocked them down faster than they could get back up. Why, it wasn't even two minutes before they were begging like dogs—and how the other group did yell and laugh and clap their hands all the way through, and shout 'Go get them, Corpse-Maker!' 'Hit him again, Child of Calamity!' 'Good for you, little Davy!' Well, it was complete chaos for a while. Bob and the Child had bloody noses and black eyes when they were finished. Little Davy made them admit that they were sneaks and cowards and not fit to eat with a dog or drink with anyone; then Bob and the Child shook hands with each other, very seriously, and said they had always respected each other and were willing to let bygones be bygones. So then they washed their faces in the river; and just then there was a loud order to stand by for a crossing, and some of them went forward to man the sweeps there, and the rest went aft to handle the after-sweeps.

I lay still and waited for fifteen minutes, and smoked from a pipe that one of them had left within reach; then the crossing was finished, and they trudged back and had a drink together and went back to talking and singing. Next they brought out an old fiddle, and one played while another clapped rhythmically, and the rest let themselves go in a traditional old-fashioned riverboat dance. They couldn't keep that up very long without getting out of breath, so eventually they gathered around the jug again.

They sang "jolly, jolly raftsman's the life for me," with an energetic chorus, and then they started talking about the differences between hogs and their various kinds of habits; and then about women and their different ways; and then about the best methods to put out houses that were on fire; and then about what should be done with the Indians; and then about what a king had to do and how much he earned; and then about how to make cats fight; and then about what to do when a man has seizures; and then about differences between clear-water rivers and muddy-water ones. The man they called Ed said the muddy Mississippi water was healthier to drink than the clear water of the Ohio; he said if you let a pint of this yellow Mississippi water settle, you

27

would have about a half to three-quarters of an inch of mud at the bottom, depending on the stage of the river, and then it wasn't any better than Ohio water—what you needed to do was to keep it stirred up—and when the river was low, keep mud on hand to put in and thicken the water up the way it should be.

The Child of Calamity agreed with that statement; he claimed there were nutrients in the mud, and anyone who drank Mississippi water could grow corn in their stomach if they chose to. He said—

'You look at the graveyards; that tells the whole story. Trees won't grow worth a damn in a Cincinnati graveyard, but in a St. Louis graveyard they grow over eight hundred feet high. It's all because of the water the people drank before they died. A Cincinnati corpse doesn't enrich the soil at all.'

And they discussed how Ohio water refused to blend with Mississippi water. Ed explained that if you catch the Mississippi during high water when the Ohio runs low, you'll discover a broad strip of clear water stretching along the entire eastern shore of the Mississippi for a hundred miles or beyond, and the moment you venture a quarter mile from the bank and cross that boundary, everything becomes thick and yellow for the remainder of the distance across. After that they discussed methods for preventing tobacco from becoming moldy, and from there they moved on to spirits and shared stories about numerous sightings that other people had experienced; but Ed says—

'Why don't you tell something that you've seen yourselves? Now let me have a say. Five years ago I was on a raft as big as this one, and right along here it was a bright moonlit night, and I was on watch and in charge of the starboard oar at the front, and one of my friends was a man named Dick Allbright, and he came along to where I was sitting at the front—yawning and stretching, he was—and bent down on the edge of the raft and washed his face in the river, and came and sat down by me and pulled out his pipe, and had just got it filled, when he looks up and says—

"Look over there," he says, "isn't that Buck Miller's place, over in the bend."

"Yes," I said, "it is—why?" He set his pipe down and rested his head on his hand, and said—

"I thought we'd be further down," I said—

"I thought the same thing when I finished my watch"—we were working six hours on and six hours off—"but the guys told me," I said, "that the raft barely seemed to move during the last hour," I said, "though it's moving along just fine now," I said. He let out a kind of groan and said—

"I've seen a raft behave like that before around here," he says. "It seems to me the current has mostly stopped above the head of this bend during the last two years," he says.

"Well, he stood up two or three times and looked far off across the water in all directions. That got me doing the same thing. A person always ends up copying what they see someone else doing, even when it doesn't make any sense. Before long I spotted something black floating on the water far off to the right side and somewhat behind us. I could see he was watching it too. I said"

"What's that?" he says, somewhat irritably,

"It's nothing but an old empty barrel."

"An empty barrel!" I said. "Why," I continued, "a spyglass is nothing compared to your eyes. How can you tell it's an empty barrel?" He said—

"I don't know; I think it's not a barrel, but I thought it might be," he says.

"Yes," I said, "that could be it, but it could be anything else too. You can't tell what something is from that far away," I said.

"We didn't have anything else to do, so we kept on watching it. After a while I said "

"Hey, look here, Dick Allbright, that thing is gaining on us, I think."

'He never said a word. The thing kept getting closer and closer, and I figured it must be a dog that was nearly exhausted. Well, we swung down into the crossing, and the thing drifted across the bright strip of moonlight, and by George, it was a barrel. I said—

"Dick Allbright, what made you think that thing was a barrel when it was half a mile away?" I asked. He said—

"I don't know," I said—

"You tell me, Dick Allbright," he says—

"Well, I knew it was a barrel; I've seen it before; lots of people have seen it; they say it's a haunted barrel."

I called the rest of the watch, and they came and stood there, and I told them what Dick had said. It floated right alongside us now, and didn't gain any more distance. It was about twenty feet away. Some wanted to bring it aboard, but the others didn't want to. Dick Allbright said rafts that had messed with it had gotten bad luck from it. The captain of the watch said he didn't believe in it. He said he figured the barrel had gained on us because it was in a slightly better current than we were. He said it would leave eventually.

So then we started talking about other things, and we had a song, and then a breakdown; and after that the captain of the watch called for another song; but it was getting cloudy now, and the barrel remained stuck right there in the same place, and the song didn't seem to have much energy to it, somehow, and so they didn't finish it, and there weren't any cheers, but it sort of fell flat, and nobody said anything for a minute. Then everybody tried to talk at once, and one fellow told a joke, but it was no use, they didn't laugh, and even the fellow who made the joke didn't laugh at it, which isn't usual. We all just settled down glumly, and watched the barrel, and felt uneasy and uncomfortable. Well, sir, it became completely dark and still, and then the wind began to moan around, and next the lightning began to flash and the thunder to rumble. And pretty soon there was a regular storm, and in the middle of it a man who was running toward the back stumbled and fell and sprained his ankle so that he had to rest up. This made the boys shake their heads. And every time the lightning came, there was that barrel with the blue lights flickering around it. We were always on the lookout for it. But gradually, towards dawn, it was gone. When the day came we couldn't see it anywhere, and we weren't sorry, either.

But the next night around half past nine, when there were songs and celebrations going on, she came back again and took her usual position on the starboard side. There were no more celebrations after that. Everyone became serious; nobody talked; you couldn't get anyone to do anything except sit around gloomily and stare at the barrel. The sky began to cloud over again. When the watch changed, the off-duty crew stayed awake instead of going to sleep. The storm raged and howled all night long, and in the middle of it another man stumbled and sprained his ankle, forcing him to stop working. The barrel disappeared toward dawn, and nobody saw it leave.

Everyone was serious and dejected all day long. I don't mean the kind of seriousness that comes from avoiding alcohol—not that kind. They were quiet, but they all drank more than usual—not together—but each man slipped away and drank privately, by himself.

After dark the off-duty crew didn't go to bed; nobody sang, nobody talked; the men didn't spread out around the raft either; they kind of huddled together toward the front; and for two hours they sat there, completely still, staring steadily in one direction, and letting out a sigh now and then. And then, here comes the barrel again. It took up its old position. It stayed there all night; nobody went to sleep. The storm returned after midnight. It became terribly dark; the rain came down in torrents; hail fell too; the thunder boomed and roared and rumbled, the wind blew like a hurricane; and the lightning spread across everything in huge sheets of brightness, and revealed the entire raft as clear as daylight; and the river churned up white as milk as far as you could see for miles, and there was that barrel bobbing along, just the same as always. The captain ordered the watch to man the rear sweeps for a river crossing, and nobody would go—no more sprained ankles for them, they said. They wouldn't even walk toward the back of the raft. Well then, right at that moment the sky split wide open, with a tremendous crash, and the lightning struck and killed two men from the rear watch, and injured two others. Injured them how, you ask? Why, it sprained their ankles!

The barrel disappeared in the darkness between lightning flashes, just before dawn. Well, nobody ate a single bite at breakfast that morning. After that, the men wandered around aimlessly in small groups of two and three, speaking quietly among themselves. But none of them stayed near Dick Allbright. They all gave him the cold shoulder. If he approached wherever any of the men were gathered, they would break apart and drift away. They refused to work the oars with him. The captain had all the small boats pulled up onto the raft next to his shelter, and wouldn't allow the dead men to be taken to shore for burial; he didn't believe that anyone who went ashore would return; and he was correct.

After nightfall, you could see quite clearly that there would be trouble if that barrel appeared again; there was so much muttering going on. Many of the men wanted to kill Dick Allbright, because he had seen the barrel on other trips, and that looked suspicious. Some wanted to put him ashore. Others said, let's all go ashore together, if the barrel comes again.

'This kind of whispering was still happening, with the men gathered together at the front of the ship watching for the barrel, when suddenly, there it was again. Down it came, slow and steady, settling back into its familiar path. You could have heard a pin drop. Then the captain came up and said:—

"Listen up, boys, don't act like a bunch of kids and idiots; I don't want this barrel following us all the way to New Orleans, and neither do you; so then, what's the best way to stop it? Burn it up—that's how. I'm going to bring it on board," he says. And before anyone could say a word, in he went.

He swam to it, and as he came pushing it to the raft, the men spread to one side. But the old man got it aboard and smashed in the head, and there was a baby in it! Yes, sir, a completely naked baby. It was Dick Allbright's baby; he admitted it and said so.

"Yes," he says, leaning over it, "yes, it is my own beloved darling, my poor lost Charles William Allbright deceased," says he—for he could wrap his tongue around the finest words in the language when he set his mind to it, and deliver them to you without a single stumble, anywhere. Yes, he said he used to live up at the head of this bend, and one night he choked his child, which was crying, not meaning to kill it—which was probably a lie—and then he was frightened, and buried it in a barrel, before his wife got home, and off he went, and took the northern trail and went to rafting; and this was the third year that the barrel had chased him. He said the bad luck always started light, and lasted until four men were killed, and then the barrel didn't come anymore after that. He said if the men would endure it one more night—and was going on like that—but the men had had enough. They started to get out a boat to take him ashore and lynch him, but he grabbed the little child all of a sudden and jumped overboard with it clutched to his chest and crying tears, and we never saw him again in this life, poor old suffering soul, nor Charles William either.

"Who was crying?" Bob asks. "Was it Allbright or the baby?"

'Why, Allbright, of course; didn't I tell you the baby was dead? It's been dead for three years—how could it cry?'

"Well, forget about how it could cry—how could it survive all that time?" Davy says. "You answer me that."

"I don't know how it did it," says Ed. "It did it though—that's all I know about it."

"Say—what did they do with the barrel?" says the Child of Calamity.

"Well, they threw it overboard, and it sank like a piece of lead."

"Edward, did the child look like it had been strangled?" asks one of them.

"Did it have its hair parted?" asks another.

"What brand was on that barrel, Eddy?" asked a guy they called Bill.

"Do you have the paperwork for those statistics, Edmund?" Jimmy asks.

"Tell me, Edwin, were you one of the men who got killed by lightning?" Davy asks.

"Him? Oh, no, he was both of them," says Bob. Then they all burst out laughing.

"Listen, Edward, don't you think you should take some medicine? You look terrible—don't you feel sick?" says the Child of Calamity.

"Oh, come on now, Eddy," Jimmy says, "show us the proof; you must have kept part of that barrel to prove what you're saying. Show us the bunghole—go ahead—and we'll all believe you."

"Listen, boys," Bill says, "let's divide it up. There are thirteen of us. I can handle a thirteenth of the story, if you can manage the rest."

Ed stood up angrily and told them they could all go to hell, which he said quite viciously, and then stormed off toward the back of the boat cursing under his breath, while they shouted and mocked him, laughing so loudly you could hear them from a mile away.

"Boys, we'll split a watermelon on that," says the Child of Calamity, and he came searching around in the dark among the wooden bundles where I was, and put his hand on me. I was warm and soft and naked, so he says "Ouch!" and jumped back.

'Bring a lantern or some fire over here, boys—there's a snake here as big as a cow!'

So they rushed over there carrying a lantern, gathered around, and peered in at me.

"Get out of there, you beggar!" says one.

"Who are you?" asks another.

"What do you want here? Speak up quickly, or you're going overboard."

"Pull him out, boys. Drag him out by his heels."

I started to plead, and crawled out among them shaking. They examined me with curiosity, and the Child of Calamity said—

"A damned thief! Give me a hand and let's throw him overboard!"

"No," says Big Bob, "let's get out the paint pot and paint him sky blue all over from head to toe, and then throw him overboard!"

"Good, that's it. Go for the paint, Jimmy."

When the paint arrived, and Bob picked up the brush and was about to start, with the others laughing and rubbing their hands together, I started to cry, and that seemed to affect Davy, so he said—

"Stop right there! He's nothing but a young boy. I'll beat up anyone who touches him!"

So I glanced around at them, and a few of them complained and grumbled under their breath, and Bob set down the paintbrush, while the others refused to pick it up.

"Come over here by the fire, and let's see what you're doing," says Davy. "Now sit down there and explain yourself. How long have you been on board here?"

"Not even fifteen seconds, sir," I said.

"How did you dry off so quickly?"

"I don't know, sir. I'm always that way, mostly."

"Oh, you are, are you? What's your name?"

I wasn't going to tell my name. I didn't know what to say, so I just said—

"Charles William Allbright, sir."

Then they roared with laughter—the entire crowd; and I was extremely glad I had said that, because perhaps laughing would put them in a better mood.

When they finished laughing, Davy said—

"This just won't work, Charles William. You couldn't have grown this much in five years, and you were a baby when you came out of the barrel, you know, and dead at that. Come on now, tell the truth, and nobody will hurt you, if you're not up to anything wrong. What is your name?"

'Aleck Hopkins, sir. Aleck James Hopkins.'

"Well, Aleck, where did you come from, here?"

'From a trading boat. She's anchored around the bend over there. I was born on that boat. My father has been trading up and down this river his whole life, and he told me to swim out here because when you passed by, he said he'd like one of you to talk to a Mr. Jonas Turner in Cairo and tell him—'

"Oh, come on!"

"Yes, sir; it's as true as anything; Dad always says—"

"Oh, your grandmother!"

They all burst into laughter, and I attempted once more to speak, but they interrupted me and cut me off.

"Now, look here," says Davy, "you're scared, and that's why you're talking crazy. Tell me the truth now, do you really live on a scow, or are you lying?"

"Yes, sir, on a trading boat. She's docked at the top of the river bend. But I wasn't born on her. This is our first trip."

"Now you're talking! What did you come aboard here for? To steal?"

"No, sir, I didn't. I was just trying to get a ride on the raft. All boys do that."

"Well, I know that. But what did you hide for?"

"Sometimes they chase the boys away."

"That's true. They might steal. Listen here; if we let you go this time, will you stay out of this kind of trouble from now on?"

"I certainly will, boss. Just give me a chance."

"All right, then. You're not far from shore. Jump overboard, and don't make a fool of yourself like this again. Damn it, boy, some raftsmen would beat you until you were black and blue!"

I didn't wait to say goodbye with a kiss, but jumped overboard and headed for the shore. When Jim came along later, the big raft had disappeared from sight around the point. I swam out and climbed aboard, and was extremely happy to see home again.

The boy didn't get the information he was looking for, but his adventure has provided the glimpse of the vanished raftsman and keelboatman that I want to present here.

I now turn to a period in Mississippi River life during the golden age of steamboat travel that I believe deserves thorough exploration—the remarkable skill of river piloting as it was practiced there. I believe nothing comparable has existed anywhere else in the world.

Chapter 4: The Boys' Ambition

When I was a child, there was only one lasting dream shared by all my friends in our village on the western shore of the Mississippi River. That dream was to become a steamboat worker. We experienced fleeting desires for other careers, but these were temporary. Whenever a circus visited and departed, it left all of us eager to become performers; the first blackface minstrel performance that reached our area made us all long to pursue that lifestyle; occasionally we hoped that if we survived and behaved well, God might allow us to become pirates. These dreams gradually disappeared, one after another; however, the desire to work on steamboats never left us.

Once a day a cheap, flashy steamboat arrived heading upriver from St. Louis, and another came downriver from Keokuk. Before these events, the day was filled with glorious anticipation; after them, the day became dead and empty. Not only the boys, but the entire village, felt this. After all these years I can picture that old time to myself now, just as it was then: the white town dozing in the sunshine of a summer morning; the streets empty, or nearly so; one or two clerks sitting in front of the Water Street stores, with their woven-seat chairs tilted back against the wall, chins resting on their chests, hats pulled down over their faces, sleeping—with wood shavings scattered around to show what had worn them out; a sow and her litter of pigs wandering along the sidewalk, making good use of watermelon rinds and seeds; two or three small, isolated freight piles scattered about the wharf; a pile of wooden planks on the slope of the stone-paved dock, and the well-known town drunk asleep in their shadow; two or three timber rafts at the head of the wharf, but nobody around to listen to the peaceful lapping of the small waves against them; the great Mississippi, the majestic, the magnificent Mississippi, rolling its mile-wide current along, gleaming in the sun; the thick forest far away on the other side; the bend above the town, and the bend below, framing the river view and turning it into a kind of sea, and altogether a very still and brilliant and lonely one. Soon a wisp of dark smoke appears above one of those distant bends; instantly a Black dock worker, famous for his sharp eye and powerful voice, calls out, 'S-t-e-a-m-boat a-comin'!' and the scene transforms! The town drunk stirs, the clerks wake up, a wild clattering of carts follows, every house and store sends out people, and in an instant the dead town comes alive and springs into motion.

Wagons, carts, men, and boys all rush from various directions toward a shared destination: the wharf. Once gathered there, the crowd fixes their gaze on the approaching steamboat as if witnessing a marvel for the very first time. The vessel truly makes for an impressive sight. She stretches long and sleek with graceful lines; two towering smokestacks rise elegantly, adorned with ornate tops and some sort of golden decoration suspended between them; an elaborate pilot house, constructed of glass and decorative woodwork, sits perched atop the texas deck just behind the stacks; the paddle-wheel housings display magnificent artwork or golden sunburst designs above the boat's name; the boiler deck, hurricane deck, and texas deck feature pristine white railings that serve both as barriers and ornamentation; a flag waves proudly from the jackstaff; the furnace doors stand open, revealing flames that burn with fierce intensity; passengers crowd the upper decks until they appear completely black; the captain positions himself beside the large bell, composed and commanding, drawing the admiration of everyone present; massive clouds of the darkest smoke pour and roll from the smokestacks—a carefully orchestrated display of magnificence achieved by adding pitch pine just before reaching port; crew members gather on the forecastle; the wide gangplank extends far out over the port bow, where an admired deckhand stands in a striking pose at its end, holding a coiled rope; pressurized steam shrieks through the safety valves, the captain raises his hand, a bell chimes, and the paddle wheels cease their motion; then they reverse direction, churning the water into white foam, and the steamboat comes to rest. What follows is a frantic rush as people scramble to board and disembark while freight gets loaded and unloaded all simultaneously; the mates orchestrate this chaos with tremendous shouting and swearing! Ten minutes pass, and the steamer departs once more, now without its flag on the jackstaff and no dark smoke billowing from its chimneys. After another ten minutes, the town returns to its lifeless state, and the local drunk lies sleeping beside the wooden platforms once again.

My father served as a justice of the peace, and I believed he held the power of life and death over everyone and could execute anyone who crossed him. This distinction satisfied me most of the time; however, the longing to become a steamboat worker kept creeping back into my thoughts. Initially, I wanted to work as a cabin boy so I could appear wearing a white apron and shake out a tablecloth over the boat's edge where all my childhood friends could witness me; afterward, I decided I'd prefer being the deckhand who positioned himself at the end of the stage plank holding a coiled rope, since he drew particular attention. Yet these remained mere fantasies—they seemed too wonderful to consider as actual possibilities. Eventually, one of the local boys departed. No one heard from him for an extended period. Finally, he reappeared working as an apprentice engineer or 'striker' aboard a steamboat. This development completely undermined everything I'd learned in Sunday school. That boy had been famously immoral, while I represented the complete opposite; still, he had risen to this elevated position while I remained stuck in anonymity and wretchedness. This fellow showed no kindness despite his success. He always found some rusty bolt to clean whenever his boat stopped at our town, positioning himself on the inner guard to scrub it where we could all observe him, envy him, and despise him. Whenever his vessel was docked for repairs, he would return home and strut through town wearing his darkest and most oil-stained clothing, ensuring everyone remembered his status as a steamboat worker; he peppered his conversations with steamboat terminology, acting as though he used these terms so regularly that he forgot ordinary people couldn't comprehend them. He would mention the 'larboard' side of a horse in such a casual, natural manner that it made you wish for his demise. He constantly discussed 'St. Louis' like a longtime resident; he would casually reference times when he 'traveled down Fourth Street,' or when he 'walked past the Planter's House,' or when a fire broke out and he operated the brakes on 'the old Big Missouri;' then he would continue fabricating stories about how many towns our size had burned down there on any given day. Two or three local boys had long commanded respect among us because they had visited St. Louis once and possessed some general understanding of its marvels, but their moment of fame had ended. They retreated into modest silence and learned to vanish whenever the merciless 'cub' engineer appeared. This fellow also had money and hair oil. Additionally, he owned a cheap silver watch and a flashy brass watch chain. He wore a leather belt instead of suspenders. If any young man was ever simultaneously admired and despised by his peers, it was him. No girl could resist his appeal. He 'stole away' every boy's romantic interest in the village. When his boat finally exploded, it spread a peaceful satisfaction among us that we hadn't experienced in months. However, when he returned home the following week, alive and famous, appearing in church all bruised and bandaged like a glorious hero, stared at and marveled over by everyone, it appeared to us that Providence's favoritism toward such an unworthy scoundrel had reached a level that deserved criticism.

This situation could only lead to one outcome, and it quickly came to pass. One boy after another managed to find work on the river. The minister's son became an engineer. The doctor's and the postmaster's sons became mud clerks. The wholesale liquor dealer's son became a bartender on a boat. Four sons of the chief merchant, and two sons of the county judge, became pilots. Pilot was the most prestigious position of all. The pilot, even in those days of modest wages, earned a generous salary—from one hundred and fifty to two hundred and fifty dollars a month, with no room and board expenses. Two months of his wages could cover a preacher's salary for an entire year. Now some of us were left heartbroken. We couldn't get work on the river—at least our parents wouldn't allow us to.

So eventually I ran away. I declared I would never return home until I became a pilot and could arrive in triumph. However, I somehow couldn't make it happen. I went humbly aboard several of the boats that were crowded together like sardines at the lengthy St. Louis wharf, and very modestly asked for the pilots, but received only cold treatment and brief responses from mates and clerks. I had to accept this kind of treatment for now, but I enjoyed comforting fantasies of a future when I would be a great and respected pilot, with lots of money, and could eliminate some of these mates and clerks and compensate for them.

Chapter 5: I Want to be a Cub-pilot

Months later, the hope inside me slowly died a reluctant death, and I discovered myself without any ambition. However, I felt too embarrassed to return home. I was in Cincinnati, and I began working to plan out a new career path. I had been reading about the recent exploration of the Amazon River by an expedition our government had sent out. Reports indicated that the expedition, due to various difficulties, had not fully explored a section of the country located near the headwaters, approximately four thousand miles from the river's mouth. It was only about fifteen hundred miles from Cincinnati to New Orleans, where I could surely find a ship. I had thirty dollars remaining; I would go and finish the exploration of the Amazon. This was the extent of my thinking on the matter. I was never particularly good with details. I packed my suitcase and bought passage on an old vessel called the 'Paul Jones,' bound for New Orleans. For sixteen dollars, I had the worn and faded grandeur of her main salon mostly to myself, since she wasn't the type of boat that would catch the attention of more sensible travelers.

When we finally set off and began drifting down the wide Ohio River, I transformed into a completely different person and became fascinated with myself. I was a traveler! That word had never tasted so delicious before. I felt an overwhelming excitement about heading toward mysterious territories and faraway places that I've never experienced to such an inspiring extent since then. I was in such an elevated state that all petty emotions left me entirely, and I could look down and feel sorry for those who had never traveled with a sympathy that contained barely a hint of scorn. Even so, when we stopped at small towns and lumber yards, I couldn't resist lounging casually against the railings of the boiler deck to soak up the jealousy of the local boys standing on the shore. If they didn't seem to notice me, I would soon cough to get their attention, or shift to a spot where they couldn't possibly miss seeing me. And once I was certain they had spotted me, I yawned and stretched, and displayed other signs of being tremendously tired of traveling.

I kept my hat off the entire time and remained where the wind and sun could hit me, because I wanted to achieve the tanned and weathered appearance of a seasoned traveler. Before the second day was halfway over, I felt a joy that filled me with the deepest gratitude; I could see that my skin had started to blister and peel on my face and neck. I wished the boys and girls back home could see me at that moment.

We reached Louisville in time—at least the neighborhood of it. We got stuck hard and fast on the rocks in the middle of the river, and stayed there four days. I was now beginning to feel a strong sense of being part of the boat's family, like an infant son to the captain and younger brother to the officers. There's no way to measure the pride I felt in this grandeur, or the affection that began to swell and grow in me for those people. I couldn't know how the lordly steamboatman looks down on that sort of presumption in a mere landsman. I particularly longed to get the smallest bit of notice from the big stormy mate, and I was watching for an opportunity to do him a service toward that end. It came at last. The wild commotion of setting a spar was going on down on the forecastle, and I went down there and stood around in the way—or mostly jumping out of it—until the mate suddenly shouted a general order for somebody to bring him a capstan bar. I jumped to his side and said: 'Tell me where it is—I'll get it!'

If a trash collector had offered to provide diplomatic services to the Emperor of Russia, the monarch couldn't have been more shocked than the mate was. He even stopped cursing. He stood there staring down at me. It took him ten seconds to pull himself back together again. Then he said with emphasis: 'Well, if this doesn't beat everything!' and returned to his work with the manner of someone who had just encountered a problem too complex to solve.

I slipped away and sought solitude for the remainder of the day. I skipped dinner and avoided supper until everyone else had finished eating. I no longer felt like part of the boat's family as I had before. Nevertheless, my spirits gradually returned as we continued our journey down the river. I regretted hating the mate so intensely, because it went against human nature not to admire him. He was enormous and muscular, with a face completely covered in beard and whiskers; he had a red woman and a blue woman tattooed on his right arm—one on each side of a blue anchor with a red rope attached; and when it came to swearing, he was magnificent. Whenever he was unloading cargo at a landing, I always positioned myself where I could watch and listen. He felt the full dignity of his important position and made sure the world recognized it too. When he gave even the most basic command, he delivered it like a lightning bolt and followed it with a long, echoing burst of profanity that thundered afterward. I couldn't help comparing how an ordinary person on land would give an order with the mate's method of doing it. If someone on land wanted the gangplank moved a foot further forward, he would likely say: 'James, or William, would one of you please push that plank forward;' but put the mate in that situation and he would bellow: 'Here, now, move that gangplank forward! Quickly, now! what are you doing! Grab it! GRAB it! There! there! Back again! back again! don't you hear me. Damn it to hell! are you going to fall asleep doing it! Stop pulling. Stop pulling, I'm telling you! Are you going to pull it completely to the stern? Where are you taking that barrel! Forward with it before I make you swallow it, you damn-damn-damn-damned cross between a tired mud-turtle and a crippled hearse-horse!'

I wished I could speak like that.

When the pain from my encounter with the mate had mostly faded, I cautiously began trying to befriend the lowest-ranking crew member on the boat—the night watchman. At first, he rejected my attempts to get close, but I eventually worked up the courage to offer him a new chalk pipe, which softened his attitude toward me. He then let me sit beside him next to the large bell on the hurricane deck, and gradually he warmed up enough to start talking. He really couldn't have avoided conversation, since I hung on his every word with such reverence and clearly showed how honored I felt by his attention. He told me the names of distant headlands and shadowy islands as we drifted past them in the quiet darkness of night, beneath the twinkling stars, and eventually began talking about his own life. He seemed overly emotional for someone earning six dollars a week—or at least he might have appeared that way to someone older than me. But I absorbed his words eagerly, with a belief that could have moved mountains if it had been put to better use. What did it matter to me that he was dirty and shabby and reeked of gin? What did it matter that his grammar was poor, his sentence structure even worse, and his swearing so lacking in skill that it weakened rather than strengthened his speech? He was a man who had been wronged, someone who had experienced hardship, and that was all I needed to know. As he grew more emotional while telling his sad story, his tears fell onto the lantern resting in his lap, and I wept too, out of sympathy.

He claimed to be the son of an English nobleman—either an earl or an alderman, he couldn't recall which, but thought he was both; his father, the nobleman, loved him, but his mother despised him from birth; and so while he was still a young boy he was sent to 'one of those old, ancient colleges'—he couldn't remember which one; and eventually his father died and his mother took control of the property and 'cast him out' as he put it. After his mother cast him out, members of the nobility who knew him used their connections to secure him a position as 'ship's assistant in a vessel;' and from that moment my watchman abandoned all constraints of time and place and launched into a story that was packed throughout with unbelievable adventures; a tale that was so drenched with violence and so filled with narrow escapes and the most captivating and unintentional personal misdeeds, that I sat silent, delighting, trembling, marveling, admiring.

It was deeply disappointing to discover later that he was a crude, coarse, ignorant, overly emotional, simple-minded fraud—an inexperienced local from the remote areas of Illinois who had consumed sensational stories and claimed their wonders as his own, until eventually he had pieced together fragments of this nonsense into his tale, and then continued telling it to newcomers like me, until he had actually started believing it himself.

———————

Chapter 6: A Cub-pilot's Experience

Spending four days stuck on the rocks at Louisville, along with various other delays, caused the poor old 'Paul Jones' to waste approximately two weeks completing the journey from Cincinnati to New Orleans. This provided me with an opportunity to become familiar with one of the pilots, who instructed me in steering the vessel, making river life even more captivating for me than it had been before.

It also gave me a chance to get to know a young man who had taken deck passage—unfortunately for me; he easily borrowed six dollars from me with a promise to return to the boat and pay me back the day after we arrived. But he probably died or forgot, because he never showed up. It was most likely the former, since he had mentioned that his parents were wealthy, and he only traveled deck passage because it was cooler.[1]

I quickly learned two things. First, no ship would likely sail to the Amazon's mouth for at least ten to twelve years. Second, the nine or ten dollars remaining in my pocket wouldn't cover such an ambitious expedition as I had envisioned, even if I could wait that long for a vessel. This meant I needed to find a different path forward. The 'Paul Jones' was heading to St. Louis. I launched a campaign to win over my pilot, and after three challenging days, he gave in. He agreed to teach me the Mississippi River from New Orleans to St. Louis for five hundred dollars, to be paid from my first earnings after completing my training. I embarked on the modest venture of mastering twelve or thirteen hundred miles of the mighty Mississippi River with all the casual confidence that comes with youth. Had I truly understood what I was asking of my abilities, I wouldn't have found the nerve to start. I assumed

---

[1] 'Deck' Passage, i.e. steerage passage.

that a pilot simply needed to keep his boat within the river's boundaries, and I didn't think that could be particularly difficult, given how broad the river was.

The steamboat pulled away from New Orleans at four in the afternoon, and it was our shift until eight o'clock. Mr. Bixby, my supervisor, got the boat moving straight, steered her past the rear ends of the other vessels docked at the wharf, and then told me, "Here, you take control; pass those steamships as closely as you would peel an apple." I grabbed the steering wheel, and my heartbeat shot up dramatically; it felt like we were going to scrape against every ship in the row because we were so close. I held my breath and started pulling the boat away from the danger; I had my own thoughts about the pilot who didn't know any better than to put us in such a dangerous situation, but I was smart enough not to say anything. Within thirty seconds I had created a safe distance between the 'Paul Jones' and the other ships; less than ten seconds later I was pushed aside in shame, and Mr. Bixby was heading back into danger while verbally attacking me for being a coward. I felt hurt, but I had to respect the calm confidence with which my supervisor moved casually from one side of his wheel to the other, steering so close to the ships that a crash seemed constantly about to happen. After he had calmed down a bit, he explained that the calm water was near the shore and the strong current was farther out, so we needed to stay close to the bank when going upstream to benefit from the easier water, and keep well away from shore when going downstream to take advantage of the current. In my mind, I decided I would become a downstream pilot and leave the upstream navigation to people who didn't care about being careful.

Occasionally, Mr. Bixby would point out various landmarks to me. He would say, "This is Six-Mile Point." I nodded in agreement. The information was pleasant enough, but I couldn't understand why it mattered. I wasn't aware that it held any significance for me.

At another moment, he announced, "This is Nine-Mile Point." Later on, he declared, "This is Twelve-Mile Point." All of these points sat roughly at water level; they all appeared virtually identical to me; they were tediously unremarkable. I wished Mr. Bixby would switch topics. However, he persisted; he would navigate closely around each point, staying near the shoreline with obvious care, and then announce: "The calm water stops here, alongside this cluster of China-trees; now we move across." And so he would cross over. He handed me control of the wheel on a few occasions, but I had no success. I would either nearly scrape the edge of a sugar plantation, or I would drift too far from the shore, which meant I fell back into disfavor once more and received criticism.

The watch finally came to an end, and we had our evening meal before heading to bed. At midnight, the bright light from a lantern blazed into my eyes, and the night watchman spoke—

"Come on! Get out!"

And then he left. I couldn't understand this strange behavior, so I eventually stopped trying to figure it out and drifted off to sleep. Soon enough, the watchman returned, and this time he was irritated. I was annoyed. I said:

"What do you want to come bothering around here in the middle of the night for? Now I probably won't be able to get back to sleep tonight."

The watchman said—

"Well, if this isn't good, I'll be damned."

The crew members who had just finished their shift were heading to bed, and I could hear their harsh laughter along with comments like "Hey there, watchman! Hasn't that new rookie come out yet? He's probably too delicate. Give him some sugar wrapped in cloth and call for the maid to sing him a lullaby."

Around this time, Mr. Bixby showed up. About a minute later, I found myself hurrying up the pilot-house stairs with some of my clothes on and the rest clutched in my arms. Mr. Bixby followed close behind, making remarks. This was something completely new—having to wake up in the middle of the night to go to work. This was an aspect of piloting that had never crossed my mind before. I understood that boats operated through the night, but somehow it had never dawned on me that someone actually had to climb out of a warm bed to keep them running. I started to worry that piloting might not be as romantic as I had pictured it; there was something very practical and labor-intensive about this new side of it.

It was quite a gloomy night, though a good number of stars were visible. The large first mate was steering the boat, and he had the old vessel aimed at a star while keeping her straight down the center of the river. The banks on both sides were no more than half a mile apart, but they appeared remarkably distant and extremely hazy and unclear. The mate said:—

"We need to land at Jones's plantation, sir."

The vengeful spirit inside me rejoiced. I told myself, I hope you enjoy your work, Mr. Bixby; you're going to have a wonderful time trying to locate Mr. Jones's plantation on a night like this; and I hope you never find it for as long as you live.

Mr. Bixby said to the mate:—

"The upper end of the plantation, or the lower?"

"Upper."

"I can't do it. The tree stumps over there are above water right now. It's not far to the lower area, and you'll have to make do with that."

"All right, sir. If Jones doesn't like it, he'll just have to deal with it, I suppose."

And then the mate departed. My excitement started to fade and my curiosity began to rise. Here was a man who not only intended to locate this plantation on such a night, but to find whichever end of it you wanted. I desperately wanted to ask a question, but I was already carrying about as many curt responses as my patience could handle, so I kept quiet. All I wanted to ask Mr. Bixby was the straightforward question of whether he was foolish enough to actually believe he could find that plantation on a night when all plantations looked exactly the same and were all the same color. But I restrained myself. I used to have excellent moments of wisdom in those days.

Mr. Bixby headed toward the shore and soon was scraping against it, exactly as if it had been broad daylight. And not only that, but he was singing—

"Father in heaven, the day is declining," etc.

It felt like I had placed my life in the hands of an especially reckless outcast. Soon he turned toward me and said:

"What's the name of the first point above New Orleans?"

I was pleased to be able to respond quickly, and I did. I said I didn't know.

"Don't know?"

This attitude shocked me. I was back down at the bottom again, instantly. But I had to say exactly what I had said before.

"Well, you're a smart one," said Mr. Bixby. "What's the name of the next point?"

Once again, I had no idea.

"Well, this is unbelievable. Tell me the name of any point or place I mentioned to you."

I spent some time thinking about it and concluded that it wasn't possible for me.

"Listen! Where do you begin from, above Twelve-Mile Point, when you're crossing over?"

"I—I—don't know."

"You—you—don't know?" he said, imitating my slow way of speaking. "What do you know?"

"I—I—nothing, for certain."

"By the great Caesar's ghost, I believe you! You're the most foolish blockhead I've ever seen or heard of, so help me Moses! The thought of you being a pilot—you! Why, you don't know enough to guide a cow down a lane."

Oh, but he was furious! He was an anxious man, and he paced back and forth at his steering wheel as if the deck was burning beneath his feet. He would simmer quietly for a moment, then erupt and lash out at me once more.

"Listen! Why do you think I told you the names of those points?"

I hesitated for a moment, trembling, and then the devil of temptation urged me to say:—

"Well—to—to—be entertaining, I thought."

This was like waving a red flag in front of a bull. He became so furious and enraged (he was navigating across the river at that moment) that I believe it blinded him with anger, causing him to crash into the steering oar of a merchant boat. Naturally, the traders unleashed a barrage of blazing profanity. No man was ever as thankful as Mr. Bixby was at that moment: he was bursting with rage, and here were people who would argue back. He flung open a window, stuck his head outside, and such an explosion of words erupted as I had never witnessed before. The more distant and faint the boat workers' curses became, the louder Mr. Bixby raised his voice and the more powerful his insults grew. When he shut the window, he was completely drained. You could have dragged a fishing net through his entire being and not gathered enough curse words to upset your mother. Soon after, he spoke to me in the most gentle manner—

"Son, you need to get yourself a small notebook, and whenever I teach you something, write it down immediately. There's only one way to become a pilot, and that's to memorize this entire river completely. You have to know it as well as you know the alphabet."

That revelation hit me hard, since my memory had never been

good at retaining anything useful. Still, I didn't stay discouraged for long. I figured I should make some allowances, since Mr. Bixby was probably exaggerating. Soon he pulled a rope and rang the big bell several times. All the stars had disappeared by now, and the night was pitch black. I could hear the paddle wheels churning along the riverbank, but I wasn't completely sure I could actually see the shore. The voice of the unseen watchman called out from the hurricane deck—

"What's this, sir?"

'Jones's plantation.'

I thought to myself that I'd like to make a small wager that it wasn't, but I kept quiet and simply waited to see what would happen. Mr. Bixby operated the engine bells, and soon the boat's front reached the shore, a torch appeared from the front deck, a man jumped onto land, and a Black man's voice from the bank called out, "Give me the carpet bag, Mr. Jones." The next moment we were heading back up the river, everything perfectly calm. I thought deeply for a while, then said to myself—though not out loud—"Well, finding that plantation was the most fortunate coincidence that could have occurred, but something like that couldn't happen again in a hundred years." And I truly believed it had been pure chance.

After traveling seven or eight hundred miles up the river, I had become a reasonably skilled upstream pilot during daylight hours, and by the time we reached St. Louis, I had made some small progress with nighttime navigation, though not much. My notebook was packed with the names of towns, points, sandbars, islands, bends, stretches, and other landmarks; however, all this information existed only on paper—none of it had stuck in my memory. It broke my heart to realize I had only recorded half the river's features; since our shifts ran four hours on and four hours off, both day and night, there was a four-hour gap in my notes for every period I had been asleep since the journey started.

My supervisor was soon hired to work on a large New Orleans steamboat, and I packed my bag and went along with him. She was a magnificent vessel. When I stood in her pilot-house, I was so high above the water that I felt like I was perched on a mountaintop; and her decks extended so far in both directions below me that I couldn't understand how I had ever thought the little 'Paul Jones' was a big ship. There were other differences as well. The 'Paul Jones's' pilot-house was a cheap, grimy, worn-out wreck, cramped for space: but this was a luxurious glass sanctuary; spacious enough to hold a dance in; flashy red and gold window curtains; an impressive sofa; leather cushions and a backrest for the high bench where visiting pilots sit to tell stories and 'watch the river;' bright, decorative spittoons instead of a wide wooden box filled with sawdust; fresh new oilcloth on the floor; a welcoming large stove for winter; a wheel as tall as my head, expensive with inlaid craftsmanship; a wire steering rope; shiny brass knobs for the bells; and a neat, white-aproned, black 'texas-tender,' to bring up pastries and ice cream and coffee during the middle watch, day and night. Now this was 'really something,' and so I started to feel encouraged again to believe that piloting was a romantic kind of job after all. The moment we started moving I began to wander around the great steamboat and fill myself with delight. She was as spotless and as elegant as a living room; when I looked down her long, golden salon, it was like staring through a magnificent tunnel; she had an oil painting, by some talented sign-painter, on every cabin door; she sparkled with countless crystal-fringed chandeliers; the clerk's office was refined, the bar was amazing, and the bartender had been groomed and outfitted at unbelievable expense. The boiler deck (that is, the second level of the boat, so to speak) was as roomy as a church, it seemed to me; the same with the forecastle; and there wasn't a pitiful small group of deckhands, firemen, and laborers down there, but an entire army of men. The fires were blazing intensely from a long line of furnaces, and above them were eight enormous boilers! This was indescribable grandeur. The powerful engines—but enough of this. I had never felt so wonderful before. And when I discovered that the crew of well-dressed servants respectfully called me 'sir,' my contentment was complete.

Chapter 7: A Daring Deed

When I got back to the pilot-house, St. Louis had disappeared and I was completely lost. Here was a section of river that was fully documented in my book, but I couldn't make sense of it at all: you see, it was reversed. I had observed it while traveling upstream, but I had never turned around to see what it looked like when it was behind me. My heart sank once more, because it was clear that I would have to learn this difficult river in both directions.

The pilot-house was packed with pilots heading downstream to examine the river. The section known as the 'upper river' (the two hundred miles stretching between St. Louis and Cairo, where the Ohio River flows in) was running low; and since the Mississippi shifts its channel so frequently, pilots always found it essential to travel down to Cairo for a fresh inspection whenever their boats would remain docked for a week; this was particularly true when water levels were low. Much of this 'river examination' was carried out by unfortunate men who rarely secured employment, and whose only chance of finding work depended on staying constantly informed and thus being prepared to step into the role of some respected pilot for a single journey, due to that pilot's unexpected illness or other urgent circumstances. Many of these men continuously traveled up and down studying the river, not because they truly expected to find employment, but because (since they were guests aboard the vessel) it cost less to 'examine the river' than to remain on shore and pay for lodging. Eventually these men became particular about their preferences, and only frequented boats that had earned a solid reputation for serving excellent meals. All visiting pilots proved valuable, since they were always prepared and eager, regardless of season or time of day, to take the small boat out and help mark the channel or support the boat's pilots in whatever way possible. They were also welcomed because all pilots become endless conversationalists when they gather together, and since they discuss only the river, they always understand each other and remain consistently fascinating. A genuine pilot cares about nothing else in the world except the river, and his professional pride exceeds that of royalty.

We had an excellent group of these river inspectors with us on this journey. There were eight or ten of them, and our spacious pilot-house had plenty of room to accommodate them all. Two or three of them wore shiny silk hats, fancy dress shirts, diamond pins on their chests, leather gloves, and polished patent-leather boots. They spoke with refined English and carried themselves with the dignity befitting men of substantial wealth and enormous reputation as pilots. The others dressed more casually and wore tall felt cone-shaped hats on their heads that reminded one of the Commonwealth era.

I was nothing in this distinguished group, and felt diminished, even sluggish. I wasn't even important enough to help steer when we needed to quickly turn the rudder; the guest standing closest would do that when needed—and this happened almost constantly, because of how winding the channel was and how shallow the water. I stood in a corner; and the conversation I overheard completely discouraged me. One visitor said to another—

"Jim, how did you navigate Plum Point on your way up?"

'It happened at night, and I navigated it the way one of the crew members on the "Diana" had instructed me; I began about fifty yards upstream from the woodpile on the false point, and stayed on course toward the cabin below Plum Point until I reached the reef—just under two and a quarter fathoms deep—then I straightened my course toward the middle sandbar until I was directly alongside the old one-armed cottonwood tree in the river bend, then I positioned my boat's stern toward the cottonwood and the bow toward the shallow area above the point, and came through at full speed—nine and a half fathoms deep.'

"Pretty square crossing, isn't it?"

"Yes, but the upper bar is working down fast."

Another pilot spoke up and said—

'I had access to better water conditions than that, and I navigated it further downstream; I began from the misleading landmark—mark twain—lifted the second reef alongside the large submerged tree trunk in the river's curve, and measured quarter less twain.'

One of the beautiful ones commented—

"I don't want to criticize your leadsmen, but that seems like quite a lot of water for Plum Point, if you ask me."

There was an approving nod all around as this quiet insult landed on the show-off and put him in his place. And so they continued their endless chatter. Meanwhile, what was running through my mind was, 'Now if my ears are hearing correctly, I not only have to memorize the names of all the towns and islands and curves, and so on, but I must even develop a close personal familiarity with every old tree stump and one-armed cottonwood and hidden woodpile that decorates the banks of this river for twelve hundred miles; and more than that, I must actually know where these things are in complete darkness, unless these pilots are blessed with eyes that can see through two miles of total blackness; I wish the piloting profession was in Jericho and I had never considered it.'

At dusk Mr. Bixby rang the large bell three times, which was the signal to land, and the captain came out of his quarters at the front of the texas deck and looked up with a questioning expression. Mr. Bixby said—

"We'll stay here for the night, captain."

"Very well, sir."

That was all. The boat reached the shore and was secured for the night. It struck me as remarkable that the pilot could act on his own authority, without needing to ask permission from such an important captain. I ate my dinner and went straight to bed, feeling disheartened by what I had observed and experienced that day. My recent trip's notes were nothing but a jumbled mess of meaningless names. Every time I had examined them during the day, they had left me completely confused and frustrated. I hoped that sleep would give me some relief, but instead, those thoughts churned relentlessly through my mind until dawn broke again, creating a wild and exhausting nightmare.

The next morning I felt quite worn out and dejected. We traveled rapidly downstream, taking considerable risks because we were eager to reach Cairo before nightfall. However, Mr. Bixby's partner, the other pilot, soon ran the boat aground, and we lost so much time getting her free that it became clear darkness would catch us well before we reached the mouth of the river. This was a serious setback, particularly for some of our visiting pilots, whose boats would have to wait for their return, regardless of how long that might take. This development considerably dampened the conversation in the pilot-house. When traveling upstream, pilots weren't concerned about low water or darkness of any kind; only fog could stop them. But downstream navigation was entirely different; a boat became nearly uncontrollable with a strong current pushing from behind; therefore it wasn't standard practice to run downstream at night when the water was low.

There seemed to be one small hope, however: if we could get through the complex and treacherous Hat Island crossing before nightfall, we could risk the remainder, since we would have clearer sailing and calmer waters. But it would be madness to try Hat Island at night. So there was plenty of watch-checking for the rest of the day, and constant calculations about our speed; Hat Island became the endless topic of conversation; at times hope ran high and at other moments we were held up in a difficult crossing, and spirits dropped once more. For hours everyone remained under the weight of this barely contained tension; it even spread to me, and I became so anxious about Hat Island, and felt such tremendous pressure and responsibility, that I longed for just five minutes on land to take a deep, full, calming breath and begin fresh. We weren't keeping regular shifts. Each of our pilots navigated the sections of the river he had traveled on the upstream journey, due to his better knowledge of those areas; but both stayed in the pilot house continuously.

An hour before sunset, Mr. Bixby took control of the wheel while Mr. W—— stepped to the side. For the following thirty minutes, every man clutched his watch and remained restless, quiet, and anxious. Finally, someone spoke up with an ominous sigh—

'Well, there's Hat Island—and we can't reach it.' All the pocket watches snapped shut at once, everyone sighed and grumbled something about it being 'such a shame, such a shame—oh, if only we could have arrived here thirty minutes earlier!' and the area was heavy with disappointment. Some people began to leave, but they lingered, hearing no bell signal to dock. The sun disappeared below the horizon, and the boat continued on. Questioning glances passed between the passengers; one person who had grabbed the door handle and turned it paused, then eventually released his grip and let the handle rotate back to its original position. We moved steadily around the river bend. More glances were shared, along with nods of amazed respect—but nobody spoke. Gradually the men gathered behind Mr. Bixby, as darkness fell and a few faint stars appeared. The complete silence and feeling of anticipation became overwhelming. Mr. Bixby pulled the rope, and two deep, rich tones from the large bell drifted into the night. Then there was a pause, and one additional note rang out. The watchman's voice came next, from the hurricane deck—

"Port side lead, there! Starboard lead!"

The shouts from the crew members taking depth measurements started to echo from far away, and were roughly passed along by the sailors relaying messages on the upper deck.

'M-a-r-k three!... M-a-r-k three!... Quarter-less three!... Half twain!... Quarter twain!... M-a-r-k twain!... Quarter-less—'

Mr. Bixby pulled two bell-ropes, and faint jinglings from deep in the engine room answered him, causing our speed to slow down. Steam started whistling through the gauge-cocks. The leadsmen continued their calls—a sound that always seems eerie in the darkness. Every pilot on board was now watching intently, their eyes focused and voices reduced to whispers. No one remained calm and relaxed except Mr. Bixby. He would turn his wheel and position himself on a spoke, and as the steamboat swung toward what appeared to me as completely invisible markers—since we seemed to be surrounded by a vast and dark sea—he would intercept and secure her position there. From the mumble of barely audible conversation, you could occasionally make out a clear sentence—like—

"There! She's cleared the first reef safely!"

After a pause, another quiet voice—

"Her stern is coming down just exactly right, by George!"

"Now she's hitting her marks; over she goes!"

Someone else muttered—

"Oh, it was done beautifully—beautifully!"

Now the engines had stopped completely, and we drifted along with the current. I couldn't actually see the boat moving, though, because all the stars had disappeared by then. This drifting felt like the most depressing thing imaginable; it made your heart feel like it had stopped beating. Soon I noticed an even darker shadow than the blackness that surrounded us everywhere. It was the tip of the island. We were heading straight toward it. We moved into its deeper shadow, and the danger seemed so immediate that I felt like I might suffocate; I had an overwhelming urge to do something, anything at all, to save the boat. But Mr. Bixby just kept standing at his wheel, quiet and focused like a cat, while all the other pilots stood right behind him, shoulder to shoulder.

"She's not going to make it!" someone whispered.

The water became shallower and shallower, according to the leadsman's calls, until it was down to—

"Eight and a half feet!.... E-i-g-h-t feet!.... E-i-g-h-t feet!.... Seven and—"

Mr. Bixby called out a warning through his speaking tube to the engineer—

"Get ready, now!"

"Yes, sir!"

"Seven and a half feet! Seven feet! Six and—"

We hit the bottom! Right away Mr. Bixby started ringing all the bells, yelled through the speaking tube, 'NOW, give her everything you've got—every ounce!' then called to his partner, 'Put her hard down! grab her! grab her!' The boat scraped and ground its way through the sand, balanced on the edge of disaster for one incredible moment, and then over she went! And the cheer that erupted behind Mr. Bixby had never before threatened to blow the roof off a pilot-house!

There was no more trouble after that. Mr. Bixby became a hero that night, and it took quite a while before river men stopped talking about what he had accomplished.

To fully understand the incredible precision needed to navigate the massive steamboat through its designated route in that dark, murky expanse of water, one must realize that the vessel not only has to carefully thread its way through submerged logs and hidden reefs, then pass so close to the island's tip that the overhanging branches brush against its stern, but at one particular spot it must glide almost within touching distance of a sunken and unseen wreck that would tear the hull planks right out from beneath the boat if it were to collide with it, destroying a quarter million dollars worth of steamboat and cargo within five minutes, and possibly taking a hundred and fifty human lives along with it.

The final comment I heard that evening was a compliment directed at Mr. Bixby, spoken as a soliloquy with great feeling by one of our guests. He said—

"By the Shadow of Death, but he's a lightning pilot!"

Chapter 8: Perplexing Lessons

After what felt like an endless period of time, I had succeeded in cramming my mind with islands, towns, sandbars, points, and river bends; though it formed a strangely lifeless collection of information. Still, since I could close my eyes and recite a lengthy series of these names while missing no more than ten miles of river out of every fifty, I started to believe I could pilot a steamboat down to New Orleans if I could just navigate around those small missing sections. But naturally, my self-satisfaction could barely begin to make me feel a bit proud before Mr. Bixby would come up with something to bring me back down to earth. One day he suddenly confronted me with this crushing blow—

"What is the shape of Walnut Bend?"

He might as well have asked me what my grandmother thought about protoplasm. I thought carefully about it, and then told him I didn't realize it had any specific shape. My explosive boss naturally blew up right away, and then kept ranting and raving until he ran out of insults to throw at me.

I had discovered long ago that he only carried a limited amount of ammunition, and I was certain he would calm down into a very peaceful and even apologetic old smooth-bore once he had used it all up. That word 'old' is simply a term of endearment; he was no more than thirty-four. I waited. Eventually he said—

'Son, you need to know the river's shape perfectly. That's all you have to guide you on a pitch-black night. Everything else disappears completely. But remember, the river doesn't look the same at night as it does during the day.'

"How on earth am I ever going to learn it, then?"

"How do you navigate through a hallway at home in the dark? It's because you know its layout. You can't see it, but you know where everything is."

'Are you telling me that I have to learn every single tiny change in the shape of the banks along this endless river just as well as I know the layout of the front hallway in my own house?'

"I swear, you must know them better than anyone has ever known the layout of the rooms in their own home."

"I wish I was dead!"

"Now I don't want to discourage you, but—"

"Well, go ahead and tell me everything; I might as well hear it now instead of later."

'You see, this has to be learned; there's no way around it. A clear starlit night creates such deep shadows that if you didn't know the shape of a shoreline perfectly, you would steer away from every cluster of trees, because you would mistake the black shadow for a solid headland; and you can see you would be getting terrified every fifteen minutes by your watch. You would stay fifty yards from shore the entire time when you should be within fifty feet of it. You can't see a snag in one of those shadows, but you know exactly where it is, and the shape of the river tells you when you're approaching it. Then there's your pitch-black night; the river has a very different shape on a pitch-black night than what it has on a starlit night. All shores appear to be straight lines then, and very faint ones too; and you'd treat them as straight lines

63

except you know better. You confidently steer your boat right into what appears to be a solid, straight wall (knowing very well that in reality there is a curve there), and that wall retreats and makes way for you. Then there's your gray mist. You take a night when there's one of these eerie, drizzling, gray mists, and then there isn't any particular shape to a shore. A gray mist would confuse the mind of the oldest man who ever lived. Well, then, different types of moonlight alter the shape of the river in different ways. You see'

"Oh, please don't say anything more! Do I really have to memorize the shape of the river in all these five hundred thousand different ways? If I tried to store all that information in my head, it would weigh me down so much I'd be walking hunched over."

'No! You only learn the shape of the river, and you learn it with such complete certainty that you can always navigate by the shape that's in your mind, and never pay attention to the one that's right in front of you.'

"Alright, I'll give it a try; but once I've learned it, can I count on it staying the same? Will it maintain its form and not change unpredictably?"

Before Mr. Bixby could respond, Mr. W—— entered to take over the watch, and he said—

'Bixby, you'll need to watch out for President's Island and all that area stretching way up past the Old Hen and Chickens. The riverbanks are collapsing and the shoreline is changing constantly. You wouldn't even recognize the point above mile marker 40 anymore. You can now navigate up inside the old sycamore snag.[2]

So that question was answered. Here were miles of shoreline constantly changing shape. My spirits sank into the mud again. Two things seemed quite clear to me. First, that to become a pilot a person had to learn more than any individual should be expected

---

[2] It may not be necessary, but it still can't hurt to explain that 'inside' means between the snag and the shore.—M.T.

to know; and second, that he must relearn it all in a completely different way every single day.

That night we were on watch duty until midnight. It was a long-standing tradition on the river for the two pilots to have a brief conversation when they switched shifts. As the incoming pilot pulled on his gloves and lit his cigar, his colleague, the pilot going off duty, would typically say something like this—

'I believe the sandbar upstream is shifting down slightly near Hale's Point; we measured two and a quarter fathoms with the lower lead line and two fathoms[3] with the other one.'

"Yes, I thought it was getting a bit shallower on my last trip. Did you encounter any other boats?"

"I encountered one ship positioned alongside the front of number 21, but she was positioned far over near the shore, and I couldn't get a complete view of her. I assumed she was the 'Sunny South'—she didn't have any skylights in front of the smokestacks."

And so on. When the relieving pilot took control of the wheel, his partner would tell him which bend they were in and point out that they were passing by a particular person's wood-yard or plantation. I thought this was just being polite, but I assumed it was actually necessary. However, Mr. W—— showed up for his watch a full twelve minutes late that particular night—a serious violation of proper conduct; in fact, it's the worst offense a pilot can commit. So Mr. Bixby didn't greet him at all, but simply handed over the wheel and walked out of the pilot-house without saying a word. I was shocked; it was an extremely dark night, we were in an especially wide and confusing section of the river where you couldn't make out any shapes or landmarks, and it seemed unbelievable that Mr. Bixby would leave that poor man to wreck the boat while trying to figure out where he was. But I decided I

---

[3] Two fathoms. 'Quarter twain' is two-and-a-quarter fathoms, thirteen-and-a-half feet. 'Mark three' is three fathoms.

would support him no matter what. He would discover that he wasn't completely without friends. So I stayed nearby and waited for him to ask where we were. But Mr. W—— continued calmly through the thick wall of darkness that surrounded us like an atmosphere, and never said a word. What an arrogant fool, I thought; here's a devil who would rather send us all to our deaths than feel indebted to me, because I'm not yet one of the experienced crew members with the privilege to disrespect captains and boss around everything living and dead on a steamboat. Eventually I climbed up onto the bench; I didn't think it was safe to fall asleep while this madman was on duty.

However, I must have fallen asleep at some point, because the next thing I knew was that dawn was breaking, Mr. W—— had left, and Mr. Bixby was back at the wheel. So it was four o'clock and everything was fine—except for me; I felt like a bag of dry bones with all of them trying to ache at the same time.

Mr. Bixby asked me why I had stayed up there. I admitted that it was to do Mr. W—— a favor—to tell him where he was. It took five minutes for the complete absurdity of the situation to sink into Mr. Bixby's mind, and then I think it filled him nearly to the brim; because he gave me a compliment—and not much of one either. He said,

"Well, all things considered, you seem to be more different kinds of a fool than any person I've ever encountered before. What did you think he wanted to know that for?"

I mentioned that I believed it could be helpful for him.

'Convenience D-nation! Didn't I tell you that a man's got to know the river in the night the same as he'd know his own front hall?'

'Well, I can navigate the front hallway in the dark if I know it's the front hallway; but imagine you place me in the middle of it in the dark without telling me which hallway it is; how would I know?'

"Well, you have to on the river!"

"All right. Then I'm glad I never said anything to Mr. W—"

"I should say so. Why, he would have slammed you right through the window and completely destroyed a hundred dollars' worth of window frame and glass."

I was relieved that this damage had been prevented, because it would have made me unpopular with the owners. They always despised anyone who had a reputation for being careless and damaging property.

I began working to learn the shape of the river, and of all the elusive and impossible-to-grasp objects I had ever tried to understand or get a handle on, this was the most challenging. I would fix my gaze on a sharp, tree-covered point that jutted far out into the river several miles ahead of me, and work hard to imprint its shape in my memory; but just as I was starting to feel satisfied with my progress, we would approach it and the frustrating thing would start to dissolve and fold back into the riverbank! If there had been a noticeable dead tree standing right at the tip of the cape, I would discover that tree had blended inconspicuously into the surrounding forest and was now positioned in the middle of a straight shoreline when I drew alongside it! No distinctive hill would maintain its shape long enough for me to determine what its actual form was, but instead it kept dissolving and changing as if it were a mountain of butter sitting in the hottest part of the tropics. Nothing ever looked the same when I was traveling downstream as it had appeared when I went upstream. I brought up these small challenges with Mr. Bixby. He said

'That's exactly what makes it so valuable. If those shapes didn't shift every few seconds, they'd be completely useless. Take this spot where we are right now, for example. As long as that hill over there stays as just one hill, I can keep moving straight ahead the way I'm going; but the second it splits at the top and creates a V shape, I know I need to steer quickly to the right, or I'll smash this boat to pieces against a rock; and then the instant one side of the V swings behind the other, I have to turn sharply to the left again, or I'll collide with a snag that would rip the backbone right out of this steamboat as cleanly as pulling a splinter from your hand. If that hill didn't change its shape during dangerous nights, there would be a terrible steamboat graveyard around here within a year.'

It was clear that I needed to learn the shape of the river in every possible way imaginable—upside down, backwards, inside out, from front to back, and sideways—and then figure out what to do on foggy nights when it had no visible shape at all. So I began working on it. Over time I started to master this difficult lesson, and my confidence returned once again. Mr. Bixby was prepared and ready to knock it back down. He came at me like this—

"How much water did we encounter during the middle crossing at Hole-in-the-Wall on our second-to-last trip?"

I found this completely unacceptable. I said—

"Every trip, going downstream and upstream, the leadsmen sing out the depths through that complicated area for three-quarters of an hour straight. How do you think I can remember such a confusing mess like that?"

'Son, you need to memorize this. You have to remember the precise location and the exact landmarks where the boat was positioned when we encountered the shallowest water in every single one of the five hundred shallow spots between St. Louis and New Orleans; and you can't confuse the shallow depth measurements and markers from one journey with the shallow depth measurements and markers from another trip, because they're rarely the same twice. You must keep them distinct.'

When I regained consciousness, I said—

"When I reach the point where I can do that, I'll be capable of bringing the dead back to life, and then I won't need to pilot a steamboat to earn my living. I want to quit this profession. I want a slop bucket and a brush; I'm only suited to be a deck hand. I don't have enough intelligence to be a pilot; and even if I did, I wouldn't have the physical strength to handle the responsibility, unless I walked around on crutches."

'Now stop that! When I say I'll teach a man the river, I mean it. And you can count on it, I'll teach him or it'll be the death of him.'

Chapter 9: Ongoing Confusion

There was no point in arguing with someone like this. I quickly put so much pressure on my memory that eventually even the shallow water and the numerous crossing-marks started to stick with me. But the outcome was exactly the same. I could never manage to learn more than one difficult thing before another one appeared. Now I had frequently observed pilots staring at the water and acting as if they were reading it like a book; but it was a book that meant nothing to me. Eventually, though, a time arrived when Mr. Bixby seemed to believe I had progressed far enough to handle a lesson on water-reading. So he started—

'Do you see that long diagonal line on the water's surface? That's a reef. What's more, it's a bluff reef. There's a solid sandbar underneath it that rises almost as vertically as a house wall. There's plenty of water right up against it, but very little water over the top of it. If you were to strike it, you would smash the boat to pieces. Do you see where the line spreads out at the upper end and starts to disappear?'

"Yes, sir."

"Well, that's a shallow spot; that's where the reef begins. You can go over that area without damaging anything. Cross over now, and stay close along the reef—the water's calm there—not much of a current."

I followed the reef until I reached the area where it ended in a fringe. Then Mr. Bixby said—

'Now get ready. Wait until I give the signal. She won't want to climb onto the reef; a boat despises shallow water. Stand by— wait—WAIT—keep her under control. NOW force her down! Grab her! grab her!'

He grabbed the other side of the wheel and helped turn it until it was completely down, and then we held it in that position. The boat fought back and wouldn't respond for a moment, but then it suddenly swung to starboard, climbed over the reef, and created a long, furious ridge of foaming water that rushed away from its bow.

'Now watch her carefully; watch her like a cat, or she'll slip away from you. When she fights hard and the steering wheel jerks a little, in a rough, slippery kind of way, ease up on her slightly; that's how she tells you at night that the water is too shallow; but keep moving her forward, little by little, toward the point. You're well up on the sandbar now; there's a sandbar under every point, because the water that flows down around it creates a whirlpool and lets the sediment settle. Do you see those thin lines on the surface of the water that spread out like the ribs of a fan? Well, those are small reefs; you want to just barely miss the ends of them, but pass them pretty close. Now watch out—watch out! Don't you get too close to that smooth, slippery-looking area; there aren't nine feet of water there; she won't make it through. She's starting to sense it; pay attention, I'm telling you! Oh damn, there you go! Stop the right wheel! Quick! Shift into reverse! Back her up!'

The engine bells rang out and the engines responded immediately, sending tall white columns of steam high into the air through the exhaust pipes, but it was too late. The boat had truly "smelled" the sandbar; the foamy waves that spread out from her bow suddenly vanished, a massive motionless swell came rolling forward and swept ahead of her, she tilted far over to the left side, and went racing toward the opposite shore as if she were terrified. We were a good mile from where we should have been when we finally regained control of her.

During the afternoon watch the following day, Mr. Bixby asked me if I knew how to navigate the next few miles. I replied—

'Go inside the first snag above the point, outside the next one, start out from the lower end of Higgins's wood-yard, make a square crossing and—'

"That's fine. I'll return before you finish up at the next location."

But he wasn't. He was still below deck when I rounded the bend and entered a stretch of river that made me nervous. I didn't realize he was hiding behind a smokestack to watch how I would handle things. I sailed along cheerfully, growing more and more confident, since he had never left the boat under my complete control for such a long time before. I even started showing off by letting go of the wheel entirely while I arrogantly turned my back to check the wake and hummed a song, displaying the kind of casual confidence I had greatly admired in Bixby and other skilled pilots. At one point I looked away for quite a while, and when I turned back to face forward, my heart jumped into my throat so suddenly that if I hadn't clenched my teeth together I would have lost it. One of those terrifying rocky reefs was stretching its dangerous length directly across our path! I panicked completely; I didn't know which way was up; I gasped and couldn't catch my breath; I spun the wheel so frantically that it twisted together like a spider's web; the boat responded and turned sharply away from the reef, but the reef seemed to follow us! I ran from it, and still it pursued us, still it remained—right in front of our bow! I never looked to see where I was heading, I just fled. The terrible collision was about to happen—why wouldn't that scoundrel come! If I broke the rules by ringing a bell, I might get thrown overboard. But that would be better than destroying the boat. So in desperate panic I created such a clanging racket down below as I imagine had never amazed an engineer in this world before. Amid the

71

chaos of the bells, the engines began backing and filling frantically, and I lost my mind completely—we were about to crash into the forest on the far side of the river. Just then Mr. Bixby stepped calmly into sight on the hurricane deck. I felt overwhelming gratitude toward him. My panic disappeared; I would have felt secure on the edge of Niagara Falls with Mr. Bixby on the hurricane deck. He casually and gently removed his toothpick from his mouth with his fingers, as if it were a cigar—we were just about to climb into an overhanging large tree, and the passengers were scurrying toward the stern like rats—and called up these instructions to me very softly—

"Stop the right engine. Stop the left engine. Reverse both engines."

The boat paused, came to a stop, pushed its front end into the branches for a tense moment, then unwillingly started to retreat.

"Stop the left side. Move forward on it. Stop the right side. Move forward on it. Aim her toward the sandbar."

I sailed away as peacefully as a summer morning. Mr. Bixby walked in and spoke with pretended innocence—

"When you spot a ship, son, you should ring the large bell three times before you dock, so the engineers can prepare."

I felt my face turn red from the sarcasm, and I told him I hadn't experienced any hail.

"Ah! Then it was for wood, I suppose. The officer on watch will tell you when he wants to take on wood."

I continued eating and said I wasn't looking for wood.

"Really? Well, what could you possibly want over here in the bend, then? Have you ever heard of a boat following a bend upstream at this point in the river?"

"No sir—and I wasn't trying to follow it. I was getting away from a bluff reef."

"No, it wasn't a bluff reef; there isn't one within three miles of where you were."

"But I saw it. It was just as steep and high as that cliff over there."

"Just about. Run over it!"

"Are you giving me an order?"

"Yes. Go through it again."

"If I don't, I wish I may die."

"All right; I'm taking responsibility." I was now just as eager to wreck the boat as I had been to save it before. I burned my orders into my memory to use at the inquest, and headed straight for the reef. As it vanished beneath our bow, I held my breath; but we glided over it smoothly like oil.

"Now don't you see the difference? It was nothing but a wind reef. The wind does that."

"I understand now. But it looks exactly like a bluff reef. How will I ever be able to tell the difference between them?"

"I can't explain it to you. It's just instinct. Eventually, you'll naturally learn to tell one from the other, but you'll never be able to explain why or how you can distinguish between them."

It turned out to be true. The surface of the water, over time, became an amazing book—a book that was like a dead language to the untrained passenger, but which revealed its thoughts to me without holding back, sharing its most precious secrets as clearly as if it spoke them aloud. And it wasn't a book to be read once and tossed away, because it had a new story to tell every day. Throughout the entire twelve hundred miles there was never a page that lacked interest, never one that you could skip without missing something important, never one that you would want to pass over, thinking you could find better entertainment elsewhere. There has never been such a wonderful book written by humans; never one whose fascination was so captivating, so constant, so brilliantly refreshed with every new reading. The passenger who couldn't read it was delighted by a strange kind of faint ripple on its surface (on the rare times when he didn't miss it completely); but to the pilot that was like text in italics; in fact, it was more than that, it was like a warning in the largest letters, with a series of urgent exclamation points at the end; because it meant that a wreck or a rock was hidden there that could destroy the life out of the strongest ship that ever sailed. It is the most subtle and basic sign the water ever gives, and the most terrifying to a pilot's eye. In reality, the passenger who couldn't read this book saw nothing but all kinds of beautiful images in it created by the sun and shadowed by the clouds, while to the experienced eye these weren't pictures at all, but the most serious and urgent kind of information.

Once I had learned the language of this water and come to know every small detail that lined the great river as well as I knew the letters of the alphabet, I had gained something valuable. But I had also lost something. I had lost something that could never be given back to me as long as I lived. All the grace, the beauty, the poetry had disappeared from the magnificent river! I still remember a particular amazing sunset that I saw when steamboating was still new to me. A wide stretch of the river had turned to blood; in the middle distance the red color brightened into gold, through which a single log came floating, dark and noticeable; in one spot a long, slanted mark lay sparkling on the water; in another place the surface was broken by bubbling, rolling rings that were as colorful as an opal; where the reddish glow was weakest, there was a smooth area covered with elegant circles and spreading lines, traced so delicately; the shore on our left was thickly wooded, and the dark shadow cast by this forest was interrupted in one place by a long, rippled trail that gleamed like silver; and high above the forest wall a smooth-trunked dead tree waved a single leafy branch that glowed like a flame in the clear splendor flowing from the sun. There were elegant curves, reflected images, wooded heights, soft distances; and over the entire scene, both far and near, the fading lights drifted steadily, enriching it every passing moment with new wonders of color.

I stood there as if under a spell. I absorbed it all in silent wonder. The world felt completely new to me, and I had never witnessed anything like this back home. But as I mentioned, a day arrived when I started to stop noticing the magnificent beauty that the moon and sun and dusk created on the river's surface; another day came when I stopped noticing them entirely. Then, if that same sunset scene had appeared again, I would have observed it without any sense of wonder, and would have remarked about it to myself in this way: This sun indicates that we're going to have wind tomorrow; that drifting log shows that the river is rising, no surprise there; that diagonal mark on the water points to a sharp reef that's going to destroy someone's steamboat one of these nights, if it continues extending out like that; those churning 'boils' reveal a dissolving sandbar and a shifting channel in that spot; the lines and circles in the smooth water over there serve as a warning that that problematic area is becoming dangerously shallow; that silver line in the forest's shadow is the 'break' from a new fallen tree, and it has positioned itself in the perfect spot it could have chosen to catch steamboats; that tall dead tree, with just one living branch, isn't going to survive much longer, and then how will anyone ever navigate through this treacherous stretch at night without that familiar old landmark.

No, all the romance and beauty had vanished from the river. The only value any part of it held for me now was how useful it could be for safely navigating a steamboat. Ever since then, I've felt genuine sympathy for doctors. What does that lovely glow on a beautiful woman's face mean to a doctor except a warning sign that hints at some fatal illness lurking beneath? Aren't all her visible attractions filled with what he recognizes as indicators of hidden sickness? Does he ever truly see her beauty, or does he only examine her with professional eyes, silently noting her unhealthy symptoms? And doesn't he sometimes question whether mastering his profession has brought him more gain or more loss?

Chapter 10: Completing My Education

Anyone who has taken the time to read the chapters I've written before this one might wonder why I'm examining piloting in such detail as a science. That was exactly what I intended with those chapters, and I'm not finished yet. I want to demonstrate, with the utmost care and thoroughness, what an incredible science it truly is. Ship channels have buoys and lights marking them, which makes learning to navigate them relatively straightforward; clear-water rivers with gravel bottoms shift their channels very slowly, so you only need to learn them once; but piloting becomes an entirely different challenge when you're dealing with massive rivers like the Mississippi and the Missouri, whose muddy banks constantly collapse and shift, whose fallen trees are always moving to new locations, whose sandbars never stay put, whose channels are constantly changing course and avoiding their previous paths, and whose obstacles must be faced during all hours of the night and in every kind of weather without the help of a single lighthouse or a single buoy; because there isn't a single light or buoy to be found anywhere along the entire three or four thousand miles of this treacherous river.[4] I believe I'm justified in spending so much time on this remarkable science because I'm confident that no one has ever written even a single paragraph about it who had actually piloted a steamboat themselves, and therefore had hands-on knowledge of the subject. If this topic had been written about extensively before, I would need to be more considerate of the reader's patience; but since it's completely unexplored territory, I've felt free to devote a substantial amount of space to it.

---

[4] True at the time referred to; not true now (1882).

When I had memorized the name and location of every visible landmark along the river; when I had mastered its contours so thoroughly that I could close my eyes and mentally trace its path from St. Louis to New Orleans; when I had learned to interpret the water's surface the way someone reads the morning newspaper; and finally, when I had trained my sluggish memory to store countless depth measurements and navigation markers, holding them firmly in mind, I believed my education was finished: so I started tilting my cap to one side and keeping a toothpick in my mouth while at the wheel. Mr. Bixby noticed these pretentious behaviors. One day he said—

"What's the height of that riverbank over there, near Burgess's place?"

"How can I tell, sir? It's three-quarters of a mile away."

"Very poor eyesight—very poor. Take the magnifying glass."

I took the glass and said right away, "I can't tell. I suppose that bank is about a foot and a half high."

"A foot and a half! That's a six-foot bank. How high was the bank along here on our last trip?"

"I don't know; I never noticed."

"You didn't? Well, you must always do it from now on."

'Why?'

"You'll need to learn many things that it reveals to you. For instance, it shows you the river's level—it tells you whether there's more or less water in the river along this stretch compared to the last trip."

"The leads tell me that." I figured I had gotten the better of him with that response.

"Yes, but what if the depth readings are wrong? The bank would show you that, and then you'd give those leadsmen a good talking-to. There was a ten-foot bank here on the last trip, and now there's only a six-foot bank. What does that mean?"

"The river is four feet higher than it was on our last trip."

"Very good. Is the river rising or falling?"

'Rising.'

"No it isn't."

"I think I'm right, sir. Over there is some driftwood floating down the stream."

'When the river rises, it lifts the driftwood, but the debris continues floating for some time even after the water stops rising. The riverbank will show you evidence of this. Wait until you reach a spot where the bank slopes gently downward. Right here—do you notice this thin strip of fine sediment? That material settled there when the water level was higher. You can see that the driftwood starts getting stranded there as well. The bank provides clues in other ways too. Do you see that tree stump on the false point?'

"Yes, yes, sir."

"Well, the water reaches right up to the roots. You need to make a note of that."

'Why?'

"Because that means there are seven feet in the chute of 103."

"But 103 is still a long way up the river."

'That's where having the riverbank helps us out. There's plenty of water at mile marker 103 right now, but there might not be enough by the time we reach it; however, the bank will keep us informed the entire way. You don't navigate narrow channels on a dropping river when heading upstream, and there are very few of those passages you're permitted to run when going downstream. There's a federal law prohibiting it. The river might be rising by the time we reach 103, and if that happens, we'll take that route. We're drawing—how much water?'

"Six feet toward the back—six and a half toward the front."

"Well, you do seem to know something."

'But what I really want to know is, do I have to keep constantly measuring the banks of this river, twelve hundred miles, month after month?'

"Of course!"

My feelings were too overwhelming to express in words for a moment. Soon I said—

"And what about these chutes? Are there many of them?"

'Absolutely. I think we won't navigate any part of the river on this trip the way you've ever seen it flow before—if you know what I mean. If the river starts rising again, we'll travel behind sandbars that you've always seen sticking up out of the water, high and dry like a house roof; we'll cut across shallow areas that you've never even noticed, straight through the middle of sandbars that spread across three hundred acres of river; we'll slip through narrow channels where you've always believed there was solid ground; we'll shoot through the forests and bypass twenty-five miles of river completely; we'll see the back side of every island between New Orleans and Cairo.'

"Then I have to go to work and learn just as much more about the river as I already know."

"About twice as much more, as close as you can estimate it."

"Well, you live and learn. I think I was an idiot when I got into this business."

"Yes, that's true. And you still are. But you won't be once you've learned it."

"Oh, I'll never be able to learn this."

"I will see that you do."

Eventually I dared to try again—

"Do I have to learn all of this just like I know the rest of the river—every shape and detail—so I can navigate it at night?"

'Yes. And you need to have reliable, accurate markers from one end of the river to the other that will help the riverbank tell you when there's enough water in each of these countless spots—like that tree stump, you understand. When the river first starts to rise, you can navigate half a dozen of the deepest channels; when it rises another foot you can navigate another dozen; the next foot will add a couple dozen more, and so on: so you can see you have to know your banks and markers with absolute certainty, and never confuse them; because when you start through one of those narrow passages, there's no turning back, unlike on the main river; you have to go through completely, or stay there six months if you get trapped on a falling river. There are about fifty of these narrow passages that you can't navigate at all except when the river is completely full and overflowing its banks.'

"This new lesson offers a promising outlook."

'Cheerful enough. And remember what I just told you; when you enter one of those places, you have to go all the way through. They're too narrow to turn around in, too winding to back out of, and the shallow water is always at the far end; never anywhere else. And the far end of them is always likely to be silting up, bit by bit, so that the markers you use to judge their depth this season might not be accurate next time.'

"Should I learn a new set every year, then?"

"Exactly. Pull her tight to the bar! Why are you standing in the middle of the river?"

The following months revealed extraordinary sights to me. On the very day we had the conversation I just described, we encountered a massive flood surge moving down the river. The entire enormous surface of the water was dark with floating dead logs, broken branches, and massive trees that had collapsed and been swept away. It took the most careful navigation to find our way through this rushing mass of debris, even during daylight hours when traveling from one point to another; and at night the challenge became enormously greater; repeatedly a enormous log, floating deep beneath the surface, would suddenly emerge directly in front of our bow, heading straight toward us; there was no point in trying to dodge it then; we could only shut down the engines, and one paddle wheel would roll over that log from end to end, creating a thunderous noise and tilting the boat in a manner that made passengers very uneasy. Occasionally we would strike one of these submerged logs with a tremendous crash, right in the middle, at full steam power, and it would shock the boat as though she had collided with a landmass. Sometimes this log would get stuck and remain directly across our front, causing the Mississippi to back up behind it; we would need to do some reverse maneuvering then to escape from the blockage. We frequently struck pale logs in the darkness, since we couldn't spot them until we were directly upon them; but a dark log stands out quite clearly at night. A white snag becomes a dangerous threat once daylight disappears.

Of course, during the major flood season, down came a massive swarm of enormous timber rafts from the headwaters of the Mississippi, coal barges from Pittsburgh, small trading boats from all over, and flatboats from 'Posey County,' Indiana, loaded with 'fruit and furniture'—the standard phrase used to describe their cargo, though in simple English the freight given this fancy name was actually hoop-poles and pumpkins. Pilots had a deadly hatred for these vessels; and the feeling was returned with interest. The law required all such vulnerable traders to keep a light burning, but it was a law that was frequently violated. All of a sudden, on a dark night, a light would appear, right under our bow, almost, and a panicked voice, with the backwoods 'twang' to it, would cry out—

"Where the hell are you going! Can't you see anything, you damn egg-sucking, sheep-stealing, one-eyed son of a stuffed monkey!"

Then for a moment, as we rushed past with our whistle blowing, the red glow from our furnaces would illuminate the flatboat and the figure of the wildly gesturing speaker as if lit by a flash of lightning, and in that moment our firemen and deck-hands would exchange a storm of thrown objects and curses, one of our paddle wheels would carry away the splintered pieces of a steering oar, and then the complete darkness would close in again. And that flatboatman would certainly go to New Orleans and file a lawsuit against our steamboat, swearing emphatically that he had kept a light burning the entire time, when the truth was that his crew had taken the lantern below deck to sing and tell lies and drink and gamble by its light, leaving no one on watch above.

Once, during the night, in one of those forest-lined ravines behind an island that steamboat workers vividly describe as "dark as the inside of a cow," we nearly crashed into a Posey County family and destroyed their fruit, furniture, and everything else they owned. Fortunately, they happened to be playing music down below, and we caught the sound just in time to steer away. We didn't cause any serious damage, which was disappointing, though we came close enough that we felt hopeful for a moment. These people then brought up their lantern, naturally, and as we reversed and maneuvered to get away, the entire family stood in its light— men and women of all ages—and swore at us until the air turned blue. On another occasion, a coal barge worker fired a bullet through our pilot house when we borrowed a steering oar from him in an extremely tight spot.

Chapter 11: The River Rises

During this major flood, these small amateur boats were an unbearable annoyance. We were navigating one narrow channel after another—a completely new experience for me—and whenever we encountered a particularly tight spot in a channel, we were almost certain to run into a flatboat there; and if it wasn't blocking that location, we would discover it in an even worse position, specifically at the entrance of the channel, stuck in the shallow water. And then there would be endless exchanges of vulgar pleasantries.

Sometimes, on the big river, when we were carefully feeling our way through thick fog, the deep silence would suddenly shatter with shouting and the clatter of tin pans, and instantly a log raft would emerge dimly through the misty curtain, bearing down on us; and then we didn't wait around to exchange pleasantries, but yanked our engine bells frantically and threw on every bit of steam we could muster to get out of the way! You don't ram a rock or a solid log raft with a steamboat if you can possibly avoid it.

You'll find it hard to believe, but many steamboat clerks always carried a large collection of religious pamphlets with them during those bygone steamboat days. They really did. Twenty times each day we would be maneuvering around a sandbar, while a line of these small-time troublemakers were floating down toward the head of the bend several miles above and beyond us. Then a small boat would shoot out from one of them and come struggling its difficult way across the vast stretch of water. It would slow down completely in the shadow of our front deck, and the breathless rowers would yell, "Give me a paper!" as the boat drifted quickly behind us. The clerk would toss over a bundle of New Orleans newspapers. If these were grabbed without any remarks, you might observe that suddenly a dozen other small boats had been drifting toward us without making a sound. You see, they had been waiting to watch how the first one would be treated. Since the first boat made no complaints, all the others would lean into their oars and approach now; and as quickly as they arrived the clerk would throw over tidy bundles of religious pamphlets, tied to wooden shingles. The volume of intense cursing that twelve packages of religious literature will inspire when fairly distributed among twelve raftsmen's crews, who have rowed a heavy boat two miles on a sweltering day to obtain them, is absolutely unbelievable.

As I mentioned before, the major flood revealed an entirely new world to me. Once the river had overflowed its banks, we abandoned our familiar routes and found ourselves constantly navigating over sandbars that had previously stood ten feet above the waterline. We were skimming along stubby shorelines, like the one at the base of Madrid Bend, which I had always seen pilots avoid in the past. We were racing through narrow channels like the one at 82, where the opening at the bottom had been a solid wall of trees until our bow nearly reached that exact location. Some of these channels were completely isolated. The thick, undisturbed forest hung over both sides of the winding narrow passage, and you could easily imagine that no human being had ever ventured into these places before. The swaying grapevines, the grassy alcoves and scenic views we caught glimpses of as we rushed past, the blooming vines displaying their crimson flowers from the crowns of dead tree trunks, and all the lavish abundance of the woodland vegetation were simply wasted and discarded in these remote spots. These channels were beautiful places to navigate through; they ran deep everywhere except at the entrance; the current flowed gently; beneath the jutting land formations the water was completely still, and the hidden banks rose so steeply that where the delicate willow groves extended outward, you could plunge your boat's side directly into them as you sped along, making it feel as though you were actually flying.

Behind other islands we discovered miserable little farms and even more miserable little log cabins. There were rickety rail fences poking a foot or two above the water, with one or two men in jeans perched on the top rail—shivering, sickly, and yellow-faced in their wretchedness. They sat with elbows resting on their knees and jaws cupped in their hands, chewing tobacco and spitting the juice at floating wood chips through the gaps left by missing teeth. Meanwhile, the rest of their families and their few farm animals were crowded together in an empty wooden flatboat moored nearby. In this flatboat, the family would have to cook, eat, and sleep for days or possibly weeks, until the river dropped two or three feet and allowed them to return to their log cabin and their fever chills—those chills being a merciful gift from an all-wise Providence that let them get exercise without any real effort. This kind of watery camping was something these people could expect to endure a couple of times each year: once during the December flood from the Ohio River, and again during the June flood from the Mississippi. Yet these were actually kind blessings, because they at least allowed these poor souls to come back to life occasionally and witness something interesting when a steamboat passed by. They truly valued this gift, opening their mouths and eyes wide to make the most of these rare moments. But what could these exiled people possibly find to do to keep from dying of depression during the low-water season?

Once, while navigating through one of these beautiful island channels, we discovered our path completely blocked by a massive fallen tree. This gives you an idea of just how narrow some of these waterways were. The passengers enjoyed an hour of leisure time in an untouched wilderness while the crew members cut away the obstruction; there was simply no possibility of turning around, you understand.

From Cairo to Baton Rouge, when the river overflows its banks, you don't face much difficulty navigating at night because the thousand-mile wall of thick forest protecting both sides is only broken by occasional farm or wood-yard openings, making it nearly impossible to 'lose the river' any more than you could wander out of a fenced pathway. However, from Baton Rouge to New Orleans, the situation changes completely. The river stretches more than a mile across and runs very deep—reaching depths of two hundred feet in some areas. For well over a hundred miles, both riverbanks have been stripped of their trees and lined with unbroken sugar plantations, with only scattered saplings or rows of decorative China-trees appearing occasionally. The timber has been cleared completely to the back edges of the plantations, extending two to four miles inland. When the first frost threatens to arrive, the plantation owners rush to harvest their crops. After they finish processing the sugar cane, they pile up the leftover stalks (called bagasse) into enormous heaps and burn them, even though in other sugar-producing regions this bagasse serves as fuel for the sugar mill furnaces. These piles of wet bagasse burn slowly and produce smoke like the devil's own kitchen.

An embankment ten or fifteen feet high protects both sides of the Mississippi River all the way down the lower section of the waterway, and this embankment sits back from the water's edge anywhere from ten to perhaps a hundred feet, depending on the situation; typically around thirty or forty feet. Fill that entire area with thick, impenetrable darkness from smoke created by a hundred miles of burning bagasse piles when the river has overflowed its banks, then send a steamboat through there at midnight and see how it will feel. And see how you will feel as well! You find yourself far out in the middle of a hazy, dim ocean that has no visible shores, that disappears and vanishes into the dark distances; because you cannot make out the narrow ridge of the embankment, and you constantly think you see a scattered tree when you actually don't. The plantations themselves are changed by the smoke and appear to be part of the ocean. Throughout your entire watch, you suffer from the intense agony of not knowing where you are. You hope you're staying within the river, but you have no way of knowing for certain. All you can be sure of is that you're likely to be within six feet of the bank and disaster when you believe you're a good half-mile from shore. And you're also certain that if you happen to suddenly crash into the embankment and knock your smokestacks into the water, you'll have the small consolation of knowing that this is exactly what you expected would happen. One of the major Vicksburg steamboats shot out into a sugar plantation one night during such conditions and had to remain there for a week. But there was nothing unusual about it; this had happened many times before.

I thought I had finished this chapter, but I want to add something curious while it's fresh in my mind. It's only relevant because it connects to piloting. There used to be an excellent pilot on the river, a Mr. X., who was a sleepwalker. People said that if his mind was troubled about a dangerous stretch of river, he was almost certain to get up and walk in his sleep and do strange things. He once served as fellow-pilot for a trip or two with George Ealer, on a large New Orleans passenger steamboat. During much of the first trip George felt uneasy, but eventually got over it as X. seemed content to stay in his bed while sleeping. Late one night the boat was approaching Helena, Arkansas; the water was low, and the crossing above the town was in a very confusing and treacherous condition. X. had seen the crossing more recently than Ealer had, and since the night was particularly drizzly, gloomy, and dark, Ealer was wondering whether he should have X. called to help navigate the area, when the door opened and X. walked in. Now on very dark nights, light is a deadly enemy to piloting; you know that if you stand in a lighted room on such a night, you cannot see things in the street clearly; but if you turn out the lights and stand in the darkness you can make out objects in the street quite well. So, on very dark nights, pilots do not smoke; they allow no fire in the pilot-house stove if there is even a crack that might let the smallest ray escape; they order the furnaces to be covered with huge tarpaulins and the skylights to be tightly sealed. Then no light whatsoever comes from the boat. The unclear figure that now entered the pilot-house had Mr. X.'s voice. This said—

"Let me handle her, George; I've been watching this place longer than you have, and it's so winding that I think I can navigate it myself more easily than I could explain to you how to do it."

"That's very kind of you, and I promise I'm ready to help. I don't have another drop of sweat left in me. I've been spinning around and around the wheel like a squirrel. It's so dark I can't tell which direction she's turning until she comes spinning around like a top."

So Ealer sat down on the bench, gasping and out of breath. The dark figure took control of the wheel without uttering a word, stabilized the swaying steamboat with a couple of adjustments, and then stood relaxed, guiding it gently from one side to the other, as smoothly and gracefully as if it were broad daylight. When Ealer witnessed this incredible display of navigation, he regretted having admitted his limitations! He gazed in amazement, pondered what he was seeing, and eventually spoke—

"Well, I thought I knew how to steer a steamboat, but that was another mistake of mine."

X. said nothing, but continued serenely with his work. He called for the depth soundings; he signaled to reduce the steam; he maneuvered the boat carefully and precisely into invisible markers, then positioned himself at the center of the wheel and gazed calmly out into the darkness, forward and backward, to confirm his location; as the soundings showed shallower and shallower water, he stopped the engines completely, and the complete silence and tension of 'drifting' ensued when the shallowest water was reached, he increased the steam, carried her skillfully across, and then began to navigate her cautiously into the next series of shallow-water markers; the same careful, attentive use of soundings and engines continued, the boat glided through without scraping bottom, and entered the third and final complexity of the crossing; barely perceptibly she moved through the darkness, advanced inch by inch into her markers, drifted slowly until the shallowest water was called out, and then, under an enormous pressure of steam, went sweeping over the reef and away into deep water and safety!

Ealer released his long-held breath in a deep, relieving sigh and said—

"That's the most skillful piece of piloting that has ever been done on the Mississippi River! I wouldn't have believed it could be done if I hadn't seen it myself."

There was no response, and he continued—

"Just keep her steady for five more minutes, partner, and let me run down and grab a cup of coffee."

A minute later, Ealer was biting into a pie down in the texas and comforting himself with coffee. Just then the night watchman happened to come in, and was about to leave again, when he noticed Ealer and exclaimed—

"Who is at the wheel, sir?"

'X.'

"Head for the pilot-house, faster than lightning!"

The next moment both men were racing up the pilot-house stairway, taking three steps at once! No one was there! The massive steamboat was speeding down the center of the river completely on its own! The watchman bolted from the area again; Ealer grabbed the wheel, threw an engine into reverse with full force, and held his breath as the boat slowly turned away from a small island it was about to smash into the middle of the Gulf of Mexico!

Eventually the watchman returned and said—

"Didn't that crazy person tell you he was asleep when he first came up here?"

'No.'

'Well, he was. I discovered him strolling along the top of the railings as casually as any other person would walk down a sidewalk; and I helped him to bed; just now he was there again, back at the stern, performing that same kind of tightrope mischief as before.'

"Well, I think I'll stick around the next time he has one of those episodes. But I hope he has them frequently. You should have seen him navigate this boat through Helena crossing. I've never witnessed anything so spectacular before. And if he can perform such flawless, elegant, masterful piloting while he's completely asleep, imagine what he could accomplish if he were dead!"

Chapter 12: Sounding

When the river runs extremely low and your steamboat needs every bit of water available in the channel—or sometimes even a few inches more than what's actually there, which happened frequently in earlier days—you have to be incredibly careful with your navigation. We regularly had to measure the depth at several especially dangerous spots on almost every journey when the river reached very low levels.

Sounding is conducted in this manner. The steamboat moors at the riverbank, just upstream from the shallow crossing; the off-duty pilot takes his apprentice or helmsman along with a selected crew of men (occasionally an officer as well), and heads out in the small boat—assuming the steamboat doesn't possess that uncommon and luxurious feature, a specially designed sounding vessel—and begins searching for the deepest channel. Meanwhile, the pilot on duty observes their movements through a telescope, and sometimes helps by using the steamboat's whistle signals, indicating 'search further upstream' or 'try further downstream.' This is because the water's surface, much like an oil painting, reveals more detail and meaning when viewed from some distance rather than up close. These whistle signals are rarely needed, though; probably never, except when wind disturbs the telltale ripples on the water's surface. Once the small boat reaches the shallow area, they reduce speed, and the pilot starts measuring the depth using a pole ten or twelve feet in length, while the helmsman at the rudder follows commands to 'steer her toward starboard' or 'let her drift toward larboard' or 'hold steady—maintain your current course.'

When the measurements show that the yawl is getting close to the shallowest section of the reef, the command is given to 'ease all!' At this point, the crew stops rowing and the yawl drifts along with the current. The following order is, 'Stand by with the buoy!' The instant the shallowest point is reached, the pilot calls out the order, 'Let go the buoy!' and overboard it goes. If the pilot isn't satisfied, he measures the depth of that spot again; if he discovers better water upstream or downstream, he moves the buoy to that location. Once he's finally satisfied, he gives the command, and all the crew members hold their oars straight up in the air, aligned in a row; a whistle blast from the boat signals that the signal has been spotted; then the crew 'give way' on their oars and position the yawl next to the buoy; the steamboat approaches slowly and cautiously, aims directly at the buoy, conserves her power for the upcoming challenge, and soon, at the crucial moment, unleashes all her steam and goes grinding and wallowing over the buoy and the sand, reaching the deep water on the other side. Or perhaps she doesn't; perhaps she 'strikes and swings.' Then she must spend several hours (or days) working to free herself.

Sometimes no buoy is placed at all, but the small boat moves forward, searching for the deepest water, and the steamboat follows behind in its path. There's often a lot of fun and excitement involved in measuring water depth, especially on a beautiful summer day or during a stormy night. However, in winter the cold weather and danger remove most of the enjoyment from it.

A buoy is simply a board measuring four or five feet in length, with one end curved upward; it resembles an upside down schoolhouse bench where one support remains while the other has been taken away. It sits anchored at the shallowest section of the reef using a rope that has a heavy stone secured to its end. Without the resistance provided by the upturned end of this inverted bench, the current would drag the buoy beneath the water's surface. During nighttime, a paper lantern containing a candle gets attached to the top of the buoy, and this light can be spotted from a mile away or farther, appearing as a small twinkling point of light in the vast darkness.

Nothing thrills a novice pilot more than the chance to go out taking depth measurements. There's such a sense of adventure surrounding it; danger often lurks nearby; it feels so spectacular and warship-like to sit in the stern and steer a fast boat; there's something magnificent about the triumphant surge of the vessel when a seasoned sailor crew puts their hearts into rowing; it's beautiful to watch the white foam flow away from the front; there's melody in the rushing water; it's wonderfully thrilling, during summer, to race across the windy stretches of the river when countless small waves dance in the sunlight. It's also such magnificence for the novice to get an opportunity to give commands; the pilot will often simply say, 'Turn her around!' and leave everything else to the novice, who immediately shouts, in his most authoritative commanding voice, 'Easy on the right! Hard on the left! Right side, pull away! Put your backs into it, men!' The novice enjoys taking soundings for another reason: the passengers' eyes follow every movement of the boat with complete fascination during daylight hours; and when night falls, he knows those same curious eyes remain fixed on the boat's lantern as it moves out into the darkness and fades away in the far distance.

One trip a pretty sixteen-year-old girl spent her time in our pilot-house with her uncle and aunt, every day and all day long. I fell in love with her. So did Mr. Thornburg's apprentice, Tom G——. Tom and I had been close friends until this time; but now a tension began to develop. I told the girl many of my river adventures, and portrayed myself as quite the hero; Tom tried to make himself appear heroic as well, and succeeded to some degree, but he always had a tendency to exaggerate. However, virtue is its own reward, so I was a barely noticeable bit ahead in the competition. Around this time something happened which looked very promising for me: the pilots decided to measure the depth at the crossing at the head of 21. This would happen around nine or ten o'clock at night, when the passengers would still be awake; it would be Mr. Thornburg's shift, therefore my supervisor would have to do the depth measuring. We had an absolutely beautiful sounding-boat—long, sleek, graceful, and as fast as a greyhound; her seats were cushioned; she carried twelve rowers; one of the officers was always sent in her to relay orders to her crew, for ours was a steamboat where a great deal of 'style' was displayed.

We docked at the shore above 21 and prepared ourselves. The night was terrible, and the river stretched so wide at that point that an inexperienced person's untrained eyes couldn't make out the far bank through such darkness. The passengers were awake and engaged; everything was going well. As I rushed through the engine room, dramatically dressed in storm gear, I encountered Tom and couldn't resist making a petty remark—

"Aren't you glad you don't have to go out sounding?"

Tom was walking away, but he quickly turned around and said—

'Now just for that, you can go and get the sounding-pole yourself. I was going to go after it, but I'd rather see you in Halifax before I'd do it now.'

"Who wants you to get it? I don't. It's in the sounding-boat."

"It's not old at all. It's been freshly painted, and it's been sitting up on the ladies' cabin railings for two days, drying."

I flew back and soon found myself among the group of ladies who were watching and wondering, arriving just in time to hear the command:

"Make way, men!"

I glanced over, and there was the impressive survey boat

thundering along, with the unscrupulous Tom commanding the helm, and my supervisor sitting beside him holding the depth-measuring pole that I had been sent on a pointless mission to retrieve. Then that young woman said to me—

"Oh, how terrible it must be to go out in that small boat on a night like this! Do you think there's any danger?"

I would have preferred being stabbed. I walked away, filled with anger, to assist in the pilot-house. Soon the boat's lantern vanished, and after some time a tiny light flickered on the water's surface a mile in the distance. Mr. Thornburg sounded the whistle in response, reversed the steamer, and headed toward it. We raced along for a period, then reduced steam and carefully drifted toward the light. Shortly after, Mr. Thornburg called out—

"Hello, the buoy light is out!"

He turned off the engines. A moment or two later he said—

"Why, there it is again!"

So he moved forward using the engines once more and called for the depth measurements. Gradually the water became shallower, and then it started to get deeper again! Mr. Thornburg muttered—

"Well, I don't get this. I think that buoy has moved away from the reef. It looks like it's a bit too far to the left. Doesn't matter, it's still safest to go over it anyway."

So, in that dense world of darkness we continued moving slowly down toward the light. Just as our bow was about to cut through it, Mr. Thornburg grabbed the bell-ropes, rang an alarming series of chimes, and shouted—

"My soul, it's the sounding-boat!"

A sudden chorus of wild alarms erupted far below—a pause— and then came the sound of grinding and crashing. Mr. Thornburg exclaimed—

"Look! The paddle wheel has crushed the sounding boat into splinters! Hurry! Go see who's been killed!"

I reached the main deck in an instant. My supervisor and the third mate, along with nearly all the crew members, were unharmed. They had realized the danger when it was already too late to get out of the way; however, when the massive paddle guards cast their shadow over them moments later, they were ready and understood what needed to be done; following my supervisor's command, they jumped at precisely the right moment, grabbed hold of the guard, and were pulled safely on board. The following instant, the sounding boat was swept toward the stern near the pilot wheel and was hit and shattered into pieces. Two crew members and the apprentice Tom were unaccounted for—news that spread rapidly throughout the vessel. The passengers rushed to the front gangway, women included, with worried expressions and pale faces, speaking in hushed, reverent tones about the terrible incident. Time and again I heard them saying, 'Poor fellows! poor boy, poor boy!'

By this time the boat's small rescue boat was crewed and launched to search for the missing person. A weak call could now be heard coming from the left side. The rescue boat had vanished in the opposite direction. Half the crowd rushed to one side to encourage the swimmer with their shouting; the other half hurried the other way to yell at the rescue boat to turn around. Based on the calls, the swimmer was getting closer, but some people said the sound indicated weakening strength. The crowd gathered against the boiler-deck railings, leaning over and peering into the darkness; and every faint and increasingly weaker cry drew from them words like, 'Oh, poor fellow, poor fellow! isn't there any way to save him?'

But the cries continued, growing closer, and soon the voice spoke with determination—

"I can make it! Stand by with a rope!"

What an enthusiastic cheer they gave him! The first officer positioned himself in the bright glow of a torch-basket, holding a coiled rope, with his crew gathered around him. The next moment the swimmer's face emerged in the circle of light, and seconds later the person was pulled aboard, exhausted and soaking wet, while cheer after cheer erupted. It was that devil Tom.

The yawl crew looked everywhere, but they couldn't find any trace of the two men. They most likely missed their grab for the guard rail, fell backward, and got hit by the paddle wheel, which killed them. Tom hadn't even tried to jump for the guard rail at all—instead, he had dove headfirst into the river and swum under the wheel. It was nothing special; I could have easily done the same thing, and I told everyone so. But everybody kept going on and on, making such a big fuss over that fool, as though he had accomplished something amazing. That girl seemed like she couldn't get enough of that pathetic 'hero' for the rest of the journey, but I didn't care one bit—I couldn't stand her anyway.

The way we ended up confusing the sounding-boat's lantern with the buoy-light happened like this. My chief explained that after placing the buoy, he moved away and kept watching it until it appeared to be stable; then he positioned himself about a hundred yards downstream from it and slightly to one side of the steamer's path, pointed the sounding-boat upstream, and waited. Since he had to wait for quite a while, he and the officer started talking; he looked up when he estimated that the steamer was roughly over the reef; he saw that the buoy had disappeared, but assumed that the steamer had already passed over it; he continued his conversation; he observed that the steamer was getting extremely close to him, but that was normal; it was the steamer's job to pass very close to him, making it easier to bring him aboard; he expected her to turn away at the last second; then it suddenly occurred to him that she was attempting to run him down, confusing his lantern with the buoy-light; so he shouted, 'Stand by to spring for the guard, men!' and the very next moment they made the jump.

Chapter 13: A Pilot's Needs

BUT I am straying from what I intended to do, which is to make clearer than perhaps shown in the previous chapters, some of the unique requirements of the science of piloting. First of all, there is one ability which a pilot must constantly develop until he has brought it to absolute perfection. Nothing less than perfection will do. That ability is memory. He cannot stop with merely thinking something is so and so; he must know it; for this is definitely one of the 'exact' sciences. With what contempt a pilot was regarded, in the old days, if he ever dared to use that weak phrase 'I think,' instead of the strong one 'I know!' One cannot easily understand what a tremendous thing it is to know every minor detail of twelve hundred miles of river and know it with absolute precision. If you will take the longest street in New York, and travel up and down it, studying its features carefully until you know every house and window and door and lamp-post and big and little sign by heart, and know them so precisely that you can instantly name the one you are beside when you are placed at random in that street in the middle of a pitch black night, you will then have a reasonable idea of the amount and the precision of a pilot's knowledge who carries the Mississippi River in his head. And then if you will go on until you know every street crossing, the character, size, and position of the crossing-stones, and the varying depth of mud in each of those countless places, you will have some idea of what the pilot must know in order to keep a Mississippi steamer out of trouble. Next, if you will take half of the signs in that long street, and change their places once a month, and still manage to know their new positions precisely on dark nights, and keep up with these repeated changes without making any mistakes, you will understand what is required of a pilot's exceptional memory by the unpredictable Mississippi.

I believe a pilot's memory is one of the most remarkable things in the world. To memorize the Old and New Testaments completely and recite them smoothly, whether forward or backward, or to start at any random point in the book and recite in either direction without stumbling or making an error, represents no extraordinary amount of knowledge and no amazing skill when compared to a pilot's comprehensive understanding of the Mississippi River and his incredible ability to navigate it. I make this comparison intentionally, and I believe I'm not exaggerating the truth when I say this. Many people will consider my comparison too bold, but pilots will not.

The pilot's memory works with remarkable ease and comfort, operating in a smooth and effortless manner while unconsciously building up enormous stores of information hour after hour, day after day, without ever losing or misplacing a single valuable piece of data. Consider this example. Imagine a leadsman calling out, 'Half twain! half twain! half twain! half twain! half twain!' until the sound becomes as repetitive as a clock's ticking; meanwhile, conversation continues constantly, with the pilot participating in the discussion and no longer consciously paying attention to the leadsman's calls; then, in the middle of this endless series of half twains, a single 'quarter twain!' gets inserted without any special emphasis, after which the half twain calls resume exactly as before: two or three weeks later, that same pilot can accurately describe the boat's exact position on the river when that quarter twain was called out, providing you with so many detailed head-marks, stern-marks, and side-marks for navigation that you should be able to take the boat to that precise location and position her in that identical spot again! The call of 'quarter twain' didn't actually divert his attention from his conversation, but his well-trained abilities immediately captured the surroundings like a photograph, recorded the depth change, and stored away the crucial details for later use without needing any conscious effort from him. If you were walking and chatting with a friend while another companion beside you kept repeating the vowel sound A monotonously for several blocks, and then suddenly inserted an R in the middle, like this: A, A, A, A, A, R, A, A, A, and so on, without emphasizing the R, you wouldn't be able to recall two or three weeks later that the R had been included, nor could you identify what you were passing when it happened. However, you could accomplish this if your memory had been carefully and systematically trained to perform that kind of task automatically.

Give someone a reasonably good memory to begin with, and piloting will transform it into an enormous powerhouse of ability. However, this only applies to the subjects practiced every day. Eventually, the person's mind would automatically notice landmarks and water depths, and their memory would grip onto these details like a steel clamp; but if you asked that same person at midday what they ate for breakfast, there would be a nine-to-one chance they couldn't tell you. Remarkable feats can be accomplished with human memory when you dedicate it completely to one specific field of work.

At the time when wages reached extremely high levels on the Missouri River, my supervisor, Mr. Bixby, traveled there and mastered over a thousand miles of that waterway with remarkable ease and speed. After he had observed each section once during the day and once at night, his training was nearly finished, so he obtained a 'daylight' license; several trips afterward he earned a full license and began piloting both day and night—and he was rated as top quality as well.

Mr. Bixby assigned me to work as a steersman for a time under a pilot whose incredible feats of memory constantly amazed me. However, I believe his memory was something he was born with, not something he developed over time. For example, when someone would bring up a name, Mr. Brown would immediately interrupt—

'Oh, I knew him. Pale-faced, red-haired guy, with a small scar on the side of his neck, like a splinter beneath the skin. He only worked the Southern trade for six months. That was thirteen years ago. I took a trip with him. There were five feet of water in the upper river back then; the "Henry Blake" ran aground at the foot of Tower Island while drawing four and a half feet; the "George Elliott" lost her rudder on the wreck of the "Sunflower"—'

"Why, the 'Sunflower' didn't sink until—"

'I know when she went down; it was three years before that, on December 2nd; Asa Hardy was her captain, and his brother John was first clerk; and it was his first trip on her, too; Tom Jones told me these things a week later in New Orleans; he was first mate of the "Sunflower." Captain Hardy stepped on a nail the 6th of July the following year, and died of lockjaw on the 15th. His brother died two years later on March 3rd,—from erysipelas. I never met either of the Hardy brothers,—they were Alleghany River men,—but people who knew them told me all these details. And they said Captain Hardy wore wool socks winter and summer just the same, and his first wife's name was Jane Shook—she was from New England—and his second wife died in a mental institution. It ran in the family. She was from Lexington, Kentucky. Her maiden name was Horton.'

And so it went, hour after hour, the man's tongue never stopping. He couldn't forget anything at all. It was completely impossible for him. The most insignificant details stayed as clear and bright in his mind, even after sitting there for years, as the most unforgettable experiences. This wasn't just a pilot's memory; it covered everything. If he happened to be discussing some unimportant letter he'd gotten seven years earlier, he would almost certainly recite the whole thing word for word from memory. And then, without realizing he was straying from his original topic, he would very likely throw in a lengthy side story about the life of whoever wrote that letter; and you'd consider yourself fortunate if he didn't also start going through that writer's family members, one after another, telling you all about their lives as well.

Having such a memory is a terrible burden. To someone with this condition, every event carries equal weight. The person cannot tell the difference between something fascinating and something completely mundane. When telling stories, they're destined to bog down their tales with exhausting details and become unbearably tedious. What's worse, they can never stay focused on their topic. They grab onto every tiny fragment of memory they encounter along the way, which constantly pulls them off track. Mr. Brown might begin with the genuine goal of sharing a hilarious story about a dog. He would be so overcome with laughter that he could barely get started; then his memory would kick in with details about the dog's breed and what it looked like; this would drift into the history of the dog's owner; then into the owner's family history, complete with descriptions of weddings and funerals that had taken place, along with recitations of congratulatory poems and funeral verses inspired by these occasions: then his memory would recall that one of these events happened during the famous 'harsh winter' of a particular year, and a detailed account of that winter would follow, including the names of people who froze to death, and statistics showing how high the prices of pork and hay climbed. Pork and hay would bring to mind corn and animal feed; corn and animal feed would lead to cows and horses; cows and horses would bring up the circus and famous bareback riders; the jump from circus to traveling zoo was simple and logical; from the elephant to equatorial Africa was just a small leap; then naturally the primitive tribes would bring up religion; and after three or four hours of mind-numbing chatter, the shift would end, and Brown would leave the pilot house mumbling excerpts from sermons he had heard years earlier about the power of prayer as a source of divine grace. And that original brief mention would be all you had discovered about that dog, despite all this waiting and anticipation.

A pilot needs to have a good memory, but there are two even more important qualities he must possess. He must have sound and quick judgment and decision-making abilities, along with cool, calm courage that no danger can disturb. Give a man even the smallest amount of bravery to begin with, and by the time he becomes a pilot, no danger that a steamboat might encounter can intimidate him; however, the same cannot quite be said about judgment. Judgment is a matter of intelligence, and a person must begin with a good supply of that quality or he will never succeed as a pilot.

The development of courage in the pilot-house happens gradually over time, but it doesn't reach a high and satisfactory level until some time after the young pilot has been 'standing his own watch,' working alone while carrying the overwhelming burden of all the responsibilities that come with the job. When an apprentice has become fairly well acquainted with the river, he travels along so confidently with his steamboat, whether during the day or night, that he soon starts to believe that it's his own courage driving him forward; but the first time the pilot steps away and leaves him to handle things on his own, he realizes it was actually the other man's courage all along. He finds out that this quality has been completely missing from his own character. The entire river suddenly becomes filled with urgent situations; he isn't ready for them; he doesn't know how to handle them; all his knowledge abandons him; and within fifteen minutes he becomes as pale as a sheet and frightened nearly to death. For this reason, pilots wisely prepare these newcomers through various clever methods to face danger with a bit more composure. One of their preferred approaches is to play a harmless trick on the candidate.

Mr. Bixby treated me this way once, and for years afterward I would blush even in my sleep whenever I remembered it. I had become a skilled pilot; so skilled, in fact, that I handled all the work during our shift, both day and night; Mr. Bixby rarely offered me any advice; all he ever did was take control during especially difficult nights or particularly challenging river crossings, dock the boat when it needed docking, act like a gentleman of leisure ninety percent of the time, and collect his pay. The lower river was nearly at flood level, and if anyone had questioned my ability to navigate any crossing between Cairo and New Orleans without assistance or guidance, I would have felt deeply offended. The thought of being scared of any crossing during daylight hours was too ridiculous to even consider. Well, on one perfect summer day I was cruising down the bend above island 66, completely full of myself and holding my head as high as a giraffe's, when Mr. Bixby said—

"I'm going downstairs for a bit. I assume you know about the next crossing?"

This felt almost like an insult. It was the most straightforward and easiest crossing in the entire river. Nobody could get into trouble there, regardless of whether they navigated it correctly or not; and when it came to the depth, there had never been any bottom at that spot. I understood all of this completely.

"Know how to operate it? Well, I can operate it with my eyes closed."

"How much water is in it?"

"Well, that's a strange question. I couldn't reach the bottom there even with a church steeple."

"You think so, do you?"

The very tone of the question shattered my confidence. That was exactly what Mr. Bixby had been expecting. He walked away without saying another word. My mind started racing with all kinds of possibilities. Without my knowledge, Mr. Bixby sent someone down to the forecastle with mysterious instructions for the leadsmen, dispatched another messenger to whisper among the officers, and then hid himself behind a smokestack where he could watch what would happen. Soon the captain emerged onto the hurricane deck; then the chief mate showed up; followed by a clerk. Every minute or two another person joined my audience; and by the time I reached the head of the island, fifteen or twenty people had gathered down there right beneath me. I started wondering what was wrong. As I began crossing, the captain looked up at me and spoke with fake concern in his voice—

"Where is Mr. Bixby?"

"Gone below, sir."

But that was enough to ruin everything for me. My imagination started creating dangers where none existed, and they grew faster than I could keep track of them. Suddenly I thought I saw shallow water up ahead! The wave of terrified panic that rushed through me nearly knocked every joint out of place. All my confidence in that river crossing disappeared completely. I grabbed the bell-rope; let it go, feeling embarrassed; grabbed it again; dropped it once more; clutched it with shaking hands yet again, and pulled it so weakly that I could barely hear the sound myself. The captain and mate shouted out immediately, both at the same time—

"Starboard lead there! And make it quick!"

This came as another shock. I started climbing the wheel like a squirrel; but I had barely gotten the boat turning to port when I spotted new dangers on that side, and I would spin away to the other direction; only to discover perils building up to starboard, and become frantic to get back to port again. Then the leadsman's ghostly cry rang out—

"D-e-e-p four!"

The water was four fathoms deep at a crossing with no bottom in sight! The sheer terror of it left me breathless.

'M-a-r-k three!... M-a-r-k three... Quarter less three!... Half twain!'

This was terrifying! I grabbed the bell-ropes and shut down the engines.

"Quarter twain! Quarter twain! Mark twain!"

I felt completely powerless. I had absolutely no idea what to do. I was trembling all over, and my eyes were bulging out so much that I could have hung my hat on them.

"Quarter to two! Nine-thirty!"

We were approaching nine o'clock! My hands were shaking uncontrollably. I couldn't ring a bell clearly with them trembling like that. I rushed to the speaking tube and yelled to the engineer—

"Oh, Ben, if you love me, support her! Quickly, Ben! Oh, help her immortal soul get out of there!"

I heard the door close softly. I glanced around, and there was Mr. Bixby, wearing a mild, pleasant smile. Then the crowd on the hurricane deck erupted in a thunderous roar of humiliating laughter. I understood everything now, and I felt lower than the lowest person who had ever lived. I dropped the lead line, positioned the boat at her markers, moved the engines forward, and said—

"It was a cruel trick to play on an orphan, wasn't it? I suppose I'll never stop hearing about how I was stupid enough to throw the lead weight at number 66's head."

"Well, no, you probably won't. Actually, I hope you don't, because I want you to learn something from that experience. Didn't you realize there was no bottom at that crossing?"

"Yes, sir, I did."

"Alright, then. You shouldn't have let me or anyone else undermine your confidence in what you know. Try to keep that in mind. And one more thing: when you find yourself in a dangerous situation, don't lose your nerve. That's not going to make things any better."

It was a valuable lesson, though one that came at a steep price. The most difficult part of the whole experience was having to endure, month after month, hearing a phrase that I had grown to particularly despise. That phrase was, 'Oh, Ben, if you love me, back her!'

Chapter 14: Rank and Dignity of Piloting

In my earlier chapters, I've attempted to take the reader through the detailed aspects of piloting science, guiding them step by step toward understanding what this science truly involves. At the same time, I've tried to demonstrate that it's a fascinating and remarkable science that deserves attention. If I've appeared to be passionate about my subject, that shouldn't come as a surprise, since I loved that profession far more than any I've pursued since, and I felt immense pride in it. The explanation is simple: a pilot in those days was the only completely free and truly independent person living on earth. Kings are merely restricted servants of parliament and the people; parliaments operate in chains created by their constituents; a newspaper editor cannot maintain independence but must work with one hand restrained by political parties and financial backers, forced to express only half or two-thirds of their thoughts; no minister is truly free and able to speak complete truth, regardless of their congregation's views; writers of every type are constrained servants of the public. We write openly and boldly, but then we make changes before we publish. In reality, every man, woman, and child has someone in authority over them, experiencing anxiety and frustration in their servitude; but during the time I'm describing, the Mississippi pilot answered to no one. The captain might stand on the hurricane deck, displaying the grandeur of very temporary power, issuing five or six commands while the boat reversed into the current, and then that captain's authority would end.

The moment the boat began moving down the river, it came under the complete and unquestionable authority of the pilot. He could do whatever he wanted with the vessel, operate it when and where he decided, and dock it at the riverbank whenever he judged that action to be the best choice. His actions were completely unrestricted; he didn't consult anyone, took orders from no one, and quickly showed irritation at even the slightest recommendations. In fact, United States law prohibited him from accepting commands or suggestions, wisely recognizing that the pilot naturally understood how to manage the boat better than anyone else could advise him. So this created the unusual situation of a ruler without a guardian, a supreme leader who held genuine absolute power rather than authority that existed only in name. I witnessed an eighteen-year-old boy calmly steering a large steamboat toward what appeared to be almost inevitable disaster, while the elderly captain stood silently nearby, filled with worry but unable to step in. His intervention, in that specific case, might have been beneficial, but allowing it would have set an extremely dangerous example. Given the pilot's unlimited power, it's easy to understand that he held an important position during the golden age of steamboat travel. The captain treated him with obvious respect and all the officers and crew showed him clear deference; this respectful attitude quickly spread to the passengers as well. I believe pilots were probably the only people I ever encountered who didn't display any level of discomfort when meeting traveling foreign royalty. But then again, people from one's own social class typically aren't intimidating figures.

Through years of practice, pilots developed the habit of expressing all their desires as direct commands. Even today, it bothers me to phrase my intentions as polite requests rather than delivering them with the sharp clarity of an order. During that era, loading a steamboat in St. Louis, sailing it to New Orleans and back, then unloading the cargo typically took around twenty-five days. The vessel would spend seven or eight of those days docked at the St. Louis and New Orleans wharves, where everyone aboard worked tirelessly—except for the two pilots, who did nothing but enjoy themselves as gentlemen about town while earning the same pay as if they were actively working. The instant the boat reached either city's wharf, they went ashore, and no one expected to see them again until the final bell rang and everything was prepared for the next journey.

When a captain found a pilot with an exceptionally strong reputation, he made every effort to retain him. During times when wages reached four hundred dollars a month on the Upper Mississippi, I've witnessed captains keeping such pilots completely idle, receiving their full salary, for three months straight while the river remained frozen. One must keep in mind that during those economical times, four hundred dollars represented a salary of nearly unimaginable magnificence. Very few men working on land earned such wages, and those who did were held in tremendous esteem. When pilots from either section of the river happened to visit our small Missouri town, they were pursued by the most distinguished and attractive people, and received the highest level of respect. Remaining docked while still collecting wages was something many pilots thoroughly enjoyed and valued; this was particularly true for those who worked the Missouri River during its golden period (the Kansas era), earning nine hundred dollars per trip, which amounted to roughly eighteen hundred dollars monthly. Here's a conversation from that time period. A fellow from the Illinois River, operating a small stern-wheel boat, approaches a pair of elaborately dressed and decorated Missouri River pilots—

"Gentlemen, I have a very good trip planned for the interior regions, and I'll need you for about a month. What will the cost be?"

'Eighteen hundred dollars each.'

"Good heavens! You take my boat, let me have your wages, and I'll split them!"

I should mention, by the way, that Mississippi steamboat workers were considered important in the eyes of people on land (and to some extent in their own eyes as well) based on how prestigious the boat was that they worked on. For example, it was a source of great pride to be part of the crew on such magnificent vessels as the 'Aleck Scott' or the 'Grand Turk.' Black firemen, deck hands, and barbers who worked on those boats were respected figures within their social circle, and they were quite aware of this status as well. A strong Black man once caused trouble at a Black dance in New Orleans by acting very pretentious. Eventually one of the organizers approached him and said—

"Who are you, anyway? Who are you? That's what I want to know!"

The offender wasn't embarrassed at all, but puffed himself up and put something in his voice that showed he knew he wasn't putting on all those airs without having the means to back them up.

'Who am I? Who am I? I'll let you know real quick who I am! I want you all to understand that I fire the middle door on the "Aleck Scott!"

That was enough.

The barber of the 'Grand Turk' was a well-dressed young Black man who displayed his self-importance with smooth satisfaction and was highly sought after by the social circle he belonged to. The young Black residents of New Orleans had a strong tendency to flirt during the evening hours on the sidewalks of the back streets. Someone witnessed and overheard something similar to what follows one evening in one of those neighborhoods. A middle-aged Black woman stuck her head out through a cracked window pane and yelled (quite happy for the neighbors to listen and feel jealous), 'You Mary Ann, get in this house right now! Standing out there fooling around with that worthless crowd, and here's the barber from the "Grand Turk" who wants to talk with you!'

My mention just now of how a pilot's unique official status put him beyond criticism or orders naturally brings Stephen W——— to mind. He was a talented pilot, a decent man, an endless talker, and possessed both cleverness and humor. He also had a thoroughly irreverent independence and was wonderfully relaxed and at ease around age, official authority, and even the most impressive wealth. He always found work, he never saved a cent, he was an extremely convincing borrower, he owed money to every pilot on the river, and to most of the captains. He could cast a kind of glamour around reckless, carefree piloting that made it almost captivating—but not to everyone. He made one trip with good old Captain Y——, and was 'relieved' from duty when the boat reached New Orleans. Someone expressed surprise at his dismissal. Captain Y—— shuddered at the simple mention of Stephen. Then his frail, thin old voice squeaked out something like this:—

'Good heavens! I wouldn't have such a wild man on my boat for anything—not for anything in the world! He curses, he sings, he whistles, he shouts—I've never seen such a man yell like that. At all hours of the night—it didn't matter to him one bit. He would just yell that way, not for any particular reason, but simply because of some kind of wicked pleasure he got from it. I could never get a good night's sleep because he would wake me up, drenched in cold sweat, with one of those terrible war cries. A strange man—very strange indeed; no respect for anything or anyone. Sometimes he called me "Johnny." And he kept a fiddle, and a cat. He played terribly. This seemed to upset the cat, so the cat would howl. Nobody could sleep where that man—and his family—was staying. And reckless. There was never anything like it. Now you can believe it or not, but as sure as I'm sitting here, he brought my boat tilting down through those terrible snags at Chicot under full steam, with the wind blowing like crazy! My officers will confirm this. They witnessed it. And, sir, while he was tearing right down through those snags, and I was trembling in my boots and praying, I swear if he didn't purse his lips and start whistling! Yes, sir; whistling "Buffalo gals, can't you come out tonight, can't you come out tonight, can't you come out tonight;" and doing it as calmly as if we were at a funeral and weren't related to the deceased. And when I protested about it, he smiled down at me as if I were his child, and told me to go inside and try to behave, and stop interfering with my betters!'

Once a particularly ruthless captain found Stephen in New Orleans without work and, as always, without money. He persistently pressured Stephen, who was in a very tight spot, and eventually convinced him to sign on at one hundred and twenty-five dollars per month—exactly half the normal wages—with the captain promising not to reveal this arrangement and thereby subject the poor man to the scorn of the entire profession. However, the boat had barely been out of New Orleans for a day when Stephen realized that the captain was bragging about his bargain, and that all the officers had been informed. Stephen flinched inwardly but remained silent. Around the middle of the afternoon, the captain walked out onto the hurricane deck, surveyed the area, and appeared quite puzzled. He looked up questioningly at Stephen, but Stephen was whistling calmly while tending to his duties. The captain lingered nearby, clearly uncomfortable, and seemed on the verge of speaking up once or twice; however, river protocol warned him against such impulsiveness, so he managed to keep quiet. He fidgeted and pondered for several more minutes before retreating to his quarters. Soon enough, he emerged again, seemingly even more confused than before. Eventually, he dared to speak up respectfully—

"The river's looking pretty good right now, isn't it, sir?"

"Well, I should say so! When the river is bank-full, that's quite a generous water level."

"There appears to be quite a strong current flowing here."

"Good deal don't describe it! It's worse than a mill-race."

"Isn't it easier closer to shore than it is out here in the middle?"

"Yes, I think it is; but a person can't be too careful with a steamboat. It's pretty safe out here; can't hit any bottom here, you can count on that."

The captain left, looking quite dejected. At this pace, he would likely die of old age before his boat reached St. Louis. The following day he came up on deck and once again discovered Stephen dutifully maintaining his position in the center of the river, battling against the entire mighty force of the Mississippi, and whistling the same calm melody. This situation was becoming serious. Near the shore, a slower vessel was moving smoothly through the calmer waters and steadily gaining ground; she started heading toward an island passage; Stephen remained in the middle of the river. The captain was compelled to speak. He said—

"Mr. W——, doesn't that chute cut off a good deal of distance?"

"I think it does, but I don't know."

"I don't know! Well, isn't there enough water in it now to get through?"

"I think there probably is, but I'm not sure."

"I swear this is strange! Look, those pilots on that boat over there are going to attempt it. Are you telling me that you don't know as much as they do?"

"They! Why, they're two-hundred-and-fifty-dollar pilots! But don't worry; I know as much as any man can afford to know for a hundred and twenty-five!"

The captain gave up.

Five minutes later, Stephen was racing through the narrow channel and leaving the competing boat far behind with his expensive two-hundred-and-fifty-dollar boots.

———————————

Chapter 15: The Pilots' Monopoly

One day, while aboard the 'Aleck Scott,' my supervisor, Mr. Bixby, was navigating carefully through a narrow passage at Cat Island, with both depth-measuring lines in use and everyone holding their breath. The captain, a nervous and anxious man, stayed quiet as long as he could manage, but eventually lost his composure and yelled from the hurricane deck—

"For heaven's sake, give her steam, Mr. Bixby! Give her steam! She'll never clear the reef at this speed!"

For all the impact this had on Mr. Bixby, you would have thought that nothing had been said at all. However, five minutes later, once the danger had passed and the leads were secured, he immediately exploded into an intense rage and delivered to the captain the most impressive verbal assault I have ever heard. No violence followed, but that was only because the captain's position was indefensible; normally he wasn't the type of man to accept criticism without a fight.

Having now explained in detail the nature of the science of piloting, and also described the position that the pilot held among the community of steamboat workers, this appears to be an appropriate place to discuss an organization that the pilots once created to protect their profession. It was interesting and remarkable because it was possibly the most tightly organized, most complete, and most powerful commercial organization ever established among people.

For a long time, wages had been two hundred and fifty dollars a month; but strangely enough, as steamboats multiplied and business increased, the wages began to drop little by little. It was easy to figure out why this was happening. Too many pilots were being trained. It was convenient to have an apprentice, a steersman, to do all the hard work for a couple of years, for free, while his master sat on a high bench and smoked; all pilots and captains had sons or nephews who wanted to become pilots. Eventually it happened that nearly every pilot on the river had a steersman. When a steersman had made enough progress that satisfied any two pilots in the trade, they could get a pilot's license for him by signing an application directed to the United States Inspector. Nothing more was needed; usually no questions were asked, no proof of ability required.

Very well, this growing crowd of new pilots soon started to drive down wages in order to secure jobs. Too late—it seemed—the experienced pilots realized their error. Clearly, something needed to be done, and fast; but what should that necessary action be. A tight organization. Nothing else would work. To achieve this seemed impossible; so it was discussed, and discussed, and then abandoned. It was too likely to destroy whoever dared to take action on the matter. But finally about a dozen of the most courageous—and some of them the finest—pilots on the river threw themselves into the venture and accepted all the risks. They obtained a special charter from the legislature, with extensive powers, under the name of the Pilots' Benevolent Association; elected their officers, finished their organization, pooled capital, raised 'association' wages to two hundred and fifty dollars immediately—and then went back to their homes, because they were quickly fired from their jobs. But there were two or three overlooked details in their by-laws which contained the potential for growth. For example, all inactive members of the association, in good standing, were eligible for a pension of twenty-five dollars per month. This started to attract one straggler after another from the ranks of the newly trained pilots, during the slow (summer) season. Better to have twenty-five dollars than go hungry; the initiation fee was only twelve dollars, and no dues were required from the unemployed.

Also, the widows of deceased members who were in good standing could receive twenty-five dollars each month, along with a specific amount for each of their children. Additionally, the deceased member would be buried at the association's expense. These benefits brought back to life all the retired and forgotten pilots throughout the Mississippi Valley. They arrived from farms, they traveled from small inland towns, they journeyed from all corners of the region. They arrived on crutches, they came on wagons, they were transported in ambulances—whatever it took to get there. They paid their twelve-dollar fee and immediately started collecting twenty-five dollars monthly while calculating their future funeral costs.

Eventually, all the incompetent, useless pilots, along with about twelve excellent ones, had joined the association, while nine-tenths of the best pilots remained outside of it and mocked it. The association became the laughingstock of the entire river. Everyone made jokes about the rule requiring members to contribute ten percent of their earnings each month to the association's treasury, especially since all the members were outcasts and blacklisted, with no one willing to hire them. Everyone mockingly thanked the association for removing all the worthless pilots from the market and leaving the entire field open to the skilled and deserving pilots; and everyone was not only sarcastically grateful for this outcome, but also for the natural consequence that followed—the steady increase in wages as the busy season drew near. Wages had risen from the low rate of one hundred dollars per month to one hundred and twenty-five dollars, and in some instances to one hundred and fifty dollars; and people found it highly amusing to emphasize that this wonderful development had been achieved by a group of men, not one of whom gained any benefit from it. Some of the jokers would visit the association headquarters to have a good time teasing the members and mockingly offering them the charity of hiring them as assistants for a single trip, so they could see what the river they had forgotten looked like. Nevertheless, the association appeared satisfied; or at least it showed no signs of discontent. Occasionally it recruited a pilot who was down on his luck and added him to its roster; and these newer recruits were quite valuable, since they were skilled pilots—all the incompetent ones had already been taken in earlier. As business picked up, wages gradually climbed to two hundred and fifty dollars—the association's target rate—and remained steady at that level; and still without benefiting any member of that organization, since no member was being hired. The mockery at the association's expense now knew no limits. There was no end to the ridicule that poor victim had to endure.

However, it's true that every long road eventually has a turn. As winter drew near, business doubled and then tripled, and a flood of boats from Missouri, Illinois, and the Upper Mississippi River came rushing down to try their luck in the New Orleans trade. Suddenly, pilots were desperately needed, and there weren't nearly enough to go around. The moment for payback had arrived. It was a hard truth to swallow—having to finally accept association pilots—but captains and boat owners realized they had no choice. Yet none of these outcasts stepped forward to offer their services! This meant an even more bitter reality had to be faced: they would have to seek out these pilots and actually ask for their help. Captain —— was the first person who found himself forced to take this medicine, and he had been the loudest critic of the organization. He tracked down one of the association's finest pilots and said—

"Well, you boys have gotten the better of us for now, so I'll give in as gracefully as I can. I've come to hire you; get your trunk on board right away. I want to leave at twelve o'clock."

"I'm not sure about that. Who is your other pilot?"

"I've got I. S——. Why?"

"I can't go with him. He doesn't belong to the association."

'What!'

"That's how it is."

"Are you seriously telling me that you refuse to work with one of the finest and most experienced pilots on the river just because he's not a member of your association?"

"Yes, I do."

"Well, if this isn't putting on airs! I thought I was doing you a favor, but I'm starting to think that I'm the one who needs something from you. Are you following some rule of the company?"

'Yes.'

"Show it to me."

So they walked into the association rooms, and the secretary quickly satisfied the captain, who said—

"Well, what am I supposed to do? I've already hired Mr. S—— for the whole season."

"I'll take care of you," the secretary said. "I'll assign a pilot to accompany you, and he'll be on board at twelve o'clock."

"But if I fire S——, he'll demand payment for the entire season's wages."

"Of course that's a matter between you and Mr. S——, captain. We can't interfere in your private affairs."

The captain raged furiously, but it accomplished nothing. Eventually he was forced to let S—— go, pay him roughly a thousand dollars, and hire an association pilot to replace him. The laughter was starting to shift to the other side now. From that point forward, each day brought a new casualty; daily, some furious captain would fire a non-association favorite amid tears and curses, then reluctantly install a despised association member in that position. Very quickly, unemployed non-association pilots became quite common, despite how busy business was and how much their services were wanted. The laughter was clearly moving to the other side of their mouths. These casualties, along with the captains and owners, soon stopped laughing entirely and started fuming about the revenge they would exact once the current business boom came to an end.

Soon all the remaining people who were laughing were the owners and crews of boats that employed two pilots who weren't part of the association. However, their victory didn't last very long. Here's why: The association had a strict rule that its members must never, under any circumstances, share information about the channel with any 'outsider.' By this point, about half the boats had only association pilots, while the other half had only outsiders. At first glance, one might think that when it came to withholding information about the river, these two groups could play the same game equally well; but this wasn't the case. At every major town from one end of the river to the other, there was a 'wharf-boat' for landing, rather than a wharf or pier. Cargo was stored in it for shipping; passengers waiting for transport slept in its cabins. On each of these wharf-boats, the association's officers installed a strongbox secured with a special lock that was used in only one other service—the United States mail service. It was the mail-bag lock, a protected government item. Through persistent pleading, the government had been convinced to allow the association to use this lock. Every association member carried a key that could open these boxes. That key, or more precisely a specific way of holding it when its owner was asked for river information by a stranger—since the success of the St. Louis and New Orleans association had now created reasonably successful branches in a dozen nearby steamboat trades—served as the association member's badge and certificate of membership; and if the stranger didn't respond by producing a similar key and holding it in the properly prescribed manner, his question was politely ignored.

From the association's secretary, each member received a package containing more or less elaborate blank forms, printed like an invoice header on high-quality paper with properly ruled columns; an invoice header that read something like this—

These blank forms were completed day by day as the journey continued and placed in the various wharf-boat storage boxes. For example, once the first river crossing departing from St. Louis was finished, the information would be recorded on the form under the proper headings, like this—

'St. Louis. Nine and a half feet. Keep the stern aligned with the courthouse and the head pointed toward the dead cottonwood tree above the wood-yard, until you reach the first reef, then pull up straight.' Then under the heading of Remarks: 'Stay just outside the wrecks; this is crucial. There's a new snag right where you straighten your course; pass above it.'

The pilot who placed that blank form in the Cairo box (after filling in the details of every river crossing from St. Louis all the way down) removed and read half a dozen new reports from steamers heading upstream about the river conditions between Cairo and Memphis, studied them completely, put them back in the box, and returned to his boat so well-prepared against potential problems that he couldn't possibly get his vessel into danger without deliberately acting with extraordinary recklessness.

Imagine the advantages of such an excellent system on a river stretching twelve or thirteen hundred miles, where the channel changed every single day! The pilot who previously had to settle for observing a shallow area once or maybe twice a month now had a hundred keen eyes monitoring it for him, along with countless intelligent minds to guide him on how to navigate it. His information about conditions was rarely more than twenty-four hours old. If the reports in the most recent box happened to create any doubts in his mind about a dangerous crossing, he had a solution available; he sounded his steam whistle in a distinctive pattern as soon as he spotted another boat approaching; the signal received a distinctive response if that boat's pilots belonged to the association; and then the two steamboats pulled up side by side and all uncertainties disappeared through fresh information provided to the questioning pilot through direct conversation and with precise details.

The first thing a pilot did when he arrived in New Orleans or St. Louis was to deliver his detailed final report to the association meeting rooms and post it there—only after completing this task was he free to see his family. In these meeting rooms, a group was always gathered, discussing changes in the river channel, and the moment a new pilot arrived, everyone would stop their conversations until this eyewitness had shared the latest news and resolved any recent uncertainties. Other tradesmen can sometimes 'forget about work' and focus their attention on different topics. This wasn't the case with a pilot; he had to dedicate himself completely to his profession and speak of nothing else, because there would be little benefit in being flawless one day and inadequate the next. He couldn't afford to waste time or conversation if he wanted to stay 'informed.'

But the outsiders faced serious difficulties. They had no specific place to gather and share information, no wharf-boat reports, and only random and unreliable methods of obtaining news. The result was that a person would sometimes have to navigate five hundred miles of river based on information that was a week or ten days outdated. During normal river conditions this might have worked; but when extremely low water levels arrived it became disastrous.

Now another completely logical outcome followed. The outsiders started running steamboats aground, sinking them, and encountering all kinds of difficulties, while accidents seemed to completely avoid the association members. Therefore, even the owners and captains of boats staffed entirely with outsiders, who had previously thought themselves completely independent of the association and free to console themselves with boasting and mockery, began to feel quite uneasy. Nevertheless, they continued to put on a show of maintaining their boasting, until one dark day when every captain in the group was officially ordered to immediately dismiss his outsiders and hire association pilots instead. And who had the bold audacity to issue such an order? Unfortunately, it came from a force behind the scenes that was more powerful than the authority itself. It was the insurance companies!

It wasn't the time to change tactics. Every outsider had to immediately take their belongings and leave. Naturally, people assumed there was some secret agreement between the association and the insurance companies, but that wasn't the case. The insurance companies had come to understand how excellent the association's reporting system was and how much safety it provided, so they had made their decision independently based on straightforward business reasoning.

There was crying and lamenting and grinding of teeth in the camp of the outsiders now. But it didn't matter, there was only one path for them to follow, and they followed it. They came forward in pairs and groups, and offered their twelve dollars and requested membership. They were shocked to discover that several new regulations had been added long ago. For example, the initiation fee had been increased to fifty dollars; that amount had to be paid, and also ten percent of the wages which the applicant had earned each and every month since the founding of the association. In many cases this totaled three or four hundred dollars. Still, the association would not consider the application until the money was available. Even then a single negative vote destroyed the application. Every member had to vote 'Yes' or 'No' in person and before witnesses; so it took weeks to decide a candidacy, because many pilots were away on voyages for such long periods. However, the regretful sinners gathered their savings together, and one by one, through our slow voting process, they were admitted to the group. A time arrived, at last, when only about ten remained outside. They said they would starve before they would apply. They stayed unemployed for a long while, because naturally nobody could dare to hire them.

Eventually the association announced that starting on a specific date, wages would be increased to five hundred dollars per month. All the branch associations had become powerful by this point, and the Red River branch had already raised wages to seven hundred dollars monthly. Faced with these developments, the ten holdouts reluctantly gave in and submitted their applications. By this time, there was another new rule that required them to pay dues not only on all the wages they had earned since the association was established, but also on what they would have earned if they had kept working up until they applied, rather than going off to sulk in unemployment. It proved to be a challenging process to elect them, but it was eventually achieved. The most stubborn holdout in this group had stayed away and let his dues pile up for so long that he had to submit six hundred and twenty-five dollars along with his application.

The association now had a healthy bank account and had become very powerful. There were no longer any outsiders. They added a new rule that prohibited accepting any new trainees or apprentices for five years; after that period, they would accept only a limited number, not through individual pilots, but through the association itself, under these conditions: the candidate had to be at least eighteen years old, come from a respectable family, and have good character; he had to pass an educational exam, pay a thousand dollars upfront for the privilege of becoming an apprentice, and had to remain under the association's control until a large portion of the membership (more than half, I believe) would agree to sign his application for a pilot's license.

All apprentices who had previously signed articles were now removed from their masters and taken in by the association. The president and secretary assigned them to work on whichever boat they selected, and transferred them from one boat to another following specific regulations. If a pilot could demonstrate that he was in poor health and required help, one of the trainees would be directed to accompany him.

The list of widows and orphans continued to expand, but the association's financial resources grew as well. The association attended its members' funerals with full ceremony and covered all the expenses. When circumstances required it, the organization sent members downstream to search for the bodies of fellow members who had perished in steamboat accidents; such a search could sometimes cost a thousand dollars.

The association obtained a charter and entered the insurance business as well. It not only provided life insurance for its members, but also took on risks related to steamboats.

The organization appeared unbreakable. It held the most secure monopoly anywhere in the world. According to United States law, no person could become a pilot without the signatures of two properly licensed pilots on his application; and at this point there was no one outside the association qualified to provide those signatures. As a result, the creation of new pilots had come to a complete stop. Each year some pilots would pass away and others would become unable to work due to age and poor health; there would be no newcomers to fill their positions. Eventually, the association could raise wages to whatever amount it wanted; and as long as it remained smart enough not to push things too far and anger the federal government into changing the licensing regulations, steamboat owners would be forced to accept these terms, since they would have no other choice.

The owners and captains were the only barrier standing between the association and complete control; eventually, this final obstacle was eliminated. As unbelievable as it might sound, the owners and captains actually brought this about themselves. When the pilots' association declared, several months in advance, that starting September 1, 1861, wages would increase to five hundred dollars per month, the owners and captains immediately raised freight rates by a few cents and justified this to the farmers along the river by pointing out the heavy wage costs that were about to take effect. This was quite a weak justification, but the farmers didn't appear to notice the flaw in the reasoning. It seemed logical to them that adding five cents to the freight cost per bushel of corn was reasonable given the situation, failing to realize that this increase on a shipment of forty thousand sacks amounted to far more than what was needed to pay for the higher wages.

So, immediately the captains and owners formed their own association and suggested raising captains' wages to five hundred dollars as well, while also pushing for another increase in freight rates. This was a fresh concept, but naturally an outcome that had been achieved once could be achieved again. The new association declared (since this happened before all the independent operators had joined the pilots' association) that if any captain hired a pilot who wasn't part of the association, he would be required to dismiss him and also pay a five hundred dollar penalty. Several of these substantial fines were collected before the captains' organization became powerful enough to exercise complete control over its members; but that practice eventually stopped. The captains attempted to convince the pilots to rule that no member of their organization should work under a captain who wasn't part of the association; however, this proposal was rejected. The pilots realized they would have the support of the captains and the underwriters regardless, so they wisely chose not to get involved in complicated partnerships.

As I mentioned earlier, the pilots' association had become perhaps the most tightly controlled monopoly in the world and appeared to be completely unbreakable. However, its days of greatness were already numbered. First, the new railroad line extending through Mississippi, Tennessee, and Kentucky to connect with Northern railway hubs started pulling passenger traffic away from the steamboats; then the war arrived and nearly wiped out the entire steamboat industry for several years, leaving most pilots without work while the cost of living kept rising; after that, the treasurer of the St. Louis association reached into the treasury and disappeared with every penny of their substantial fund; and finally, with railroads expanding everywhere, there was little left for steamboats to do once the war ended except haul cargo; so immediately some clever person from the Atlantic coast brought in the idea of pulling a dozen steamboat loads down to New Orleans behind a common little tugboat; and suddenly, in what seemed like an instant, both the association and the distinguished art of piloting had become relics of a bygone and melancholy era!

Chapter 16: Racing Days

It was always the custom for the boats to leave New Orleans between four and five o'clock in the afternoon. From three o'clock onward they would be burning rosin and pitch pine as a sign of preparation, creating the picturesque spectacle of a line stretching two or three miles long, filled with tall, rising columns of coal-black smoke. This formed a colonnade that supported a dark roof of the same smoke, all blended together and spreading out over the city. Every outbound boat had its flag flying at the jack-staff, and sometimes a duplicate flag on the stern staff at the back. For two or three miles, mates were shouting commands and cursing with more than usual intensity. Countless processions of freight barrels and boxes were spinning across the levee and flying aboard the loading planks, while late passengers dodged and weaved among these frantic activities, hoping to reach the front deck stairway alive, though having serious doubts about their chances.

Women carrying handbags and hatboxes were trying to keep up with husbands loaded down with travel bags and crying babies, failing miserably as they lost their composure in the whirl and roar and general chaos. Carts and baggage wagons were clattering back and forth in wild haste, constantly getting blocked and jammed together, and during those moments one could barely see them through the profanity, except vaguely and dimly. Every winch connected to every cargo hatch, from one end of that long array of steamboats to the other, was keeping up a deafening whiz and whir, lowering freight into the hold, and the half-naked crews of sweating workers who operated them were singing songs like "The Last Sack! The Last Sack!"—inspired to unimaginable excitement by the chaos of turmoil and noise that was driving everybody else mad.

By this time the hurricane and boiler decks of the steamboats would be crowded and filled with passengers. The final bells would start ringing all along the line, and then the commotion seemed to intensify; within a moment or two the last warning came—a chorus of Chinese gongs accompanied by the shout, "All that ain't going, please get ashore!"—and suddenly, the chaos increased fourfold! People came flooding onto the shore, knocking over excited stragglers who were attempting to rush aboard. Just one moment later, a long row of gangplanks was being pulled in, each carrying its typical last-minute passenger hanging onto the end with teeth, fingernails, and every possible grip, while the usual final procrastinator made a desperate leap toward shore right over his head.

Now several boats slide backward into the stream, creating wide gaps in the tightly packed row of steamers. Citizens crowd the decks of boats that aren't departing so they can watch the spectacle. One steamer after another straightens up, gathers all her power, and soon comes swinging by under tremendous steam pressure, with flags flying and black smoke billowing, while her entire crew of firemen and deck-hands (usually dark-skinned African Americans) gather together on the front deck, with the best singer among them standing tall in the center (positioned on the capstan), waving his hat or a flag, and all of them roaring out a powerful chorus, while the farewell cannons thunder and the countless spectators wave their hats and cheer! One steamer after another falls into formation, and the majestic procession goes soaring up the river.

In earlier days, when two speedy boats began a race with large crowds of spectators watching, it was thrilling to listen to the crews singing, particularly during evening hours when the ship's front section glowed with the bright red light from flaming torch containers. Racing provided magnificent entertainment. The audience always believed that racing posed risks; however, the truth was quite different—especially after regulations were established that limited each vessel to a specific amount of steam pressure per square inch. No engineer was ever drowsy or negligent when he was passionate about a race. He remained constantly vigilant, testing pressure valves and monitoring equipment. The hazardous situation occurred on slow, methodical boats, where engineers became sleepy and permitted debris to enter the feed-water heater, blocking the water flow to the boilers.

During the golden age of steamboat travel, a race between two famously fast steamers was an event of enormous significance. The date would be scheduled several weeks ahead of time, and from that moment on, the entire Mississippi Valley would be consumed with excitement. Political discussions and weather talk were abandoned, and people spoke only of the upcoming race. As the time drew near, both steamers would prepare themselves by stripping down and getting ready. Every piece of equipment that added weight or created resistance against wind or water was removed, provided the boat could function without it. The spars, and sometimes even the derricks that supported them, were taken ashore, leaving no way to refloat the vessel if it ran aground. When the 'Eclipse' and the 'A. L. Shotwell' held their famous race many years ago, people claimed that great care was taken to scrape the gold paint off the decorative ornament that hung between the 'Eclipse's' smokestacks, and that for that single journey the captain went without his leather gloves and had his hair completely shaved off. However, I always had my doubts about these stories.

If the boat was known to perform at its peak speed when drawing five and a half feet forward and five feet aft, it was meticulously loaded to that precise measurement—it wouldn't accept even a container of homeopathic pills on its cargo list after reaching that point. Very few passengers were brought aboard, since they not only increase weight but they refuse to help 'balance the boat.' They constantly rush to one side whenever there's something worth seeing, while a dedicated and seasoned steamboat operator would remain at the boat's center and part his hair down the middle using a spirit level.

No cargo or passengers could be picked up along the route, since the racing boats would only stop at major cities, and even then just briefly. Coal barges and wood barges were arranged in advance and kept ready to be quickly attached to the speeding steamboats at a moment's notice. Each boat carried double crews to ensure all tasks could be completed rapidly.

When the chosen date arrived and everything was ready, the two massive steamers backed into the river and positioned themselves there, maneuvering for a moment and seemingly observing each other's every move like living beings. Their flags hung limp, trapped steam screamed through the safety valves, and thick black smoke billowed and churned from the smokestacks, darkening the entire sky. Crowds of people were everywhere—filling the riverbanks, covering the rooftops, packing the steamboats and ships—and you could tell that the edges of the mighty Mississippi would be lined with spectators from here all the way north for twelve hundred miles, ready to cheer on these racing vessels.

Soon tall columns of steam shoot up from the escape pipes of both steamboats, two cannons fire their farewell salute, two red-shirted crew members standing on the capstans wave their small flags above the gathered crews on the front decks, two mournful solos hang in the air for a few lingering moments, two powerful choruses explode into song—and here they come! Brass bands blare out Hail Columbia, cheer after cheer roars from the shoreline, and the magnificent vessels go racing past like the wind.

Those boats never stop for even a moment between New Orleans and St. Louis, except for a second or two at major towns, or to attach thirty-cord wood-boats to their sides. You should be on board when they take a couple of those wood-boats in tow and send a swarm of men into each one; by the time you've cleaned your glasses and put them back on, you'll be wondering what happened to all that wood.

Two well-matched steamboats will remain within sight of each other for days on end. They could even travel side by side, except that pilots aren't all the same, and the most skilled pilots will win the race. If one boat has a brilliant pilot whose partner is slightly less capable, you can determine who's on duty by observing whether that boat has gained or lost distance during each four-hour shift. The most cunning pilot can slow down a boat if he lacks exceptional talent for steering. Steering is an extremely refined skill. A person shouldn't keep a rudder dragging against a boat's stern if he wants to travel upriver quickly.

There's a huge difference between boats, naturally. For quite a while I worked on a boat that moved so slowly we'd actually forget what year we had departed from port. Though this only happened occasionally. Ferry boats would miss profitable runs because their passengers aged and passed away while waiting for us to move out of the way. This happened even less frequently. I kept records of these incidents, but I carelessly lost them somewhere along the way. This vessel, the 'John J. Roe,' crawled along at such a sluggish pace that when she eventually went down in Madrid Bend, it took five years before her owners got word of the disaster. That detail always puzzled me, but that's what the official records show, regardless. She was depressingly slow; even so, we frequently enjoyed thrilling competitions racing against islands, rafts, and similar obstacles. On one particular journey, though, we performed reasonably well. We reached St. Louis in sixteen days. But even at this breakneck speed, I believe we switched watch crews three times while traveling through Fort Adams reach, which stretches only five miles. A 'reach' refers to a straight section of river, and naturally the current flows through such areas with considerable force.

That trip we took to Grand Gulf from New Orleans took us four days to cover three hundred and forty miles, while the 'Eclipse' and 'Shotwell' completed it in just one day. We spent nine days traveling through the chute of 63, covering seven hundred miles, but the 'Eclipse' and 'Shotwell' made that journey in only two days. More than a generation ago, a steamboat called the 'J. M. White' traveled from New Orleans to Cairo in three days, six hours, and forty-four minutes. In 1853, the 'Eclipse' completed the same route in three days, three hours, and twenty minutes.[5] In 1870, the 'R. E. Lee' accomplished it in three days and one hour. This final time is considered the fastest trip on record. I will attempt to demonstrate that it was not. Here's my reasoning: when the 'J. M. White' made her run, the distance between New Orleans and Cairo was approximately eleven hundred and six miles, which means her average speed was slightly over fourteen miles per hour. During the 'Eclipse's' era, the distance between these two ports had been reduced to one thousand and eighty miles, making her average

---

[5] Time disputed. Some authorities add 1 hour and 16 minutes to this.

speed just under fourteen and three-eighths miles per hour. By the time of the 'R. E. Lee's' run, the distance had decreased to about one thousand and thirty miles, giving her an average of approximately fourteen and one-eighth miles per hour. Therefore, the 'Eclipse's' time was clearly the fastest that has ever been achieved.

Chapter 17: Cut-offs and Stephen

These technical details matter for one specific reason. They allow me to explain one of the Mississippi's strangest characteristics— its tendency to shorten itself over time. If you toss a long, flexible apple peel over your shoulder, it will roughly form the shape of a typical section of the Mississippi River; specifically, the nine or ten hundred miles that extend from Cairo, Illinois, down south to New Orleans, which is remarkably winding, with occasional short straight segments scattered at great distances. The two-hundred-mile section from Cairo north to St. Louis isn't nearly as winding, since that area has rocky terrain that the river can't erode very much.

The water carves the soft banks of the lower river into deep horseshoe-shaped bends; these curves are so pronounced that in some locations, if you stepped off your boat at one end of the horseshoe and walked across the narrow strip of land—perhaps half to three-quarters of a mile—you could sit down and relax for a couple of hours while your steamboat traveled around the long curve at ten miles per hour to pick you up again. When the river is rising rapidly, some unscrupulous person whose plantation sits back from the water, and is therefore less valuable, only needs to wait for the right moment, dig a small channel across the narrow neck of land on some dark night, and direct the water into it, and in an amazingly short time a miracle occurs: namely, the entire

Mississippi has claimed that little ditch as its own, placing the country dweller's plantation directly on its banks (increasing its value fourfold), while that other person's previously valuable plantation suddenly finds itself stranded far away on a large island; the old river channel around it will quickly become shallow, boats won't be able to come within ten miles of it, and its value plummets to a quarter of what it once was. Guards are posted at these narrow strips of land when necessary, and if someone happens to be caught digging a channel across them, the odds are heavily against them ever getting another chance to dig such a ditch.

Take a look at some of the results of this channel-cutting activity. There used to be a narrow strip of land across from Port Hudson, Louisiana, that measured only half a mile at its thinnest point. You could walk across it in just fifteen minutes, but if you took a raft around the bend, you'd have to travel thirty-five miles to reach the same destination. In 1722, the river broke through that narrow strip, abandoned its original course, and cut thirty-five miles off its length. Similarly, it reduced its length by twenty-five miles at Black Hawk Point in 1699. Below Red River Landing, the Raccourci cut-off was created (I believe this happened forty or fifty years ago). This cut twenty-eight miles from the river's length. Today, if you travel by river from the southernmost of these three cut-offs to the northernmost one, you cover only seventy miles. To make that same trip one hundred and seventy-six years ago, someone would have had to travel one hundred and fifty-eight miles—a reduction of eighty-eight miles over that relatively short stretch. At some point in the distant past, cut-offs were created above Vidalia, Louisiana, at island 92, at island 84, and at Hale's Point. These cut-offs collectively shortened the river by seventy-seven miles.

Since I was on the Mississippi, new shortcuts have been created at Hurricane Island, at Island 100, at Napoleon, Arkansas, at Walnut Bend, and at Council Bend. These changes made the river shorter by a total of sixty-seven miles. During my time there, a shortcut was also made at American Bend, which reduced the river's length by ten miles or more.

Therefore, the Mississippi River between Cairo and New Orleans stretched twelve hundred and fifteen miles in length one hundred and seventy-six years ago. After the cut-off in 1722, it measured eleven hundred and eighty miles. Following the American Bend cut-off, it was reduced to one thousand and forty miles. Since then, it has shortened by sixty-seven miles. As a result, its current length is only nine hundred and seventy-three miles.

Now, if I wanted to be one of those heavy-handed scientific people and pretend to prove what happened in the distant past by what happened during a specific period in recent times, or what will happen in the far future by what has taken place in recent years, what an incredible opportunity this presents! Geology has never had such a chance, nor such precise data to work with! Neither has the 'development of species'! Ice ages are significant phenomena, but they are unclear—unclear. Please note:—

Over the course of one hundred and seventy-six years, the Lower Mississippi has made itself two hundred and forty-two miles shorter. This works out to an average of just over one mile and a third each year. So any reasonable person who isn't blind or foolish can clearly see that during the Old Oolitic Silurian Period, exactly one million years ago this coming November, the Lower Mississippi River stretched more than one million three hundred thousand miles long and jutted out over the Gulf of Mexico like a fishing pole. By the same logic, anyone can see that in seven hundred and forty-two years from now, the Lower Mississippi will measure only a mile and three-quarters in length, and Cairo and New Orleans will have connected their streets and will be moving along peacefully under one mayor and a shared board of aldermen. Science has something captivating about it. You get such enormous amounts of speculation from such a small investment of actual facts.

When the water starts to flow through one of those channels I've been talking about, it's time for the people in that area to relocate. The water cuts away the banks like a blade. By the time the channel has grown to twelve or fifteen feet wide, the disaster is essentially complete, because no force on earth can halt it at that point. When the width reaches a hundred yards, the banks start to break away in chunks half an acre wide. The current flowing around the bend previously traveled only five miles per hour; now it has increased tremendously due to the shortened distance. I was aboard the first boat that attempted to navigate through the cut-off at American Bend, but we didn't make it through. It was approaching midnight, and it was a fierce night—thunder, lightning, and heavy rain pouring down. It was estimated that the current in the cut-off was moving at about fifteen or twenty miles per hour; twelve or thirteen was the maximum our boat could manage, even in relatively calm water, so perhaps we were unwise to attempt the cut-off. Nevertheless, Mr. Brown was determined, and he continued trying. The eddy rushing up the bank, beneath the 'point,' was nearly as fast as the current out in the center; so we would go racing up the shore like a lightning express train, build up a substantial head of steam, and 'prepare for a surge' when we hit the current that was spinning past the point. But all our preparations proved futile. The moment the current struck us it whirled us around like a spinning top, the water flooded the forecastle, and the boat tilted so far over that a person could barely maintain their footing. The next moment we were far down the river, struggling with all our strength to stay out of the woods. We attempted the experiment four times. I stood on the forecastle companionway to watch. It was remarkable to see how quickly the boat would spin around and turn tail the instant she emerged from the eddy and the current hit her bow. The jarring impact and the shaking would have been roughly the same if she had struck a sandbar at full speed. Under the lightning flashes one could see the plantation cabins and the fertile acres tumbling into the river; and the crash they produced was a decent imitation of thunder. Once, when we spun around, we barely missed a house by about twenty feet, which had a light glowing in the window; and at that same moment that house went into the water. Nobody could remain on our forecastle; the water rushed across it like a flood every time we plunged across the current. At the conclusion of our fourth attempt we ended up in the woods two miles below the cut-off; all the countryside there was flooded, naturally. A day or two later the cut-off was three-quarters of a mile wide, and boats passed up through it without much trouble, and thus saved ten miles.

The old Raccourci cut-off shortened the river by twenty-eight miles. A tradition grew up around this place. People said that one night a steamboat came through and followed the massive bend in the usual way, with the pilots unaware that the cut-off had been created. It was a ghastly, terrible night, and everything looked unclear and twisted. The old bend had already started filling in with sediment, so the boat found itself dodging strange underwater obstacles and sometimes striking them. The confused pilots began cursing, and eventually made the completely pointless wish that they would never escape from that location. As typically occurs in such situations, that specific prayer was granted while the others were ignored. So even today that ghostly steamboat continues wandering around in that abandoned waterway, attempting to find its way out. More than one serious night watchman has told me that on foggy, gloomy nights, he has looked nervously down that forgotten river while passing the tip of the island, and spotted the dim light of the phantom steamboat's lanterns moving through the far-off darkness, and heard the muted sound of her steam pipes and the sorrowful calls of her depth-sounders.

In the absence of additional statistics, I would like to close this chapter with one more memory of 'Stephen.'

Most of the ship captains and pilots held Stephen's promissory notes for money he had borrowed, with amounts starting at two hundred and fifty dollars and going higher. Stephen never actually paid back any of these notes, but he was extremely punctual and enthusiastic about renewing them every twelve months.

Of course, there eventually came a time when Stephen could no longer borrow money from his longtime creditors, so he was forced to seek out new people who didn't know his reputation. One such victim was the good-hearted, simple-natured young Yates (I'm using a made-up name, but the actual name started with a Y, just like this one does). Young Yates graduated as a pilot, landed a job, and when the month ended and he walked up to the clerk's office to collect his two hundred and fifty dollars in crisp new bills, Stephen was waiting there! His smooth tongue started working, and within a very short time, Yates's two hundred and fifty dollars had switched hands. Word of this quickly spread around pilot headquarters, and the old creditors found great amusement and satisfaction in the news. But innocent Yates never suspected that Stephen's promise to pay him back promptly by the end of the week was completely worthless. Yates showed up for his money at the agreed-upon time; Stephen sweet-talked him and convinced him to wait another week. Yates returned then, as they had arranged, and left feeling placated once again, but now facing yet another delay. This pattern continued. Yates tracked down Stephen week after week, getting nowhere, and finally gave up trying. And then immediately, Stephen began tracking down Yates! Wherever Yates showed up, there was Stephen, without fail. And not only was he there, but he was radiating warmth and pouring out apologies for being unable to pay. Before long, whenever poor Yates spotted him approaching, he would turn around and run away, dragging along anyone who was with him if he had company;

but it didn't help; his debtor would chase him down and trap him. Breathing heavily and red-faced, Stephen would arrive with his hands stretched out and his eyes eager, interrupt whatever conversation was happening, shake both of Yates's arms until they felt loose in their sockets, and start talking—

'Wow, what a chase I've had! I could see you didn't notice me, so I put on full speed because I was afraid I'd miss you completely. And here you are! There, just stand like that, and let me get a good look at you! That same wonderful face.' [To Yates's friend:] 'Just look at him! Look at him! Isn't it wonderful to see him! Isn't it? Isn't he just a sight to behold! Some people call him a sight; I call him a whole spectacle! That's what he is—a complete spectacle. And now I remember! How I wish I could have found you an hour sooner! For twenty-four hours I've been holding onto that two hundred and fifty dollars for you; I've been searching for you everywhere. I waited at the Planter's from six yesterday evening until two o'clock this morning, without rest or food; my wife asks, "Where have you been all night?" I told her, "This debt weighs heavily on my conscience." She says, "In all my years I've never seen a man worry about a debt the way you do." I said, "It's just who I am; how can I change that?" She says, "Well, please go to bed and get some sleep." I said, "Not until that poor, honorable young man gets his money." So I stayed up all night, and this morning I rushed out, and the first person I ran into told me you had boarded the "Grand Turk" and sailed to New Orleans. Well, sir, I had to lean against a building and weep. So help me God, I couldn't control myself. The man who owned the place came out cleaning with a cloth, and said he didn't appreciate people crying against his building, and then it felt like the entire world had turned against me, and there was no point in living anymore; and walking along an hour ago, suffering agony that no one can imagine, I ran into Jim Wilson and paid him the two hundred and fifty dollars on account; and to think that you're here now, and I don't have a penny! But as certain as I'm standing here on this ground on this specific brick,—there, I've made a mark on the brick to remember it by,—I'll borrow that money and pay it to you at exactly twelve o'clock tomorrow! Now, stand there; let me look at you just one more time.'

Yates's life became unbearable. He couldn't escape his debtor or the terrible suffering his debtor endured from being unable to pay what he owed. Yates was afraid to appear in public, terrified that he might discover Stephen lurking around the corner, waiting for him.

Bogart's pool hall was a popular hangout for riverboat pilots back then. They gathered there as much to share news about the river as they did to play games. One morning Yates was there; Stephen was also present, but he stayed hidden from view. Eventually, when nearly all the pilots who were in town had shown up, Stephen suddenly emerged from his hiding spot and rushed toward Yates as if greeting a long-lost brother.

'Oh, I'm so happy to see you! My goodness, just looking at you brings such relief to my eyes! Gentlemen, I owe money to every one of you; altogether I probably owe about forty thousand dollars. I want to pay it back; I plan to pay back every single cent of it. You all understand, without me having to explain, how much pain it has caused me to stay in debt for so long to such patient and generous friends; but the worst pain I feel—by far the worst— comes from the money I owe to this wonderful young man here; and I came to this place this morning specifically to announce that I have finally discovered a way to pay off all my debts! And I especially wanted him to be present when I made this announcement. Yes, my loyal friend—my benefactor, I've discovered the way! I've found the method to pay off all my debts, and you'll get your money!' Hope appeared in Yates's eyes; then Stephen, smiling kindly and placing his hand on Yates's head, added, 'I'm going to pay them off in alphabetical order!'

Then he turned and vanished. The complete meaning of Stephen's 'approach' didn't become clear to the confused and thoughtful crowd for about two minutes; and then Yates whispered with a sigh—

"Well, the Y's have a slim chance. He won't make it past the C's in this world, and I figure that even after a great deal of eternity has passed in the next one, I'll still be called up there as 'that poor, ragged pilot who came here from St. Louis in the early days!'"

Chapter 18: I Take a Few Extra Lessons

During my two or two and a half years as an apprentice, I worked under many pilots and encountered numerous types of steamboat workers and various kinds of steamboats. It wasn't always practical for Mr. Bixby to keep me with him, so during those times he would assign me to work with someone else. To this day, I continue to benefit from that experience. In that brief but intense period of learning, I became personally and intimately familiar with nearly every different type of human personality that you might encounter in fiction, biography, or history. I'm reminded daily that typical shore-based jobs require as much as forty years to provide a person with this kind of education. When I mention that I'm still benefiting from this experience, I don't mean it has made me a good judge of character—no, it hasn't accomplished that, because good judges of character are born with that ability, not trained to have it. The benefits I've gained vary in both type and extent, but the aspect I treasure most is the enthusiasm that early experience has brought to my reading in later years. Whenever I come across a well-developed character in fiction or biography, I usually develop a strong personal connection with them, simply because I feel like I've known them before—I've encountered them on the river.

The person who appears most frequently in my mind from the shadows of that lost time is Brown from the steamboat 'Pennsylvania'—the man I mentioned in an earlier chapter, whose memory was both exceptional and exhausting. He was a middle-aged, tall, thin, bony, clean-shaven, horse-faced, ignorant, cheap, spiteful, snarling, fault-finding, flaw-obsessing tyrant. I quickly developed the habit of starting my watch shifts with fear weighing on my heart. Regardless of how enjoyable my time had been with the off-duty crew below deck, and no matter how cheerful my mood when I began climbing up, my spirit turned to lead within my body the instant I neared the pilot-house.

I still remember the first time I ever walked into that man's presence. The steamboat had pulled away from St. Louis and was heading downstream in a straight line. I climbed up to the pilot house feeling excited and very proud to be somewhat officially part of the leadership crew of such a fast and well-known steamboat. Brown was steering the wheel. I stopped in the center of the room, ready to give my respectful greeting, but Brown didn't turn around. I thought he glanced at me quickly from the corner of his eye, but since he didn't even do that again, I figured I must have been wrong. At that moment he was carefully navigating through some dangerous shallow spots near the wood supply yards, so it wouldn't have been appropriate to disturb him. I quietly walked over to the tall bench and sat down.

There was silence for ten minutes; then my new boss turned and examined me carefully and thoroughly from head to toe for what felt like—to me—about fifteen minutes. After that he turned his face away and I didn't see it for several seconds; then it appeared again, and this question met me—

"Are you Horace Bigsby's apprentice?"

"Yes, sir."

After this there was a pause and another inspection. Then—

"What's your name?"

I told him. He repeated it back to me. It was probably the only thing he ever forgot; because even though I was with him for many months, he never spoke to me in any other way than 'Here!' followed by whatever he wanted me to do.

"Where were you born?"

"In Florida, Missouri."

A pause. Then—

"Would've been a hell of a lot better if he'd stayed there!"

Through about a dozen fairly straightforward questions, he extracted my entire family history from me.

The electrical wires were being installed now, during the first crossing. This disrupted the investigation. Once the wires had been put in place, he continued—

"How long have you been on the river?"

I told him. After a pause—

"Where did you get those shoes?"

I provided him with the information.

"Lift up your foot!"

I followed his instructions. He took a step back and examined the shoe with careful attention and obvious disdain, scratching his head as he pondered the situation and pushing his tall, cone-shaped hat forward to make the thinking process easier, then exclaimed, 'Well, I'll be dod derned!' before going back to his wheel.

What reason there was to be so upset about it remains just as much a mystery to me now as it was back then. It must have been a full fifteen minutes—fifteen minutes of boring, homesick silence—before that long horse-like face turned toward me again—and then, what a transformation! It was as red as fire, and every muscle in it was twitching. Then came this scream—

"Hey! Are you planning to sit there all day?"

I landed in the middle of the floor, thrown there by the electric shock of the surprise. As soon as I could find my voice, I said apologetically, "I have had no orders, sir."

"You haven't received any orders! My, what a fine gentleman we think we are! We must have orders! Our father was a gentleman who owned slaves, and we've been to school. Yes, we're a gentleman too, and we have to have orders! Orders, is that it? Orders are what you want! Damn my hide, I'll teach you not to puff yourself up and strut around here talking about your damned orders! Get away from the wheel!" (I had walked up to it without realizing it.)

I took a step or two backward and stood there as if in a dream, with all my senses numbed by this wild attack.

"Why are you just standing there? Take that ice pitcher down to the texas tender—come on, get moving, and don't take all day doing it!"

The moment I returned to the pilot-house, Brown said—

"Hey! What were you doing down there all this time?"

"I couldn't find the texas-tender; I had to go all the way to the pantry."

"What a ridiculous story! Fill up the stove."

I went ahead and did exactly that. He watched me with the intense focus of a cat. Soon after, he shouted—

"Put down that shovel! You're the biggest fool I've ever seen—you don't even have enough sense to load up a stove."

Throughout the entire watch, this kind of behavior continued. Indeed, the following watches were very similar during a period that lasted for months. As I mentioned earlier, I quickly developed the habit of reporting for duty with a sense of dread. The instant I was present, even on the darkest nights, I could sense those yellow eyes fixed on me, and I knew their owner was looking for an excuse to unleash some poison in my direction. As a preliminary, he would say—

"Here! Take the wheel."

Two minutes later—

"Where in the world are you going? Pull her down! Pull her down!"

After another moment—

"Hey! Are you planning to hold onto her all day? Let her go— meet her! Meet her!"

Then he would leap up from the bench, grab the steering wheel away from me, and handle the situation himself, all while unleashing his fury on me the entire time.

George Ritchie was the other pilot's apprentice. He was having a great time now because his boss, George Ealer, was as kind-hearted as Brown was cruel. Ritchie had worked under Brown the previous season, so he knew exactly how to amuse himself and torment me with a single activity. Whenever I took control of the wheel for a moment during Ealer's watch, Ritchie would lean back on the bench and imitate Brown, constantly shouting things like "Grab her! Grab her! Worst steamboat pilot I've ever seen!" "Hey! Where are you heading now? Are you going to hit that fallen tree?" "Pull her back! Don't you hear me? Pull her back!" "There she goes! Just like I thought! I told you not to cut that sandbar so close. Get away from the wheel!"

So I always struggled, regardless of who was on duty; and at times it felt like Ritchie's well-meaning harassment was almost as irritating as Brown's relentless criticism.

I frequently felt the urge to kill Brown, but this wouldn't solve anything. A trainee had to endure whatever his supervisor dished out in terms of harsh commentary and criticism; and we all believed there was a federal law that made striking or threatening a pilot while on duty a crime punishable by prison time. Still, I could picture myself killing Brown; there was no law against imagining it; and that's exactly what I would do the moment I got into bed. Rather than mentally reviewing my river route as I was supposed to, I set work aside for entertainment, and murdered

Brown. I killed Brown every single night for months; not in tired, old, ordinary methods, but in fresh and vivid ways—methods that were sometimes remarkable for their creative originality and the horrifying nature of the circumstances and setting.

Brown constantly looked for any excuse to criticize; and when he couldn't find a reasonable excuse, he would create one. He would reprimand you for staying close to the shore, and for not staying close to it; for keeping near a sandbar, and for not keeping near it; for slowing down when you weren't told to, and for not slowing down when you weren't told to; for increasing speed without being ordered, and for waiting to be ordered. In short, his unchanging practice was to criticize everything you did; and another unchanging practice of his was to deliver all his comments to you in the form of an insult.

One day we were approaching New Madrid, heading downstream with a heavy cargo load. Brown was positioned on one side of the steering wheel; I stood on the other side, ready to "pull down" or "shove up" as needed. Every so often, he would steal a quick glance in my direction. I had figured out long ago what those looks meant—he was scheming to set some kind of trap for me. I found myself wondering what form his latest scheme would take. Eventually, he stepped away from the wheel and spoke in his typical snarling manner—

"Here! Let's see if you have enough courage to turn her around."

This was destined to be a success; nothing could stop it; since he had never permitted me to turn the boat around before; therefore, regardless of how I might handle the task, he could easily criticize it. He positioned himself behind me with his eager eye watching, and the outcome was predictable: I panicked within fifteen seconds and lost track of what I was doing; I began turning the boat around too soon, but noticed a flash of satisfaction in

Brown's eye and fixed my error; I started the turn again while positioned too high, but managed to correct myself in time; I made additional mistakes and still succeeded in recovering; but eventually I became so bewildered and nervous that I committed the worst error of all—I went too far downstream before starting to bring the boat around. Brown's opportunity had arrived.

His face flushed red with anger; he leaped forward, threw me across the room with one powerful swing of his arm, spun the steering wheel down, and unleashed a torrent of harsh words that continued until he ran out of breath. During this outburst he called me every type of insulting name he could come up with, and a couple of times I thought he was about to curse—but he held back this time. 'Dod dern' was as close as he dared come to the pleasure of swearing, since he had been raised with a healthy fear of eternal fire and brimstone.

That was an uncomfortable hour, since there was a large audience gathered on the hurricane deck. When I went to bed that night, I imagined killing Brown in seventeen different ways—all of them completely new.

Chapter 19: Brown and I Exchange Compliments

Two trips later, I found myself in serious trouble. Brown was at the helm; I was working the engine controls. My younger brother appeared on the upper deck and yelled to Brown to stop at a particular landing about a mile downstream. Brown showed no sign that he had heard anything. But that was typical of him: he never bothered to acknowledge a junior clerk. The wind was howling; Brown was hard of hearing (though he always acted like he wasn't), and I seriously doubted whether he had caught the instruction. If I had been expendable, I would have spoken up; but since I wasn't, it seemed wise to protect myself; so I remained silent.

Soon enough, we sailed past that plantation. Captain Klinefelter came up on deck and said—

"Let her come around, sir, let her come around. Didn't Henry tell you to land here?"

"No, sir!"

"I sent him up to do it."

"He did come up; and that's all the good it did, the damn fool. He never said anything."

"Didn't you hear him?" the captain asked me.

Of course I didn't want to get involved in this situation, but there was no way to avoid it; so I said—

"Yes, sir."

I knew what Brown would say next before he even spoke; it was—

"Shut your mouth! You never heard anything like that."

I shut my mouth as I was told. An hour later, Henry walked into the pilot-house, completely unaware of what had been happening. He was a completely harmless boy, and I felt bad seeing him arrive, because I knew Brown wouldn't show him any mercy. Brown started in right away—

"Hey! Why didn't you tell me we had to stop at that plantation?"

"I did tell you, Mr. Brown."

"It's a lie!"

I said—

"You're lying. He did tell you."

Brown stared at me with genuine surprise, and for a full moment he was completely speechless; then he yelled at me—

"I'll take care of your situation in just a moment!" then to Henry, "And you get out of the pilot-house; leave now!"

The pilot's orders had to be followed—it was the law. The boy began to leave and had already placed his foot on the top step outside the door when Brown, suddenly overcome with rage, grabbed a ten-pound chunk of coal and lunged after him. However, I stood between them with a heavy stool in my hands, and I struck Brown with a solid, direct blow that knocked him flat.

I had committed the most serious offense possible—I had raised my hand against a pilot while he was working! I figured I was definitely headed for prison, and I couldn't be in any worse trouble if I continued and settled my long-standing grievances with this man while I had the opportunity; therefore I stayed with him and beat him with my fists for quite some time—I don't know exactly how long, the satisfaction of it probably made it feel longer than it actually was;—but eventually he broke free and jumped up and lunged toward the wheel: a completely understandable concern, since during all this time, the steamboat had been racing down the river at fifteen miles per hour with no one steering! Fortunately, Eagle Bend was two miles wide at this flood stage, and proportionally long and deep; and the boat was guiding herself straight down the center and avoiding any risks. Even so, that was just good fortune—someone might have discovered her crashing into the forest.

Seeing immediately that the 'Pennsylvania' wasn't in any danger, Brown grabbed the large telescope like a weapon and commanded me to leave the pilot-house with more aggression than a Comanche warrior. However, I wasn't intimidated by him anymore; so instead of leaving, I stayed and pointed out his poor grammar. I corrected his angry outbursts for him and translated them into proper English, explaining to him how much better clear English was compared to the crude dialect from the Pennsylvania coal mines where he came from. He certainly could have held his own in a simple exchange of insults; but he wasn't prepared for this type of argument. Soon he set down his telescope and took control of the wheel, grumbling and shaking his head, while I went back to the bench. The commotion had drawn everyone to the hurricane deck, and I felt anxious when I spotted the old captain looking up from the middle of the gathering. I thought to myself, 'Now I'm finished!' Even though he was typically kind and tolerant with the boat's crew and patient with small mistakes, he could be quite strict when the offense warranted it.

I tried to picture what he would do to a trainee pilot who had committed such a serious offense as I had, especially on a steamboat loaded with expensive cargo and crowded with passengers. Our shift was almost over. I figured I would find somewhere to hide until I could find an opportunity to sneak off the boat. So I quietly left the pilot house, went down the stairs, and made my way around to the officers' quarters door—and was just about to slip inside when the captain appeared right in front of me! I lowered my head, and he stood there looking down at me without saying anything for a moment or two, then spoke with great emphasis—

"Follow me."

I followed behind him as he led the way to his sitting room at the front of the officers' quarters. We were by ourselves now. He shut the rear door, then walked slowly to the front door and closed that one too. He took a seat while I remained standing in front of him. He studied me for a short while, then spoke—

"So you've been fighting Mr. Brown?"

I responded humbly—

"Yes, sir."

"Do you realize that this is a very serious matter?"

"Yes, sir."

"Do you realize that this boat was racing down the river for a full five minutes with nobody steering it?"

"Yes, sir."

"Did you hit him first?"

"Yes, sir."

"What with?"

"A stool, sir."

'Hard?'

"Not too bad, sir."

"Did it knock him down?"

"He—he fell, sir."

"Did you follow it up? Did you do anything further?"

"Yes, sir."

"What did you do?"

"Beat him up, sir."

"Beat him up?"

"Yes, sir."

"Did you beat him badly—I mean, severely?"

"You could call it that, sir, I suppose."

"I'm extremely glad about it! Listen, never mention that I said that. You have committed a serious offense; and don't you ever commit it again on this boat. But—wait for him on shore! Give him a good solid beating, do you understand? I'll cover the costs. Now go—and remember, not a word of this to anyone. Get out of here!—you've committed a serious offense, you scoundrel!"

I slipped away, thrilled by the feeling of having narrowly escaped and been powerfully rescued; and I could hear him chuckling to himself and smacking his heavy thighs after I had shut his door.

When Brown finished his watch, he went directly to the captain, who was speaking with some passengers on the boiler deck, and insisted that I be put ashore in New Orleans—and he added—

"I'll never operate this boat again as long as that inexperienced pilot remains aboard."

The captain said—

"But he doesn't need to come around when you're on watch, Mr. Brown."

"I refuse to remain on the same vessel as that man. Either he leaves or I do."

"Very well," said the captain, "let it be yourself," and he continued his conversation with the passengers.

During the short time left in the trip, I understood exactly how a freed slave must feel, because I had become a freed slave myself. When we stopped at the docks, I would listen to George Ealer playing his flute, or hear him read from his two favorite books—what he called his bibles—which were works by Goldsmith and Shakespeare. Sometimes I played chess with him, and I might have won a few games if he hadn't always taken back his final move and played the ending differently.

Chapter 20: A Catastrophe

We spent three days in New Orleans, but the captain couldn't find another pilot. He suggested that I take the daytime watch while George Ealer handled the night shifts. However, I was scared—I had never worked a watch alone before, and I was certain I would run into trouble at the entrance of some channel or run the boat aground trying to navigate through a sandbar. Brown kept his position, but he refused to work with me. So the captain wrote me an order for passage aboard the 'A. T. Lacey' to St. Louis, explaining that he would locate a new pilot there and I could return to my steersman position afterward. The 'Lacey' was scheduled to depart a few days after the 'Pennsylvania.'

The night before the 'Pennsylvania' departed, Henry and I sat talking on a pile of freight on the levee until midnight. Our conversation focused mainly on a topic I believe we had never discussed before—steamboat disasters. One was heading our way at that very moment, though we had no idea; the water that would create the steam that would cause it was flowing past some point fifteen hundred miles upriver while we talked—but it would reach us at exactly the right time and place. We wondered whether people without official authority could be much help during disasters and the panic that follows; even so, they might serve some purpose; therefore we decided that if we ever encountered a disaster, we would at least stay with the boat and provide whatever small assistance circumstances might offer. Henry recalled this conversation later, when the disaster struck, and he responded just as we had agreed.

The 'Lacey' began its journey up the river two days after the 'Pennsylvania.' A couple of days into our trip, we stopped at Greenville, Mississippi, and someone yelled—

"The Pennsylvania exploded at Ship Island, killing one hundred and fifty people!"

At Napoleon, Arkansas, that same evening, we received an extra edition published by a Memphis newspaper that provided additional details. The paper mentioned my brother and reported that he had not been injured.

Further up the river, we received another newspaper update. My brother was mentioned once more, but this time he was described as being injured beyond recovery. We didn't receive the complete details of the disaster until we arrived in Memphis. This is the tragic story—

It was six o'clock on a hot summer morning. The 'Pennsylvania' was slowly moving north of Ship Island, about sixty miles below Memphis, running on half steam while towing a wood barge that was nearly empty. George Ealer was alone in the pilot house, I believe; the second engineer and a striker were on duty in the engine room; the second mate was keeping watch on deck; George Black, Mr. Wood, and my brother, who were clerks, were sleeping, along with Brown and the head engineer, the carpenter, the chief mate, and one striker; Captain Klinefelter was sitting in the barber's chair, and the barber was getting ready to shave him. There were quite a few cabin passengers on board, and three or four hundred deck passengers—at least that's what people said at the time—and not many of them were awake yet. Since the wood was almost completely unloaded from the barge, Ealer signaled to go 'full steam ahead,' and the next instant four of the eight boilers exploded with a deafening roar, and the entire front third of the boat was blown high into the air! The main portion of the wreckage, including the smokestacks, crashed back down onto the boat, creating a mountain of torn and twisted debris—and then, shortly after, flames erupted.

Many people were thrown great distances and landed in the river, including Mr. Wood, my brother, and the carpenter. The carpenter was still lying on his mattress when he hit the water seventy-five feet away from the boat. Brown, the pilot, and George Black, the chief clerk, were never seen or heard from again after the explosion. The barber's chair, with Captain Klinefelter sitting in it unharmed, remained with its back hanging over empty space—everything in front of it, including the floor, had vanished; and the dazed barber, who was also uninjured, stood with one toe extending over the void, still mindlessly stirring his shaving cream without saying a word.

When George Ealer saw the smokestacks shooting upward in front of him, he understood what was happening; so he buried his face in the collar of his coat, and pressed both hands there firmly to hold this shield in place so that no steam could reach his nose or mouth. He had plenty of time to take care of these precautions while he was rising up and coming back down. He soon landed on top of the unexploded boilers, forty feet below where the pilot-house used to be, along with his steering wheel and a shower of other debris, and surrounded by a cloud of burning steam. All of the many people who inhaled that steam died; no one survived.

But Ealer breathed none of it. He made his way to the fresh air as quickly as possible; and when the steam cleared away he came back and climbed up on the boilers again, and carefully searched for each and every one of his chess pieces and the various sections of his flute.

By this point, the fire was starting to pose a serious threat. Screams and moans echoed through the air. Many people had suffered severe burns, and many others were injured; the explosion had sent an iron crowbar straight through one man's body—I believe they mentioned he was a priest. He didn't die immediately, and his agony was terrible to witness. A fifteen-year-old French naval cadet, the son of a French admiral, was horribly burned but endured his pain with courage. Both officers were severely scalded as well, yet they remained at their stations despite their injuries. They pulled the wood-boat toward the stern, and together with the captain, they held back the panicked crowd of terrified immigrants until the wounded could be brought to safety and given priority treatment.

When Mr. Wood and Henry fell into the water, they began swimming toward shore, which was only a few hundred yards away. However, Henry soon said he thought he wasn't injured (what a puzzling mistake!), and therefore decided he would swim back to the boat to help rescue the wounded. So they separated, and Henry turned back.

By this time the fire was spreading rapidly and aggressively, and several people who were trapped beneath the debris were desperately pleading for rescue. Every attempt to extinguish the fire proved unsuccessful; so the buckets were soon abandoned and the officers began working with axes, trying to cut the trapped victims free. One of the prisoners was a striker; he reported that he wasn't hurt, but couldn't escape on his own; and when he realized that the fire would probably force the rescuers to retreat, he pleaded for someone to shoot him, which would spare him from a more horrific death. The fire did indeed force the axemen to withdraw, and they were left powerless, having to listen to this unfortunate man's desperate appeals until the flames put an end to his suffering.

The fire forced everyone who could fit onto the wood-flat; it was then set loose to drift, and both it and the burning steamboat floated down the river toward Ship Island. They tied the flat at the top of the island, and there, exposed to the scorching sun, the barely clothed survivors had to stay without food, medicine, or treatment for their wounds for the remainder of the day. Eventually, a steamboat arrived and transported the victims to Memphis, where generous help was immediately provided. By this point, Henry had lost consciousness. The doctors examined his wounds and determined they were fatal, so they naturally focused their primary efforts on patients who had a chance of survival.

Forty wounded men were laid on makeshift beds across the floor of a large public hall, and Henry was among them. Each day, the women of Memphis arrived carrying flowers, fresh fruit, and all manner of treats and delicacies, staying to care for the injured. Every doctor in the city took turns keeping watch, along with all the medical students, while the rest of the community provided money and whatever supplies were needed. Memphis had mastered this kind of compassionate response, having witnessed many disasters similar to the Pennsylvania incident near its shores, making it more experienced than any other river city in performing the noble work of the Good Samaritan.

The scene that greeted me when I walked into that enormous hall was unlike anything I had ever witnessed before. Two lengthy rows of people lying face down—more than forty in total—and every face and head wrapped in shapeless bundles of loose, unprocessed cotton. It was a horrifying sight. I remained there for six days and nights, and it proved to be an extremely sorrowful experience. There was one daily occurrence that was especially disheartening: the transfer of those who were dying to a separate room. This was carried out so that the spirits of the remaining patients wouldn't be harmfully affected by witnessing one of their fellow sufferers in their final moments. The doomed person was always transported with minimal disturbance, and the stretcher was consistently concealed from view by a barrier of medical staff; but it made no difference: everyone understood what that group of hunched figures, moving with muted footsteps and deliberate pace, signified; and all eyes followed it longingly, while a tremor of fear spread alongside it like a ripple.

I witnessed many unfortunate men taken to the 'death-room,' never to be seen again. However, I observed our chief mate being carried there on multiple occasions. His injuries were terrible, particularly his burns. He was covered in linseed oil and raw cotton from the waist up, barely resembling anything human. His mind frequently wandered; during these episodes, his agony would cause him to rant and yell and sometimes scream. Following periods of silent exhaustion, his confused mind would suddenly imagine the large hospital ward as a ship's forecastle, with the bustling crowd of nurses transformed into his crew; he would sit upright and bellow, 'Move yourselves, move yourselves, you fossils, slugs, undertakers! Are you going to spend all day moving that small load of cargo?' He would follow this outburst with an earth-shattering explosion of profanity that nothing could halt or silence until he had completely vented his rage. During these wild episodes, he would sometimes rip away chunks of cotton, revealing his burned flesh beneath. The sight was horrifying. Naturally, this commotion and these disturbing displays were harmful to the other patients; therefore, the physicians attempted to administer morphine to calm him. Whether lucid or delirious, he refused to take it. He claimed his wife had died from that dangerous drug, and he would rather die than consume it. He became suspicious that the doctors were hiding it in his regular medications and drinking water—so he stopped consuming either. On one occasion, after going without water for two scorching days, he picked up the ladle, and the sight of the clear liquid, combined with his desperate thirst, nearly overwhelmed his resolve; but he controlled himself and cast it aside, and from that point forward he refused to allow any water near him. On three separate occasions I watched him carried to the death-room, unconscious and believed to be dying; but each time he recovered, cursed his caretakers, and insisted on being returned to his bed. He survived to serve as a steamboat mate once again.

But he was the only one who went to the death-room and came back alive. Dr. Peyton, a leading physician who possessed all the qualities that make up an outstanding and perfect character, did everything that medical knowledge and professional expertise could do for Henry; however, as the newspapers had stated from the start, his injuries were beyond healing. On the evening of the sixth day, his confused mind focused on distant matters, and his weak fingers picked at his bedcover. His time had come; we carried him to the death-room, poor boy.

Chapter 21: A Section in My Biography

In due course I received my license. I was now a pilot, fully qualified. I took on casual jobs; since no misfortunes occurred, intermittent work gave way to steady and extended assignments. Time passed smoothly and successfully, and I assumed—and hoped—that I would follow the river for the remainder of my life, and die at the wheel when my mission was complete. But eventually the war arrived, commerce was halted, my occupation was lost.

I needed to find another way to make a living. So I became a silver miner in Nevada; then, a newspaper reporter; then, a gold miner in California; then, a reporter in San Francisco; then, a special correspondent in the Sandwich Islands; then, a traveling correspondent in Europe and the East; then, an educational speaker on the lecture circuit; and, finally, I became a writer of books, and a permanent resident among the other steadfast people of New England.

In just a few words, I have summarized the twenty-one slowly passing years that have come and gone since I last looked out from the windows of a pilot-house.

Let's continue now.

Chapter 22: I Return to My Muttons

After being away for twenty-one years, I felt an overwhelming urge to see the river once more, along with the steamboats and whatever friends from my youth might still be around, so I decided to make the journey back there. I recruited a poet to keep me company and hired a stenographer to record his words, then set off toward the west around mid-April.

When I decided to take notes for eventual publication, I gave careful consideration to how I should proceed. I realized that if people recognized me on the river, I wouldn't have the same freedom to move around, talk with people, ask questions, and observe things as I would if I remained anonymous. I remembered how steamboat workers in earlier days had a habit of entertaining unsuspecting strangers with the most colorful and elaborate tall tales, while they would bore their more experienced acquaintances with plain and uninteresting facts. So I decided that from a practical standpoint, it would be beneficial to have our group use fake names. The concept was definitely sound, but it created endless trouble. While names like Smith, Jones, and Johnson are simple to remember when you don't actually need to remember them, it becomes nearly impossible to recall them when you actually need them. How do criminals manage to keep a completely new false identity straight in their heads? This remains a great puzzle to me. I was completely innocent, yet I could rarely remember my assumed name when I needed it. It seemed to me that if I had actually committed a crime to further muddle my thinking, I never would have been able to keep track of the name at all.

We departed on the Pennsylvania Railroad at 8 A.M. on April 18.

"EVENING. Speaking of dress. Grace and picturesqueness gradually disappear from it as one travels away from New York."

I found this observation among my notes. It doesn't matter which direction you travel—the fact stays the same. Whether you head north, south, east, or west makes no difference: you can wake up in the morning and estimate how far you've traveled by observing how much grace and elegance has disappeared from the clothing of the new passengers—and I'm not talking only about women, but about both men and women. I believe posture and bearing are at the heart of this phenomenon, and I think that's exactly what it is; there are many ladies and gentlemen in smaller cities whose clothes are all made by the finest tailors and dressmakers in New York; yet this doesn't have any noticeable impact on the overall truth: a trained eye never confuses these people with actual New Yorkers. No, there's an effortless grace, energy, and style about someone born and raised in New York that clothing alone simply cannot create.

'APRIL 19. This morning, I entered an area where men wore full goatees—sometimes paired with a mustache, but not very often.'

It was strange to encounter this dense collection of an outdated and unattractive style; it felt like suddenly running into a forgotten friend you had assumed was dead for an entire generation. The goatee spreads across a vast area of the country and comes with an unwavering belief in Adam and the biblical account of creation, which remains unshaken by the attacks of scientists.

'AFTERNOON. At the train stations, the idle people keep both hands in their pants pockets; it was noticeable before that one hand was sometimes outside—here, never. This is an important fact in geography.'

If lazy people determined the character of a country, it would be even more important, naturally.

'Until now, all this time, the station loafer has often been seen scratching one shin with the other foot; here, these signs of activity are missing. This has an ominous look.'

Gradually, we entered the tobacco-chewing region. Fifty years ago, the tobacco-chewing region covered the entire Union. It has been greatly reduced now.

Next, boots started showing up. They weren't very common at first, though. Later on—farther down the Mississippi—they became standard. They vanished from other parts of the country along with the mud; without a doubt they'll disappear from the river towns as well, once proper paved streets arrive.

We arrived in St. Louis at ten o'clock that night. At the hotel's front desk, I offered a hastily made-up fake name, trying desperately to appear relaxed and casual. The desk clerk stopped and looked me over with the kind of sympathetic expression someone gives to a decent person caught in questionable circumstances; then he said—

"It's all right; I know what kind of room you're looking for. I used to work as a clerk at the St. James in New York."

An unpromising start for a career built on deception. We headed to the dining room, where we encountered two other men I had met before. How strange and unjust it is: dishonest fraudsters travel around giving lectures using my pen name and no one doubts them; but when an honest person tries to pull off a deception, he gets caught immediately.

One thing was clear: we had to head down the river the next day, since people who couldn't be fooled were showing up at this pace—a bitter letdown, because we'd planned to spend a week in St. Louis. The Southern was an excellent hotel, and we could have enjoyed a pleasant stay there. It's spacious and well-managed, and its décor doesn't make you want to weep, unlike that of the enormous Palmer House in Chicago. Admittedly, the billiard tables belonged to the Old Silurian Period, and the cues and balls to the Post-Pliocene era; but this was actually refreshing rather than uncomfortable, since there's something soothing and restorative about observing ancient things.

The most striking absence I noticed in the billiard room was the lack of river men. If any were present, they had hidden their identity and were keeping a low profile. I didn't see any of the flashy attitudes and pretentious behavior, the showy displays of wealth, and the extravagant spending that used to set the steamboat workers apart from the landlubbers in the crowded billiard rooms of St. Louis during earlier times. Back then, the main saloons were always filled with river men; out of fifty players, thirty or thirty-five would typically be from the river trade. But I suspected their numbers had dwindled significantly, and steamboat workers were no longer part of the elite class. Why, in my day they used to address the bartender as Bill, or Joe, or Tom, and give him a friendly slap on the shoulder; I kept watching for that kind of familiarity. But none of these people behaved that way. Clearly, a prestige that once existed had faded and disappeared completely over these twenty-one years.

When I went up to my room, I discovered the young man named Rogers there, crying. Rogers wasn't actually his real name; neither was Jones, Brown, Dexter, Ferguson, Bascom, or Thompson; but he would respond to any of these names that someone found convenient in a pinch, or to any other name, really, if he realized you were talking to him. He said—

'What is someone supposed to do here when they want a drink of water?—drink this slush?'

"Can't you drink it?"

"I could if I had some other water to wash it with."

Here was something that hadn't changed at all; twenty years hadn't altered this water's muddy brown color in the slightest; twenty decades might not succeed any better, most likely. It flows out of the churning, shore-eroding Missouri River, and every glassful of it contains nearly an acre of soil dissolved within it. I learned this information from the bishop of the diocese. If you let your glass sit for thirty minutes, you can divide the soil from the water as easily as in Genesis; and afterward you'll discover that both are excellent: one perfect for eating, the other perfect for drinking. The soil provides great nutrition, while the water is completely healthy. One satisfies hunger; the other quenches thirst. However, the local people don't consume them separately, but combined, just as nature blended them. When they discover an inch of sediment at the bottom of a glass, they mix it up, and then drink the mixture like they would porridge. It's challenging for an outsider to become accustomed to this thick liquid, but once he gets used to it, he'll choose it over plain water. This is actually true. It works well for steamboat operations, and it's good for drinking; but it's unclean for every other purpose, except for baptizing.

The next morning, we drove around the city in the rain. The place seemed barely changed. It had actually transformed dramatically, but it didn't appear that way; because in St. Louis, just like in London and Pittsburgh, you can't make anything new look fresh—the coal smoke ages everything the instant you finish building it. The city had roughly doubled in size since I had lived there, and had grown into a metropolis of 400,000 people; yet, in the established business districts, it looked much the same as it had before. Still, I'm certain there isn't as much smoke in St. Louis now as there once was. The smoke used to pile up in a thick, rolling black dome over the city, completely blocking out the sky. This covering is much thinner these days; even so, there's still plenty of smoke around, I believe. I didn't hear anyone complaining about it.

However, changes were clearly visible on the outskirts, particularly in residential architecture. The beautiful new houses are impressive, attractive, and contemporary. These homes also stand independently, surrounded by green lawns, while the houses from earlier times are crowded together in blocks and follow identical designs, with matching windows set within arched frameworks of carved stone—a style of house that was quite appealing when it was less common.

There was another change—Forest Park. This was new to me. It is beautiful and very extensive, and has the excellent merit of having been created mainly by nature. There are other parks, and fine ones, notably Tower Grove and the Botanical Gardens; for St. Louis took interest in such improvements at an earlier time than most of our cities did.

The first time I ever saw St. Louis, I could have bought it for six million dollars, and it was the biggest mistake of my life that I didn't do it. It was painful now to look out over this domed and towering metropolis, this vast stretch of brick and mortar extending in every direction into hazy, immeasurable distances, and remember that I had let that opportunity slip away. Why I should have let it slip away seems, naturally, foolish and impossible to understand today, at first glance; yet there were reasons at the time that justified this decision.

A Scottish gentleman, the Honorable Charles Augustus Murray, writing approximately forty-five to fifty years ago, observed—'The streets are narrow, poorly paved and poorly lit.' Those streets remain narrow to this day, naturally; many of them are still poorly paved; however, the criticism of poor lighting can no longer be made. The 'Catholic New Church' was the only remarkable building at that time, and Mr. Murray was enthusiastically urged to admire it, with its 'type of Greek-style portico, topped by a sort of steeple, far too small in its proportions, and crowned by various decorations' which the practical Scotsman found himself 'completely unable to describe;' and thus was thankful when a German visitor assisted him with the exclamation—'By —, they look exactly like bed-posts!' St. Louis is now well supplied with impressive and magnificent public buildings, and the small church, which the residents once took such pride in, lost its significance long ago. Nevertheless, this would not astonish Mr. Murray, if he could return; for he predicted the future greatness of St. Louis with firm confidence.

The farther we traveled on our inspection tour, the more clearly I understood how much the city had expanded since my last visit; detailed changes became increasingly obvious and common as we continued: changes that consistently showed progress, vitality, and prosperity.

But the most dramatic change of all was at the levee. This time, it broke from the usual pattern. Half a dozen sleeping steamboats sat where I once witnessed a solid mile of bustling, active vessels! This sight was depressing, truly heartbreaking. The absence of the ever-present and cheerful steamboat workers from the billiard hall now made sense. They were gone because they no longer existed in their former role. Their jobs had vanished, their influence had disappeared, they had been absorbed into the general population, now working ordinary jobs like everyone else, like a weakened Samson, stripped of strength and barely noticeable. Half a dozen lifeless steamboats, a mile of deserted docks, a Black man exhausted from drinking lying asleep in a vast and silent emptiness, where once the organized armies of commerce used to compete![6] This was truly desolation.

> *The ancient, ancient sea, like someone weeping,*
> *Comes murmuring, with foamy lips,*
> *And knocking at the empty piers,*
> *Calls for his long-lost multitude of ships.'*

The towboat and the railroad had completed their task thoroughly and effectively. The massive bridge stretching above us had played its part in the destruction and ruin. Former steamboat workers told me with grim satisfaction that the bridge wasn't profitable. However, it provides little comfort to a dead man to learn that the dynamite that killed him wasn't as high-quality as people had thought it would be.

The sidewalks along the riverfront were in poor condition: the walkways were quite damaged; there was plenty of mud everywhere. All of this felt familiar and comforting; but the old armies of cargo wagons, and struggling crowds of people, and huge piles of goods, had disappeared; and Sunday quiet had taken their place. The age-old stretch of cheap, filthy taverns was still there, but business was slow for them; the crowds of liquor-drinking Irishmen had left, and in their place were a few scattered groups of ragged Black men, some drinking, some drunk, some dozing, others sleeping. St. Louis is a large and successful and growing city; but its riverfront appears dead beyond any hope of revival.

Mississippi steamboat travel began around 1812; after thirty years, it had expanded to enormous proportions; and in fewer than

---

[6] Capt. Marryat, writing forty-five years ago says: 'St. Louis has 20,000 inhabitants. The river abreast of the town is crowded with steamboats, lying in two or three tiers.'

thirty additional years, it had died! An unusually brief existence for such a magnificent enterprise. Naturally it isn't completely dead, just as a disabled eighty-year-old who once could leap twenty-two feet on flat ground isn't entirely finished; but when compared with what it was during its peak strength, Mississippi steamboat travel can be considered dead.

It destroyed the traditional keel-boat industry by cutting the freight journey to New Orleans to under a week. The railroads eliminated steamboat passenger service by accomplishing in two or three days what steamboats took a week to complete; and the towing fleets wiped out the long-distance freight business by pulling six or seven steamboat loads of cargo down the river simultaneously, at such a low cost that steamboats couldn't possibly compete.

Freight and passenger transportation by water continues to belong to the steamships. This business is controlled—across the two thousand miles of river between St. Paul and New Orleans— by two or three tightly-knit corporations that are well-equipped with capital; and through skilled and thoroughly professional management and organization, these companies earn adequate profits from what remains of the once enormous steamboat industry. I imagine that St. Louis and New Orleans have not been significantly harmed by this transformation, but what a tragedy for the wood-yard worker!

He used to line the entire river; his densely packed merchandise extended from one city to another along the banks, and he sold countless cords of it every year for immediate cash payment; but all the scattered boats that remain burn coal now, and the rarest sight on the Mississippi today is a wood-pile. Where is the former wood-yard man now?

Chapter 23: Traveling Incognito

My plan was to spend some time in every town between St. Louis and New Orleans. To accomplish this, I would need to travel from place to place using the short packet boat lines. It was a simple plan to create, and it would have been easy to carry out twenty years ago—but not anymore. There are long gaps between boats these days.

I wanted to start with the fascinating old French settlements of St. Genevieve and Kaskaskia, sixty miles downstream from St. Louis. Only one boat was advertised for that route—a Grand Tower packet. Still, one boat was all we needed, so we went down to take a look at her. She was an ancient pile of junk, and a fake on top of that; she was pretending to be personal property, when in reality the honest dirt was caked so thickly all over her that she could rightfully be taxed as real estate. There are spots in New England where her hurricane deck would be worth a hundred and fifty dollars per acre. The soil on her forecastle was quite fertile— the new wheat crop was already sprouting from the cracks in sheltered areas. The companionway had a dry, sandy quality and would have been perfect for growing grapes, with a southern exposure and a bit of deep plowing. The soil of the boiler deck was shallow and rocky, but adequate for grazing livestock. A colored boy was standing watch there—no one else was in sight. We learned from him that this peaceful vessel would depart as advertised 'if she got her trip;' if she didn't get it, she would wait for it.

"Does she have any of her trip left?"

"Bless you, no, boss. She hasn't been unloaded yet. She only came in this morning."

He wasn't sure when she would be able to make her trip, but he thought it might be tomorrow or possibly the next day. This wouldn't work for us at all, so we had to abandon our novel plan of sailing down the river on a farm vessel. We had one more option available to us: a Vicksburg steamboat called the 'Gold Dust' was scheduled to depart at 5 P.M. We booked passage on her bound for Memphis and gave up our idea of making stops along the way, since it wasn't practical. The boat was tidy, clean, and comfortable. We set up camp on the boiler deck and purchased some inexpensive reading material to pass the time. The seller was an elderly Irishman with a kind face and a tongue that moved smoothly, and from him we discovered that he had lived in St. Louis for thirty-four years without ever crossing the river during that entire time. Then he launched into a very eloquent speech filled with classical names and references, which was quite impressive in its fluency until it became fairly obvious that this wasn't the first time, or perhaps even the fiftieth time, that he had delivered this presentation. He was quite a character and much better entertainment than the mediocre literature he was peddling. A casual comment linking Irishmen and beer drew this piece of information from him—

"They don't drink it, sir. They can't drink it, sir. Give an Irishman lager for a month, and he's a dead man. An Irishman has copper lining inside him, and the beer eats away at it. But whiskey shines up that copper and saves his life, sir."

At eight o'clock sharp, we backed out and crossed the river. As we slowly approached the shore through the thick darkness, a brilliant burst of white electric light suddenly blazed from our front deck, illuminating the water and warehouses with the brightness of midday. This represented another major change— no more flickering, smoky, tar-dripping, useless torch baskets; their time had passed. Next, rather than calling out twenty men to handle the gangplank, just a couple of workers and some steam power lowered it from the crane where it hung, launched it, and placed it in exactly the right position. The entire operation was completed before a ship's officer from the old days could have even gotten his swearing routine warmed up to begin the preliminary work. Why this new and straightforward method of managing the gangplanks wasn't conceived when the first steamboat was constructed remains a puzzle that helps one understand just how slow-thinking the average person really is.

We finally departed at two in the morning, and when I woke up at six, we were turning toward a rocky point where an old stone warehouse stood—or at least what remained of it. Two or three crumbling houses sat nearby, protected by the tree-covered hills, but there were no signs of human or animal life anywhere. I began to wonder if I had mixed up the river, since I had absolutely no memory of this location. The river's shape also seemed strange to me. Nothing was visible anywhere that I could recall having seen before. I felt surprised, disappointed, and frustrated.

We dropped off a well-dressed lady and gentleman, along with two well-dressed, refined young women, together with various Russian leather bags. What an odd place for people like this! No carriage was there waiting for them. The group walked away as though they hadn't expected one, and headed down a winding country road on foot.

But the mystery became clear when we started moving again; these people were obviously heading to a large town that was hidden behind a sandbar (a new island) about two miles downstream from this landing. I couldn't recall that town; I couldn't identify it or remember its name. This made me lose some of my patience. I thought it might be St. Genevieve—and that's exactly what it turned out to be. Look at what this unpredictable river had done: it had created this enormous useless sandbar right in front of this town, cutting off its river access, completely isolating it, and turning it into an inland town. It's a beautiful old place, too, and it deserved better treatment. The French established it, and it remains from an era when someone could travel from the Mississippi Delta all the way to Quebec while staying on French land and living under French authority the entire journey.

I soon climbed up to the hurricane deck and looked longingly toward the pilot-house.

Chapter 24: My Cover is Blown

After carefully studying the face of the pilot on duty, I was confident that I had never seen him before, so I went up there. The pilot looked me over while I looked him over in return. Once these usual introductions were finished, I sat down on the high bench, and he turned around and continued with his work. Every detail of the pilot-house was familiar to me, except for one thing— a wide-mouthed tube beneath the instrument panel. I wondered about that device for quite some time, then gave up and asked what it was used for.

"To hear the engine bells through."

It was another clever invention that should have been created fifty years earlier. That's what I was thinking when the pilot asked—

"Do you know what this rope is for?"

I managed to avoid answering this question without making any commitments.

"Is this the first time you've ever been in a pilot-house?"

I crawled underneath that one.

"Where are you from?"

'New England.'

"Is this your first time traveling out West?"

I climbed over this one.

"If you're curious about these things, I can explain what they're all used for."

I said I would like it.

'This,' he said, placing his hand on a backing-bell rope, 'sounds the fire alarm; this,' he continued, putting his hand on a go-ahead bell, 'calls the texas-tender; this one,' he explained, pointing to the whistle-lever, 'calls the captain'—and he continued in this manner, touching each item one by one, spinning out his calm web of deceptions.

I had never felt so much like a passenger before. I thanked him emotionally for each new piece of information and wrote it down in my notebook. The pilot became enthusiastic about his chance to share knowledge and began filling me with details in the traditional manner. Sometimes I worried he might stretch his storytelling too far, but his tales always held up, and he managed to get through them successfully. He gradually moved into revealing the river's amazing peculiarities of various kinds and supported them with some quite enormous examples. For instance—

"Do you see that small boulder jutting out of the water over there? Well, when I first arrived on the river, that was a solid ridge of rock, more than sixty feet high and two miles long. Everything has been washed away except for that." [This with a sigh.]

I felt an overwhelming urge to destroy him, but it struck me that killing him through any conventional means would be far too merciful for someone like him.

Once, when a strange-looking vessel with an enormous coal bucket tilted upward at the end of a pole was passing by in the distance, he casually pointed it out, the way someone might mention an object that had become tiresome through repeated exposure, and remarked that it was an 'alligator boat.'

"An alligator boat? What's it for?"

"To dredge out alligators with."

"Are they so dense that they become a problem?"

"Well, not anymore, because the Government controls them now. But they used to be there. Not in every spot, but in the preferred locations, scattered here and there, where the river spreads out wide and shallow—like Plum Point, and Stack Island, and similar places—areas they refer to as alligator beds."

"Did they actually interfere with ship traffic?"

"Years ago, yes, when the water was extremely low; there was barely a trip back then where we didn't run aground on alligators."

It seemed to me that I would definitely need to pull out my tomahawk. However, I held myself back and said—

"It must have been terrible."

'Yes, that was one of the main challenges of piloting. It was incredibly difficult to read the water because those cursed things kept shifting around constantly—they never stayed in one place for more than five minutes. You could easily identify a wind-reef just by looking at it; you could spot a break; you could recognize a sand-reef—all of that was simple enough; but an alligator reef barely showed itself at all. Nine times out of ten you couldn't tell where the water was; and when you finally figured out where it was, chances were it wouldn't be there by the time you arrived because those devils had moved around in the meantime. Of course there were a few pilots who could read alligator water almost as well as they could read any other type, but they needed natural talent for it; it wasn't something a person could learn through practice—you had to be born with that ability. Let me think: there was Ben Thornburg, and Beck Jolly, and Squire Bell, and Horace Bixby, and Major Downing, and John Stevenson, and Billy Gordon, and Jim Brady, and George Ealer, and Billy Youngblood—all top-notch alligator pilots. They could read alligator water as clearly as any other person could identify whiskey. Read it?—Oh, couldn't they just! I only wish I had as many dollars as they could read alligator water from a mile and a half away. Yes, and it was profitable for them too. A skilled alligator pilot could always earn fifteen hundred dollars a month. At night, other people had to stop and wait because of alligators, but those men never stopped for alligators; they only stopped for fog. They could supposedly smell the best alligator water; I don't know if that was true or not, and I think a person has enough to handle if he sticks to what he knows firsthand, without going around supporting other people's claims, though there are plenty who aren't shy about doing exactly that, as long as they can dig up something amazing to share. Which is definitely not the way of Robert Styles, not by three fathoms—maybe a quarter less.'

[My goodness! Was this really Rob Styles?—This distinguished figure with a mustache?—He was quite a skinny young man back in my day. How much his appearance has improved over twenty-five years, along with his remarkable skill at exaggerating the truth.] After these thoughts, I said out loud—

"I would think that removing the alligators by dredging wouldn't have accomplished much, since they could return immediately."

'If you had as much experience with alligators as I do, you wouldn't speak that way. You dredge an alligator just once and he learns his lesson. That's the last time you'll see him. He wouldn't return even for pie. If there's anything an alligator hates more than everything else, it's getting dredged. Furthermore, they weren't just pushed aside; most of each shovelful was scooped up onto the boat; they dumped them into the cargo hold; and once they had collected a full load, they transported them to New Orleans to the Government facilities.'

"What for?"

'Why, to make soldier-shoes out of their hides. All the Government shoes are made of alligator hide. It makes the best shoes in the world. They last five years, and they won't absorb water. The alligator fishery is a Government monopoly. All the alligators are Government property—just like the live-oaks. You cut down a live-oak, and Government fines you fifty dollars; you kill an alligator, and up you go for misprision of treason—lucky

172

duck if they don't hang you, too. And they will, if you're a Democrat. The buzzard is the sacred bird of the South, and you can't touch him; the alligator is the sacred bird of the Government, and you've got to let him alone.'

"Do you ever run aground on the alligators these days?"

"Oh, no! That hasn't happened in years."

"Well, then, why do they still keep the alligator boats in service?"

"Just for police duty—nothing more. They simply patrol back and forth occasionally. Today's alligators recognize them as easily as a thief recognizes a beat cop; when they spot one approaching, they scatter and head for the forest."

After wrapping up and completing the alligator story with a flourish, he slipped naturally and effortlessly into telling historical tales, recounting some incredible achievements of half a dozen old steamboats he had known, spending considerable time describing a particularly remarkable feat performed by his favorite vessel among this notable collection of boats—and then he continued by saying—

'That boat was the "Cyclone"—the last trip she ever made—she sank on that very trip—the captain was Tom Ballou, the biggest liar I ever encountered. He never seemed able to tell the truth, no matter what the circumstances. He would absolutely make you cringe. He was the most outrageous liar! I finally left him; I couldn't take it anymore. The saying goes, "like master, like man;" and if you stick with that type of person, you'll eventually fall under suspicion yourself, as sure as you're alive. He paid top wages; but I said to myself, What good are wages when your reputation is at risk? So I gave up the wages and held onto my reputation. And I've never regretted that decision. Reputation is worth everything, isn't it? That's how I see it. He had more selfish tendencies than any seven men in the world—all crammed into the back of his skull, naturally, where they belonged. They weighed down the back of his head so much that it made his nose point up in the air. People thought it was vanity, but it wasn't—it was spite. If you only saw his foot, you'd think he was nineteen feet tall, but he wasn't; it was because his foot was out of proportion. He was probably meant to be nineteen feet tall, no doubt, if his foot was made first, but he didn't reach that height; he was only five feet ten. That's what he was, and that's what he remains. Take the lies out of him, and he'll shrink to the size of your hat; take the spite out of him, and he'll vanish completely. That "Cyclone" was incredible to operate, and the smoothest thing to steer that ever sailed the waters. Position her in the middle of a big river, and just let her go; that was all you needed to do. She would stay on course all night long, if you left her alone. You couldn't even feel her rudder. It took no more effort to steer her than it does to count the Republican votes in a South Carolina election. One morning, just at dawn, on the last trip she ever made, they brought her rudder aboard to repair it; I didn't know anything about it; I backed her out from the wood-yard and went weaving down the river without a care. When I had traveled about twenty-three miles, and made four terribly crooked crossings—'

"Without any rudder?"

"Yes—old Captain Tom showed up on the roof and started criticizing me for sailing on such a dark night—"

"Such a dark night? But you said—"

'Forget what I said—it was pitch black now, though pretty soon the moon started to rise, and—'

"You mean the sun—because you started out just at daybreak—wait a minute! Was this before you left the captain because of his lying, or—"

"It happened before—oh, a very long time before. And as I was explaining, he—"

"But was this the trip she sank, or was—"

"Oh, no! That was months later. And so the old man, he—"

"Then she made two final trips, because you said—"

He stepped back from the wheel, wiping away his sweat, and said—

'Here!' (calling me by name), 'you take control and steer for a while—you're better at it than I am. Trying to pretend you're a stranger and don't know anything!—well, I recognized you before you'd said seven words; and I decided to figure out what your little scheme was. It was to get me talking. Well, I let you do it, didn't I? Now take the wheel and finish the watch; and next time be honest, and you won't have to work for your passage.'

Thus ended the fake-name situation. And we weren't even six hours away from St. Louis! But I had gained something valuable anyway, because I had been eager to get my hands on the wheel from the very start. I seemed to have forgotten the river, but I hadn't forgotten how to steer a steamboat, or how to enjoy doing it, either.

Chapter 25: From Cairo to Hickman

The landscape from St. Louis to Cairo—a distance of two hundred miles—offers diverse and stunning views. The hills were now dressed in the vibrant green leaves of spring, creating an elegant and fitting backdrop for the wide river flowing between them. Our journey started favorably, blessed with an ideal day of gentle breezes and bright sunshine, while our steamboat covered the miles behind us with impressive speed.

We discovered a railway cutting through Chester, Illinois; Chester now also has a penitentiary and is progressing in other ways as well. At Grand Tower, there was also a railway; and another one at Cape Girardeau. The first town gets its name from a massive, stocky column of rock that rises up from the water on the Missouri side of the river—a creation of nature's imaginative craftsmanship—and stands as one of the most beautiful features of that region's landscape. As nearby or distant neighbors, the Tower has the Devil's Bake Oven—called that, perhaps, because it doesn't strongly look like anyone else's bake oven; and the Devil's Tea Table—this last one being a large, smooth-surfaced chunk of rock with a tapering wine-glass base, positioned some fifty or sixty feet above the river, next to a cliff decorated with flowers and garlands, and resembling a tea table enough to serve anyone, whether Devil or Christian. Further down the river we have the Devil's Elbow and the Devil's Race-course, and many other pieces of his property that I can't remember right now.

The Town of Grand Tower was clearly a busier place than it had been in earlier times, but it appeared to need some repairs in various spots, and a fresh coat of whitewash throughout. Nevertheless, it was enjoyable for me to see the old place once again. 'Uncle' Mumford, our second officer, explained that the town had been dealing with flooding, and as a result wasn't looking its best at the moment. However, he mentioned it wasn't surprising that the town didn't spend money on whitewash for itself, since more lime was produced there, and of superior quality, than anywhere else in the West; and he added—'On a dairy farm you can never get any milk for your coffee, nor any sugar for it on a sugar plantation; and it goes against common sense to visit a lime town looking for whitewash.' From my own experience I knew the first two examples to be accurate; and also that people who sell candy don't have a taste for candy; therefore there was logic in Uncle Mumford's concluding observation that 'people who make lime lean more toward religion than whitewash.' Uncle Mumford went on to say that Grand Tower was a major coaling center and a thriving community.

Cape Girardeau sits on a hillside and presents an attractive appearance. A large Jesuit school for boys stands at the base of the town near the river. Uncle Mumford mentioned that it enjoyed as strong a reputation for academic rigor as any comparable institution in Missouri. Another college occupied a higher position on an elevated summit—a gleaming new building with distinctive towers and spires that resembled an enormous cruet set with all its pieces intact. Uncle Mumford declared that Cape Girardeau was Missouri's Athens, housing several additional colleges beyond those he had already pointed out, all founded on various religious principles. He drew my attention to what he described as the town's "pronounced and widespread religious character," though I couldn't perceive that it appeared any more religious than other hillside communities with similar slopes constructed from the same type of brick. Personal preferences often lead people to observe more than what actually exists.

Uncle Mumford has spent thirty years working as a mate on the river. He's a man with practical sense and a level head who has observed life closely and gained extensive experience in various matters. He holds strong opinions and possesses just a hint of poetry in his nature, along with an easy way with words, a thick growl in his voice, and a few choice curse words that he can access when his duties demand some spiritual motivation. He represents the blessed old-school type of mate, and when there's work to be done, he goes about seriously cursing in a manner that fills the former steamboat worker's heart with sweet, gentle yearnings for those bygone days that will never return. "Get up there, you! Are you planning to take all day? Why didn't you just say you were paralyzed in your back legs before you signed on!"

He's a reliable captain with his crew; he treats them with kindness and fairness while maintaining authority, which is why they respect him and remain loyal. He still wears the casual, unkempt clothing typical of the older generation of ship officers, but on his next voyage, the Anchor Line will put him in a proper uniform—a sharp blue naval uniform with brass buttons, just like all the other officers in the company—and then he'll present a completely different appearance from what he does today.

Uniforms on the Mississippi! This change surpasses all other transformations combined when it comes to being unexpected. Yet there's another surprise—that this wasn't implemented fifty years earlier. The idea is so clearly logical that one would think it should have been considered much sooner. For fifty decades out there, unsuspecting passengers seeking assistance and guidance have been confusing the first mate with the cook and mistaking the captain for the barber—and receiving harsh treatment as a result. However, their difficulties have now come to an end. The significantly enhanced appearance of the boat's crew represents another benefit accomplished during this period of uniform reform.

We navigated down the curve below Cape Girardeau. People used to call it 'Steersman's Bend' - it was easy sailing with plenty of deep water, always. It was just about the only spot on the Upper River where a new apprentice was permitted to pilot a boat through during low water conditions.

Thebes, located at the beginning of the Grand Chain, and Commerce at its end, were towns that were easy to remember since they hadn't changed much in any noticeable way. The Chain itself hadn't changed either—which makes sense given its nature; it's a series of underwater rocks perfectly positioned to trap and destroy steamboats during stormy nights. Many steamboat wrecks lie buried there, hidden from view; among them was my first friend, the 'Paul Jones.' She smashed her hull and sank like a stone, according to the historian who told me this story—Uncle Mumford. He mentioned that she had a gray mare on board, along with a preacher. To me, this explanation was enough to account for the disaster; it certainly was for Mumford, who went on to say—

'But there are many uninformed people who would mock such a thing and dismiss it as superstition. However, you'll always find that these are people who have never journeyed with a gray mare and a preacher. I once traveled down the river in exactly that kind of company. We ran aground at Bloody Island; we ran aground at Hanging Dog; we ran aground just below this very same Commerce; we struck Beaver Dam Rock; we hit one of the most dangerous spots in the 'Graveyard' behind Goose Island; we had a deck hand killed in a brawl; we burned out a boiler; snapped a shaft; had a flue cave in; and limped into Cairo with nine feet of water flooding the hold—could have been more, could have been less. I recall it as clearly as if it happened yesterday. The crew panicked with fear. They painted the mare blue, within sight of the town, and threw the preacher into the river, or we never would have made it at all. The preacher was pulled from the water and rescued. He admitted, himself, that he had been responsible for the trouble. I remember every detail, as if it were yesterday.'

That this combination—of preacher and gray mare—would create disaster seems odd and initially hard to believe; however, the evidence is backed by so much solid proof that doubting it would be unreasonable. I personally recall an incident where a captain received warnings from many friends about bringing both a gray mare and a preacher aboard with him, yet he stuck to his decision despite everything they told him; and that very day—it might have been the following day, and some claim it was, although I believe it happened the same day—he became intoxicated and tumbled down the hatchway, and was carried home dead. This is absolutely true.

No trace of Hat Island remains today; every piece of it has been washed away. I can't even recall which part of the river it used to occupy, except that it was located somewhere between St. Louis and Cairo. It was a dangerous area—all around Hat Island, in the early days. A farmer who lived along the Illinois shore mentioned that twenty-nine steamboats had left their remains scattered within view of his home. Between St. Louis and Cairo, steamboat wrecks average one per mile—two hundred wrecks in total.

I could see major changes starting from Commerce and continuing downstream. Beaver Dam Rock now sits in the middle of the river, creating an enormous wave break; it used to be near the shore, and boats would pass on the outside of it. A large island that once stood far out in the middle of the river has moved back to the Missouri shore, and boats no longer travel near it. The island known as Jacket Pattern has been worn down to just a narrow wedge and is destined for complete destruction soon. Goose Island has almost entirely disappeared, leaving only a small piece about the size of a steamboat. The dangerous area called the 'Graveyard,' where we used to navigate so carefully and cautiously among countless wrecks, is now far from the main channel and poses no threat to anyone. One of the islands that was once known as the Two Sisters has completely vanished; the other, which used to sit close to the Illinois shore, is now on the Missouri side, a full mile away; it has become permanently connected to the shore, and you need keen eyesight to spot where they join—but it's still technically Illinois territory, and the residents living there must ferry themselves across to work on Illinois roads and pay Illinois taxes: what a strange situation!

Near the mouth of the river, several islands had disappeared—swept away by the water. Cairo remained in place—clearly visible across the long, flat point where it sits on the far edge; however, we had to take a lengthy route around to reach it. Darkness came as we left the 'Upper River' and encountered the flooding waters of the Ohio. We moved forward confidently; the submerged rock that once blocked our path directly had shifted upstream a considerable distance away from the channel; or more accurately, roughly one county's worth of land from the Missouri point had been carried into the river, while the Cairo point had extended downward and expanded its long strip of land by the same amount.

The Mississippi operates as a fair and balanced river; it never sweeps away one person's farm without creating an identical new farm for that person's neighbor. This prevents bitter disputes.

Heading into Cairo, we nearly collided with a steamboat that ignored our whistle and then attempted to cut across our path. Through some vigorous reversing, we managed to avoid hitting it, which was unfortunate since the collision would have provided excellent material for writing.

Cairo is a bustling town today, built with solid construction and possessing an urban appearance that stands in striking contrast to its previous condition, as described in Mr. Dickens's depiction of it. Nevertheless, it was already being constructed with bricks when I last saw it—which was during the time when Colonel (now General) Grant was training his first regiment there. Uncle Mumford mentions that the libraries and Sunday schools have accomplished valuable work in Cairo, just as the brick masons have. Cairo enjoys substantial railroad and river commerce, and its location at the meeting point of the two major rivers is so beneficial that it can hardly fail to thrive.

When I woke up in the morning, we had already passed Columbus, Kentucky, and were getting close to Hickman, a beautiful town sitting on top of an attractive hill. Hickman is located in an area rich with tobacco farming, and in the past it had a thriving and profitable tobacco business, gathering the crop in its warehouses from a wide surrounding region and sending it out by riverboat; but Uncle Mumford says the town built a railroad to make this trade a bit easier, and he believes it made things easier in the wrong way—it took most of the business away from the town by 'grabbing it all along the railway line instead of bringing it to the town's doorstep.'

Chapter 26: Under Fire

The conversation turned to the war, since we were now approaching the northern edge of what had once been a battlefield. Columbus lay just behind us, which sparked considerable discussion about the famous Battle of Belmont. Several of the boat's officers had served actively in the Mississippi war fleet. From what I could tell, they had initially found themselves completely out of their depth in that type of warfare, but eventually grew accustomed to it, made peace with it, and became somewhat comfortable with their roles. One of our pilots had gotten his first taste of combat during the Belmont engagement, serving as a pilot on a Confederate vessel. I had always been curious about how an inexperienced person might feel during his first battle, positioned all alone high up in a pilot house, exposed as a target for anyone and everyone, with no one beside him to prevent him from showing cowardice when the situation became dangerous and threatening around him. His account was therefore precious to me—it filled a void that all the history books had left unfilled until that moment.

THE PILOT'S FIRST BATTLE

He said—

It was November 7th. The battle started at seven in the morning. I was aboard the 'R. H. W. Hill.' We picked up a group of soldiers from Columbus. We returned and then loaded a battery of artillery. My partner told me he was going to watch the battle and wanted me to come with him. I told him no, I wasn't eager to go, and that I would observe it from the pilot-house. He called me a coward and walked away.

That battle was a terrible thing to witness. General Cheatham ordered his soldiers to remove their coats and pile them up, then declared, "Now follow me to hell or victory!" I heard him shout those words from the pilot-house, and then he charged forward, leading his troops into battle. Old General Pillow, with his white hair flowing, rode in on a white horse, guiding his men with the energy of a young man. Eventually the Union forces drove the Confederate soldiers back, and here they came rushing toward us! Everyone was running for their lives, each man looking out for himself with no concern for anyone else, and they scrambled down beneath the riverbank to find cover. I was seated with my legs dangling outside the pilot-house window. Suddenly I heard a whistling noise zip past my ear. I figured it must be a bullet. I didn't pause to consider what to do—I simply threw myself backward and hit the floor, where I remained. The projectiles kept flying all around us. Three cannonballs tore through the smokestack; another shot blasted away part of the pilot-house; explosive shells were shrieking and exploding everywhere. It was an extremely dangerous situation—I really regretted being there.

I lay there on the pilot-house floor while the gunfire came faster and faster. I crawled behind the large stove in the center of the pilot-house. Soon a bullet came through the stove and barely missed my head, cutting through my hat. I decided it was time to get out of there. The captain was on the roof with a red-headed major from Memphis—a distinguished-looking man. I heard him say he wanted to leave, but "that pilot is killed." I crawled over to the starboard side to pull the bell to reverse the boat; I raised up and looked around, and I saw about fifteen bullet holes through the window panes; the shooting had been so intense I hadn't noticed them before. I looked out at the water, and the scattered gunfire was like a hailstorm. I thought it best to get out of that place. I went down the pilot-house rope, head first—not feet first but head first—sliding down—before I hit the deck, the captain said we had to leave. So I climbed back up the rope and got on the floor again. Around that time, they grabbed my partner and were

183

bringing him up to the pilot-house between two soldiers. Someone had said I was killed. He stuck his head in and saw me on the floor reaching for the reverse bells. He said, "Oh, hell, he ain't shot," and pulled away from the men who had him by the collar, and ran below. We stayed there until three o'clock in the afternoon, and then got away safely.

The next time I saw my partner, I said, "Now, come on, be honest with me and tell me the truth. Where did you go when you went to see that battle?" He said, "I went down into the hold."

Throughout that entire battle, I was terrified almost to the point of death. I barely understood what was happening around me because I was so frightened; however, nobody else knew this except for me. The following day, General Polk summoned me and commended me for my courage and heroic behavior. I remained silent and accepted his praise. I believed his assessment wasn't accurate, but it wasn't my place to argue with a general officer.

Shortly after that, I became ill and exhausted, and had to travel to the Hot Springs for treatment. While I was there, I received numerous letters from commanders requesting that I return to service. I turned them down because I wasn't healthy enough or strong enough to resume my duties; however, I remained quiet about my condition and maintained the reputation I had established.

A simple story, told in a straightforward manner; but Mumford informed me that the pilot had "embellished that frightening experience of his, in places;" that his later career during the war was evidence of this.

We traveled down through the passage of Island No. 8, and I went below deck and started talking with a passenger, an attractive man with a relaxed manner and a sharp face. We were getting close to Island No. 10, a location that became famous during the war. This gentleman lived on the mainland nearby. I chatted with him about the wartime period, but soon our conversation turned to 'feuds,' because nowhere in the South had family vendettas thrived more vigorously, or lasted longer between fighting families, than in this specific area. This gentleman said—

There have been several feuds in this area over the years, but I believe the worst one was between the Darnells and the Watsons. Nobody knows anymore what started the original fight—it happened so long ago that even the Darnells and Watsons don't remember, assuming any of them are still alive, which I doubt they are. Some people say it began over a horse or a cow—regardless, it was something trivial; the money involved didn't matter at all— both families were wealthy. The dispute could have been resolved easily enough, but that wasn't acceptable to them. Harsh words had been exchanged, and after that, nothing but bloodshed could settle it. That horse or cow, whatever it was, led to sixty years of killing and violence! Every year or so, someone got shot from one side or the other, and as soon as one generation was wiped out, their sons picked up the feud and continued it. And it's exactly as I'm telling you—they kept shooting each other year after year, turning it into something like a religion, until they had long forgotten what originally caused the conflict. Whenever a Darnell encountered a Watson, or a Watson encountered a Darnell, one of them was going to get hurt—the only question was which one would get the advantage over the other. They would gun each other down right in front of their families. They didn't actively hunt for each other, but when they happened to cross paths, they would get angry and start fighting. Men would shoot boys, and boys would shoot men. One man shot a twelve-year-old boy— came across him in the woods and didn't give him any opportunity to defend himself. If he had given the boy a chance, the boy would have shot him instead. Both families attended the same church (everyone in this area is religious); throughout this entire fifty or sixty-year conflict, both groups showed up every Sunday to worship. They lived on opposite sides of the state line, and the church was located at a dock called Compromise. Half the church building and half the center aisle were in Kentucky, while the other half were in Tennessee. On Sundays you would see the families arrive, all dressed in their finest clothes—men, women, and children—and they would walk up the aisle and sit down quietly and peacefully, one group on the Tennessee side of the church and the other on the Kentucky side. The men and boys would prop their rifles against the wall within easy reach, and then everyone would participate in the prayers and hymns. However, people say that the man sitting closest to the aisle wouldn't kneel down with the rest of his family but would remain standing guard instead. I'm not certain about that detail since I've never attended that church in my life, but I remember that's what people used to say.

Twenty or twenty-five years ago, one of the feuding families caught a nineteen-year-old young man and killed him. I don't remember if it was the Darnells and Watsons, or one of the other feuds, but either way, this young man rode up—there was a steamboat docked there at the time—and the first thing he saw was a whole gang of his enemies. He jumped down behind a pile of wood, but they rode around and started attacking him while he fired back, and they were galloping and prancing around, yelling and shooting with everything they had. I think he wounded a couple of them, but they closed in on him and chased him into the river. As he swam downstream, they followed along the bank and kept shooting at him, and when he reached the shore he was dead. Windy Marshall told me about it. He witnessed the whole thing. He was the captain of the boat.

Years ago, the Darnell family had been so reduced in numbers that the old man and his two sons decided they would leave the country. They started to board a steamboat just above No. 10, but the Watsons learned about their plan, and they arrived just as the two young Darnells were walking up the gangway with their wives on their arms. The fight started right then, and they never made it any further—both of them were killed. After that, old Darnell got into a conflict with the man who operated the ferry, and the ferryman came out worse in the encounter—and died. But his friends shot old Darnell repeatedly—filled him full of bullets, and finished him off.

The country gentleman who shared these stories with me had grown up in comfort and luxury, possessed considerable intelligence, and had received a college education. His careless grammar resulted from sloppy habits rather than lack of knowledge. This tendency among educated men in the West isn't universal, but it's widespread—certainly common in towns, if not in cities—to a degree that one can't help but notice and find remarkable. I heard a Westerner who would be considered highly educated in any nation say "never mind, it don't make no difference, anyway." A lifelong local resident who was there heard this, but it didn't register with her at all. She could remember it later when I brought it up, but she admitted that the words hadn't bothered her ears at the time—an admission that suggests if educated people can listen to such terrible grammar from such a source and remain unaware of what happened, the offense must be quite common—so widespread that people's ears have become numbed by constant exposure to it, and are no longer sharp, no longer bothered by such linguistic assaults.

No one in the world speaks perfect grammar; no one has ever written it—no one, either in the world or beyond it (using the Scriptures as evidence for the latter point); therefore it would not be fair to demand grammatical perfection from the people of the Valley; but they and all other people may rightfully be expected to avoid knowingly and deliberately corrupting their grammar.

I discovered that the river had undergone dramatic changes at Island No. 10. The island I recalled from memory stretched about three miles in length and a quarter-mile in width, covered with dense timber, and sat close to the Kentucky shoreline—I'd estimate within two hundred yards of it. However, now you needed a telescope just to locate it. All that remained was a tiny, unremarkable patch of land, and it was no longer positioned near the Kentucky shore; instead, it had shifted completely to the opposite side, a full mile away. During wartime, this island had served as a strategically crucial location because it controlled the surrounding area; with its heavy fortifications, no one could pass by it. The island sat between the upper and lower sections of the Union forces, keeping them divided, until they eventually managed to connect across the Missouri strip of land; but since the island has now become part of that strip, the broad river flows freely without any barriers.

In this area, the river flows from Kentucky into Tennessee, then back into Missouri, before returning to Kentucky, and finally flowing into Tennessee once more. As a result, a mile or two of Missouri extends into Tennessee.

The town of New Madrid looked quite unhealthy, but otherwise remained unchanged from its previous condition and appearance. Its clusters of wooden houses were still arranged on the same old flat plain, surrounded by the same old forests. The town was as peaceful as before, and apparently had neither grown nor shrunk in size. People said that the recent high water had flooded it and damaged its appearance. This was surprising news, because during low water the riverbank is very high there (fifty feet), and in my time an overflow had always been considered impossible. This current flood of 1882 will undoubtedly be remembered in the river's history for several generations before another deluge of similar magnitude is seen. It submerged all the unprotected lowlands from Cairo to the mouth of the river; it broke through the levees in many places on both sides of the river; and in some southern regions, when the flood reached its peak, the Mississippi was seventy miles wide! Several lives were lost, and the destruction of property was terrible. The crops were ruined, houses were swept away, and homeless people and cattle were forced to seek shelter on scattered high ground here and there in fields and forests, waiting in danger and hardship until boats commissioned by the national and local governments and by newspaper organizations could come and rescue them. The property of countless people remained underwater for months, and the poorer residents would have starved by the hundreds if help had not been quickly provided.[7] The water had been receding for quite some time now, yet as a rule we found the banks still underwater.

Chapter 27: Some Imported Articles

We encountered two steamboats at New Madrid. Two steamboats visible at the same time! This has become a rare sight on the lonely Mississippi River. The isolation of this magnificent, enormous waterway is both striking and melancholy. Mile after mile, and then mile after mile again, it flows with its muddy brown current between walls of dense forest and nearly deserted banks, rarely showing a sail or any moving thing to disturb the water's surface and interrupt the sameness of this empty, watery wilderness. The day passes this way, night arrives, and then day returns—and everything remains the same, night following night and day following day—a grand, constant sameness of peace, stillness, calm, sluggishness, emptiness—a symbol of eternity, the actual fulfillment of the paradise described by priests and prophets, and yearned for by both the virtuous and the naive!

Immediately after the War of 1812, tourists began arriving in

---

[7] For a detailed and interesting description of the great flood, written on board of the New Orleans Times-Democrat's relief-boat, see Appendix A

America from England; scattered individuals at first, then something like a steady stream of them—a procession that continued its persistent, determined journey through the country for many, many years. Each tourist took notes, returned home, and published a book—a book that was typically measured, honest, sensible, and generous; but which appeared to be exactly the opposite to our sensitive ancestors. A look at these travel books reveals that in certain respects the Mississippi has experienced no change since those foreigners visited it, and remains today much as it was then. The feelings stirred in those foreign hearts by these sights were not all cut from the same mold, naturally; they had to vary, at least initially, because the early tourists were forced to create their own emotional responses, while in older countries one can always draw upon the emotions of previous visitors. And remember, emotions are among the most difficult things in the world to create from nothing; it's easier to produce seven facts than one genuine emotion. Captain Basil Hall, R.N., writing fifty-five years ago, says—

Here I caught my first glimpse of what I had longed to see for so long, and in that moment I felt completely rewarded for all the difficulties I had endured to travel this far; I stood there watching the river flow by until darkness made it impossible to make out anything. However, it wasn't until I had returned to this same place a dozen times that I truly understood the magnificence of what lay before me.

Following are Mrs. Trollope's emotions. She is writing a few months later in the same year, 1827, and is arriving at the mouth of the Mississippi—

The first sign that we were approaching land was the sight of this massive river flowing out with its muddy waters, mixing with the deep blue of the Gulf of Mexico. I had never seen a scene as completely desolate as this entrance to the Mississippi. If Dante had witnessed it, he could have created images of another infernal realm from its terrors. Only one object rises above the swirling waters; this is the mast of a ship that was wrecked long ago while trying to cross the sandbar, and it still stands there, a grim reminder of the destruction that has already occurred, and an ominous warning of what is yet to come.

Emotions of Hon. Charles Augustus Murray (near St. Louis), seven years later—

'Only when you travel up the powerful current for fifty or a hundred miles, using both your imagination and your natural sight, do you begin to grasp all of its power and grandeur. You witness it nourishing an endless valley, carrying along in its flow the spoils of its countless triumphs over the broken forest—sometimes sweeping away enormous chunks of earth along with everything growing on them, and other times creating islands that will one day become home to people; and while you contemplate this scene, it becomes time for deeper thought to remind you that the current flowing before you has already journeyed through two or three thousand miles, and still has one thousand three hundred more miles to travel before it reaches its final ocean destination.'

Receive, now, the emotions of Captain Marryat, R.N. author of the sea tales, writing in 1837, three years after Mr. Murray—

'Perhaps never in the history of nations has there been an example of a century marked by such constant and relentless crime as can be found in the history of the violent and bloodstained Mississippi. The river itself seems perfectly suited for the terrible acts that have taken place along its banks. Unlike most rivers, it is not beautiful to look at or life-giving as it flows; it is not a river that draws the eye as it moves along, nor can you walk safely along its shores or trust yourself to its waters without danger. It is a violent, swift, destructive torrent, heavy with muddy soil; and few of those who fall into its waters ever surface again,[8] or can keep themselves afloat on its surface for long without help from some helpful piece of driftwood. It holds the roughest and most inedible fish, like catfish and similar types, and as you travel downstream, its banks are home to the stinking alligator, while panthers sun themselves at its edges in the cane thickets, almost unreachable by humans. Rushing its violent waters through wild areas covered with trees of little worth except as firewood, it tears down entire forests as it flows, which vanish in chaotic disorder, swept away by the current now heavy with the masses of earth that once fed their roots, often blocking and temporarily changing the river's path, which, as if furious at being resisted, floods and destroys the entire surrounding countryside; and as soon as it forces its way back through its original channel, it plants everywhere the torn-up giants of the forest (on whose branches birds will never again rest, or raccoons, opossums, or squirrels climb) as traps for the bold steamboat navigators of its waters, who, crashing into these hidden dangers that punch through their hulls, very often do not have time to steer toward and reach the shore before they sink to the bottom. There are no pleasant memories connected with this great sewage drain of Western America, which dumps its mud into the Gulf of Mexico, contaminating the clear blue sea for many miles beyond where it empties. It is a river of destruction; and instead of reminding you, like other beautiful rivers, of an angel that has come down for humanity's benefit, you picture it as a devil, whose forces have only been controlled by the amazing power of steam.'

This is rather rough writing for someone used to wielding a pen; nevertheless, as a sweeping view of the feelings that churned

---

[8] There was a foolish superstition of some little prevalence in that day, that the Mississippi would neither buoy up a swimmer, nor permit a drowned person's body to rise to the surface.

through this famous visitor's heart when confronted with the appearance and history of the 'great common sewer,' it holds significance. It has worth, though its statistical content is damaged by errors; for the catfish is a perfectly good fish for anyone, and there are no panthers that are 'impervious to man.'

Later on comes Alexander Mackay, of the Middle Temple, Barrister at Law, with better digestion and no catfish dinner on board, and he feels as follows—

'The Mississippi! I felt emotions beyond description when I first found myself floating on its waters. How many times during my school days, and in my daytime dreams afterward, had my mind envisioned this majestic river, flowing with its turbulent current through the vast region that bears its name, and collecting along its path to the ocean the tributary waters from nearly every latitude in the temperate zone! Here it was at last in reality, and I was finally traveling upstream against its current. I gazed upon it with the same reverence that anyone must feel when encountering a magnificent feature of the natural world.'

So much for the emotions. Every single tourist comments on the profound, contemplative isolation and emptiness of the enormous river. Captain Basil Hall, who observed it during flood season, states—

'Sometimes we traveled twenty or thirty miles without seeing a single home. An artist looking for inspiration to paint the great flood would have found plenty of ideas here.'

Just two hundred years ago, the original and most courageous of all foreign explorers, the pioneer who led the way, completed his exhausting and lengthy voyage of discovery down the majestic stretches of the great river—La Salle, whose name will endure as long as the river itself exists. We quote from Mr. Parkman—

And now they approached the end of their journey. On April sixth, the river split into three wide channels. La Salle took the western route, and D'Autray chose the eastern one, while Tonty navigated through the middle passage. As he floated down the muddy current between the low, swampy banks, the slightly salty water transformed into ocean brine, and the wind became fresh with the sea's salty scent. Then the vast expanse of the great Gulf spread before him, its endless waves rolling restlessly, boundless, silent, and as solitary as when it first emerged from chaos, without a single sail or any sign of life.

Then, on a patch of firm ground, La Salle erected a column displaying the coat of arms of France; the French soldiers assembled in formation with their weapons; and while the New England Native Americans and their women watched in amazed silence, they sang the Te Deum, The Exaudiat, and the Domine Salvum Fac Regem.

Then, while musket fire erupted in volleys and celebratory shouts rang out, the triumphant explorer erected the column and declared in a booming voice, formally claiming possession of the river and the enormous territories it watered, in the name of the King. The column carried this inscription—

LOUIS THE GREAT, KING OF FRANCE AND NAVARRE, REIGNS; THE NINTH OF APRIL, 1682.

New Orleans planned to properly commemorate the two-hundredth anniversary of this distinguished event this year; however, when the time arrived, all the city's resources and extra funds were needed elsewhere, as flooding had struck the region, causing destruction and devastation throughout the area.

Chapter 28: Uncle Mumford Speaks His Mind

We spent the entire day traveling down the river, with the

waterway almost completely to ourselves. In the past, when the water was at this level, we would have encountered acres of lumber rafts and dozens of large coal barges, along with occasional small trading boats that moved from farm to farm with the merchant's family living aboard. We might have also seen a random boat carrying a modest theatrical troupe like Hamlet and Company on a traveling performance tour. However, all of these were nowhere to be found. Late in the day, we spotted a single steamboat—just one, and that was all. The vessel was resting in the shade at the tree-lined entrance to the Obion River. Through our telescope, we discovered that the boat had been named after me—or perhaps I should say he was named after me, depending on how you look at it. Since this was my first experience with this type of recognition, it seems reasonable to mention it here, while also drawing the authorities' attention to how long it took for me to notice this honor.

I noticed a major change in the river at Island 21. It had been a very large island that used to sit out toward the middle of the stream, but now it's permanently connected to the main shore and is no longer functioning as an island.

As we neared the famous and intimidating Plum Point, night began to fall, but that wasn't something to worry about—not in these modern times. The federal government has now transformed the Mississippi into something like a two-thousand-mile torch-lit parade. At the beginning of every river crossing and at the end of every crossing, the government has installed a bright-burning light. You're never completely in darkness anymore; there's always a guiding light visible, whether ahead of you, behind you, or alongside. One could almost say that lights have been used lavishly there. Numerous crossings are illuminated that weren't shallow when they were first established, and have never become shallow since; crossings so clear and also so direct that a steamboat can navigate through them on its own, once it has passed through them before. Lights in such locations are certainly not wasteful; it's much more practical and pleasant for a pilot to steer by them rather than by an expanse of shapeless darkness that keeps shifting; and money is saved for the boat at the same time, since she can naturally cover more distance with her rudder centered than she can with it turned sideways across her stern and slowing her down.

But this development has largely stripped piloting of its romance. Combined with several other changes, it has completely eliminated the romantic appeal of the profession. Take, for example, the danger from snags, which is nothing like what it used to be. In today's practical world, government snag-boats patrol up and down the river, pulling out the river's teeth; they have cleared away all the old clusters that once made many areas so treacherous, and they prevent new ones from forming. In the past, if your boat escaped your control on a pitch-black night and headed for the woods, you would experience tremendous anxiety; the same was true when you were feeling your way through thick darkness in a narrow channel; but all of that has changed now—you simply turn on your electric light, instantly transforming night into day, and your dangers and worries disappear. Horace Bixby and George Ritchie have mapped the crossings and plotted the routes using compass bearings; they have created a lamp to accompany the chart and have secured a patent for the entire system. With these tools, a pilot can now navigate through fog with considerable safety and with a level of confidence that was impossible in earlier times.

With all these plentiful navigation aids, the removal of dangerous obstacles, ample artificial lighting available at the flip of a switch whenever required, and maps and compasses to combat poor visibility, steering a riverboat during favorable water conditions is now almost as safe and straightforward as driving a stagecoach, though it retains barely three times the romance.

And now in these modern times, these days of endless change, the Anchor Line has elevated the captain above the pilot by paying him higher wages than the pilot receives. This was a significant step, but they haven't stopped there. They have ordered that the pilot must stay at his station and maintain his watch continuously, whether the boat is moving or docked at the shore. We, who were once the elite of the river, can no longer go to bed as we used to and sleep while a hundred tons of cargo are loaded aboard; instead, we must remain in the pilot-house and stay alert as well. Truly we are being treated like a bunch of mates and engineers. The Government has stripped away the romance from our profession; the Company has removed its prestige and dignity.

Plum Point looked the same as it always had at night, except now there were beacons marking the crossings, along with many other lights on the Point and along its shoreline; these lights came from the United States River Commission's fleet and from a village that officials had built on the land for offices and service employees. The Commission's military engineers have taken on the massive task of remaking the Mississippi River—a job surpassed in scale only by the original work of creating it. They are constructing wing-dams in various locations to redirect the current; building dikes to contain it within narrower boundaries; and creating additional dikes to keep it in place; and for countless miles along the Mississippi, they are cutting down timber fifty yards back from the water's edge, planning to slope the bank down to low-water level at the angle of a house roof and reinforce it with stones; and in many areas they have protected the eroding shores with rows of wooden piles. Anyone familiar with the Mississippi will immediately declare—not out loud, but to themselves—that ten thousand River Commissions, backed by all the world's resources, cannot tame that unruly river, cannot control or contain it, cannot command it to go here or there and expect obedience; cannot save a shoreline it has condemned; cannot block its path with any barrier it won't tear down, dance over, and mock. But a wise person won't voice these thoughts aloud; for the West Point engineers have no equals anywhere; they possess complete knowledge of their complex science; and so, since they believe they can restrain and control that river and dominate it, it's only sensible for the non-scientific person to stay quiet, keep a low profile, and wait to see them accomplish it. Captain Eads, with his jetties, completed work at the Mississippi's mouth that seemed clearly impossible; so we don't feel entirely confident now in predicting against similar impossibilities. Otherwise one would speak up and say the Commission might as well intimidate the comets in their orbits and try to make them behave, as attempt to force the Mississippi into proper and reasonable conduct.

I spoke with Uncle Mumford about this and related topics, and I'm presenting the results here as they were recorded in shorthand, so you can trust that this account is complete and accurate. However, I've occasionally omitted remarks that were directed at the workers, like "where the hell are you taking that barrel?" These comments seemed to interrupt the flow of the written record without adding any useful information or clarity. I haven't removed all such interruptions though—only the ones that were clearly unrelated to the main discussion. Whenever I wasn't sure whether a comment should stay or go, I decided it was better to leave it in.

UNCLE MUMFORD'S IMPRESSIONS

Uncle Mumford said—

'For as long as I've been a steamboat mate—thirty years—I've watched this river and studied it. Maybe I could have learned more about it at West Point, but if I believe that I wish I may be what are you sucking your fingers there for?—grab that barrel of nails! Four years at West Point, with plenty of books and schooling, will teach a man a good deal, I suppose, but it won't teach him the river. You hand one of those little European rivers over to this Commission, with its hard bottom and clear water, and it would just be an easy job for them to wall it up, pile it up, build dikes around it, tame it down, boss it around, and make it go wherever they wanted it to go, stay where they put it, and do exactly as they said, every time. But this isn't that kind of river. They've started in here with great confidence and the best intentions in the world, but they're going to be left behind. What does Ecclesiastes vii. 13 say? Says enough to knock their little scheme completely off course, doesn't it? Now take a look at their methods. There at Devil's Island, in the Upper River, they wanted the water to go one way, but the water wanted to go another. So they built a stone wall. But what does the river care about a stone wall? When it was ready, it just burst right through it. Maybe they can build another one that will hold—that is, up there—but not down here they can't. Down here in the Lower River, they drive some stakes to turn the water away from the shore and stop it from cutting away the bank; well, doesn't it go straight over and cut somebody else's bank? Certainly. Are they going to stake all the banks? Why, they could buy land and build a new Mississippi cheaper. They're staking Bulletin Tow-head now. It won't do any good. If the river has a claim on that island, it will take it back, for sure, stakes or no stakes. Way down there, they've driven two rows of piles straight through the middle of a dry sandbar half a mile long, which is forty feet out of the water when the river is low. What do you think that's for? If I know, I wish I may land in—move yourself, you son of an undertaker!—get that kerosene out, now, quickly, quickly! And just look at what they're trying to do down there at Milliken's Bend. There's been a cut-off in that section, and Vicksburg is left out in the cold. It's a country town now. The river flows in below it, and a boat can't go up to the town except when the water is high. Well, they're going to build wing-dams in the bend opposite the foot of 103, and throw the water over and cut off the foot of the island

199

and plow down into an old channel where the river used to be in ancient times; and they think they can persuade the water to go around that way, and get it to flow in above Vicksburg, as it used to do, and bring the town back into the world again. That is, they're going to take this whole Mississippi, and twist it around and make it run several miles upstream. Well you've got to admire men who deal in ideas of that size and can carry them around without crutches; but you don't have to believe they can perform such miracles, do you! And yet you're not absolutely required to believe they can't. I think the safe way, where a man can afford it, is to bet against the operation, and at the same time buy enough property in Vicksburg to cover yourself in case they win. The Government is doing a lot for the Mississippi now—spending loads of money on her. When there used to be four thousand steamboats and ten thousand acres of coal-barges, and rafts and trading boats, there wasn't a lantern from St. Paul to New Orleans, and the snags were thicker than bristles on a hog's back; and now when there are three dozen steamboats and not a single barge or raft, the Government has pulled out all the snags, and lit up the shores like Broadway, and a boat's as safe on the river as she'd be in heaven. And I think that by the time there aren't any boats left at all, the Commission will have the old thing all reorganized, and dredged out, and fenced in, and cleaned up, to a degree that will make navigation just simply perfect, and absolutely safe and profitable; and all the days will be Sundays, and all the mates will be Sunday-school su——what-in-the-nation-are-you-fooling-around-there-for, you sons of unrighteousness, heirs of perdition! is it going to take a year to get that barrel ashore?'

During our journey to New Orleans and back, we engaged in numerous conversations with river workers, plantation owners, journalists, and officials from the River Commission—leading to contradictory and bewildering outcomes. Specifically:—

Some people believed in the Commission's plan to randomly

and permanently restrict (and therefore deepen) the channel, protect endangered shorelines, and so on.

Some people believed that the Commission's funds should only be used for constructing and maintaining the extensive levee system.

Some people believed that the taller you construct your levee, the higher the riverbed will become; and that as a result the levee system is fundamentally flawed.

Some people believed in the plan to ease pressure on the river during flood season by diverting its excess waters into Lake Borgne and other areas.

Some people believed in the plan to create northern lake reservoirs that would refill the Mississippi River during periods of low water.

Whenever you encounter someone down there who believes in one of these theories, you can turn to the next person and base your conversation on the assumption that they don't believe in that particular theory; and once you've gained experience, you don't take this approach with doubt or hesitation, but with the confidence of a converted murderer on his deathbed—a reformed one, I mean. You will come to understand, with deep and peaceful certainty, that you're not going to encounter two people afflicted with the same theory one right after another. No, there will always be one or two people with different intellectual ailments in between. As you continue, you'll discover one or two additional things. You'll learn that every disorder in this collection is contagious; and you cannot go where it exists without catching it yourself. You may inoculate yourself with preventive facts as much as you want—it won't help; it will appear to work, but it doesn't; the moment you come into contact with any one of those theorists, prepare yourself for the fact that it's time to display your quarantine flag.

Yes, you are definitely his victim, but his work doesn't completely harm you—only partially. He's like your family doctor who shows up to treat your mumps but leaves you with scarlet fever. If your person happens to be a Lake Borgne relief theorist, for example, he'll breathe out a cloud of lethal facts and statistics that will definitely knock you down with that particular condition. However, at the same time, he'll cure you of any of the other five theories that might have already infected your thinking.

I have experienced all five types, and I had them severely, but don't ask me to tell you in sorrowful detail which one caused me the most suffering, or which one affected the most people, because I don't know. Honestly, no one can answer that second question. Improving the Mississippi River is a major subject of discussion down there. Every person living along the riverbanks south of Cairo talks about it daily, during whatever time they can spare from discussing the war, and each of the main theories has its dedicated group of passionate supporters, but as I mentioned, it's impossible to determine which cause attracts the most followers.

Everyone agreed on one thing, though: if Congress would provide enough funding, the results would be enormous. Fine; the funding has since been approved—probably adequate, and certainly not excessive. Let's hope this prediction proves completely accurate.

One thing readers will easily accept is that an opinion from Mr. Edward Atkinson on any major national commercial issue comes as close to being authoritative as any individual's opinion in the United States. What he has to say about Mississippi River Improvement can be found in the Appendix.[9]

Sometimes, half a dozen statistics will reveal, like a lightning flash, the importance of a topic that ten thousand carefully crafted

---

[9] See Appendix B.

words, written with the same goal in mind, had ultimately left unclear and uncertain. Here's an example of this kind—a paragraph from the 'Cincinnati Commercial'—

The towboat "Jos. B. Williams" is heading to New Orleans with a tow of thirty-two barges, carrying six hundred thousand bushels of coal (at seventy-six pounds per bushel) not including her own fuel, making this the largest tow ever transported to New Orleans or anywhere else in the world. Her freight charges, at 3 cents per bushel, total $18,000. It would require eighteen hundred railroad cars, with three hundred and thirty-three bushels per car, to move this quantity of coal. At $10 per ton, or $100 per car, which would be a reasonable rate for this distance by rail, the freight costs would reach $180,000, or $162,000 more by rail than by river. The tow will travel from Pittsburgh to New Orleans in fourteen or fifteen days. It would require one hundred trains of eighteen cars each to transport this single tow of six hundred thousand bushels of coal, and even if it maintained the typical speed of fast freight lines, it would take an entire summer to complete the journey by rail.

When a river in excellent condition allows someone to save $162,000 and an entire summer's worth of time on just one shipment, the wisdom of taking steps to maintain the river in good condition becomes clear even to those who aren't business-minded.

Chapter 29: A Few Sample Bricks

We traveled through the Plum Point area, rounded Craighead's Point, and sailed past without interference by what had once been the powerful Fort Pillow, which is remembered for the massacre that took place there during the war. Massacres appear quite regularly throughout the histories of various Christian nations, but this is nearly the only one that can be discovered in American history; it may well be the only one that matches the scale suggested by that enormous and dark title. We have the 'Boston Massacre,' where two or three people lost their lives; but we would need to combine all of Anglo-Saxon history to find something comparable to the Fort Pillow tragedy; and most likely even then we would have to go back to the era and the actions of Richard the Lionheart, that celebrated 'hero,' before we could achieve it.

More of the river's unusual changes. In the past, the channel used to flow above Island 37, past Brandywine Bar, and down toward Island 39. Later, it changed its path and went from Brandywine down through Vogelman's chute in the Devil's Elbow, to Island 39—part of this route reversing the previous direction; the river flowing upstream for four or five miles, rather than downstream, and eliminating about fifteen miles of distance altogether. This happened in 1876. That entire area is now known as Centennial Island.

There is a tradition that Island 37 was one of the main hideouts of the once famous 'Murel's Gang.' This was an enormous organization of robbers, horse thieves, slave stealers, and counterfeiters who operated along the river about fifty or sixty years ago. During our journey across the country toward St. Louis, we had heard endless stories about Jesse James and his dramatic history, since he had just been murdered by an agent of the Missouri Governor and was therefore taking up considerable space in the newspapers. Inexpensive biographies of him were being sold by train vendors. According to these accounts, he was the most extraordinary criminal of his type who had ever lived. This was wrong. Murel was his equal in daring, in courage, in greed, in cruelty, brutality, callousness, and betrayal, and in overall comprehensive wickedness and shamelessness; and he was far superior in some broader ways. James was a small-time criminal; Murel operated on a massive scale. James's limited imagination never dreamed of anything grander than planning attacks on trains, stagecoaches, and rural banks; Murel planned slave uprisings and the conquest of New Orleans; and beyond that, when the occasion called for it, this Murel could step into a pulpit and inspire the congregation. What are James and his handful of common criminals compared with this dignified old-fashioned outlaw, with his sermons, his planned rebellions and city conquests, and his impressive army of one thousand men, sworn to carry out his wicked commands!

Here is a paragraph or two about this major operator, from a now forgotten book that was published fifty years ago—

He seems to have been an extremely skilled and thoroughly corrupt criminal. When he traveled, he typically disguised himself as a traveling preacher, and it's reported that his sermons were very emotionally powerful—captivating his audiences so completely that they neglected to watch their horses, which his accomplices would steal while he was delivering his sermon. However, stealing horses in one state and selling them in another was only a minor part of their operation; their most profitable scheme involved convincing enslaved people to escape from their owners so they could sell them elsewhere. This system worked as follows: they would tell an enslaved person that if he escaped from his master and allowed them to sell him, he would receive part of the money they got for him, and when he returned to them a second time, they would help him reach a free state where he would be safe.

The unfortunate victims went along with this demand, hoping they would receive money and their freedom. They would be sold to a different owner and then escape back to their original employers. Sometimes they would be sold this way three or four times until the criminals had made three or four thousand dollars from them. However, since there was always the risk of being caught after this, the standard practice was to eliminate the only witness who could testify against them—the enslaved person himself—by killing him and dumping his body in the Mississippi River. Even when it could be proven that they had stolen an enslaved person before he was killed, they were always ready to avoid punishment. They would hide the person who had escaped until he was advertised and a reward was posted for anyone who would capture him. This type of advertisement gives the person legal authority to take the property when found. The enslaved person then becomes property held in trust, so when they sold him, it only constituted a breach of trust rather than theft. For a breach of trust, the property owner could only seek compensation through a civil lawsuit, which was pointless since the damages were never actually paid. One might wonder how Murel managed to escape lynch law under these conditions. This becomes clear when you understand that he had more than a thousand sworn accomplices, all prepared at a moment's notice to support any gang member who might be in danger. The names of all Murel's main accomplices were obtained from him personally, in a way that I will explain shortly. The gang consisted of two groups: the Heads or Council, as they called themselves, who made plans and organized operations but rarely took direct action. They numbered about four hundred. The second group were the active operatives, called strikers, and there were approximately six hundred and fifty of them. These men served as instruments for the others. They took all the risks and received only a small share of the profits. They were completely under the control of the gang leaders, who would sacrifice them at any moment by turning them over to the authorities or drowning their bodies in the Mississippi. The main meeting place for this group of criminals was on the Arkansas side of the river, where they hid their captives in the swamps and dense cane fields.

The damage caused by this vast criminal organization was severely felt, but their plans were so well organized that although Murel, who was always active, was suspected everywhere, no proof could be obtained. It happened, however, that a young man named Stewart, who was searching for two slaves that Murel had lured away, encountered him and gained his trust, took the oath, and was accepted into the gang as one of the General Council. Through this means everything was discovered, for Stewart became a traitor, although he had taken the oath, and having obtained all the information, he exposed the entire operation, the names of all the participants, and finally succeeded in gathering sufficient evidence against Murel to secure his conviction and sentencing to the Penitentiary (Murel was sentenced to fourteen years' imprisonment). So many people who were thought to be honest and held respectable reputations in the different States were found to be among the list of the Grand Council as published by Stewart, that every effort was made to discredit his claims—his character was attacked, and more than one attempt was made to kill him. He was forced to leave the Southern States as a result. It is, however, now well established to have been entirely true, and although some criticize Mr. Stewart for having broken his oath, they no longer try to deny that his revelations were accurate. I will quote one or two portions of Murel's confessions to Mr. Stewart, made to him when they were traveling together. I should have mentioned that the ultimate intentions of Murel and his associates were, by his own account, on a very large scale, having no less an objective in view than inciting the blacks against the whites, taking control of and plundering New Orleans, and making themselves masters of the territory. The following are a few extracts:

I gathered all my friends around New Orleans at one of our companions' homes in that city, and we held council for three days before we finalized all our plans to our satisfaction; we then decided to launch the rebellion at any cost, and recruit as many allies as we could for that purpose. With every man's role assigned to him, I set out for Natchez on foot, having sold my horse in New Orleans—with the plan of stealing another one after I departed. I walked for four days, and no chance presented itself for me to acquire a horse. On the fifth day, around noon, I had grown weary, and stopped at a creek to get some water and rest briefly. While I was sitting on a log, looking down the road in the direction from which I had come, a man appeared in sight riding a fine-looking horse. The instant I spotted him, I decided to take his horse, if he appeared to be a traveler. He rode up, and I could tell from his gear that he was indeed a traveler. I stood up and drew an elegant rifle pistol on him and commanded him to get down. He complied, and I grabbed his horse by the bridle and pointed down the creek, and ordered him to walk ahead of me. He went a few hundred yards and came to a stop. I tied up his horse, and then forced him to remove his clothes, everything except his shirt and drawers, and commanded him to turn his back to me. He said, 'If you are determined to kill me, allow me time to pray before I die,' I told him I had no time to listen to him pray. He turned around and fell to his knees, and I shot him through the back of the head.

I cut open his stomach and removed his internal organs, then threw his body into the creek. I searched through his pockets and discovered four hundred dollars and thirty-seven cents, along with several documents that I didn't have time to look through. I threw the wallet, papers, and his hat into the creek. His boots were completely new and fit me perfectly, so I put them on and threw my old shoes into the creek to replace them. I bundled up his clothes and packed them into his travel bag, since they were brand-new fabric of the finest quality. I climbed onto as magnificent a horse as I had ever ridden, and headed toward Natchez in much better condition than I had been in for the past five days.

Crenshaw and I gathered four good horses and headed for Georgia. Just before we reached Cumberland Mountain, we met up with a young man from South Carolina, and Crenshaw quickly learned all about his business. The man had traveled to Tennessee to buy a herd of hogs, but when he arrived, pork cost more than he had expected, so he decided not to make the purchase. We figured he would make a good target. Crenshaw winked at me, and I understood what he had in mind. Crenshaw had traveled this road before, but I never had. We had ridden several miles up the mountain when we passed near a steep cliff. Just before we reached it, Crenshaw asked me for my whip, which had a pound of lead in the handle. I handed it to him, and he rode up alongside the South Carolinian and struck him on the side of the head, knocking him off his horse. We jumped down from our horses and searched his pockets, finding twelve hundred and sixty-two dollars. Crenshaw said he knew a place to hide the body. He grabbed the man under his arms while I took his feet, and we carried him to a deep crack in the edge of the cliff and threw him in, where he disappeared from sight. We then threw in his saddle and took his horse with us, which was worth two hundred dollars.

We were held up for several days, and during that time our companion traveled to a nearby small village where he spotted a posted notice advertising the enslaved person we had with us. The advertisement included descriptions of the two men who had supposedly purchased him and expressed doubts about these men's legitimacy. The situation was becoming dangerous, but we had to make the best of desperate circumstances. That night, we brought the enslaved person to the bank of a creek that flows past our friend's farm, where Crenshaw shot him in the head. We removed his internal organs and submerged his body in the creek.

'He had sold the other enslaved man for the third time on the Arkansas River for more than five hundred dollars; and then stole him back and handed him over to his accomplice, who took him to a swamp and concealed the horrific act, securing the final profits and a sacred oath of silence; since a scheme of that nature won't work unless it remains a mystery to everyone except those involved. He sold the enslaved man, from beginning to end, for nearly two thousand dollars, and then permanently removed him from the reach of all who might pursue him; and they can never catch him unless they can find the enslaved man; and that they cannot do, for his body has fed many a turtle and catfish by now, and the frogs have sung for many a long day over the silent rest of his bones.'

We were getting close to Memphis, and right in front of that city, with its residents watching, the most famous river battle of the Civil War took place. Two men I had worked under during my time on the river participated in that fight: Mr. Bixby, who served as head pilot of the Union fleet, and Montgomery, who was Commodore of the Confederate fleet. Both men saw extensive active duty throughout the war and earned outstanding reputations for their courage and skill.

As we approached Memphis, we started looking for a reason to remain aboard the 'Gold Dust' until she reached her final destination—Vicksburg. Our accommodations were so comfortable that we had no desire to make any changes. I had some important business to handle in Napoleon, Arkansas, but I thought I might be able to take care of it without leaving the 'Gold Dust.' I mentioned this possibility, so we chose to stay in our current quarters.

The boat would stay docked at Memphis until ten o'clock the following morning. It's a stunning city, magnificently positioned on a towering bluff that overlooks the river. The streets run straight and wide, although the paving doesn't inspire overwhelming praise. No, the real admiration should be saved for the city's sewage system, which is considered flawless; this is a recent improvement, though, since conditions were completely opposite just a few years earlier—a transformation that came about after learning from a devastating yellow fever outbreak. During those terrible days, people died by the hundreds and thousands; the combined impact of residents fleeing and dying was so severe that the population dropped by three-quarters and stayed that low for some time. Commerce nearly came to a halt, and the streets took on the deserted appearance of a Sunday.

Here is a picture of Memphis during that catastrophic period, described by a German tourist who appears to have personally witnessed the events he recounts. This comes from Chapter VII of his recently published book in Leipzig, 'Mississippi-Fahrten, von Ernst von Hesse-Wartegg.'—

In August, the yellow fever had reached its peak intensity. Every day, hundreds of people died from the terrible epidemic. The city had become an enormous cemetery, with two-thirds of the population having fled the area, leaving only the poor, the elderly, and the sick behind as certain victims for the deadly disease. The houses were shut up tight, with small lamps glowing in front of many of them—a signal that death had visited there. Frequently, multiple bodies lay dead inside a single house, with black mourning cloth hanging from the windows. The shops were boarded up because their owners had either left town or died.

'Terrifying plague! In the shortest time, it struck down and destroyed even the strongest victims. A minor illness, then an hour of fever, then the horrifying delirium, then—the Yellow Death! On street corners and in the squares, sick people lay dying, suddenly overcome by the disease; and even corpses, twisted and stiff. Food ran out. Meat rotted within hours in the foul and disease-ridden air, turning black.

Terrifying screams echo from countless homes; then after some time they fall silent, and everything becomes quiet: honorable, selfless men arrive with the coffin, seal it shut, and take it away to the cemetery. In the nighttime silence prevails. Only the doctors and the funeral carriages rush through the streets; and from far away, at regular intervals, comes the muted rumbling of the railway train, which with the speed of the wind, and as if chased by demons, races past the plague-stricken city without stopping.

But there's plenty of life there now. The population has grown beyond forty thousand people and continues to increase, while business is thriving. We toured the city, stopped by the park with its friendly crowd of squirrels, admired the beautiful homes covered in roses and appealing to the eye in many other ways, and enjoyed an excellent breakfast at the hotel.

A thriving place is the Good Samaritan City of the Mississippi: it has a great wholesale distribution trade; foundries, machine shops; and factories that produce wagons, carriages, and cotton-seed oil; and will soon have cotton mills and elevators.

Her cotton receipts reached five hundred thousand bales last year—an increase of sixty thousand over the previous year. Five major railway trunk lines extend outward from her thriving commercial center, and a sixth line is currently being constructed.

This Memphis is completely different from the one that the long-gone and forgotten parade of foreign tourists used to describe in their books many years ago. Back in the era of the now-forgotten but once-famous and intensely disliked Mrs. Trollope, Memphis appeared to be made up mostly of a single long street lined with log houses, along with scattered cabins spread out behind toward the forest; occasionally there was a pig, and endless amounts of mud. That was fifty-five years ago. She stayed at the hotel. Clearly it wasn't the same one where we had our breakfast. She writes—

'The table was set for fifty people and was almost completely full. They ate in complete silence, and with such incredible speed that their dinner was finished literally before ours had even started; the only sounds that could be heard were those made by the knives and forks, along with the constant chorus of coughing and other noises.'

'Coughing, and so on.' The 'and so on' represents an offensive word in that context, a word she doesn't always politely conceal, but occasionally puts in print. You'll discover it in the next account of a steamboat dinner she shared with numerous aristocratic plantation owners; they were wealthy, well-bred, uneducated show-offs, decorated with the typical meaningless military and legal titles from that bygone era of false appearances and empty boasting—

'The complete absence of basic table manners; the greedy speed with which food was grabbed and consumed; the bizarre crude expressions and way of speaking; the disgusting spitting, which made it absolutely impossible to keep our clothes clean; the horrifying way they ate with their knives, pushing the entire blade into their mouths; and the even more horrifying way they cleaned their teeth afterwards with a pocket knife, quickly made us realize that we were not dining with the generals, colonels, and majors of the old world; and that the dinner hour would be anything but pleasant.'

Chapter 30: Sketches by the Way

It was a massive river, downstream from Memphis; the banks were completely full everywhere, and very often overflowing, with waters spilling out across the land, flooding the forests and fields for miles inland; and in some places, reaching a depth of fifteen feet; there were signs everywhere of people's hard work destroyed, and everything would have to be rebuilt with limited resources and diminished spirit. It was a depressing sight, and it stretched continuously for hundreds of miles. Sometimes the beacon lights stood in three feet of water, at the edge of thick forests that extended for miles without any farm, lumber yard, clearing, or opening of any kind; this meant that the person responsible for the light had to travel a great distance by small boat to fulfill their duty, often in terrible weather conditions. Yet I was told that this work is carried out faithfully in all kinds of weather; and it's not always done by men, sometimes by women, when the man is ill or away. The Government provides oil and pays ten or fifteen dollars per month for the lighting and maintenance. A Government boat delivers oil and distributes wages once a month.

The Ship Island area remained as heavily forested and uninhabited as it had always been. The island no longer exists as an island; it has permanently connected itself to the mainland, and now wagons travel across the same waters where steamboats once sailed. No traces remain of the wrecked 'Pennsylvania.' Some farmer will likely uncover her remains with his plow someday and be startled by the discovery.

We were now entering the region where Black people frequently migrated. These individuals had been unable to travel during slavery, so they were making up for that lost opportunity now. They would remain on a plantation until the urge to travel took hold of them; then they would pack their belongings, flag down a steamboat, and leave. They weren't heading to any specific destination; almost any location would suffice; they simply wanted to be in motion. The amount of money they had available would determine the rest of their journey. If their funds could take them fifty miles, that was fine; let it be fifty miles. If not, a shorter journey would work just as well.

During a few days, we often responded to these calls. Sometimes there was a cluster of flood-stained, run-down cabins, filled with Black residents, with no white people in sight; featuring bare patches of dry earth scattered about; several fallen trees, with skeletal cattle, mules, and horses eating the leaves and chewing the bark—no other sustenance available to them in the flood-ravaged territory. Sometimes there was a single isolated landing-cabin; nearby stood the Black family that had called out to us; young and old, small and large, perched on the meager pile of household belongings; these items included a rusty rifle, some mattress covers, trunks, metal cookware, stools, a damaged mirror, an old armchair, and six or eight worthless and listless yellow dogs, tied to the family with ropes. They had to bring their dogs; couldn't leave without their dogs. Yet the dogs were never cooperative; they always resisted; so, one by one, in an absurd parade, they were pulled aboard; all four paws planted firmly and sliding across the platform, heads nearly yanked off; but the person pulling marched steadily forward, leaning into the task, with the rope across his shoulder for better grip. Sometimes a child was overlooked and left on the shore; but never a dog.

The typical river chatter was happening in the pilot-house. Island No. 63—an island that had a beautiful chute, or passage, behind it in earlier days. They told the story of how Jesse Jamieson, on the 'Skylark,' had a visiting pilot with him on one journey—a poor old worn-out, retired fellow—and left him at the wheel at the foot of 63 to finish out the watch. The old sailor went up through the chute and down the river on the outside; then up the chute and down the river again; and yet again and again; and turned the boat over to the relief pilot after three hours of sincere effort, at the very same foot of the island where he had first taken the wheel! A black man on shore who had watched the boat pass by about thirteen times said, "I declare, I wouldn't be surprised if there's a whole line of them Skylarks!"

The following story shows how reputation can influence people's opinions. The 'Eclipse' was famous for being incredibly fast. One day the steamboat passed by, and an elderly Black man on the shore, busy with his own affairs, didn't pay attention to which steamboat it was. Soon after, someone asked him—

"Has any boat gone upstream?"

"Yes, sir."

"Was she going fast?"

"Oh, just okay—taking it easy."

"Now, do you know what boat that was?"

"No, sir."

'Why, uncle, that was the "Eclipse."'

"No! Is that so? Well, I bet it was—because she just went by here sparkling!"

A piece of history that shows the violent nature of some people in this area. During the early weeks of flooding, A's fence rails were washed down onto B's property, while B's rails were swept up in the current and deposited on A's land. A suggested, "Let's leave things as they are; I'll use your rails, and you can use mine." However, B refused—he wouldn't accept this arrangement. One day, A went onto B's property to retrieve his rails. B threatened, "I'll kill you!" and approached him with his gun drawn. A responded, "I'm not carrying a weapon." Since B wanted to act fairly, he threw down his gun, then drew a knife and slashed A's throat all the way around, focusing mainly on the front but failing to cut the jugular vein. While struggling, A managed to grab the abandoned gun and shot B dead—and eventually recovered from his wounds.

Further gossip followed, after which everyone went below to get their afternoon coffee, leaving me alone at the wheel. Something soon reminded me of our final hour in St. Louis, part of which I had spent on this boat's hurricane deck at the stern. A stranger had joined me there, striking up a conversation—an energetic young man who told me he was born in a town in Wisconsin's interior and had never seen a steamboat until the week before. He also mentioned that during his trip down from La Crosse, he had inspected and examined the boat so thoroughly and with such intense interest that he had learned everything from bow to rudder-blade. He asked where I was from. I replied, New England. "Oh, a Yankee!" he said, and continued talking without waiting for me to confirm or deny it. He immediately offered to show me around the entire boat, tell me the names of its different parts, and explain what they were used for. Before I could protest or make an excuse, he was already talking rapidly as he began his helpful task. When I realized he was giving the wrong names for things and amusing himself at the expense of an innocent stranger from a distant place, I remained quiet and let him continue. He provided me with a wealth of false information, and the longer he went on, the more his imagination grew, and the more he enjoyed his cruel deception. Sometimes, after telling me a particularly ridiculous and outrageous lie, he was so overcome with laughter that he had to step away for a moment, using one excuse or another, to prevent me from becoming suspicious. I stayed with him faithfully until his performance was complete. Then he commented that he had promised to teach me everything about a steamboat and had accomplished that goal, but if he had missed anything, I should just ask him and he would fill in the gaps. "Anything about this boat that you don't know the name of or what it's for, you come to me and I'll tell you." I said I would, then left. I disappeared and approached him from a different direction where he couldn't see me. There he sat, completely alone, doubled over and twisting back and forth, consumed by uncontrollable laughter. He must have made himself ill, because he wasn't seen in public for several days afterward. Meanwhile, I forgot about the entire incident.

The thing that brought it back to my mind now, as I stood alone at the wheel, was the sight of this young man standing in the pilot-house doorway, his hand on the doorknob, silently and sternly studying me. I can't remember when I've seen anyone look so hurt as he did. He didn't say a word—just stood there and stared; looked at me with reproach and thought it over. Eventually he closed the door and walked away; stopped on the texas for a moment; came slowly back and stood in the doorway again, with that wounded expression on his face; looked at me for a while with quiet disapproval, then said—

"You taught me everything about steamboats, didn't you?"

"Yes," I admitted.

"Yes, you did—didn't you?"

'Yes.'

"You're the guy who—who—"

Language failed him completely. He paused—struggling helplessly to find more words—then he gave up entirely, muttered a deep, forceful curse, and left for good. I saw him several times afterward on the lower decks during the voyage, but he remained cold toward me—refusing even to look in my direction. The fool—if he hadn't been so eager to play his stupid practical joke on me from the start, I could have guided his thoughts in a different direction and prevented him from committing such a pointless and foolish act of rudeness.

I made sure to wake up with the four o'clock watch every morning, because you can never witness too many summer sunrises on the Mississippi River. They are absolutely captivating. First, there's the powerful eloquence found in complete silence; a deep quiet settles over everything. Then comes the haunting feeling of solitude, isolation, and distance from all the world's worries and commotion. The dawn arrives quietly and secretly; the solid black walls of forest gradually soften into gray, and enormous sections of the river open up and show themselves; the water becomes smooth as glass, releasing ghostly little spirals of white mist, with not even the slightest breeze or movement of leaves; the peacefulness is deep and endlessly fulfilling. Then one bird begins to sing, another joins in, and soon these individual songs grow into a joyful explosion of music. You can't see any of the birds; you simply travel through a world of song that seems to create itself. When the light grows a bit stronger, you witness one of the most beautiful and gentle scenes you could ever imagine. You see the brilliant green of the thick, densely packed leaves nearby; you watch it gradually fade shade by shade as it stretches ahead of you; on the next jutting cape, a mile away or farther, the color has softened to the delicate fresh green of springtime; the cape beyond that has nearly lost all color, and the most distant one, miles away beneath the horizon, rests on the water like a faint wisp of vapor, barely distinguishable from the sky above and around it. This entire stretch of river acts like a mirror, showing you the shadowy reflections of the foliage, the curving shorelines, and the distant capes painted across its surface. All of this is truly beautiful; gentle and rich and stunning; and when the sun climbs higher and spreads a pink glow here, scatters golden dust there, and creates a purple haze wherever it will produce the most striking effect, you have to admit that you've witnessed something truly worth remembering.

We passed through the Kentucky Bend region in the early morning—the site of a bizarre and heartbreaking tragedy from years past. Captain Poe owned a small steamboat with a stern paddle wheel, which had served as home for him and his wife for many years. One evening the vessel hit a submerged tree trunk at the entrance to Kentucky Bend and went down with shocking speed; by the time the captain made his way to the back of the boat, water had already risen well above the cabin floor. He began chopping through the roof into his wife's cabin from above using an ax; she was sleeping in the upper bunk, but the ceiling proved much weaker than he had realized; his first swing broke through the decayed planks and split open her head.

This bend is completely filled in now as a result of a cut-off, and the same natural force has taken the great and once heavily traveled Walnut Bend and placed it far back in isolation, away from the usual route of passing steamboats.

We visited Helena, and also a town I had never heard of before, since it was recently established—Arkansas City. The town was created because of a railway; the Little Rock, Mississippi River and Texas Railroad reaches the river at that location. We asked a passenger who lived there what kind of place it was. "Well," he said, after thinking it over, and with the manner of someone who wants to take his time and be precise, "It's a hell of a place." This description was perfectly accurate, like a photograph. There were several rows and groups of run-down wooden houses, and enough mud to keep the town supplied with that material for a hundred years, since the flood had only recently receded. Stagnant pools of water sat in the streets here and there, and about a dozen crude flat-bottomed boats were scattered around, stranded wherever they happened to be when the water drained away and people could once again visit and shop on foot. Even so, it's a prosperous place, with fertile farmland surrounding it, a grain elevator at the waterfront, and also a large mill for producing cottonseed oil. I had never seen this type of mill before.

Cotton seed had relatively little value during my era, but today it sells for $12 or $13 per ton, and nothing gets wasted. The oil extracted from it has no color, no taste, and little to no smell. Experts claim that with the right processing techniques, it can be made to look like and function as any type of oil, while being produced more cheaply than the least expensive original oils. Clever entrepreneurs shipped it to Italy, processed it there, put new labels on it, and imported it back as olive oil. This business became so threatening that Italy had to impose heavy taxes on these imports to prevent serious damage to their domestic oil industry.

Helena sits in one of the most beautiful locations along the Mississippi River. It's positioned on the last and southernmost cluster of hills visible on that side of the water. Under normal circumstances, it's a charming town, but recent flooding (or perhaps water seepage) had been devastating the area. Entire blocks of houses had been flooded with murky water, and the exterior walls of buildings were still marked with wide, dark stains that stretched upward from their foundations. Abandoned and wrecked barges were scattered everywhere. Wooden sidewalks built on four-foot-high stilts were still standing, while the regular boardwalks at ground level had become loose and unstable— when a couple of people walked quickly across them, the noise was so loud it could make a blind person think a cavalry was charging through. The mud was thick and black everywhere, and stagnant pools of water that bred disease had formed in many spots. A Mississippi River flood is almost as destructive and devastating as a fire.

We had a wonderful time here on this bright Sunday: two complete hours of freedom on land while the boat unloaded its cargo. In the side streets, only a handful of white people could be seen, but there were many Black residents—mostly women and girls; and nearly all of them dressed in vibrant new clothing of fashionable and intricate design and tailoring—a striking and cheerful contrast to the gloomy mud and the melancholy puddles.

Helena ranks as Arkansas's second-largest town by population, with approximately five thousand residents. The surrounding countryside proves remarkably fertile and productive. Helena maintains a thriving cotton trade, processing between forty and sixty thousand bales each year. The town also supports substantial lumber and grain businesses, along with a foundry, oil mills, machine shops, and wagon manufacturing facilities. In total, Helena has invested $1,000,000 in its manufacturing sectors. Two railway lines serve the community, establishing it as the commercial hub for an extensive and flourishing region. According to the New Orleans 'Times-Democrat,' Helena's total annual revenue from all sources reaches $4,000,000.

Chapter 31: A Thumbprint and What Came of It

We were getting close to Napoleon, Arkansas. That's when I started thinking about what I needed to do there. It was noon, bright and sunny. This wasn't ideal—actually, it was pretty bad, since what I had to do wasn't really the kind of thing you'd want to handle in broad daylight. The more I thought about it, the more this concern kept nagging at me—coming at me from different angles. Eventually, it crystallized into a clear question: does it make sense to handle this business during the day when, with just a small sacrifice of comfort and convenience, I could wait for nightfall when there wouldn't be any prying eyes watching? That settled the matter. A straightforward question with a straightforward answer is usually the quickest way through most complicated situations.

I brought my friends into my cabin and told them I was sorry to cause trouble and disappointment, but after thinking it over, it really seemed best that we take our luggage off the boat and stay over in Napoleon. They immediately voiced their strong disapproval; their words were rebellious. Their primary argument was one that has always been the first to emerge in such situations since the dawn of time: "But you made the decision and agreed to stay with this boat, etc.;" as if, having chosen to do something unwise, a person is therefore obligated to go forward and make it twice as foolish by following through with that choice.

I attempted several different approaches to calm them down, and these efforts worked reasonably well. Encouraged by this success, I decided to put in even more effort. To demonstrate that I hadn't created this irritating situation and wasn't responsible for it in any way, I gradually began explaining the background of what had happened—essentially telling them this story:

Toward the end of last year, I spent several months in Munich, Bavaria. In November I was staying at Fraulein Dahlweiner's boarding house at 1a, Karlstrasse; however, my workplace was a mile away, in the home of a widow who earned her living by renting rooms to tenants. She and her two young children would visit me every morning and speak German with me—at my request. One day, while exploring the city, I visited one of the two facilities where the Government stores and monitors corpses until doctors determine that they are permanently dead, rather than in a comatose state. It was a ghastly place, that large room. There were thirty-six adult corpses visible, lying on their backs on slightly tilted boards, arranged in three long rows—all of them displaying waxy-white, stiff faces, and all of them wrapped in white burial shrouds. Along the walls of the room were deep recesses, resembling bay windows; and in each of these lay several marble-faced infants, completely hidden and covered beneath mounds of fresh flowers, except for their faces and folded hands. Around one finger of each of these fifty motionless forms, both large and small, was a ring; and from the ring a wire extended to the ceiling, and from there to a bell in a monitoring room nearby, where, day and night, a watchman remains constantly vigilant and prepared to rush to assist any of that pale assembly who, awakening from death, might make a movement—for any motion, even the slightest, would pull the wire and sound that dreadful bell. I pictured myself as a death-guard dozing there alone, deep in the slow-passing hours of some howling, windy night, and having in an instant my entire body frozen into trembling terror by the sudden ringing of that horrible alarm! So I asked about this system; inquired what typically happened? whether the watchman died, and the revived corpse came and did whatever it could to ease his final moments. But I was scolded for attempting to satisfy an idle and foolish curiosity in such a serious and sorrowful place; and departed with my pride wounded.

The next morning, I was telling the widow about my adventure when she suddenly exclaimed—

"Come with me! I have a tenant who can tell you everything you want to know. He used to work as a night watchman there."

He was alive, but he certainly didn't appear to be. He lay in bed with his head propped up high on pillows; his face was gaunt and pale, his deeply sunken eyes were closed; his hand, resting on his chest, looked like a claw because it was so skeletal and long-fingered. The widow started introducing me to him. The man's eyes opened slowly and gleamed maliciously from the shadows of their hollow sockets; he scowled darkly; he raised his thin hand and dismissively waved us away. However, the widow continued speaking until she had managed to explain that I was a stranger and an American. The man's expression immediately transformed; it brightened and became almost enthusiastic—and moments later, he and I found ourselves alone together.

I started speaking in rigid, formal German; he replied in very adaptable English; from that point on, we put the German language aside for good.

This man with tuberculosis and I became close friends. I visited him every day, and we discussed all sorts of topics. At least, we talked about everything except wives and children. Whenever anyone's wife or anyone's child was brought up, three things invariably happened: first, the most gracious, loving, and tender expression would shine in the man's eyes for a brief moment; then it would fade away the next instant, replaced by that deadly look that had blazed there the first time I ever saw him open his eyes; finally, he would stop talking completely for the rest of that day; he would lie there silent, distant, and lost in thought; he seemed to hear nothing I said; he paid no attention to my farewells, and clearly had no awareness, either by sight or sound, when I left the room.

When I had been Karl Ritter's only close companion for two

months, seeing him every day, he suddenly said one day—

"I will tell you my story."

A DYING MAN'S CONFESSION

Then he continued like this:

I have never given up, until now. But now I have given up. I am going to die. I made up my mind last night that it must be, and very soon, too. You say you are going to revisit your river, by and by, when you find opportunity. Very well; that, together with a certain strange experience which happened to me last night, determines me to tell you my story—for you will see Napoleon, Arkansas; and for my sake you will stop there, and do a certain thing for me—a thing which you will willingly undertake after you have heard my story.

Let's cut the story short wherever possible, since it's going to be lengthy and will need it. You already understand how I ended up traveling to America, and how I came to make my home in that isolated area down South. But you don't know that I had a wife. My wife was young, beautiful, loving, and oh, so wonderfully good and innocent and kind! And our little daughter was exactly like her mother, only smaller. It was the most joyful of all happy homes.

One night—it was near the end of the war—I woke up from a heavy stupor and discovered I was tied up and gagged, with the air reeking of chloroform! I saw two men in the room, and one was telling the other in a rough whisper, 'I told her I would, if she made a sound, and as for the child—'

The other man cut in with a quiet, half-sobbing voice—

"You told us we were just going to tie them up and take their money, not harm them; otherwise I never would have joined you."

"Stop your complaining; I had to change the plan when they woke up; you did everything you could to protect them, so let that be enough for you; come on, help search through everything."

225

Both men wore masks and rough, tattered clothing; they carried a bull's-eye lantern, and in its light I observed that the more gentle robber was missing his right thumb. They searched through my modest cabin for a moment; the lead bandit then spoke in his theatrical whisper—

"It's a waste of time—he'll tell us where it's hidden. Remove his gag and wake him up."

The other said—

"All right—as long as there's no beating."

"No beating him with a club then—as long as he stays quiet."

They came toward me; suddenly there was a noise outside; the sound of voices and horses' hooves pounding; the robbers stopped breathing and listened carefully; the sounds gradually grew closer and closer; then came a loud shout—

"Hello, the house! Show a light, we want water."

"That's the captain's voice, by God!" said the ruffian in a harsh whisper, and both robbers escaped through the back door, turning off their lantern as they ran.

The strangers called out several more times, then continued riding past—it sounded like there were about twelve horses—and after that, I heard nothing else.

I fought against my restraints, but couldn't break free. I attempted to call out, but the gag worked perfectly; no sound would come. I strained to hear my wife's voice and my child's—listening carefully and desperately, but silence filled the space where their bed stood at the far end of the room. This quiet grew more terrifying, more threatening, with each passing moment. Do you think you could have survived an hour of such torment? Then have compassion for me, who endured three full hours. Three hours—they felt like three lifetimes! Each time the clock chimed, it seemed as though years had passed since I'd last heard it. Throughout this entire ordeal I kept fighting my restraints; finally, as dawn approached, I managed to free myself, stood up, and stretched my aching body. I could make out details fairly clearly now. The floor was scattered with items the thieves had thrown about while searching for my money. The first thing that drew my attention was a paper of mine that I had watched the more violent of the two criminals examine before tossing aside. It was stained with blood! I stumbled to the other side of the room. Oh, my poor innocent, defenseless loved ones, there they lay, their suffering over, mine just beginning!

Did I turn to the law for help? Does it satisfy a poor man's thirst when the King drinks on his behalf? Oh, no, no, no—I didn't want any unwelcome meddling from the law. Laws and the gallows couldn't settle the debt that was owed to me! Let the laws stay out of this matter and leave it in my hands, without any worries: I would track down the debtor and collect what was due. How would I accomplish this, you ask? How could I manage it and feel so certain about it, when I hadn't seen the robbers' faces, hadn't heard their real voices, and had no idea who they could be? Even so, I was sure—completely sure, totally confident. I had a clue—a clue that you wouldn't have thought much of—a clue that wouldn't have been much help even to a detective, since he would lack the secret of how to use it. I'll get to that soon—you'll see. Let's continue now, taking things in their proper order. There was one detail that pointed me in a specific direction from the start: Those two robbers were clearly soldiers dressed up as wandering beggars; and they weren't new to military service, but experienced in it—career soldiers, perhaps; they hadn't developed their military posture, movements, and bearing in a day, or a month, or even in a year. That's what I thought, but I kept it to myself. And one of them had said, 'the captain's voice, by G—!'—the one whose life I intended to take. Two miles away, several regiments were camped, along with two companies of U.3. cavalry. When I discovered that Captain Blakely, of Company C had come our way that night with an escort, I said nothing, but I decided to look for my man in that company. In conversation I carefully and consistently described the robbers as vagrants and camp followers; and the people searched uselessly among this group, with no one suspecting the soldiers except me.

Working patiently through the night in my ruined home, I created a disguise using various scraps of clothing I could find; I purchased a pair of blue goggles from the nearest village. Eventually, when the military camp disbanded and Company C received orders to move a hundred miles north to Napoleon, I hid my small collection of money in my belt and left under cover of darkness. By the time Company C reached Napoleon, I had already arrived. Indeed, I was there with a new profession—fortune-teller. To avoid appearing biased, I befriended soldiers and read fortunes for all the companies stationed there; however, I devoted most of my attention to Company C. I made myself endlessly helpful to these specific men; there was no favor they could request or risk they could impose on me that I would refuse. I allowed myself to become the target of their jokes; this enhanced my popularity and made me well-liked among them.

I quickly discovered a private who was missing a thumb—what excitement this brought me! When I realized that he was the only one in the entire company who had lost a thumb, my final doubts disappeared; I knew I was following the correct path. This soldier's name was Kruger, a German. Nine Germans served in the company. I observed carefully to see who his close friends might be; however, he didn't appear to have any particular close companions. But I became his close companion; and I made sure to strengthen that friendship. At times I felt such intense desire for my revenge that I could barely stop myself from dropping to my knees and pleading with him to identify the man who had killed my wife and child; but I succeeded in controlling my words. I waited for the right moment, and continued telling fortunes whenever the chance arose.

My equipment was straightforward: a small amount of red paint and some white paper. I would paint the ball of my client's thumb, press it onto the paper to make a print, examine it that evening, and tell him his fortune the following day. What was my reasoning behind this foolishness? It was this: During my youth, I knew an elderly Frenchman who had worked as a prison guard for thirty years, and he explained to me that there was one aspect of a person that never altered, from birth to death—the lines on the ball of the thumb; and he mentioned that these lines were never precisely identical on the thumbs of any two people. In our time, we photograph new criminals and display their pictures in the Rogues' Gallery for future identification; but that Frenchman, in his era, would take a print of the ball of a new prisoner's thumb and store that for future identification. He always maintained that photographs were unreliable—future disguises could render them worthless; 'The thumb's the only reliable method,' he would say; 'you cannot disguise that.' And he would demonstrate his theory as well, using my friends and acquaintances; it never failed.

I continued telling fortunes. Each night I locked myself away, completely alone, and examined the day's thumbprints using a magnifying glass. Picture the consuming intensity with which I studied those intricate red swirls, with that document beside me bearing the right-hand thumb and finger prints of that unknown killer, marked with the most precious blood—to me—that had ever been spilled on this earth! And time after time I found myself repeating the same old disheartened observation, 'will they never match!'

But my reward finally arrived. It was the thumbprint of the forty-third man from Company C that I had tested—Private Franz Adler. An hour earlier, I hadn't known the killer's name, voice, appearance, face, or nationality; but now I knew all of these details! I thought I could be confident; the Frenchman's repeated proofs provided such strong evidence. However, there was still a way to be absolutely certain. I had taken an impression of Kruger's left thumb. The next morning I pulled him aside when he wasn't on duty; and when we were away from anyone who could see or hear us, I said with emphasis—

"Part of your fortune is so serious that I thought it would be better for you if I didn't reveal it in public. You and another man, whose fortune I was examining last night—Private Adler—have been murdering a woman and a child! You are being hunted: within five days both of you will be killed."

He fell to his knees, terrified beyond belief, and for five minutes he kept repeating the same words over and over, like someone who had lost their mind, speaking in that same half-sobbing manner that reminded me of that deadly night in my cabin—

"I didn't do it; I swear on my soul I didn't do it; and I tried to stop him from doing it; I did, as God is my witness. He did it by himself."

This was all I wanted. And I tried to get rid of the fool; but no, he clung to me, begging me to save him from the assassin. He said—

'I have money—ten thousand dollars—hidden away, earned through stealing and robbery; save me—tell me what to do, and you can have it, every penny. Two-thirds of it belongs to my cousin Adler; but you can take it all. We hid it when we first arrived here. But I moved it to a new location yesterday, and haven't told him—won't tell him. I was planning to run away and escape with all of it. It's gold, and too heavy to carry when someone is running and hiding; but a woman who went across the river two days ago to prepare my escape route is going to follow me with it; and if I don't get a chance to describe the hiding place to her I was going to slip my silver watch into her hand, or send it to her, and she would understand. There's a piece of paper in the back of the case that explains everything. Here, take the watch—tell me what to do!'

He was attempting to force his watch on me and was showing me the document while explaining it, when Adler showed up, roughly twelve yards from where we stood. I told poor Kruger—

'Put away your watch, I don't want it. You won't be hurt. Go now; I need to tell Adler his fortune. Soon I'll explain how you can avoid the assassin; in the meantime, I'll need to examine your thumbprint again. Don't say anything to Adler about this—don't tell anyone.'

He left feeling both terrified and grateful, the poor soul. I gave Adler an extremely lengthy fortune reading—deliberately making it so long that I couldn't complete it. I promised to visit him during his guard duty that night to reveal the truly significant portion— the tragic elements, as I described them—which needed to be shared away from anyone who might overhear. The soldiers always maintained a sentry post outside the town—simply following standard military protocol and formality—there was no real need for it since no enemies were in the area.

Toward midnight I set out, armed with the password, and made my way toward the isolated area where Adler was supposed to stand guard. The darkness was so thick that I nearly stumbled into a shadowy figure before I could speak a word of protection. The guard called out and I responded, both of us speaking at the same time. I added, "It's just me—the fortune-teller." Then I moved close to the poor man's side, and without saying anything I plunged my dagger into his heart! Yes indeed, I laughed, that was certainly the tragic part of his fortune! As he tumbled from his horse, he grabbed at me, and my blue spectacles stayed clutched in his hand; and the horse bolted away, dragging him along with his foot caught in the stirrup.

I ran through the forest and successfully escaped, leaving behind the incriminating goggles in the dead man's grip.

This happened fifteen or sixteen years ago. Since that time, I have wandered without purpose across the world, sometimes working, sometimes doing nothing; sometimes having money, sometimes being broke; but always weary of living, and hoping it would end, because my purpose here was complete after what I did that night; and the only joy, comfort, or contentment I experienced during all those long years was in thinking every day, 'I have killed him!'

Four years ago, my health started to decline. I had drifted into Munich without any real purpose. Running out of money, I looked for work and found it; I performed my duties faithfully for about a year, and then was offered the position of night watchman at that morgue you recently visited. The location matched my state of mind. I enjoyed it there. I found comfort being with the dead—being alone with them. I would walk among those stiff corpses and study their stern faces for hours at a time. The later the hour, the more powerful the experience became; I favored the late hours. Sometimes I dimmed the lights: this created depth, you understand; and allowed the mind to wander; invariably, the shadowy retreating rows of the dead filled me with strange and captivating thoughts. Two years ago—I had been working there for a year by then—I was sitting completely alone in the watch-room on a windy winter's night, cold, numb, miserable; slowly drifting toward unconsciousness; the moaning of the wind and the banging of distant shutters growing weaker and weaker in my fading hearing with each passing moment, when suddenly and sharply that death-bell rang out a terrifying alarm above my head! The shock of it almost paralyzed me; it was the first time I had ever heard it ring.

I pulled myself together and rushed to the morgue. About halfway down the outer row, a covered figure was sitting upright, slowly shaking its head from side to side—a horrifying sight! It was facing sideways toward me. I hurried over to it and looked into its face. My God, it was Adler!

Can you guess what my first thought was? Put into words, it was this: 'So it appears you escaped me once before: things will turn out differently this time!'

Clearly this creature was experiencing unthinkable horrors. Imagine what it must have felt like to awaken surrounded by that silent stillness, and gaze out at that forbidding assembly of corpses! What thankfulness radiated from his gaunt pale face when he spotted a living person standing before him! And how the intensity of this wordless appreciation grew when his gaze landed on the life-restoring medicines that I held in my hands! Then picture the terror that filled this haggard face when I placed the medicines behind my back, and spoke with cruel mockery—

"Speak up, Franz Adler—call upon these dead. No doubt they will listen and show mercy, but there is no one else here who will."

He attempted to speak, but the portion of the burial cloth that secured his jaw remained tight and wouldn't allow him to. He tried to raise pleading hands, but they were folded across his chest and bound. I said—

'Shout, Franz Adler; make the people sleeping in the far-off streets hear you and bring help. Shout—and don't waste time, because there isn't much left to waste. What, you can't? That's unfortunate; but it doesn't matter—it doesn't always bring help anyway. When you and your cousin killed a defenseless woman and child in that cabin in Arkansas—my wife and my child!—they screamed for help, you remember; but it didn't do any good; you remember that it didn't help at all, don't you? Your teeth are chattering—so why can't you shout? Use your hands to loosen the bandages—then you'll be able to. Ah, I see—your hands are tied, they can't help you. How strangely things happen again, after so many years; because my hands were tied that night, you remember? Yes, tied just like yours are now—how strange that is. I couldn't break free. It didn't cross your mind to untie me; it doesn't cross my mind to untie you. Quiet—! there's a late footstep. It's coming this direction. Listen, how close it is! You can count each footfall—one—two—three. There—it's right outside. Now's your chance! Shout, man, shout!—it's the only opportunity standing between you and eternity! Ah, you see you've waited too long—it's passed by. There—it's fading away. It's gone! Think about it—consider it—you've heard a human footstep for the final time. How strange it must be, to listen to such an ordinary sound as that, and know that you'll never hear its equal again.'

Oh, my friend, the suffering in that covered face was pure joy to witness! I came up with a new form of torment and put it to use—helping myself along with a small bit of false storytelling—

'That poor Kruger tried to save my wife and child, and I repaid his kindness with a grateful favor when the opportunity arose. I convinced him to steal from you, and a woman and I helped him escape, ensuring he got away safely.' A look of surprise and triumph flickered faintly through the pain on my victim's face. I felt troubled and uneasy. I said—

"So what happened—didn't he get away?"

A negative shake of the head.

"No? What happened, then?"

The satisfaction on the covered face became even more obvious. The man attempted to mumble some words but couldn't manage it; he tried to communicate something with his restricted hands but failed; he paused for a moment, then weakly tilted his head in a meaningful way toward the dead body that lay closest to him.

"Dead?" I asked. "Failed to escape?—caught in the act and shot?"

Negative shake of the head.

"How, then?"

Again the man attempted to do something with his hands. I observed carefully, but couldn't figure out what he was trying to do. I leaned closer and watched even more closely. He had turned his thumb around and was feebly hitting his chest with it. 'Ah—stabbed, is that what you mean?'

A confirming nod, accompanied by a ghostly smile of such strange wickedness, that it sent a flash of understanding through my sluggish mind, and I shouted—

"Did I stab him, thinking he was you? That blow was intended for no one else but you."

The dying scoundrel's confirming nod was as joyful as his weakening strength could manage to express.

"Oh, wretched, wretched me, to kill the compassionate soul who stood as a friend to my beloved children when they were defenseless, and would have rescued them if he could! Wretched, oh, wretched, wretched me!"

I thought I heard the muffled sound of a mocking laugh. I lifted my face from my hands and saw my enemy settling back onto his slanted board.

He took a remarkably long time to die. He possessed incredible vitality and an extraordinary constitution. Indeed, he spent quite a considerable time in the process. I brought over a chair and a newspaper, settled down beside him, and began reading. From time to time I took a drink of brandy. This was essential because of the cold weather. However, I also did it partly because I noticed that early on, whenever I reached for the bottle, he assumed I was going to offer him some. I read out loud: primarily fictional stories about people rescued from death's door and brought back to life and strength through a few spoonfuls of alcohol and a hot bath. Yes, he endured a lengthy, difficult death—lasting three hours and six minutes from the moment he rang his bell.

It is believed that throughout all eighteen years that have passed since the corpse-watch system was established, no shrouded occupant of the Bavarian morgues has ever rung its bell. Well, it is a harmless belief. Let it remain at that.

The cold from that room of death had seeped deep into my

bones. It brought back and took hold of the illness that had been troubling me, but which, until that night, had been gradually fading away. That man killed my wife and my child; and in three days he will have put me on his list as well. It doesn't matter—God! how wonderful the memory of it is!—I caught him trying to escape from his grave, and I forced him back into it.

After that night, I was bedridden for a week; but as soon as I could move around, I went to the morgue records and obtained the address of the house where Adler had died. It was a miserable boarding house. My thinking was that he would have naturally come into possession of Kruger's belongings, being his cousin; and I hoped to retrieve Kruger's watch, if possible. However, while I was ill, Adler's possessions had been sold and dispersed, all except for a few old letters and some worthless miscellaneous items. Nevertheless, through those letters, I tracked down a son of Kruger's, the only remaining relative. He is now a thirty-year-old man, a shoemaker by profession, and lives at No. 14 Konigstrasse, Mannheim—a widower with several young children. Without explaining my reasons to him, I have provided two-thirds of his financial support ever since.

Now, regarding that watch—it's amazing how strangely things work out! I tracked it all across Germany for more than a year, spending a lot of money and dealing with endless frustration; and finally I managed to get it. I got it and felt incredibly happy; I opened it up, only to discover there was nothing inside! Of course, I should have realized that piece of paper wouldn't have remained there all this time. Naturally I gave up on that ten thousand dollars then; I abandoned it completely and put it out of my thoughts: and quite sadly too, because I had wanted that money for Kruger's son.

Last night, when I finally accepted that I was going to die, I started preparing. I began burning all the unnecessary papers, and sure enough, from a stack of Adler's documents that I hadn't thoroughly examined before, out fell that piece of paper I had been searching for so long! I recognized it immediately. Here it is—I will translate it:

'Brick livery stable, stone foundation, middle of town, corner of Orleans and Market. Corner toward Court-house. Third stone, fourth row. Stick notice there, saying how many are to come.'

There—take it and keep it safe. Kruger explained that the stone could be removed, and that it was located in the north wall of the foundation, in the fourth row from the top, and was the third stone from the west. The money is hidden behind it. He said the final sentence was meant to deceive, designed to mislead anyone if the paper happened to fall into the wrong hands. It most likely served that purpose for Adler.

Now I want to ask that when you take your planned trip down the river, you will search for that hidden money and send it to Adam Kruger at the Mannheim address I mentioned. This will make him wealthy, and I will rest more peacefully in my grave knowing that I have done everything possible for the son of the man who attempted to rescue my wife and child—even though my hand unknowingly struck him down, when my heart's true desire would have been to protect and help him.

Chapter 32: The Disposal of a Bonanza

"That was Ritter's story," I told my two friends. A deep and striking silence followed, lasting quite a while; then both men burst into a rapid series of excited and amazed exclamations about the remarkable events in the tale; and this, combined with a steady stream of questions, continued until everyone was nearly out of breath. Then my friends started to calm down and retreat, with occasional bursts of commentary, into quiet and deep contemplation. For ten minutes, there was complete stillness.

Then Rogers spoke in a dreamy voice—

'Ten thousand dollars.'

Adding, after a considerable pause—

"Ten thousand. That's a lot of money."

The poet soon asked—

"Are you going to send it to him right away?"

"Yes," I said. "It's a strange question."

No response came. After a moment, Rogers asked hesitantly:

"All of it?—That is—I mean—"

"Absolutely, all of it."

I was about to say more, but I stopped—actually, I was stopped by a series of thoughts that suddenly arose in my mind. Thompson said something, but my attention had wandered, and I didn't catch his words. However, I did hear Rogers respond—

"Yes, that's how it appears to me. It should be more than enough, since I don't see that he has accomplished anything."

The poet then said—

'When you really think about it, it's more than enough. Just consider it—five thousand dollars! He couldn't possibly spend that much money in his entire lifetime! And it would harm him as well; it might even destroy him—you need to consider that possibility. Before long he would waste every last penny, close down his business, perhaps start drinking heavily, abuse his motherless children, fall into other destructive behaviors, and steadily go from bad to worse—'

"Yes, that's exactly right," Rogers interrupted passionately. "I've witnessed it countless times—yes, far more than a hundred instances. If you want to ruin a man like that, all you need to do is put money in his hands; simply place money in his possession, and that's all it takes. If it doesn't bring him down and strip away all his usefulness, along with his self-respect and everything else, then I don't understand human nature at all—isn't that true, Thompson?

And even if we were to give him just a third of it, why, in less than six months—"

"You'd better say less than six weeks!" I said, getting heated and interrupting. "Unless he had that three thousand dollars safely stored away where he couldn't get to it, he wouldn't last you six weeks any more than—"

'Of course he wouldn't,' Thompson said. 'I've edited books for those types of people, and the moment they get their hands on the royalty money—whether it's three thousand or two thousand dollars—'

"What business does that shoemaker have with two thousand dollars, I'd like to know?" Rogers interrupted passionately. "Here's a man who's probably completely satisfied right now, living there in Mannheim, surrounded by people of his own social class, eating his meals with the kind of appetite that only comes from hard, honest work, enjoying his simple life—honest, upright, pure in heart, and blessed! Yes, I say blessed! More blessed than all the countless people who dress in fine silk and go through the meaningless, artificial motions of social nonsense—but just put that temptation in front of him once! Just place fifteen hundred dollars before a man like that and tell him—"

"Fifteen hundred devils!" I shouted. "Five hundred would corrupt his values, destroy his work ethic, pull him into the bar, then into the gutter, then into the poorhouse, and from there to—"

"Why should we burden ourselves with this wrongdoing, gentlemen?" the poet interrupted with earnest and heartfelt appeal. "He is content where he is and as he is. Every feeling of honor, every feeling of compassion, every feeling of noble and holy goodwill warns us, pleads with us, demands that we leave him in peace. That is genuine friendship, that is authentic friendship. We could pursue other paths that would be more impressive; but none that would be so truly compassionate and sensible, you can be sure of it."

After talking more about it, it became clear that each of us secretly had some doubts about how we had handled this situation. It was obvious that we all believed we should send something to the poor shoemaker. We had a long and careful discussion about this matter, and we eventually decided to send him a chromo.

Well, now that everything appeared to be settled to everyone's satisfaction, a fresh problem emerged: it became clear that these two men were anticipating an equal three-way split of the money with me. That wasn't what I had in mind. I told them that if they received half of it to divide between themselves, they should count themselves fortunate. Rogers said—

"Who would have gotten any of it if it weren't for me? I threw out the first clue—without that, everything would have ended up with the shoemaker."

Thompson said he had been thinking about the exact same thing when Rogers first brought it up.

I shot back that the idea would have come to me soon enough on my own, without anyone's assistance. Perhaps I was slow when it came to thinking, but I was certain of myself.

This issue escalated into an argument, then turned into a physical fight, and both men ended up getting severely beaten. Once I had patched myself up as best I could, I climbed up to the hurricane deck feeling quite irritated. I discovered Captain McCord was there, and I spoke to him as pleasantly as my mood would allow—

"I've come to say goodbye, Captain. I want to go ashore at Napoleon."

"Go ashore where?"

'Napoleon.'

The captain laughed, but when he saw that I wasn't in a cheerful mood, he stopped and said—

"But are you serious?"

"Serious? I certainly am."

The captain looked up at the pilot-house and said—

"He wants to get off at Napoleon!"

'Napoleon?'

"That's what he says."

'Great Caesar's ghost!'

Uncle Mumford walked across the deck toward them. The captain said—

"Uncle, here's a friend of yours who wants to get off at Napoleon!"

'Well, by —?'

I said—

"Come on, what's all this fuss about? Can't a man go ashore at Napoleon if he wants to?"

"Well, for crying out loud, don't you know? There isn't any Napoleon anymore. Hasn't been for years and years. The Arkansas River broke through it, tore it all to pieces, and washed it into the Mississippi!"

'Swept the entire town away?—banks, churches, jails, newspaper offices, courthouse, theater, fire department, livery stable—everything?'

'Everything. Just a fifteen-minute job.' or something like that. They didn't leave a trace of it, not a single piece or fragment, except for the remains of a shack and one brick chimney. This boat is floating along right now where the very center of that town used to be; over there is the brick chimney—all that remains of Napoleon. These thick woods on the right used to be a mile behind the town. Look back behind you—upstream—now you're starting to recognize this area, aren't you?'

"Yes, I recognize it now. It's the most amazing thing I've ever heard of—by far the most incredible and unexpected."

Mr. Thompson and Mr. Rogers had arrived in the meantime, carrying their bags and umbrellas, and had quietly listened to the captain's report. Thompson placed a fifty-cent piece in my palm and spoke quietly—

"For my portion of the chromolithograph."

Rogers did the same.

Yes, it was truly remarkable to watch the Mississippi River flowing between empty shores, right over the exact location where I had once seen a large, proud town twenty years earlier. This was a town that served as the county seat for a major and significant county; a town with a large United States marine hospital; a town known for countless fights—with an inquest held every single day; a town where I had once known the most beautiful girl, and the most talented in the entire Mississippi Valley; a town where we had received the first printed news of the 'Pennsylvania's' tragic disaster twenty-five years ago; a town that no longer existed—completely consumed, disappeared, gone to feed the fish; nothing remained except a piece of a shack and a crumbling brick chimney!

Chapter 33: Refreshments and Ethics

Regarding Island 74, which sits close to the former Napoleon, a quirk of the river has seriously confused human laws and turned them into something meaningless and ridiculous. When the State of Arkansas received its charter, it controlled territory "to the center of the river"—an extremely unstable boundary. The State of Mississippi claimed territory "to the channel"—another shifting and unreliable boundary. Island 74 belonged to Arkansas. Eventually, a cut-off pushed this large island out of Arkansas, yet it didn't fall within Mississippi either. The "middle of the river" lies on one side of it, while the "channel" runs on the other. That's how I understand this problem. Whether I've gotten the details correct or incorrect, this fact remains: here sits this large and extremely valuable island of four thousand acres, cast out into the cold, belonging to neither one state nor the other; paying taxes to neither, owing loyalty to neither. One man owns the entire island, and by rights he is "the man without a country."

Island 92 belongs to Arkansas. The river shifted it over and connected it to Mississippi. A man set up a whiskey shop there without a Mississippi license, and made himself wealthy serving Mississippi customers under Arkansas protection, where no license was required in those days.

We drifted smoothly down the river in our typical solitude— rarely spotting a steamboat or any other vessel in motion. The landscape remained unchanged: endless stretches of nearly continuous forest extending along both riverbanks, wrapped in silent isolation. Occasionally we glimpsed one or two cabins positioned in small clearings on the bare, gray banks—structures that had once stood a quarter to half-mile closer to the water's edge but had been gradually dragged further and further inland as the shoreline collapsed. Take Pilcher's Point, for example, where locals told us the cabins had been relocated three hundred yards backward in just three months; yet the crumbling banks had already reached them again, forcing another retreat even further inland.

Napoleon didn't think much of Greenville, Mississippi, back in the day, but look—Napoleon has vanished into obscurity, while Greenville is thriving with energy and activity, making quite an impressive showing in the Valley. The town reportedly has three thousand residents and conducts annual business worth $2,500,000 in total trade. It's a town on the rise.

There was considerable discussion on the boat regarding the Calhoun Land Company, a business venture that is anticipated to produce beneficial outcomes. Colonel Calhoun, a grandson of the prominent politician, traveled to Boston and established a syndicate that acquired an extensive piece of land along the river in Chicot County, Arkansas—approximately ten thousand acres—

intended for cotton cultivation. The goal is to operate on a cash-only system: purchase directly from original sources and manage their own crops; provide their Black workers with supplies and essential goods at a minimal markup, around 8 or 10 percent; offer them decent living accommodations, and so forth, while encouraging them to save money and stay on the property. If this venture proves financially successful, which appears quite likely, they plan to open a bank in Greenville and offer loans at a reasonable interest rate—6 percent has been mentioned.

The problem up until now has been—I'm quoting comments from planters and steamboat operators—that the planters, while they owned the land, lacked liquid capital and had to use both their land and crops as collateral to keep their operations running. As a result, the commission merchant who provides the funding assumes some risk and charges high interest rates—typically 10 percent, plus 2½ percent for arranging the loan. The planter must also purchase his supplies through this same merchant, paying both commissions and markups. Then when he ships his harvest, the merchant adds his commissions, insurance costs, and other fees. So, all things considered, from beginning to end, the merchant's portion of that crop amounts to roughly 25 percent.[10]

A cotton planter's assessment of the typical profit margin for cotton farming in his area: One worker with a mule can cultivate ten acres of cotton, producing ten bales of cotton valued at approximately $500; the production costs amount to roughly $350; resulting in a net profit of $150, which equals $15 per acre. There's now also additional income from cotton seeds, which previously held little worth—especially in areas where significant transportation was required. In sixteen hundred pounds of raw

---

[10] 'But what can the State do where the people are under subjection to rates of interest ranging from 18 to 30 per cent., and are also under the necessity of purchasing their crops in advance even of planting, at these rates, for the privilege of purchasing all their supplies at 100 per cent. profit?'—Edward Atkinson.

cotton, four hundred pounds consist of lint, valued at approximately ten cents per pound; and twelve hundred pounds of seeds, worth $12 or $13 per ton. Perhaps in the future, even the cotton stems won't be discarded as waste. Mr. Edward Atkinson explains that each bale of cotton produces fifteen hundred pounds of stems, and these stems contain high levels of phosphate of lime and potash; when these stems are ground up and combined with silage or cotton-seed meal (which is too nutrient-dense to be used as animal feed in large amounts), this stem mixture creates an excellent feed that's rich in all the essential nutrients needed for producing milk, meat, and bone development. Until now, these stems have been viewed as nothing more than a troublesome waste product.

People complain that plantation owners have remained bitter toward their former slaves since the war ended. These owners maintain only cold business relationships with them, refusing to allow any personal feelings to enter the arrangement. They won't operate a store themselves to supply what the black workers need, which would protect the workers' money and make them both able and willing to remain on the plantation—creating a mutual benefit. Instead, they allow this opportunity to go to some enterprising Jewish merchant, who encourages the thoughtless black worker and his wife to purchase all kinds of unnecessary items on credit at inflated prices, month after month, with the credit secured against the worker's portion of the growing crop. By season's end, the worker's entire share belongs to the Jewish merchant, the worker finds himself further in debt, becomes discouraged, dissatisfied, and restless, and both he and the plantation owner suffer as a result. The worker will board a steamboat and leave for elsewhere, forcing the plantation owner to find a replacement who doesn't know him, doesn't care about him, will enrich the Jewish merchant for another season, and then follow the same path as his predecessor by taking a steamboat elsewhere.

It is hoped that the Calhoun Company will demonstrate, through its humane and protective treatment of its workers, that its approach is the most profitable for both the plantation owner and the laborers; and it is believed that widespread adoption of this method will then follow.

And when so many people are sharing their opinions, shouldn't the bartender have his say too? He's a thoughtful, observant man who never drinks; he works hard to earn his wages and would succeed if there were enough customers. He explains that people throughout Mississippi and Louisiana would rather send upriver to purchase vegetables than grow them themselves, and they'll come aboard at the docks to buy fruit from the bartender. He believes they 'don't know anything except cotton;' he's convinced they don't understand how to grow vegetables and fruit—'at least most of them don't.' He mentions that 'a Black person will go to H for a watermelon' ('H' is all I can find in the stenographer's notes—probably means Halifax, though that seems like quite a distance to travel for a watermelon). The bartender purchases watermelons for five cents upriver, transports them downstream, and sells them for fifty cents. 'Why does he create such fancy and colorful drinks for the Black workers on the boat?' Because they won't accept anything else. 'They want a large drink; it doesn't matter what you make it from, they want their money's worth. If you offer a Black person a simple shot of fifty-cent brandy for five cents—will he drink it? No. It's not big enough for him. But if you mix up a pint of all sorts of worthless ingredients and throw in some red coloring to make it attractive— red is the key element—and he wouldn't set down that glass even to attend a circus.'

All the bars on this Anchor Line are rented and owned by one company. They supply the liquor from their own establishment and hire the bartenders on salary. Good liquor? Yes, on some of the boats where there are the kind of passengers who want it and can afford to pay for it. On the other boats? No. Nobody but the deck hands and firemen drink it. "Brandy? Yes, I've got brandy, plenty of it; but you don't want any of it unless you've made your will." It isn't like it used to be in the old days. Back then everybody traveled by steamboat, everybody drank, and everybody bought drinks for everybody else. "Now most everybody goes by railroad, and the rest don't drink." In the old days the bartender owned the bar himself, "and was cheerful and sharp and talkative and all decked out in jewelry, and was the most stylish aristocrat on the boat; used to make $2,000 on a trip. A father who left his son a steamboat bar left him a fortune. Now he leaves him room and board; yes, and laundry, if one shirt per trip will do. Yes, indeed, times have changed. Why, do you know, on the main line of boats on the Upper Mississippi, they don't have any bar at all! Sounds like poetry, but it's the absolute truth."

Chapter 34: Tough Yarns

STACK island. I remembered Stack Island; I also remembered Lake Providence, Louisiana—the first town with a distinctly Southern appearance that you encounter when traveling downriver; it sits flat and low, with shade trees draped in ancient gray beards of Spanish moss; 'there's a peaceful, thoughtful, Sunday quality about the place,' Uncle Mumford observes with emotion—and with accuracy.

A Mr. H. provided some minor factual details about this region that I would have been reluctant to believe if I hadn't known him to be a steamboat mate. He was traveling with us as a passenger, lived in Arkansas City, and was heading to Vicksburg to rejoin his boat, a small Sunflower packet. He was a serious man who had earned a reputation for being remarkably unworldly, especially for someone who worked on the river. Among other things, he claimed that Arkansas had been harmed and held back by generations of exaggerated stories about the mosquitoes in the area. One might laugh, he said, and dismiss the matter as trivial; but when you examine the actual effects in terms of discouraging immigration and reducing property values, it was far from trivial, or something to be dismissed or mocked. These mosquitoes had been consistently portrayed as dangerous and uncontrollable; whereas 'the truth is, they are weak, small in size, timid to a fault, delicate'—and so on, and so on; you would have thought he was describing his own family. But while he was gentle regarding the Arkansas mosquitoes, he was harsh enough about the mosquitoes of Lake Providence to compensate—'those Lake Providence giants,' as he eloquently called them. He claimed that two of them could defeat a dog, and that four of them could pin down a man; and unless help arrived, they would kill him—'slaughter him,' as he put it. He mentioned in a seemingly offhand way—yet meaningful way—'the fact that the life policy in its simplest form is unknown in Lake Providence—they take out a mosquito policy besides.' He shared many extraordinary stories about those unruly insects. Among other tales, he said he had witnessed them attempting to vote. Noticing that this claim seemed to strain our belief considerably, he softened it somewhat: said he might have been wrong about that specific detail, but was certain he had seen them around the polling places 'campaigning.'

There was another passenger—a friend of H.'s—who supported the damning testimony against those mosquitoes and shared some thrilling encounters he'd experienced with them. The tales were quite large, simply quite large; yet Mr. H. kept interrupting with a cold, relentless "Hold on—subtract twenty-five percent of that; now continue;" or, "Hold on—you're making that too intense; tone it down, tone it down—you're putting a little too much decoration on your statements: always dress a fact in simple clothing, never in fancy dress;" or, "Excuse me, once again: if you're planning to pile anything more onto that statement, you'll need to get a couple of barges and pull the rest, because it's already drawing all the water that exists in the river; stick to facts—just stick to the plain facts; what these gentlemen want for a book is the absolute truth—isn't that right, gentlemen?" He explained privately that it was essential to monitor this man constantly and keep him under control; it wouldn't do to ignore this precaution, as he, Mr. H., "knew from bitter experience." He said, "I won't mislead you; he once told me such an enormous lie that it made my left ear swell up and expand so much that I actually couldn't see around it; it stayed that way for months, and people traveled miles to watch me use it as a fan."

Chapter 35: Vicksburg During the Trouble

We used to sail past the towering hill-city of Vicksburg as we traveled downstream, but that's no longer possible. A cut-off has transformed it into a landlocked town, just like what happened to Osceola, St. Genevieve, and several other places. There's now stagnant water—along with a large island—sitting in front of Vicksburg. When you travel down the river, you go along the far side of the island, then make a turn and approach the town from there; that works when the water level is high, but during low water you can't reach the town directly and have to dock some distance downstream from it.

Signs and scars still remain as reminders of Vicksburg's enormous wartime experiences: earthworks, trees damaged by cannonballs, cave shelters carved into the clay cliffs, and more. The caves served an important purpose during the six-week bombardment of the city from May 8 to July 4, 1863. They were used by civilians, primarily women and children, not as permanent homes but as places to escape to for safety when needed. They were simply holes and tunnels dug into the vertical clay banks, then branching into a Y-shape inside the hill. Life in Vicksburg during those six weeks was perhaps—but wait; here are some materials from which to recreate it:

The population consisted of twenty-seven thousand soldiers and three thousand civilians; the city was completely isolated from the outside world—solidly walled in, with gunboats blocking the front and soldiers with artillery batteries guarding the rear; therefore, there was no trade with the outside world; no coming and going; no farewell wishes for departing guests, no warm welcomes for arriving visitors; no printed pages of worldwide news to read at breakfast each morning—instead, there was a wearisome, dull absence of such material; consequently, there was also no rushing to watch steamboats appearing in the distance, smoking as they moved up or down the river and heading toward the town—because none arrived, the river remained empty and undisturbed; there was no hustle and bustle around the train station, no chaotic struggles with confused crowds of passengers by loud groups of cab drivers—everything was quiet there; flour cost two hundred dollars per barrel, sugar thirty, corn ten dollars per bushel, bacon five dollars per pound, rum one hundred dollars per gallon; other items were priced accordingly: as a result, there was no roaring and clattering of wagons and carriages racing through the streets; they had nothing to do among that small group of financially drained civilians; at three o'clock in the morning, there was silence; silence so complete that the rhythmic footsteps of a guard could be heard from what seemed an impossible distance; beyond the range of this solitary sound, the stillness was perhaps absolute: suddenly came earth-shaking thunder-crashes of artillery, the sky became webbed with crisscrossing red streaks trailing from soaring explosive shells, and a shower of iron fragments fell upon the city; fell upon the empty streets: streets that were no longer empty a moment later, but spotted with dim shapes of panicked women and children rushing from their homes and beds toward the cave shelters—encouraged by the grimly humorous soldiers, who shouted 'Rats, to your holes!' and laughed.

The cannon thunder roars, shells shriek and explode overhead, the iron rain pours down for one hour, two hours, three, possibly six, then stops; silence follows, but the streets remain empty; the quiet continues; gradually a head emerges from a cave here and there, looking around cautiously; as the silence persists, bodies follow heads, and exhausted, half-suffocated people gather together, stretch their stiff limbs, breathe in deep gulps of the welcome fresh air, chat with neighbors from the nearby cave; perhaps they wander home eventually, or take a stroll through the town, if the calm continues; and they will rush back to their holes again, soon enough, when the storm of war breaks out once more.

Since there are only three thousand of these cave-dwellers— just the population of a small village—wouldn't they get to know each other quite well after a week or two? So much so that whatever good or bad things happened to one person would matter to everyone else?

Those are the materials that history provides. From these sources, couldn't almost anyone recreate for themselves what life was like during that period in Vicksburg? Could you, having never lived through it, come closer to bringing that experience to life for another person who wasn't there than someone from Vicksburg who actually went through it? This seems unlikely; yet there are reasons why this might actually be possible. When someone takes their first sea voyage, it becomes an experience filled with countless striking new discoveries; these new experiences contrast so sharply with everything they've known before that they seem to permanently capture their imagination and memory. Through speaking or writing, they can help someone who has never been to sea relive that extraordinary and exciting journey with them; they can make that person see it all and feel it all. But what if they wait? What if they take ten voyages one after another—what happens then? The experience loses its vividness, its excitement, its element of surprise; it becomes ordinary. That person would have nothing to share that would stir a landlubber's heart.

Years ago, I spoke with a couple of Vicksburg civilians—a man and his wife. When allowed to tell their story in their own way, these people recounted it without passion, almost without interest.

A week of their amazing life there might have made them eloquent speakers forever; but they experienced six weeks of it, and that completely wore out the novelty; they became accustomed to being bombed out of their homes and into the ground; the situation became routine. After that, any chance of their conversations about it ever being remarkably interesting was lost. What the man said amounted to this:—

'Every day felt like Sunday. Seven Sundays each week—at least that's how it seemed to us. We had nothing to do, and time dragged on endlessly. Seven Sundays, and every single one of them was interrupted at some point, whether during the day or at night, by several hours of that terrible storm of fire and thunder and iron. At first, we used to rush for the shelters much faster than we did later on. The first time it happened, I forgot about the children, and Maria had to bring them both along. Once she was safely in the cave, she fainted. Two or three weeks later, when she was running for the shelters one morning through a shower of shells, a large shell exploded near her and covered her completely with dirt, and a piece of the metal tore away her hairpiece from the back of her head. Well, she actually stopped to retrieve that hairpiece before she continued on! She was already getting used to the situation, you see. We all became able to tell quite a bit about shells, and after that we didn't always take cover if it was just a light bombardment. We men would hang around and chat, and someone would say, 'There she goes!' and identify what type of shell it was by its sound, then continue talking—if there wasn't any danger from it. If a shell was exploding close above us, we stopped talking and stood perfectly still—uncomfortable, certainly, but it wasn't safe to move. When it finished, we resumed talking, assuming no one was hurt—perhaps saying, 'That was a big one!' or some other ordinary comment before we continued; or sometimes we would see a shell hovering high in the air above us. In that situation, every guy would quickly say, 'See you later, gentlemen!' and take off. Time and time again I watched groups of women strolling through the streets, looking as pleasant as could be, while keeping one eye turned upward watching the shells; and I've seen them stop when they were unsure about what a shell was going to do, and wait to be certain; and then they would either continue walking casually or rush for cover, depending on what they decided. Streets in some cities are littered with scraps of paper and various odds and ends scattered about. Ours weren't; they were covered with metal debris. Sometimes a person would collect all the iron fragments and unexploded shells in his area and stack them into a sort of monument in his front yard—sometimes weighing a ton. No glass remained; glass couldn't survive such bombardment; it was all shattered. The windows of houses were empty—they looked like eye sockets in a skull. Intact window panes were as rare as news.

'We held church services on Sundays. There weren't many people at first, but eventually we had pretty good attendance. I've watched the service pause for a moment, with everyone sitting quietly—no voices to be heard, creating an almost funeral-like atmosphere—made even more somber by the terrible booming and crashing sounds happening outside and above us; and soon, when someone could be heard again, the service would continue. Church organs and hymns mixed with bombardment sounds created a strangely powerful combination—at least at first.

Coming out of church one morning, we had an accident—the only one that occurred near me on a Sunday. I was just having a warm handshake with a friend I hadn't seen in a while, saying, 'Stop by our cave tonight, after the bombardment; we've gotten our hands on a pint of excellent wh—.' I was about to say whiskey, you understand, but a shell cut me off. A piece of it severed the man's arm and left it hanging in my hand. And do you know what memory is going to stick with me the longest, outlasting everything else, both small and large matters, I believe? It's the selfish thought I had at that moment: 'the whiskey is safe.' And yet, you know, it was somewhat understandable; because whiskey was as rare as diamonds, and we only had that small amount; we never got another taste throughout the entire siege.

Sometimes the caves were desperately overcrowded and constantly hot and stuffy. Occasionally a cave would have twenty or twenty-five people crammed into it, with no space for anyone to turn around and air so polluted that sometimes you couldn't even light a candle in there. A baby was born in one of those caves one night. Just imagine that—it was like giving birth inside a trunk.

Twice we had sixteen people crammed into our cave, and many times we sheltered a dozen. The air became pretty stifling in there. We always had eight people; eight was the normal number who belonged there. Hunger and misery and sickness and fear and grief, along with countless other hardships, weighed so heavily on them that none of them were ever truly themselves again after the siege ended. All of them died except three of us within a few years. One night a shell exploded right in front of the entrance and caused it to collapse, sealing us inside. Things got pretty hectic for a while as we dug our way out. Some of us nearly suffocated. After that experience, we created two separate openings—we should have thought of that from the beginning.

'Mule meat. No, we only resorted to that during the final day or two. Naturally it tasted good; everything tastes good when you're starving.

This man had maintained a diary for—six weeks? No, just the first six days. On the first day, he wrote eight densely packed pages; on the second, five pages; on the third, one page—written carelessly; on the fourth, three or four lines; a line or two on the fifth and sixth days; by the seventh day, he had given up the diary entirely; life in the terrible siege of Vicksburg had now become routine and ordinary.

The war history of Vicksburg contains more elements to captivate the general reader than any other river town. It overflows with variety, brims with incidents, and abounds in dramatic scenes. Vicksburg resisted longer than any other significant river town and witnessed warfare in every form, on both land and water—the siege, the mine, the assault, the repulse, the bombardment, sickness, captivity, famine.

The most beautiful of all the national cemeteries is located here. Above the grand entrance, this inscription appears:

"HERE REST IN PEACE 16,600 WHO DIED FOR THEIR COUNTRY IN THE YEARS 1861 TO 1865."

The grounds are beautifully positioned, sitting very high and offering a sweeping view of the surrounding land and river. They are elegantly designed with wide terraces, curving roads and walkways, and there is abundant decoration featuring semi-tropical plants and flowers. In one section stands a patch of original wild forest, left exactly as it naturally grew, making it perfectly enchanting. Everything about this cemetery shows the influence of the national Government. The Government's work is always notable for its quality, strength, completeness, and precision. The Government does its work properly from the start, and then maintains it carefully.

By winding roads—which were often cut so deep between

vertical walls that they resembled tunnels without roofs—we drove out a mile or two and visited the monument that stands on the site where General Pemberton surrendered Vicksburg to General Grant. Its metal construction will protect it from the scratches and chips that so damaged its predecessor, which was made of marble; however, the brick foundations are crumbling, and it will eventually collapse. It overlooks a scenic area of forested hills and valleys; and is quite attractive itself, being well covered in blooming wildflowers. The damaged remains of the marble monument have been moved to the National Cemetery.

On the road, about a quarter mile toward town, an elderly Black man proudly showed us an unexploded artillery shell that had been lying in his yard since the day it landed there during the siege.

"I was standing here, and the dog was standing here; the dog went for the shell, going to pick a fight with it; but I didn't; I said, 'Just make yourself at home here; stay still where you are, or bust up the place, just as you have a mind to, but I've got business out in the woods, I do!'"

Vicksburg is a city with significant commercial districts and attractive residential areas; it controls the trade along the Yazoo and Sunflower Rivers; it is expanding railroad lines in multiple directions through fertile farming regions, and it has a bright future ahead filled with prosperity and importance.

It seems that almost all river towns, both large and small, have decided they must rely primarily on railroads for prosperity and growth from now on. They are putting this belief into practice. All indications suggest that the next twenty years will bring significant changes to the Valley, with increased population and wealth, along with the intellectual progress and broadening of perspectives that naturally accompany such developments. However, if we can learn anything from history, these river towns will likely find ways, here and there, to hinder and slow down their own advancement.

During the era when steamboats dominated transportation, they held themselves back through a system of dock fees that was so poorly structured it essentially prevented what could be called small-scale commercial traffic in cargo and passengers. Boats faced such steep docking charges that they couldn't afford to stop for just one or two passengers or a small shipment of goods. Rather than encouraging trade to come to their communities, these towns actively and successfully drove it away. They could have enjoyed frequent boat service and affordable rates, but their approach made infrequent service and expensive rates inevitable. This was a strategy that reached—and still reaches—from New Orleans all the way to St. Paul.

We really wanted to take a trip up the Yazoo and Sunflower rivers—a fascinating area under normal circumstances, but even more captivating at that moment because the massive flooding could still be witnessed in full effect up there—but we would almost certainly have to wait a day or longer for a boat to New Orleans on our way back, so we had to abandon the plan.

Here's a story I heard on the boat that evening. I'm including it here simply because it's a good story, not because it fits with what I've been discussing—because it really doesn't. A passenger told it—a college professor—and it came up during a wide-ranging conversation that started with discussion about horses, moved on to astronomy, then to the lynching of gamblers in Vicksburg fifty years earlier, then to dreams and superstitions; and finally concluded, well past midnight, in an argument about free trade versus protectionism.

Chapter 36: The Professor's Story

This happened in my early years. I wasn't a college professor back then. I was a modest young land-surveyor, with the entire world spread out before me—ready to be surveyed, if anyone needed that kind of work done. I had signed a contract to survey a route for a major mining ditch in California, and I was traveling there by ship—a journey that would take three or four weeks. The vessel carried quite a few passengers, but I kept mostly to myself; I was passionate about reading and daydreaming, and I stayed away from conversations so I could enjoy these pursuits. Three professional gamblers were traveling on the ship—crude, disgusting men. I never spoke with them, but I couldn't avoid seeing them regularly, since they spent their days and nights gambling in a stateroom on the upper deck, and during my walks around the ship I frequently caught sight of them through their door, which they kept slightly open to let out the excess tobacco smoke and cursing. They created an unpleasant and detestable atmosphere, but I had no choice but to tolerate it, naturally.

There was another passenger who caught my attention quite a bit, since he seemed determined to befriend me, and I couldn't have avoided him without risking hurting his feelings, which I certainly didn't want to do. Moreover, there was something appealing about his rural simplicity and his radiant good nature. When I first encountered this Mr. John Backus, I guessed from his clothing and appearance that he was a livestock farmer from the remote areas of some western state—probably Ohio—and later when he shared details about his personal background and I learned that he was indeed a cattle rancher from inland Ohio, I was so satisfied with my own insight that I grew fonder of him for confirming my intuition.

He started walking with me every day after breakfast to help me take my daily walk; and over time, his constantly moving mouth had shared with me everything about his work, his future plans, his family, his relatives, his political views—basically everything that had to do with anyone named Backus, whether alive or dead. Meanwhile, I believe he had skillfully drawn out of me everything I knew about my profession, my people, my goals, my future plans, and myself. He was a kind and convincing person, and this demonstrated it perfectly; because I wasn't someone who usually talked about my personal affairs. I mentioned something about triangulation once; the impressive word caught his attention; he asked what it meant; I explained it; after that he politely and harmlessly ignored my actual name, and always called me Triangle.

What a passionate enthusiast he was when it came to cattle! Just hearing the mention of a bull or cow would make his eyes brighten and set his eloquent tongue in motion. As long as I was willing to walk and listen, he would continue walking and talking; he was familiar with every breed, he adored every breed, and he spoke of them all with genuine affection. I trudged along in silent misery while the cattle discussion continued; when I couldn't stand it any longer, I would skillfully introduce a scientific subject into our conversation; then my eyes would light up while his grew dim; my tongue would come alive while his fell silent; life became a source of joy for me and a cause of sorrow for him.

One day he said, speaking a bit hesitantly and with some uncertainty—

"Triangle, would you mind coming down to my cabin for a minute so we can have a brief conversation about something?"

I went with him immediately. When we arrived, he stuck his head out, looked carefully up and down the hallway, then shut the door and locked it. He sat down on the couch, and he said—

'I'm going to make a little proposition to you, and if it strikes you as favorable, it'll be a pretty good thing for both of us. You're not going out to California for fun, and neither am I—it's business, isn't that right? Well, you can do me a good turn, and I can do the

259

same for you, if we're willing. I've worked and scraped and saved for quite a few years, and I've got it all here.' He unlocked an old hair trunk, pushed aside a jumble of worn clothes, and brought a short thick bag into view for a moment, then buried it again and relocked the trunk. Lowering his voice to a careful whisper, he continued, 'It's all there—a full ten thousand dollars in gold coins; now this is my little idea: What I don't know about raising cattle isn't worth knowing. There's plenty of money in it, in California. Well, I know, and you know, that all along a line that's being surveyed, there are little pieces of land that they call "gores," that go to the surveyor free of charge for nothing. All you have to do, on your end, is to survey in such a way that the "gores" will fall on good rich land, then you turn them over to me, I stock them with cattle, the cash rolls in, I pay out your share of the money regularly, right along, and—'

I felt bad about crushing his bright enthusiasm, but there was no way around it. I cut him off and said sternly—

"I'm not that type of surveyor. Let's change the subject, Mr. Backus."

It was heartbreaking to witness his bewilderment and listen to his clumsy, embarrassed apologies. I felt just as troubled as he did—particularly since he appeared completely unaware that his suggestion had been inappropriate. So I quickly moved to comfort him and help him forget his blunder by engaging in an enthusiastic discussion about livestock and meat processing. We were anchored at Acapulco, and as we stepped onto the deck, we were fortunate to see the crew starting to lift cattle aboard using rope slings. Backus's sadness disappeared immediately, and with it any recollection of his recent error.

"Just look at that!" he exclaimed. "My goodness, Triangle, what would they say about this back in Ohio? Wouldn't their eyes pop out of their heads seeing them handled like that? They sure would!"

All the passengers had come up on deck to watch—even the gamblers—and Backus was familiar with every one of them, having bothered them all with his favorite subject. As I walked away, I noticed one of the gamblers coming over to speak with him; then another one joined them; then the third. I stopped; waited; observed; the conversation went on among the four men; it became more intense; Backus slowly started backing away; the gamblers followed him, staying right beside him. I felt uneasy. But then, as they walked past me, I heard Backus speaking with a tone of harassed irritation—

"But it's no use, gentlemen; I tell you again, as I've told you half a dozen times before, I wasn't raised to it, and I'm not going to risk it."

I felt relieved. "His clear thinking will be enough to protect him," I told myself.

During the two-week journey from Acapulco to San Francisco, I witnessed the gamblers having serious conversations with Backus on multiple occasions, and at one point I offered him a subtle warning. He laughed quietly and said—

"Oh, absolutely! They follow me around quite a bit—they want me to play a little, just for fun, they say—but good heavens, if my family has told me once to watch out for that kind of person, they've told me a thousand times, I'm sure."

Eventually, we were getting close to San Francisco. It was a dark, ugly night with strong winds, though the sea wasn't too rough. I was alone on deck. Around ten o'clock, I headed below. A figure emerged from the gamblers' den and vanished into the darkness. I felt a jolt of shock because I was certain it was Backus. I rushed down the companionway, searched for him everywhere, couldn't locate him, then hurried back to the deck just in time to spot him as he went back into that damned den of thieves. Had he finally given in? I was afraid he had. What had he gone below for? His bag of money? Quite possibly. I approached the door, filled with dread. It was slightly open, and I peered inside and witnessed a scene that made me deeply regret not paying attention to saving my poor friend from the countryside, instead of wasting my time reading and daydreaming. He was gambling. Even worse, they were feeding him champagne, and it was already starting to affect him. He complimented the 'cider,' as he called it, and said that now that he'd gotten a taste of it, he almost thought he would drink it even if it were hard liquor, it was so delicious and better than anything he had ever encountered before. Secret smiles passed between the scoundrels at this, and they refilled all the glasses, and while Backus honestly emptied his completely, they pretended to do the same but poured the wine over their shoulders.

I couldn't stand watching what was happening, so I walked ahead and attempted to focus on the ocean and the sounds of the wind. However, my restless mind kept pulling me back every fifteen minutes, and each time I witnessed Backus drinking his wine honestly and completely while the others were discarding theirs. It was the most agonizing night I had ever endured.

The only hope I had was that we might reach our harbor quickly—that would end the game. I did everything I could to help the ship along with my prayers. Finally we came rushing through the Golden Gate, and my heart jumped with joy. I hurried back to that door and looked inside. Unfortunately, there was little reason for hope—Backus's eyes were heavy and bloodshot, his sweaty face was bright red, his speech was slurred and garbled, his body swayed drunkenly with the rocking motion of the ship. He emptied another glass completely while the cards were being dealt.

He took his hand, looked at it, and his lifeless eyes brightened for a moment. The gamblers noticed this and revealed their satisfaction through barely visible gestures.

"How many cards?"

"None!" said Backus.

One villain—named Hank Wiley—threw away one card, while the others each discarded three. The betting started. Up until now the bets had been small—a dollar or two; but Backus opened with an eagle this time, Wiley paused for a moment, then 'matched it' and 'raised it ten dollars.' The other two folded their hands.

Backus went twenty better. Wiley said—

'I see that, and I'll raise you a hundred!' then smiled and reached for the money.

"Leave it be," said Backus, with drunken seriousness.

"What! Do you mean to tell me you're going to cover it?"

"Cover it? Well, I think I can—and I'll put another hundred on top of that, too."

He reached into his overcoat and pulled out the money that was needed.

"Oh, so that's your little game, is it? I see your raise, and I'll raise it five hundred!" said Wiley.

'Five hundred more,' said the foolish bull-driver, and pulled out the money and threw it onto the pile. The three conspirators barely attempted to hide their excitement.

All diplomacy and pretense were abandoned now, and the harsh outbursts came rapidly one after another, while the golden pile grew taller and taller. Finally, ten thousand dollars lay visible before them. Wiley threw a bag of coins onto the table and spoke with sarcastic tenderness—

"Five thousand dollars better, my friend from the countryside—what do you say now?"

"I'm calling you!" Backus declared, throwing his golden shot-bag onto the pile. "What cards are you holding?"

'Four kings, you damn fool!' and Wiley threw down his cards and surrounded the stakes with his arms.

"Four aces, you fool!" roared Backus, aiming his loaded revolver at the man. "I'm a professional gambler myself, and I've been waiting to catch you cheaters this entire trip!"

The anchor dropped with a thunderous crash, and the long journey had come to an end.

Well—well, it's a sad world. One of the three gamblers was Backus's friend. He was the one who dealt those fateful hands. According to an agreement with the two victims, he was supposed to give Backus four queens, but unfortunately, he didn't.

A week later, I ran into Backus—dressed in the latest fashion—on Montgomery Street. He said cheerfully as we were saying goodbye—

"Oh, by the way, you don't need to worry about those cattle. I don't actually know anything about livestock, except what I managed to learn during a week's training in Jersey just before we set sail. My knowledge of cattle and my enthusiasm for them have served their purpose—I won't need them anymore."

The next day, we reluctantly said goodbye to the 'Gold Dust' and her officers, hoping to see that boat and all those officers again someday. This was something that fate would make tragically impossible!

Chapter 37: The End of the 'Gold Dust'

FOR, three months later, on August 8, while I was writing one of the previous chapters, the New York newspapers delivered this telegram—

A TERRIBLE DISASTER.

SEVENTEEN PEOPLE KILLED BY AN EXPLOSION ON THE STEAMBOAT 'GOLD DUST.'
NASHVILLE,
Aug. 7.—A dispatch from Hickman, Ky., says—

The steamboat "Gold Dust" had her boilers explode at three o'clock today, right after departing from Hickman. Forty-seven people suffered burns from scalding water and seventeen are unaccounted for. The vessel was brought to shore in the calm water just upstream from the town, and thanks to the efforts of local residents, the cabin passengers, ship's officers, and some of the crew and deck passengers were brought to safety and taken to hotels and private homes. At one point, twenty-four of the wounded were being treated in Holcomb's general store, where they received complete care before being moved to more comfortable locations.

A list of names followed, which showed that among the seventeen people who died, one was the bartender; and among the forty-seven who were injured, the casualties included the captain, first mate, second mate, and the second and third clerks; also Mr. Lem S. Gray, the pilot, and several crew members.

In response to a private telegram, we discovered that none of them had been seriously injured, with the exception of Mr. Gray. Letters that arrived later confirmed this information and indicated that Mr. Gray was recovering and would make a full recovery. Subsequent letters were less optimistic about his condition, and eventually we received one that announced his death. He was a good man, an exceptionally friendly and honorable person who deserved a more merciful end.

Chapter 38: The House Beautiful

We boarded a steamboat from Cincinnati bound for New Orleans; or we could say we boarded a Cincinnati steamboat—both ways of saying it are correct; the first version is how people in the East would phrase it, while the second is the Western way of expressing it.

Mr. Dickens refused to accept that the Mississippi steamboats were 'magnificent,' or that they were 'floating palaces'—

descriptions that had always been used to describe them; descriptions that didn't even fully capture the admiration that people felt when they saw them.

Mr. Dickens's position was perhaps unshakeable; the people's position was definitely unshakeable. If Mr. Dickens was comparing these boats with the crown jewels, or with the Taj Mahal, or with the Matterhorn, or with some other priceless or amazing thing he had witnessed, they weren't magnificent—he was correct. The people compared them with what they had experienced, and when measured this way, when judged by this standard, the boats were magnificent—the word was accurate, it wasn't too strong at all. The people were just as correct as Mr. Dickens was. The steamboats were more impressive than anything on land. When compared with fine homes and top-quality hotels in the Valley, they were undoubtedly magnificent, they were 'palaces.' To a handful of people living in New Orleans and St. Louis, they might not have been magnificent, perhaps not palaces, but to the vast majority of those populations, and to all the people living along both riverbanks between Baton Rouge and St. Louis, they were palaces. They matched what citizens imagined magnificence to be, and they fulfilled that vision completely.

Every town and village along that enormous stretch of double river-frontage had its finest home, grandest residence, mansion— the dwelling of its wealthiest and most prominent citizen. It's simple to describe: large grassy yard, with a picket fence painted white—in decent condition; brick walkway from gate to door; big, square, two-story frame house, painted white and featuring a portico like a Greek temple—with this difference, that the impressive fluted columns and Corinthian capitals were a pitiful fake, being made of white pine, and painted; iron door knocker; brass doorknob—tarnished, from lack of polishing. Inside, an uncarpeted hallway, of smooth boards; opening from it, a parlor, fifteen feet by fifteen—in some cases five or ten feet larger; ingrain carpet; mahogany center table; lamp on it, with green paper shade—resting on what looked like a gridiron, made of brightly colored yarns, by the young ladies of the house, and called a lamp-mat; several books, stacked and arranged, with mechanical precision, according to an inherited and unchanging system; among them, Tupper, heavily marked with pencil; also, 'Friendship's Offering,' and 'Affection's Wreath,' with their sentimental nonsense illustrated in fading mezzotints; also, Ossian; 'Alonzo and Melissa:' perhaps 'Ivanhoe:' also 'Album,' filled with original 'poetry' of the you-have-wounded-the-spirit-that-loved-you variety; two or three moralistic works—'Shepherd of Salisbury Plain,' etc.; current issue of the proper and harmless Godey's 'Lady's Book,' with painted fashion-plate of wax-figure women with identical mouths—lips and eyelids the same size—each five-foot woman with a two-inch wedge protruding from under her dress and pretending to be half of her foot. Polished airtight stove (new and dangerous invention), with pipe running through a board which blocks up the abandoned good old fireplace. On each end of the wooden mantel, over the fireplace, a large basket of peaches and other fruits, life-size, all made in plaster, crudely, or in wax, and painted to look like the real thing—which they don't. Over center of mantel, engraving—Washington Crossing the Delaware; on the wall by the door, copy of it done in bold crewel work by one of the young ladies—work of art which would have made Washington think twice about crossing, if he could have predicted what use was going to be made of it. Piano—disguised kettle—with music, bound and loose, stacked on it, and on a stand nearby: Battle of Prague; Bird Waltz; Arkansas Traveler; Rosin the Bow; Marseilles Hymn; On a Lone Barren Isle (St. Helena); The Last Link is Broken; She wore a Wreath of Roses the Night when last we met; Go, forget me, Why should Sorrow o'er that Brow a Shadow fling; Hours there were to Memory Dearer; Long, Long Ago; Days of Absence; A Life on the Ocean Wave, a Home on the Rolling Deep; Bird at Sea; and spread open on the rack, where the melancholy singer has left it, ro-holl on, silver moo-hoon, guide the trav-el-lerr his way, etc. Leaning thoughtfully against the piano, a guitar—guitar capable of playing the Spanish Fandango by itself, if you give it a start. Wild work of art on the wall—religious motto, made on the premises, sometimes in colored yarns, sometimes in dried grasses: ancestor of the 'God Bless Our Home' of modern commerce. Framed in black moldings on the wall, other works of art, conceived and created on the premises, by the young ladies; being stark black-and-white crayons; landscapes, mostly: lake, solitary sailboat, fossilized clouds, prehistoric trees on shore, coal-black precipice; name of perpetrator prominent in the corner. Lithograph, Napoleon Crossing the Alps. Lithograph, The Grave at St. Helena. Steel-plates, Trumbull's Battle of Bunker Hill, and the Sally from Gibraltar. Copper-plates, Moses Smiting the Rock, and Return of the Prodigal Son. In big gilt frame, misrepresentation of the family in oil: papa holding a book ('Constitution of the United States'); guitar leaning against mamma, blue ribbons fluttering from its neck; the young ladies, as children, in slippers and scalloped pantalettes, one embracing toy horse, the other charming kitten with ball of yarn, and both smiling sweetly up at mamma, who smiles back. These people all fresh, raw, and red—apparently skinned. Opposite, in gilt frame, grandpa and grandma, at thirty and twenty-two, rigid, old-fashioned, high-collared, puff-sleeved, staring palely out from a background of solid Egyptian night. Under a glass French clock dome, large bouquet of stiff flowers made in corpse-white wax. Pyramid-shaped whatnot in the corner, the shelves occupied mainly with bric-a-brac of the period, arranged with an eye to best effect: shell, with the Lord's Prayer carved on it; another shell—of the long-oval type, narrow, straight opening, three inches long, running from end to end—portrait of Washington carved on it; not well done; the shell had Washington's mouth, originally—artist should have worked with that. These two are souvenirs of the long-ago honeymoon trip to New Orleans and the French Market. Other bric-a-brac: California 'specimens'—quartz, with gold bump attached; old Guinea-gold locket, with circle of ancestral hair in it; Indian arrowheads, of flint; pair of beaded moccasins, from uncle who crossed the Plains; three 'alum' baskets of various colors— being skeleton-frame of wire, covered with cubes of crystallized alum in the rock-candy style—works of art which were created by the young ladies; their twins and copies to be found upon all whatnots in the land; collection of dried bugs and butterflies pinned to a card; painted toy-dog, seated upon bellows-attachment—drops its lower jaw and squeaks when pressed upon; sugar-candy rabbit—limbs and features blended together, not clearly defined; pewter presidential-campaign medal; miniature cardboard wood-sawyer, to be attached to the stove-pipe and operated by the heat; small Napoleon, made in wax; spread-open daguerreotypes of dim children, parents, cousins, aunts, and friends, in all poses but natural ones; no columned portico at back, and manufactured landscape stretching away in the distance—that came later, with the photograph; all these vague figures lavishly chained and ringed—metal indicated and confirmed beyond doubt by stripes and splashes of bright gold bronze; all of them too much combed, too much dressed up; and all of them uncomfortable in stiff Sunday-clothes of a style which the viewer cannot imagine could ever have been in fashion; husband and wife generally grouped together—husband sitting, wife standing, with hand on his shoulder—and both preserving, all these fading years, some traceable effect of the daguerreotypist's cheerful 'Now smile, if you please!' Mounted over whatnot—place of special holiness— an atrocity in watercolor, done by the young niece that came on a visit long ago, and died. Pity, too; for she might have regretted this in time. Horsehair chairs, horsehair sofa which keeps sliding from under you. Window shades, of oil cloth, with milkmaids and ruined castles stenciled on them in harsh colors. Lambrequins hanging from gaudy boxes of beaten tin, gilded. Bedrooms with rag carpets; bedsteads of the 'corded' type, with a sag in the middle, the cords needing tightening; musty feather-bed—not aired often enough; cane-seat chairs, splint-bottomed rocker; looking-glass on wall, school-slate size, veneered frame; inherited bureau; wash-bowl and pitcher, possibly—but not certainly; brass candlestick, tallow candle, snuffers. Nothing else in the room. Not a bathroom in the house; and no visitor likely to come along who has ever seen one.

That was the home of the most important citizen, stretching all the way from the outskirts of New Orleans to the border of St. Louis. When he boarded a large, magnificent steamboat, he entered a new and wonderful world: smokestacks designed to look like a spray of feathers—and perhaps painted red; the pilot house, hurricane deck, and boiler-deck railings, all decorated with white wooden ornamental work in elaborate designs; golden acorns crowning the derricks; golden deer antlers above the large bell; a colorful symbolic painting on the paddle-box, possibly; a spacious boiler-deck, painted blue, and equipped with Windsor armchairs; inside, a seemingly endless snow-white cabin; porcelain handles and oil paintings on every stateroom door; curved patterns of decorative work highlighted with gold, extending overhead throughout the entire converging view; large chandeliers positioned regularly, each one like an April shower of sparkling glass drops; beautiful rainbow light streaming everywhere from the colored glass of the skylights; the entire space forming an extended, magnificent tunnel, a dazzling and deeply satisfying sight! In the ladies' cabin, a pink and white Wilton carpet, as soft as pudding, and enhanced with a stunning pattern of enormous flowers. Then there was the Bridal Chamber—the person who came up with that concept was still alive and unpunished at that time—a Bridal Chamber whose elaborate nonsense was bound to overwhelm the now weakening mind of that cheering citizen. Every stateroom contained a pair of comfortable clean beds, and perhaps a mirror and a compact closet; and sometimes there was even a washbasin and water pitcher, and part of a towel that could be distinguished from mosquito netting by someone with experience—though usually these items were missing, and the passengers in rolled-up sleeves washed themselves at a long line of fixed basins in the barbershop, where there were also shared towels, shared combs, and shared soap.

Take the steamboat I just described, and you have it at its highest and finest, most pleasing, comfortable, and satisfactory condition. Now cover it with a layer of old and stubborn dirt, and you have the Cincinnati steamer I mentioned earlier. Not all over—only inside; because it was well-managed in all departments except the steward's.

But clean that boat and give her a fresh coat of paint, and she would be nearly identical to the most praised boat from the prosperous days of the past: for the design and construction of western steamboats has remained unchanged; likewise, steamboat furnishings and decorations have stayed the same.

Chapter 39: Manufactures and Miscreants

In the Vicksburg area, where the river once twisted and turned like a corkscrew, it now flows in a relatively straight path due to artificial cut-offs that shortened a former seventy-mile stretch to just thirty-five miles. This transformation displaced Vicksburg's neighboring community, Delta, Louisiana, pushing it inland and bringing its days as a river town to an end. A massive sandbar now covers the entire area where the town once faced the river, densely populated with young trees that will eventually grow into a thick forest, completely concealing the displaced town from view.

In time we passed Grand Gulf and Rodney, both famous from the war, and arrived at Natchez, the final beautiful hill city—since Baton Rouge, which still lay ahead, sits not on a hill but merely on elevated ground. The renowned Natchez-under-the-hill hasn't changed much in twenty years; in its outward appearance—based on accounts from the long line of foreign visitors who came before—it hasn't altered in sixty years, remaining small, scattered, and run-down. During the old keelboat days and early steamboat era, it had a terrible moral reputation—there was plenty of drinking, partying, brawling, and violence among the river's rough crowd back then. However, Natchez-on-top-of-the-hill is appealing; it has always been appealing. Even Mrs. Trollope (1827) was forced to acknowledge its beauty:

At one or two points, the monotonous flat landscape is broken up by bluffs, which is what they call the brief stretches of elevated terrain. The town of Natchez sits beautifully on one of these high areas. The striking contrast between its vibrant green hill and the gloomy line of dark forest extending in all directions, the lush growth of pawpaw, palmetto and orange trees, the rich variety of fragrant flowers that bloom there, all combine to make it look like an oasis in the desert. Natchez marks the northernmost point where oranges can ripen outdoors or survive the winter without protection. Apart from this delightful location, I found all the small towns and villages we passed to look extremely miserable.

Natchez, just like its neighboring river towns both near and distant, now has railroads and continues to expand them—extending these lines in every direction into the wealthy surrounding areas that naturally serve as its tributaries. Similar to Vicksburg and New Orleans, the city operates its own ice factory, producing thirty tons of ice daily. During my era in Vicksburg and Natchez, ice was considered a luxury item; only wealthy people could afford it. Today, however, anyone and everyone can obtain it. I toured one of the ice manufacturing facilities in New Orleans to observe what the polar regions might resemble when transported to the edge of tropical territory. Yet there was nothing particularly remarkable about the facility's appearance. It was simply a large building containing some harmless steam equipment at one end and several substantial porcelain pipes extending throughout the space. Actually, they weren't porcelain—they only appeared to be; they were made of iron, but the ammonia flowing through them had covered them with solid, milk-white ice as thick as a person's hand. The ice should have melted, since winter clothing wasn't necessary in that environment, but it remained frozen because the interior of the pipes was extremely cold.

Embedded in the floor were countless tin boxes, each measuring one foot square and two feet in length, with open tops. These containers held clear water, and around each box, salt and other appropriate materials were packed. Additionally, ammonia gases were somehow applied to the water through a process that will forever remain mysterious to me, since I couldn't grasp how it worked. As the water in the boxes slowly froze, workers would occasionally stir it once or twice with a stick—I believe this was to release air bubbles. Other workers continuously removed boxes whose contents had completely frozen solid. They would quickly dip each box into a vat of boiling water to free the ice block from its tin container, then slide the block onto a platform cart, making it ready for sale. These large blocks were firm, solid, and crystal-clear. Some of them contained big bouquets of fresh and vibrant tropical flowers frozen inside; others held beautiful silk-dressed French dolls and other attractive items. These blocks were meant to stand upright in platters at the center of dining tables to cool the tropical air while also serving as decoration, since the flowers and objects trapped within them could be viewed as if through clear glass. I learned that this factory could sell its ice by wagon throughout New Orleans, even in the smallest household quantities, at six or seven dollars per ton while still earning a decent profit. Given this situation, there's definitely opportunity for ice factories in the North, because we don't get ice at such favorable prices there unless someone purchases at least three hundred and fifty pounds in a single delivery.

The Rosalie Yarn Mill in Natchez has the capacity to operate 6,000 spindles and 160 looms, and it employs 100 workers. The Natchez Cotton Mills Company started its operations four years ago in a two-story building measuring 50 by 190 feet, equipped with 4,000 spindles and 128 looms, with a capital investment of $105,000, all funded by local investors in the town. Two years later, the same shareholders increased their capital to $225,000 and added a third story to the mill while extending its length to 317 feet, along with additional machinery that expanded the capacity to 10,300 spindles and 304 looms. The company currently employs 250 workers, many of whom are residents of Natchez. The mill processes 5,000 bales of cotton each year and produces the highest standard quality of brown shirtings, sheetings, and drills, manufacturing 5,000,000 yards of these products annually.[11] It operates as a close corporation with stock valued at $5,000 per share, though none is available on the market.

The changes in the Mississippi River are dramatic and remarkable, yet they were to be expected; however, I wasn't expecting to live long enough to see Natchez and these other river towns transform into manufacturing powerhouses and railroad hubs.

Speaking of manufacturing brings to mind a conversation about that subject that I heard—or rather, overheard—while aboard the Cincinnati steamboat. I woke up from a restless sleep with a jumbled mix of voices ringing in my ears. I listened carefully—two men were talking; their topic seemed to be the great flood. I peered out through the open transom window. The

---

[11] New Orleans Times-Democrat, 26 Aug, 1882.

two men were having a late breakfast, seated across from each other with no one else nearby. They wrapped up their discussion about the flood with just a few remarks—having clearly used it simply as a conversation starter and a way to get acquainted—then they shifted to business matters. It quickly became clear that they were traveling salesmen—one from Cincinnati, the other from New Orleans. They were sharp, quick-moving men with rapid speech; money was their deity, and figuring out how to earn it was their faith.

'Now regarding this product,' said Cincinnati, cutting into what appeared to be butter and holding out a piece of it on his knife blade, 'it's from our company; look at it—smell it—taste it. Apply whatever test you want to it. Take all the time you need—no rush—be thorough about it. There now—what's your verdict? It's butter, isn't it. Not by a long shot—it's oleomargarine! Yes, sir, that's exactly what it is—oleomargarine. You can't distinguish it from butter; by George, even an expert can't tell the difference. It's from our company. We supply most of the boats in the West; there's barely a pound of butter on any of them. We are moving right along—racing right along is more accurate. We are going to capture that entire market. Yes, and the hotel business, too. You are going to witness the day, very soon, when you won't be able to find an ounce of butter to save your life, in any hotel in the Mississippi and Ohio Valleys, except in the largest cities. Why, we are producing oleomargarine now by the thousands of tons. And we can sell it so incredibly cheap that the whole country will have to accept it—can't avoid it you see. Butter doesn't stand a chance—there's no possibility for competition. Butter has had its time—and from now on, butter gets pushed aside. There's more profit in oleomargarine than—why, you can't imagine the volume of business we handle. I've stopped in every town from Cincinnati to Natchez; and I've sent home large orders from every single one of them.'

And so on and so forth, for ten minutes more, in the same passionate manner. Then New Orleans spoke up and said—

"Yes, it's an excellent imitation, that's for sure; but it's not the only high-quality one out there. For example, they make olive oil from cottonseed oil these days, so you can't tell the difference between them."

"Yes, that's true," Cincinnati replied, "and it was an excellent business for a while. They shipped it overseas and brought it back from France and Italy, with the United States customs stamp on it to certify it as authentic, and there was tremendous money to be made; but France and Italy ended the scheme—naturally they would. They imposed such a heavy tariff that cottonseed olive oil couldn't handle the increase; we had to shut down and give up."

"Oh, it did, did it? You wait here a minute."

Goes to his cabin, brings back a couple of long bottles, and pulls out the corks—says:

'There you go, smell them, taste them, examine the bottles, check out the labels. One of them is from Europe, the other has never left this country. One is European olive oil, the other is American cottonseed olive oil. Can you tell them apart? Of course you can't. Nobody can. People who want to can go to the expense and trouble of shipping their oils to Europe and back—that's their choice; but our company knows a trick that's worth six times that. We produce the whole thing—right from the start—in our factory in New Orleans: labels, bottles, oil, everything. Well, no, not the labels: we've been buying those overseas—getting them dirt cheap there. You see, there's just one tiny little speck, essence, or whatever it is, in a gallon of cottonseed oil that gives it a smell, or a flavor, or something—remove that, and you're all set—it's perfectly easy then to turn the oil into any kind of oil you want, and there isn't anyone who can tell the real from the fake. Well, we know how to get that one little particle out—and we're the only company that does. And we produce an olive oil that is just simply perfect—completely undetectable! We're doing fantastic business, too—as I could easily show you with my order book for this trip. Maybe you'll supply everyone's bread pretty soon, but we'll provide cottonseed oil for their salads from the Gulf to Canada, and that's a sure thing.'

Cincinnati beamed with admiration. The two rogues exchanged business cards and stood up. As they walked away from the table, Cincinnati said—

"But you need customs stamps, don't you? How do you handle that?"

I didn't hear the answer.

We sailed past Port Hudson, the site of two of the most devastating events of the war—the nighttime naval battle fought there between Farragut's fleet and the Confederate shore batteries on April 14th, 1863; and the unforgettable ground battle two months afterward, which went on for eight hours—eight hours of extraordinarily intense and relentless combat—and concluded, ultimately, with the defeat of the Union troops amid heavy casualties.

Chapter 40: Castles and Culture

BATON ROUGE was adorned with flowers, like a bride—no, far more than that; like a greenhouse. We had reached the true South now—no modifications, no compromises, no halfway measures. The magnolia trees on the Capitol grounds were beautiful and fragrant, with their thick, rich leaves and enormous snowball-like blooms. The flower's fragrance is very sweet, but you need some distance from it because it's so intense. They don't make good bedroom flowers—they could overwhelm someone in their sleep. We were definitely in the South at last; this is where the sugar region starts, and the plantations—enormous green expanses, with sugar mills and slave quarters grouped together in the middle distance—stretched out before us. Above us blazed a tropical sun, and the air was thick with tropical heat.

And at this point, the pilot's paradise also begins: a wide river stretching from here to New Orleans, with plenty of water from shore to shore, and no sandbars, snags, fallen trees, or shipwrecks blocking his path.

Sir Walter Scott is likely responsible for the Capitol building; it's impossible to imagine that this small fake castle would have ever been constructed if he hadn't driven people to madness a few generations back with his medieval romances. The South still hasn't recovered from the weakening influence of his books. Admiration for his fantastical heroes and their absurd chivalrous deeds and romantic foolishness continues to exist here, in an environment where you can already sense the healthy and practical nineteenth-century aroma of cotton mills and trains; and remnants of its pompous language and other empty nonsense persist alongside it. It's sad enough that a whitewashed castle with towers and decorative features—materials completely fake inside and out, pretending to be something they're not—was ever constructed in this otherwise respectable location; but it's far more tragic to witness this architectural lie being restored and preserved in our time, when it would have been so simple to let dynamite complete what a merciful fire started, and then use this restoration money to build something authentic.

Baton Rouge doesn't have exclusive rights to imitation castles, though, and it certainly doesn't have a monopoly on them. Here's a picture from an advertisement for the 'Female Institute' in Columbia, Tennessee. The following comment comes from that same advertisement—

The Institute building has long been celebrated as an outstanding example of impressive and beautiful architecture. Visitors are delighted by how much it resembles the ancient castles found in songs and stories, complete with its towers, walls topped with turrets, and porches covered in ivy.

Running a school in a castle is a romantic idea; just as romantic as operating a hotel in a castle.

By itself, the replica castle is certainly harmless and acceptable enough; but as a symbol that creates and maintains sentimental medieval romanticism here in the middle of the most straightforward and strongest and infinitely greatest and most valuable of all the centuries the world has ever witnessed, it is inevitably a damaging thing and an error.

Here is an excerpt from the prospectus of a Kentucky 'Female College.' The term "Female College" sounds acceptable enough; however, since phrasing it in that questionable manner was done solely for the sake of brevity, it appears to me that "she-college" would have been even better—because it's shorter and conveys the same meaning: that is, assuming either phrase actually means anything at all—

'The president is from the South by birth, upbringing, education, and personal beliefs; the faculty members all share Southern values, and except for those born in Europe, they were all born and raised in the South. Since we believe Southern culture represents the finest form of civilization this continent has ever witnessed, our young women receive training based on Southern principles of grace, sophistication, femininity, faith, and proper conduct; therefore, we provide an exceptional women's college designed for the South and actively seek support from Southern families.'[12]

KNOXVILLE, Tenn., October 19.—This morning, just a few minutes after ten o'clock, General Joseph A. Mabry, Thomas O'Connor, and Joseph A. Mabry, Jr., were killed in a gunfight. The trouble started yesterday afternoon when General Mabry attacked

---

[12] Examples of this carelessly left out by the advertiser

Major O'Connor and threatened to kill him. This happened at the fairgrounds, and O'Connor told Mabry that it wasn't the right place to settle their dispute. Mabry then told O'Connor that he wouldn't live much longer. It appears that Mabry was carrying a weapon while O'Connor was unarmed. The source of their conflict was a long-standing feud over the transfer of some property from Mabry to O'Connor. Later that afternoon, Mabry sent word to O'Connor that he would kill him the moment he saw him. This morning, Major O'Connor was standing in the doorway of the Mechanics' National Bank, where he served as president. General Mabry and another man walked down Gay Street on the side opposite from the bank. O'Connor stepped inside the bank, grabbed a shotgun, took careful aim at General Mabry, and fired. Mabry dropped dead, struck in the left side. As he fell, O'Connor fired a second time, hitting Mabry in the thigh. O'Connor then reached back into the bank and retrieved another shotgun. At that moment, Joseph A. Mabry, Jr., General Mabry's son, came running down the street, unnoticed by O'Connor until he was within forty feet, when the young man fired a pistol that struck O'Connor in the right chest, the bullet passing through his body near the heart. The instant Mabry fired, O'Connor spun around and shot back, the blast hitting young Mabry in the right chest and side. Mabry collapsed with twenty pieces of buckshot in him, and almost immediately O'Connor fell dead without any struggle. Mabry attempted to get up but fell back dead. The entire tragedy unfolded within two minutes, and none of the three men spoke after being shot. General Mabry had approximately thirty pieces of buckshot in his body. A bystander was seriously wounded in the thigh by buckshot, and another was hit in the arm. Four other men had their clothes torn by buckshot. The incident created tremendous excitement, and Gay Street was packed with thousands of people. General Mabry and his son Joe had been acquitted just a few days earlier of murdering Moses Lusby and

Don Lusby, a father and son whom they had killed several weeks before. Will Mabry had been killed by Don Lusby last Christmas. Major Thomas O'Connor was President of the Mechanics' National Bank here and was the wealthiest man in the State.— Associated Press Telegram.

Last month, Professor Sharpe from the Somerville, Tennessee Female College, described as 'a quiet and gentlemanly man,' received word that his brother-in-law, Captain Burton, had made threats on his life. Burton had apparently already murdered one person and stabbed another with a knife. Professor Sharpe armed himself with a double-barreled shotgun, went looking for his brother-in-law, discovered him playing billiards in a saloon, and shot him in the head, killing him instantly. The 'Memphis Avalanche' reported that the Professor's actions received widespread community support; understanding that the law couldn't protect him given the current state of public opinion, he took matters into his own hands.

Around the same time, two young men in North Carolina got into a dispute over a girl, and they began exchanging threatening messages. Friends attempted to bring them together and resolve their differences, but their efforts were completely wasted. On the 24th, the young men encountered each other on a public road. One carried a heavy club, while the other wielded an ax. The man with the club fought fiercely for his survival, but the battle was doomed from the beginning. A precisely aimed strike knocked his club spinning from his hands, and moments later he lay dead.

Around the same time, two well-connected young men from Virginia, who worked as clerks in a hardware store in Charlottesville, got into a fight while fooling around. Peter Dick threw pepper into Charles Roads's eyes; Roads demanded an apology; Dick refused to give one, and they agreed that a duel was unavoidable, but a problem emerged; neither party had pistols, and it was too late at night to obtain them. One of them suggested that butcher knives would serve the purpose, and the other accepted the proposal; the outcome was that Roads collapsed to the floor with a deep cut in his stomach that may or may not prove deadly. If Dick has been arrested, the news hasn't reached us. He expressed deep regret, and we are informed by a Staunton correspondent of the Philadelphia Press that every effort has been made to keep the matter quiet.—Extracts From The Public Journals.

What, guard, hey! The man who can blow such a self-satisfied blast as that probably blows it from a castle.

From Baton Rouge to New Orleans, massive sugar plantations line both sides of the river throughout the entire journey, extending their mile-wide expanses back to the distant forest walls of moss-draped cypress trees in the background. The shores are no longer isolated. Numerous homes line the entire route on both riverbanks—positioned so closely together for extended stretches that the wide river flowing between the two rows creates a kind of broad boulevard. The area appears remarkably welcoming and cheerful. Occasionally, you'll spot a grand mansion with columns and porches, nestled among the trees. Here's what some of the many foreign visitors who traveled through this area fifty years ago had to say. Mrs. Trollope observes—

The uninterrupted flat landscape along the Mississippi River's banks stretched unchanged for many miles beyond New Orleans; however, the elegant and lush palmetto trees, the dark and majestic holly oaks, and the vibrant orange trees could be seen everywhere, and many days passed before we grew tired of admiring them.

Captain Basil Hall—

The region of countryside that borders the Mississippi River in southern Louisiana is densely populated with sugar plantation owners, whose impressive mansions, colorful verandas, well-maintained gardens, and many slave quarters, all kept clean and orderly, created a remarkably prosperous appearance along the riverbank landscape.

All the procession paints the attractive picture in the same way. The descriptions from fifty years ago don't need a single word changed to exactly describe the same region as it appears today—except for how well-maintained the houses are. The whitewash has disappeared from the slave cabins now, and many, possibly most, of the big mansions that once gleamed so brilliantly white have lost their paint and show a decayed, neglected appearance. This is the damage from the war. Twenty-one years ago everything was neat and well-kept and bright along the coast, just as it had been in 1827, as those tourists described it.

Poor tourists! People deceived them with ridiculous and foolish lies, then mocked them for believing and publishing these stories. They told Mrs. Trollope that the alligators—or crocodiles, as she referred to them—were terrifying creatures, and they supported this claim with a horrifying tale about how one of these misrepresented reptiles crawled into a settler's cabin one night and devoured a woman and five children. The woman alone would have been enough for any reasonably impossible alligator, but these storytellers insisted on making the creature consume the five children as well. One wouldn't expect that pranksters of such a bold nature would be easily offended—yet they were. It's hard to comprehend today, and impossible to defend, the treatment that the book by the serious, honest, intelligent, kind, dignified, generous, well-intentioned Captain Basil Hall received.

Chapter 41: The Metropolis of the South

The approaches to New Orleans looked familiar; the overall scenery remained the same. When someone travels quickly through London on an elevated railway supported by tall arches, they can peer into miles of upper-floor bedrooms through open windows, but the lower portions of the houses sit below their eye level and cannot be seen. In the same way, when the river runs high in the New Orleans area, the water rises to the top of the surrounding levee walls, while the flat land behind them sits much lower—like the bottom of a bowl—and as the boat glides along on the high floodwaters, passengers look down at the houses and can see into their upper-story windows. Nothing exists except that fragile wall of earth standing between the residents and complete devastation.

The old brick salt warehouses clustered at the upper end of the city appeared exactly as they always had; these were warehouses that had undergone a kind of magical transformation, though, since I had last seen them; because when the war started, the owner went to sleep one evening leaving them filled with thousands of bags of ordinary salt, valued at around two dollars per bag, and woke up the next morning to discover his pile of salt had transformed into a pile of gold, figuratively speaking, since the war news had driven the price of salt to such sudden and dizzying heights.

The extensive stretch of wooden docks stayed the same, and there were just as many ships as before: but the long line of steamboats had disappeared; not completely, naturally, but very little of it remained.

The city itself hadn't changed—at least not visibly. It had grown significantly in size and population, but the town's appearance remained the same. The streets were still covered in deep dust mixed with scattered waste paper; the deep, trough-like gutters running along the curbs were still half-filled with stagnant water topped by a dusty film; the sidewalks were still cluttered—particularly in the sugar and bacon district—with casks, barrels, and hogsheads; the massive blocks of severely plain commercial buildings looked just as dusty as they always had.

Canal Street had become more elegant, appealing, and vibrant than it used to be, with its flowing crowds of pedestrians, its multiple lines of rushing streetcars, and—as evening approached—its wide second-floor balconies packed with men and women dressed in the newest fashions.

Not that Canal Street has any real 'architecture'—speaking in broad terms, New Orleans lacks architecture entirely, except in its cemeteries. This might sound strange to say about a wealthy, forward-thinking, and dynamic city with a quarter million residents, but it's the truth. There's a massive granite U.S. Custom-house that's expensive and authentic enough, but as decoration goes, it's worse than a gas storage tank. The building resembles a state penitentiary. However, it was constructed before the war. Architecture in America could be said to have emerged after the war ended. New Orleans, I think, has experienced both the good fortune and misfortune of avoiding any major fires in recent years. This must be the case. If things had been different, I believe you could identify the 'burnt district' by the dramatic improvement in its architecture compared to the older styles. You can see this phenomenon in Boston and Chicago. Boston's 'burnt district' was unremarkable before the fire, but now no commercial district anywhere in the world can exceed it—or possibly even match it— in beauty, elegance, and refined taste.

However, New Orleans has just begun—right at this very moment, you could say. Once finished, the new Cotton Exchange will stand as an impressive and beautiful structure; solid, substantial, filled with architectural elegance; no fake elements or false appearances or unsightly features anywhere on it. For the city, it will be worth far more than what it costs, because it will inspire others like it. What has been missing until now was a model to aim for; something to train the eye and develop taste; a source of inspiration, so to speak.

The city is well equipped with forward-thinking men—intelligent, wise, and far-sighted individuals. The difference between the city's spirit and its architecture is like the difference between being awake and asleep. There seems to be a boom in everything except that one lifeless aspect. The water in the gutters used to be stagnant and slimy, creating a powerful breeding ground for disease; but now the gutters are flushed two or three times daily by powerful machinery; in many gutters the water never sits still but flows in a steady stream. Other health improvements have been implemented, and they've been so effective that New Orleans claims to be one of the healthiest cities in the country during the long periods between occasional yellow fever outbreaks. There's now plenty of ice available for everyone, manufactured right in the city. It's a thriving commercial center with extensive river, ocean, and railway business. When we visited, it was the best electrically lit city in the nation. New Orleans had more electric lights than New York, and they were much better quality. You could experience this modified daylight not only on Canal Street and some neighboring main streets, but along a five-mile stretch of the riverfront. The city now has excellent clubs—several recently established—and appealing modern pleasure destinations at West End and Spanish Fort. Telephones are everywhere. One of the most remarkable improvements is in journalism. The newspapers, as I recall them, weren't particularly impressive. Now they are. Money is invested in them generously. They gather the news regardless of cost. The editorial work isn't just routine labor, but genuine literature. As an example of New Orleans journalistic accomplishment, the Times-Democrat of August 26, 1882, featured a report on the year's business activities in Mississippi Valley towns from New Orleans all the way to St. Paul—covering two thousand miles. That newspaper edition contained forty pages with seven columns per page, totaling two hundred and eighty columns; fifteen hundred words per column, adding up to four hundred and twenty thousand words altogether. In other words, nearly three times as many words as this book contains. One can sadly compare this achievement with New Orleans' architecture.

I have been discussing only public architecture. The residential buildings in New Orleans are flawless, even though they remain unchanged from how they have always been. All the homes are made of wood—in the American section of the city, I mean—and they all have a welcoming appearance. The houses in the affluent neighborhoods are large; they are usually painted bright white and typically feature wide porches, or double porches, held up by decorative columns. These grand homes sit in the middle of expansive properties and emerge, adorned with roses, from among rolling hills of gleaming green leaves and flowers of many colors. No houses could be more in tune with their environment, or more attractive to look at, or more inviting and cozy in appearance.

One eventually gets used to the water tank; this is a large barrel, painted green, and sometimes reaching two stories high, which is supported against the corner of the house on stilts. There is something about this combination that suggests both a mansion and a brewery, which seems very strange at first. But the people cannot dig wells, so they collect rainwater instead. They also cannot easily have basements or graves, since the town is built on artificial ground; so they go without both, and few of the living complain, and none of the dead do either. The Israelites are buried in graves—with permission, I believe, not as a requirement; but no one else is, except the poor, who are buried at public expense. The graves are only three or four feet deep.

Chapter 42: Hygiene and Sentiment

They bury their dead in vaults above the ground. These vaults look like houses—sometimes like temples; they're usually built of

287

marble; they're architecturally graceful and well-proportioned; they face the walkways and driveways of the cemetery; and when someone walks among a thousand or so of them and sees their white roofs and gables stretching into the distance on all sides, the phrase 'city of the dead' suddenly takes on real meaning for them. Many of the cemeteries are beautiful and are kept in perfect condition. When someone goes from the levee or the nearby business streets to a cemetery, they notice that if those people down there would live as neatly while they're alive as they do after they're dead, they would discover many benefits in doing so; and furthermore, their neighborhood would be the wonder and admiration of the business world. Fresh flowers in water-filled vases can be seen at the entrances of many of the vaults: placed there by the devoted hands of grieving parents and children, husbands and wives, and replaced daily. A gentler form of sorrow finds its inexpensive and lasting memorial in the rough and ugly but indestructible 'immortelle'—which is a wreath or cross or some similar symbol, made of rosettes of black linen, with sometimes a yellow rosette where the cross's bars meet—a kind of sorrowful brooch, you might say. The immortelle needs no care: you simply hang it up, and there you have it; just leave it alone, it will handle your grief for you, and keep it in mind better than you can; it withstands weather excellently, and lasts like boiler-iron.

On bright, sunny days, beautiful little chameleons—the most graceful of all reptiles with legs—crawl along the marble faces of the tombs, hunting for flies. When it comes to variety, their color changes don't live up to what people say about them. They do shift colors when someone approaches and places an immortelle flower, but that's hardly impressive: any decent reptile would react the same way.

I will gradually move away from this topic of graveyards. I have been trying my best to find the sentimental aspect of it, but I cannot manage it. I believe there is no truly sentimental part to it.

It is all grotesque, ghastly, horrible. Graveyards may have been acceptable in past eras, when nobody understood that for every dead body placed into the ground, to feed the earth and the plant-roots, and the air with disease-germs, five or fifty, or perhaps a hundred people must die before their natural time; but they are barely acceptable now, when even children know that a dead saint begins a century-long career of murder the moment the earth covers his corpse. It is a grim kind of thought. The relics of St. Anne, up in Canada, have now, after nineteen hundred years, gone to healing the sick by the dozen. But it is simply a matter of course that these same relics, within a generation after St. Anne's death and burial, made several thousand people sick. Therefore these miracle-performances are simply compensation, nothing more. St. Anne is somewhat slow to pay, for a Saint, it is true; but better a debt paid after nineteen hundred years, and outlawed by the statute of limitations, than not paid at all; and most of the knights of the halo do not pay at all. Where you find one that pays—like St. Anne—you find a hundred and fifty that take the benefit of the statute. And none of them pay any more than the principal of what they owe—they pay none of the interest either simple or compound. A Saint can never quite return the principal, however; for his dead body kills people, whereas his relics heal only—they never restore the dead to life. That part of the account is always left unsettled.

Dr. F. Julius Le Moyne, after fifty years of medical practice, wrote: "Burying human bodies that have died from infectious diseases continuously fills the atmosphere and contaminates the water supply with not only the germs that come from basic decomposition, but also with the specific germs of the diseases that caused death."

The gases released from buried bodies will rise up through eight or ten feet of gravel to reach the surface, much like coal gas does, and there's virtually no limit to their ability to escape.

During the 1853 epidemic in New Orleans, Dr. E. H. Barton documented that the Fourth District experienced a death rate of four hundred and fifty-two per thousand residents—more than twice the rate of any other district. This particular district contained three large cemeteries where over three thousand bodies had been interred during the preceding year. In other areas of the city, the closeness of cemeteries appeared to worsen the severity of the disease.

In 1828, Professor Bianchi showed how the terrifying return of the plague in Modena was caused by digging in soil where, three centuries earlier, victims of the disease had been buried. Mr. Cooper, when explaining the causes of certain epidemics, notes that opening the plague burial grounds at Eyam led to an immediate outbreak of disease.—North American Review, No. 3, Vol. 135.

In a speech delivered to the Chicago Medical Society advocating for cremation, Dr. Charles W. Purdy presented some compelling comparisons to demonstrate the burden that burying the dead places on society:

Every year in the United States, people spend one and one-fourth times more money on funerals than the Government spends on public schools. In 1880, the amount this country spent on funerals was enough to cover all the debts of every business that failed in the United States that same year, and still provide each bankrupt business owner with $8,630 to start over again. Each year, funerals cost more money than the total value of all the gold and silver produced in the United States in 1880! These numbers don't even include the money invested in cemeteries or spent on tombs and monuments, or the financial losses from declining property values near burial grounds.

For wealthy people, cremation would work just as well as burial since the ceremonies surrounding it could be made as expensive and showy as a Hindu suttee. For poor people, cremation would be better than burial because it's so inexpensive[13]—so inexpensive until the poor started copying the rich, which they would eventually do. Adopting cremation would free us from a bunch of worn-out burial jokes, but on the other hand, it would bring back a lot of stale old cremation jokes that have been dormant for two thousand years.

I know a Black man who makes his living doing odd jobs and heavy physical work. He never makes more than four hundred dollars a year, and since he has a wife and several young children, they have to pinch every penny to make it through the year without going into debt. For someone like him, a funeral becomes an enormous financial catastrophe. While I was working on one of the earlier chapters, this man's young child died. He walked all over town with a friend, searching for a coffin he could afford. He purchased the cheapest one available, made of plain stained wood. It cost him twenty-six dollars. If it had been built to hold something practical, it probably would have cost less than four dollars. He and his family will feel the burden of that expense for many months to come.

Chapter 43: The Art of Burial

Around the same time, I ran into a man on the street whom I hadn't seen for six or seven years, and we had a conversation that went something like this. I said—

"But you used to look sad and old; you don't anymore. Where did you get all this youthfulness and sparkling cheerfulness? Give me the address."

He laughed cheerfully, removed his gleaming hat, pointed to a jagged pink strip of paper glued inside the crown with writing on

---

[13] Four or five dollars is the minimum cost.

it, and continued laughing while I read, 'J. B——, Undertaker.' Then he put his hat back on, gave it a disrespectful tilt to one side, and called out—

'That's exactly the problem! Times were tough for me when you knew me before—I was in the insurance business, you know; very unpredictable work. When there was a big fire, sure—business would boom for about ten days while people were scared; after that, policy sales would be slow until the next fire happened. A town like this doesn't have fires frequently enough—a guy goes through so many slow weeks in a row that he loses hope. But let me tell you, this is the real business! People don't wait around for others to die as examples. No sir, they pass away regularly—there aren't any slow periods in the funeral business. I started out with just two or three small old coffins and a rented hearse, and now look at what I've built! I've developed a business here that would satisfy anyone, no matter who they are. Five years ago, I was living in an attic; now I live in a fancy house with a mansard roof and all the modern conveniences.'

"Does a coffin pay so well? Is there much profit on a coffin?"

'Get out of here! What are you talking about!' Then, with a knowing wink, lowering his voice, and placing his hand on my arm in an impressive manner; 'Listen here; there's one thing in this world that's never cheap. That's a coffin. There's one thing in this world that a person never tries to bargain you down on. That's a coffin. There's one thing in this world that a person never says— "I'll shop around a bit, and if I can't find anything better I'll come back and buy it." That's a coffin. There's one thing in this world that a person won't settle for in pine if he can get walnut; and won't settle for in walnut if he can get mahogany; and won't settle for in mahogany if he can get an iron casket with a silver nameplate and bronze handles. That's a coffin. And there's one thing in this world that you don't have to chase after a person to get him to pay for. And that's a coffin. The funeral business?—well it's the most reliable business in all of Christendom, and the most respectable.

'Why, just look at it. A wealthy man will only accept your finest goods; and you can really load it on too—pile it on and charge him heavily—he'll never complain. And when you deal with a poor man, if you handle him correctly he'll spend everything he has on a single purchase. Or especially a woman. For example: Mrs. O'Flaherty walks in—a widow—wiping her eyes and sort of moaning. She uncovers one eye, looks around tearfully at the merchandise; she says—

"And what might you ask for that one?"

"Thirty-nine dollars, madam," I said.

"It's a fine big price, sure, but Pat shall be buried like a gentleman, as he was, if I have to work my fingers off for it. I'll have that one, sir."

"Yes, madam," I said, "and it's a very good one, too; not expensive, certainly, but in this life we must cut our coat according to our cloth, as they say." And as she begins to leave, I mention casually, "This one with the white satin lining is beautiful, but I'm afraid—well, sixty-five dollars is rather—rather—but never mind, I felt I had to mention to Mrs. O'Shaughnessy—"

"Do you mean to say that Bridget O'Shaughnessy bought the mate to that jewel box to ship that drunken devil to Purgatory in?"

"Yes, madam."

"Then Pat will go to heaven in one just like it, even if it costs the O'Flaherties their last penny; and remember, add some extra touches too, and I'll give you another dollar."

'And since I work with the livery stables, I naturally don't forget to mention that Mrs. O'Shaughnessy rented fifty-four dollars' worth of carriages and put as much elegance into Dennis's funeral as if he had been a duke or an assassin. And naturally she comes in and outdoes the O'Shaughnessys by about four carriages and a bus. That's how things used to be, but that's all finished now; at least, in this particular town. The Irish started piling up so many carriages at their funerals that a funeral left them broke and starving for two years afterward; so the priest stepped in and put an end to it all. He doesn't allow them to have more than two carriages now, and sometimes only one.'

"Well," I said, "if you're so cheerful and upbeat during normal times, what must you be like during an epidemic?"

He shook his head.

"No, you've got that wrong. We don't want to see an epidemic. An epidemic doesn't pay. Well, of course I don't mean that exactly; but it doesn't pay compared to the regular business. Doesn't it occur to you why?"

No.

'Think.'

"I can't imagine. What is it?"

"It's just two things."

"Well, what are they?"

'One's Embalming.'

"And what's the other?"

'Ice.'

"How is that?"

'Well, in normal times, when a person dies, we preserve him in ice; one day, two days, maybe three, to wait for friends to arrive. Takes a lot of it—melts quickly. We charge jewelry rates for that ice, and war-prices for attendance. Well, don't you know, when there's an epidemic, they rush them to the cemetery the minute the breath's gone. No market for ice in an epidemic. Same with embalming. You take a family that's able to embalm, and you've got an easy thing. You can mention sixteen different ways to do it—though there are only one or two ways, when you come down to the basic facts of it—and they'll take the highest-priced way, every time. It's human nature—human nature in grief. It doesn't reason, you see. At the time, it doesn't care a damn. All it wants is physical immortality for the deceased, and they're willing to pay for it. All you've got to do is just be calm and pile it up—they'll stand the expense. Why, man, you can take a dead person that you couldn't give away; and get your embalming equipment around you and go to work; and in a couple of hours he is worth a cool six hundred—that's what he's worth. There isn't anything equal to it but trading rats for diamonds in time of famine. Well, don't you see, when there's an epidemic, people don't wait to embalm. No, indeed they don't; and it hurts the business like hell-th, as we say— hurts it like hell-th, health, see?—Our little joke in the trade. Well, I must be going. Give me a call whenever you need any—I mean, when you're going by, sometime.'

In his joyful high spirits, he exaggerated things himself, if any exaggeration occurred at all. I have not embellished his story.

With these brief mentions of burial, let's move on from this topic. As for myself, I hope to be cremated. I mentioned this to my pastor once, and he responded in what he apparently believed was a striking way—

'I wouldn't worry about that if I had your opportunities.' He had no idea what he was talking about—the entire family was so against it.

Chapter 44: City Sights

The old French quarter of New Orleans—originally the Spanish quarter—looks nothing like the American section of the city: the American section that extends beyond the commercial brick district that separates them. The houses are grouped together in blocks; they are severely simple and stately; they follow the same design, with occasional variations that create a pleasing effect; all are covered with plaster on the exterior, and almost all feature long verandas with iron railings that extend along multiple floors. Their main beauty comes from the deep, rich, multicolored patina that time and weather have given to the plaster. This patina blends perfectly with everything around it, and appears as naturally suited to its place as the glow on clouds at sunset. This enchanting weathering effect cannot be replicated successfully; nor can it be found anywhere else in America.

The iron railings are also a specialty. The pattern is often extremely light and delicate, airy and graceful—featuring a large cipher or monogram in the center, creating an intricate cobweb of puzzling, complex forms crafted in steel. The old railings are handmade and are now relatively rare and correspondingly valuable. They have become collectible items.

The group had the opportunity to wander leisurely through this historic district of New Orleans with the South's greatest literary talent, the writer of 'The Grandissimes.' In this author, the South has discovered a masterful portrayal artist of its inner life and its past. Indeed, I have learned through experience that the inexperienced eye and empty mind can examine it, understand it, and evaluate it more clearly and beneficially through his books than through direct personal encounter with it.

With Mr. Cable there to observe for you, and to describe, explain, and shed light on everything, a walk through that historic district becomes a vivid pleasure. You experience a sharp awareness of things unseen or barely visible—clear, yet intermittent and shadowy; you catch glimpses of prominent features, but miss the subtle details or perceive them incompletely through your imagination: like an uninformed, near-sighted visitor traveling along the edge of vast, unclear Alpine horizons with an inspired and knowledgeable far-sighted local guide.

We visited the old St. Louis Hotel, which is now home to municipal offices. There's nothing particularly striking about the building, but you could say the same thing about it as you could about the Academy of Music in New York—if anyone has ever used a broom or shovel to clean either place, there's certainly no evidence to prove it. It's strange that cabbages, hay, and other plants don't actually sprout inside the Academy of Music, though this is probably because the seats block out the light and you couldn't possibly tend to crops except in the walkways between rows. The fact that the ushers manage to grow their boutonniere flowers right there on the property shows what could be accomplished if the place had proper agricultural management.

We also visited the venerable Cathedral, and the beautiful square in front of it; one was dim with religious light, the other bright with worldly illumination, and lovely with orange trees and flowering shrubs; then we drove in the hot sun through the maze of houses and out onto the wide flat expanse beyond, where the villas are located, and the water wheels that drain the town, and the commons filled with cows and children; passing by an old cemetery where we were told lie the remains of an early pirate; but we took their word for it, and did not visit him. He was a pirate with a tremendous and bloody history; and as long as he maintained unblemished, in retirement, the dignity of his reputation and the grandeur of his ancient profession, honor and reverence were his from high and low; but when at last he descended into politics and became a petty alderman, the public rejected him, and turned away and wept. When he died, they erected a monument over him; and little by little he has come into respect again; but it is respect for the pirate, not the alderman. Today the loyal and generous remember only what he was, and charitably forget what he became.

From there, we drove several miles across a swamp along a raised shell road, with a canal on one side and thick woods on the other. Here and there in the distance, a weathered cypress tree with angular branches and moss-covered bark stood out clearly against the sky, its distinctive shape as charming as the apple trees in Japanese artwork—this was our route and its surroundings. An alligator would occasionally swim peacefully along the canal, and now and then a picturesque person of color would stand on the bank, casting their motionless reflection on the calm water while waiting for a fish to bite.

And eventually we arrived at the West End, a cluster of hotels built in the typical style of light summer resorts, featuring wide verandas that wrapped around the buildings, with the waves of the vast blue Lake Pontchartrain washing against the doorsteps. We enjoyed dinner on a ground-level veranda overlooking the water— the main course being the famous fish known as pompano, as delicious as the more innocent varieties of temptation.

Thousands of people arrive by train and carriage to West End and Spanish Fort each evening, where they dine, listen to musical performances, take walks outdoors under the electric lighting, go boating on the lake, and enjoy themselves through many other different activities.

We had chances on other days and in different places to try the pompano. Most notably, at an editorial dinner at one of the city's clubs. There, it reached its absolute peak of perfection and lived up to its reputation. Accompanying it was a towering pyramid of bright red crayfish—large ones, as big as a person's thumb—delicate, flavorful, and appetizing. There were also deviled whitebait, premium quality shrimp, and a platter of small soft-shell crabs of exceptional quality. The remaining dishes were comparable to what you might find at Delmonico's or Buckingham Palace; however, the ones I've described can only be found in such perfect form in New Orleans, I believe.

In the West and South, they have a new organization called the Broom Brigade. It consists of young women who wear matching uniforms and perform military drills, using brooms instead of rifles. It makes for quite an attractive display when viewed privately. When they perform on a theater stage under bright colored lights, it must create a beautiful and captivating show. I watched them execute their elaborate routines with elegance, enthusiasm, and remarkable accuracy. I observed them do everything a person could possibly do with a broom, except actually sweep. I never saw them sweep. But I'm confident they could master that skill. What they've already mastered proves this point. And if they ever did learn to sweep, and if they marched down Tchoupitoulas or some of those other streets in that area, those roads would look dramatically better within just a few minutes. But the young women themselves wouldn't look as good afterward, so really nothing would be gained in the end.

The drill took place in the Washington Artillery building. Inside this building, we observed numerous fascinating artifacts from the war. We also saw an excellent oil painting that depicted Stonewall Jackson's final meeting with General Lee. Both men appear on horseback in the scene. Jackson has just arrived on his horse and is approaching Lee to speak with him. The painting holds great value because of its portraits, which are genuine and authentic. However, like many other historical paintings, it conveys no meaning without its explanatory label. Any label would serve the painting just as well as another—

First Meeting between Lee and Jackson.

Last Interview between Lee and Jackson.

Jackson Introducing Himself to Lee.

Jackson Accepts Lee's Invitation to Dinner.

Jackson Politely Declines Lee's Dinner Invitation—with Gratitude.

Jackson Apologizing for a Heavy Defeat.

Jackson Reports a Great Victory.

Jackson Asking Lee for a Match.

It tells one story, and that's enough; it clearly and effectively communicates, 'Here are Lee and Jackson together.' The artist would have made it show that this was Lee and Jackson's final meeting if he could have managed it. But he couldn't, because there was no way to accomplish it. A clear, readable label is typically worth more for conveying information than a ton of meaningful posture and facial expression in a historical painting. In Rome, people with refined and empathetic temperaments stand up and cry in front of the famous 'Beatrice Cenci the Day before her Execution.' This demonstrates what a label can accomplish. If they didn't know what the picture depicted, they would examine it without emotion and comment, 'Young woman with allergies; young woman with her head covered.'

I found the half-forgotten Southern speech patterns and dropped sounds as pleasant to my ear as they had always been. A Southerner speaks like music. At least it sounds like music to me, but then I was born in the South. The educated Southerner has no use for an r, except at the beginning of a word. He says 'honah,' and 'dinnah,' and 'Gove'nuh,' and 'befo' the waw,' and so on. The words may lack charm to the eye, in print, but they have it to the ear. When did the r disappear from Southern speech, and how did it come to disappear? The habit of dropping it was not borrowed from the North, nor inherited from England. Many Southerners— most Southerners—put a y into certain words that begin with the k sound. For instance, they say Mr. K'yahtah (Carter) and speak of playing k'yahds or of riding in the k'yahs. And they have the pleasant habit—long ago fallen into decay in the North—of frequently using the respectful 'Sir.' Instead of the curt Yes, and the abrupt No, they say 'Yes, Suh', 'No, Suh.'

But there are some language problems. Such as using 'like' instead of 'as,' and adding an 'at' where it isn't necessary. I heard an educated gentleman say, 'Like the flag-officer did.' His cook or his butler would have said, 'Like the flag-officer done.' You hear gentlemen say, 'Where have you been at?' And here is the worse form—I heard a ragged street kid say it to a friend: 'I was a-ask'n' Tom whah you was a-sett'n' at.' Even the most refined people carelessly say 'will' when they mean 'shall'; and many of them say,

'I didn't go to do it,' meaning 'I didn't mean to do it.' The Northern word 'guess'—brought from England, where it used to be common, and now considered by mocking Englishmen as a Yankee creation—is rarely used among Southerners. They say 'reckon.' They don't have any 'doesn't' in their language; they say 'don't' instead. The uneducated often use 'went' for 'gone.' It is almost as bad as the Northern 'hadn't ought.' This reminds me that a remark of a very strange nature was made here in my neighborhood (in the North) a few days ago: 'He hadn't ought to have went.' How is that? Isn't that quite a triumph? One knows the influences combined in this mixed person's speech without asking: one parent Northern, the other Southern. Today I heard a schoolteacher ask, 'Where is John gone?' This form is so common—so nearly universal, in fact—that if she had used 'whither' instead of 'where,' I think it would have sounded like pretension.

We discovered one outstanding word—a word that made the trip to New Orleans worthwhile; a flexible, expressive, useful word—'lagniappe.' People pronounce it lanny-yap. It comes from Spanish—at least that's what they told us. We found it at the top of a miscellaneous column in the Picayune on our first day; heard twenty people say it on the second; asked what it meant on the third; started using it and became skilled at incorporating it on the fourth. The word has a specific meaning, but I believe people expand its use somewhat when it suits them. It's like the thirteenth roll in a 'baker's dozen.' It represents something extra thrown in, free of charge, for good measure. This tradition began in the Spanish quarter of the city. When a child or a servant purchases something at a store—or even the mayor or the governor, for all I know—they complete the transaction by saying—

"Give me something extra as a bonus."

The shopkeeper always responds; he gives the child a piece of licorice root, gives the servant an inexpensive cigar or a spool of thread, gives the governor—I don't know what he gives the governor; support, probably.

When you receive an invitation to drink in New Orleans—something that happens from time to time—and you respond, "What, again? No, I've had enough," the other person will say, "But just one more time—this is for lagniappe." When a gentleman realizes he's piling on his compliments a bit too heavily and notices from the young woman's expression that his praise would have been better without that last remark, he transforms his "I beg your pardon—no offense intended" into the shorter phrase "Oh, that's for lagniappe." If a restaurant waiter trips and pours a quarter cup of coffee down the back of your neck, he says "For lagniappe, sir," and brings you another cup at no additional cost.

Chapter 45: Southern Sports

In the North, people mention the war in social conversation about once a month, sometimes as frequently as once a week, but as a specific topic of discussion, it was long ago retired from regular use. There are good reasons for this. Take a dinner party of six men today—it's quite possible that four of them, maybe even five, never served in combat at all. So the odds are four to two, or five to one, that the war won't come up as a conversation topic at any point during the evening. The chances are even higher that if it does become the subject, it won't stay that way for very long. If you include six women in the group, you've added six people who experienced so little of the war's terrible realities that they exhausted their conversation about it years ago, and would quickly grow tired of the war as a topic if someone brought it up.

The situation is completely different in the South. There, every man you encounter fought in the war, and every woman you meet witnessed the war firsthand. The war dominates all conversation.

People's fascination with it remains intense and unwavering, while their interest in other subjects quickly fades. Bringing up the war will energize a quiet gathering and get everyone talking, when almost any other subject would leave them silent. In the South, the war serves the same purpose that A.D. does everywhere else: it's their reference point for dating events. Throughout the day, you constantly hear things described as happening since the war, or during the war, or before the war, or right after the war, or about two years or five years or ten years before the war or after the war. This shows how deeply that monumental event touched every single person's life. It gives someone who has never experienced such things a much clearer understanding of what a massive and all-encompassing disaster an invasion truly is than they could ever gain from reading books by the fireplace.

At a club one evening, a gentleman turned to me and said quietly—

'You've probably noticed that we're almost always discussing the war. It's not that we don't have other things to talk about, but nothing else captures our attention quite as powerfully. There's another reason too: During the war, each of us personally experienced what felt like every possible type of human situation; as a result, you can't bring up any outside topic without it reminding someone of an incident from the war—and they immediately share it. Naturally, this steers the conversation right back to the war. You can try as hard as you like to keep other subjects on the table, and we might all pitch in to help, but there's only one outcome: the most unrelated topic will trigger war memories in everyone and leave them speechless; conversation will probably grind to a halt because you simply can't discuss trivial matters when you have a vivid memory or thought burning in your mind that you're desperate to share.'

The poet was sitting a short distance away, and soon he started to speak—about the moon.

The gentleman who had been speaking with me commented quietly to the side: "Look, the moon is completely removed from any battlefield, but you'll notice that it will somehow remind someone of the war; within ten minutes, the moon as a subject will be set aside."

The poet mentioned that he had observed something that surprised him; he had gotten the impression that down here, closer to the equator, the moonlight appeared much more intense and brilliant than it did up North; he had gotten the impression that when he had visited New Orleans many years earlier, the moon—

Interruption from the other end of the room—

"Let me explain that. It reminds me of a story. Everything has changed since the war, for better or for worse; but you'll find people down here who are natural complainers, who see no change except change for the worse. There was an old Black woman like this. A young New Yorker said in her presence, "What a wonderful moon you have down here!" She sighed and said, "Oh, bless your heart, honey, you should have seen that moon before the war!""

The new topic was already dead. However, the poet brought it back to life and gave it a fresh beginning.

A short argument broke out over whether there was actually a real difference between moonlight in the North and South, or if people were just imagining it. The conversation about moonlight naturally shifted to discussing artificial ways of lighting up the darkness. Then someone recalled how Admiral Farragut, when he was attacking Port Hudson on a pitch-black night, didn't want to help the Confederate gunners see their targets better, so he refused to use any battle-lanterns. Instead, he had his ship decks painted white, which created a faint but useful glow that allowed his sailors to move around much more easily. This brought the war back into the conversation once again—the ten minutes still weren't quite finished.

I wasn't disappointed, because conversations about war from men who have actually experienced combat are always fascinating; while discussions about the moon from a poet who has never been there tend to be boring.

We went to a cockfighting arena in New Orleans on a Saturday afternoon. I had never witnessed a cockfight before. Men and boys of every age and skin color were there, speaking different languages and representing various nationalities. However, I noticed something quite striking and unexpected was missing: the stereotypical cruel faces. There weren't any brutal-looking faces. Without any cockfighting taking place, you could have convinced a newcomer that this gathering was a prayer meeting; and once it started, you might have passed it off as a religious revival—as long as you covered your newcomer's eyes—because the shouting was absolutely tremendous.

A Black man and a white man were in the ring; everyone else stood outside. The roosters were brought in inside sacks; and when time was called, they were taken out by the two handlers, petted, caressed, pushed toward each other, and finally released. The large black rooster immediately lunged at the small gray one and hit him on the head with his spur. The gray one fought back with determination. Then the chaos of many different voices shouting erupted, and didn't stop after that. When the roosters had been fighting for a short while, I expected them to drop dead at any moment, since both were blind, covered in blood, and so worn out that they often collapsed. Still they wouldn't surrender, and they wouldn't die either. The Black man and the white man would pick them up every few seconds, clean them off, spray cold water on them in a fine mist, and take their heads in their mouths and hold them there briefly—perhaps to revive their fading life; I'm not sure. Then, when placed down again, the dying birds would stagger around blindly, with wings dragging, find each other, deliver a random blow or two, and collapse from exhaustion once more.

I didn't witness how the battle ended. I made myself watch for as long as possible, but the scene became too heartbreaking to bear; so I openly admitted this, and we left. Later, we learned that the black rooster had died in the ring, fighting until his final moment.

Clearly, there's tremendous fascination with this 'sport' among those who have become somewhat familiar with it. I've never witnessed people enjoy anything more than this crowd enjoyed this fight. The same was true for both elderly gray-haired men and ten-year-old boys. They became completely absorbed in wild excitement. The 'cocking-main' is certainly an inhumane form of entertainment, there's no doubt about that; however, it appears to be a much more respectable and far less cruel sport than fox-hunting—because the roosters enjoy it; they both experience and provide enjoyment; which isn't the case with the fox.

We attended—in the French sense—a mule race one day. I believe I enjoyed this competition more than any other mule there. I found it more entertaining than I recall having enjoyed any other animal race I've ever witnessed. The grandstand was packed with the beauty and the chivalry of New Orleans. That expression isn't my own creation. It belongs to the Southern reporter. He's been using it for two generations. He employs it twenty times a day, or twenty thousand times a day; or a million times a day—depending on what the situation demands. He's forced to use it a million times a day if he needs to mention respectable men and women that frequently; because he has no other expression for such purposes except that single one. He never grows weary of it; it always sounds impressive to him. There's a kind of grandiose medieval pompousness and flashiness about it that appeals to his showy primitive nature. If he had been in Palestine in ancient times, we wouldn't have heard any references to 'many people' from him. No, he would have declared 'the beauty and the chivalry of Galilee' gathered to hear the Sermon on the Mount. It's probable that the men and women of the South are thoroughly tired of that expression by now, and would welcome a change, but there's no immediate likelihood of them receiving it.

The New Orleans editor writes with a strong, compact, direct, and straightforward style; he doesn't waste words and avoids excessive emotion. His typical correspondent, however, writes quite differently. In the Appendix, I've included an excellent letter written by someone with skill; but the average correspondent uses a style that's completely different from that. For example—

The 'Times-Democrat' sent a relief steamboat up one of the bayous last April. This steamboat docked at a village somewhere up there, and the Captain invited some of the village ladies to take a short trip with him. They accepted and came on board, and the steamboat pushed off up the creek. That was all there was to it. And that's all the editor of the 'Times-Democrat' would have gotten out of it. There was nothing in the situation except statistics, and he wouldn't have extracted anything else from it. He probably would have even organized them into tables, partly to ensure complete clarity of statement, and partly to conserve space. But his special correspondent understands different methods of handling statistics. He simply abandons all restraint and indulges in them—

'On Saturday morning, the beauty of the place blessed our cabin, and proud of her lovely cargo, the brave little boat sailed up the bayou.'

Twenty-two words to describe how the ladies boarded the boat and it pushed off up the creek represents a complete waste of ten perfectly good words, and it also undermines the conciseness of the statement.

The problem with Southern reporters is women. Women unsettle them and throw them off balance. A reporter can be straightforward, sensible, and reliable until a woman appears. Then he falls apart completely; his thinking becomes confused, and he turns flowery and foolish. Reading the passage above, you might think this follower of Sir Walter Scott is a beginner who barely knows how to use a pen. Actually, he provides plenty of evidence throughout his lengthy letter that he knows perfectly well how to write when women aren't around to give him this overly decorative writing style. For example—

At 4 o'clock, threatening clouds started forming in the southeast, and soon a strong wind came from the Gulf that grew more intense with each passing moment. It wasn't safe to leave the dock at that point, so we had to wait. The oak trees shed long strands of their moss-covered branches as the wind pulled at them, and the bayou grew ambitious, creating small waves that seemed to mock much larger bodies of water. When the wind calmed briefly, we were able to depart, and we steamed toward home under a dark sky with heavy winds blowing. As night began to fall, nearly everyone on board wished they were closer to home.

There's nothing wrong with that. It's good description, written concisely. Yet there was great temptation there to fall into sensational writing.

But let's get back to the mule. Since I left that topic, I've searched around and discovered a complete account of the race. In this report, I find support for the idea I just suggested—specifically, that the problem with Southern reporters is women: women, combined with Walter Scott and his knights and beauty and chivalry, and everything that goes with it. This is a superb report, as long as the women remain absent from it. But when they interfere, we get this wild outcome—

It will probably be a long time before the ladies' section displays such a sea of foam-like beauty as it did yesterday. New Orleans women are always charming, but never more so than at this time of year, when dressed in their delicate spring outfits they bring with them a breath of gentle freshness and an indescribable aura of purity. The section was so packed with them that, walking below and seeing no way to get closer, many a man understood as never before how the Peri felt at the Gates of Paradise, and wondered what priceless gift would grant him access to their sacred presence. Gleaming on their white-dressed chests or shoulders were the colors of their favored champions, and if not for the fact that these brave heroes appeared on unromantic mules, it would have been easy to picture one of King Arthur's festive days.

There were thirteen mules in the first race; they were all different kinds of mules with various complexions, ways of moving, temperaments, and appearances. Some were beautiful animals, while others were not; some had glossy coats, while others looked like they hadn't been groomed in a while; some were playfully cheerful and energetic; others were filled with spite and mischief; judging by their expressions, some seemed to think they were heading into battle, others appeared to believe it was all fun and games, and the remaining ones treated it like a solemn ceremony. Each mule behaved according to what it believed was happening. The outcome was a complete lack of coordination that was more than made up for by a striking display of diversity—the kind of colorful and amusing variety that was quite a sight to see.

All the riders were young gentlemen from fashionable society. If the reader has been curious about why the ladies of New Orleans would attend such a modest spectacle as a mule race, this explains it. It's a trendy novelty; everyone involved belongs to high society.

It's great fun and everyone loves it. The mule race is one of the most notable events of the year. It has brought some remarkably fast mules into the spotlight. One of these had to be disqualified because he was so fast that he made it a one-mule competition and stripped it of one of its best qualities—variety. But every so often someone disguises him with a different name and a fresh appearance and enters him again.

The riders wear complete jockey outfits made of brightly colored silks, satins, and velvets.

The thirteen mules took off together after a few hesitant attempts, racing away with tremendous energy. Since every mule and every rider had their own individual ideas about how the race should be conducted, which part of the track was preferable under specific conditions, how frequently they should switch lanes, when crashes should happen, and when they should be prevented, these twenty-six competing viewpoints generated an absolutely wild and visually striking chaos, and the scene that unfolded was hilariously funny.

Mile heat; time 2:22. Eight of the thirteen mules were left behind. I had placed a bet on a mule that would have won if the order had been flipped around. The second heat was entertaining; and so was the 'consolation race for beaten mules,' which came afterward; but the first heat was the most enjoyable in that regard.

I believe that the most thrilling of all races is a steamboat race, though I also have a strong preference for the exciting and spirited mule-rush. Picture two blazing steamboats racing side by side, pushing themselves to the absolute limit—meaning every rivet in their boilers—trembling and vibrating and moaning from bow to stern, shooting white steam from their pipes, billowing black smoke from their smokestacks, showering sparks everywhere, splitting the river into long streaks of bubbling foam—this is entertainment that makes one's very soul dance with delight. A horse race seems rather dull and bland by comparison. Even so, a horse race might be acceptable in its own right, I suppose, if it weren't for the annoying false starts. However, nobody ever gets killed. At least, nobody was ever killed during any horse race I attended. People have been injured, that's true, but this hardly matters.

Chapter 46: Enchantments and Enchanters

The biggest annual event in New Orleans is something we arrived too late to experience—the Mardi Gras festivities. I witnessed the procession of the Mystic Crew of Comus there twenty-four years ago—with knights and nobles and others, dressed in silken and golden Paris-made splendor, designed and purchased for that single night's use; and following them came all kinds of giants, dwarfs, monstrosities, and other entertaining grotesque figures— a striking and marvelous kind of show, as it moved solemnly and silently down the street in the light of its smoking and flickering torches; but it's said that in recent years the spectacle has been greatly enhanced in terms of cost, magnificence, and variety. There's a main figure—'Rex;' and if I recall correctly, neither this king nor any of his large group of followers is known to any outsider. All these people are gentlemen of standing and importance; and it's an honor to belong to the organization; so the secrecy in which they conceal their identities is simply for the sake of romance, and not because of the police.

Mardi Gras is naturally a remnant from the time when the French and Spanish controlled the region, but I believe the religious aspect has been largely removed from it by now. Sir Walter has gained the upper hand over the clergy with their hoods and prayer beads, and his influence will endure. His medieval themes, enhanced by fantastical creatures, strange spectacles, and delightful beings from fairy tales, are more impressive to witness than the crude imaginative displays and activities of the celebrating masses from the priests' era, and work just as effectively, perhaps, to mark the significance of the day and remind people that the boundary between the secular season and the sacred one has been reached.

This Mardi Gras celebration was something that belonged exclusively to New Orleans until not too long ago. However, it has now expanded to Memphis, St. Louis, and Baltimore. It has likely reached as far as it can go. This is something that could barely survive in the practical North and would certainly only last for a very short time—as short as it would survive in London. The heart of it lies in romance, not in humor or the bizarre. Remove the romantic mysteries, the kings and knights and grand-sounding titles, and Mardi Gras would die down there in the South. The very element that keeps it thriving in the South—sentimental romance—would destroy it in the North or in London. Puck and Punch, along with the press everywhere, would attack it and mock it without mercy, and its first appearance would also be its final one.

When we weigh the crimes of the French Revolution and Napoleon against their positive contributions, we find two significant benefits that balance the scales: the Revolution shattered the chains of the old regime and the Church's control, transforming a nation of downtrodden subjects into a nation of free citizens; and Napoleon established a system where merit mattered more than noble birth, while also completely removing the divine mystique from monarchy, so that European rulers who had once been viewed as gods were reduced to mere mortals from that point forward, never again to reclaim godlike status but to serve only as symbolic leaders who must answer for their actions just like ordinary people. These great contributions offset the temporary damage that Napoleon and the Revolution caused, leaving the world forever in their debt for these lasting and monumental advances in liberty, human dignity, and social progress.

Then Sir Walter Scott arrived with his magical storytelling, and through his influence alone, he stopped this wave of progress and even pushed it backward. He made the world fall in love with dreams and illusions, with outdated and corrupt forms of religion, with outdated and broken systems of government, and with the foolishness and emptiness, fake grandeur, fake ornaments, and fake chivalry of a mindless and worthless society that had long since disappeared. He caused immeasurable damage—more real and lasting damage, perhaps, than any other individual who ever wrote. Most of the world has now moved beyond a good portion of these harmful effects, though certainly not all of them, but in our South they still thrive quite strongly. Not as strongly as they did half a generation ago, perhaps, but still quite strongly. There, the genuine and healthy civilization of the nineteenth century is strangely mixed and blended with Walter Scott's fake Middle Ages civilization, and so you have practical, sensible, forward-thinking ideas and progressive achievements mixed together with dueling, pompous speech, and the shallow romanticism of an ridiculous past that is dead and, out of kindness, should be buried. If not for the Sir Walter disease, the character of the Southerner—or Southron, as Sir Walter preferred to say it in his more formal way—would be completely modern, instead of a mixture of modern and medieval, and the South would be a full generation more advanced than it currently is. It was Sir Walter who made every gentleman in the South a Major or a Colonel, or a General or a Judge, before the war, and it was also he who made these gentlemen treasure these fake titles. For it was he who established rank and social class down there, and also respect for rank and social class, and pride and enjoyment in them. Enough blame is placed on slavery without also crediting it with these creations and contributions of Sir Walter.

Sir Walter played such a significant role in shaping Southern character as it existed before the war that he bears considerable responsibility for the conflict itself. It may seem somewhat unfair to blame a deceased man by claiming we never would have experienced any war if not for Sir Walter; yet one could potentially construct a reasonable argument supporting such an extreme claim. The Southerner during the American Revolution owned slaves, just as the Southerner during the Civil War did: but the former resembles the latter about as much as an Englishman resembles a Frenchman. This transformation in character can be attributed more readily to Sir Walter's influence than to any other factor or individual.

One can see, through one or two indicators, how deeply that influence reached, and how powerfully it persists. If someone picks up a Northern or Southern literary magazine from forty or fifty years ago, they will find it packed with verbose, pompous, flowery 'eloquence,' romanticism, sentimentality—all copied from Sir Walter, and quite poorly executed as well—harmless parodies of his style and techniques, really. This type of literature being popular in both regions of the country, there was a chance for fair competition; and as a result, the South was able to display as many well-known literary figures, relative to population, as the North could.

But a change has occurred, and there is no longer an opportunity for fair competition between the North and South. The North has abandoned that old inflated writing style, while Southern writers still hold onto it—they cling to it and consequently have a limited market for their work. There is certainly as much literary talent in the South now as there ever was; however, their work can only gain minimal recognition under current conditions; these authors write for the past, not the present; they use outdated forms and a language that has died. But when a Southern writer of genius writes in modern English, his book no longer moves on crutches, but on wings; and those wings carry it quickly throughout America and England, and through the major English reprint publishing houses of Germany—as demonstrated by the success of Mr. Cable and Uncle Remus, two of the very few Southern authors who do not write in the Southern style. Instead of three or four widely-known literary names, the

South should have a dozen or two—and will have them when Sir Walter's influence comes to an end.

A fascinating example of how a single book can wield tremendous power for either benefit or damage can be seen in the contrasting effects produced by 'Don Quixote' and those produced by 'Ivanhoe.' The former completely eliminated the world's fascination with the foolishness of medieval chivalry; while the latter brought it back to life. As far as our Southern states are concerned, the beneficial work accomplished by Cervantes has become virtually meaningless, so thoroughly has Scott's harmful influence destroyed it.

Chapter 47: Uncle Remus and Mr. Cable

MR. JOEL CHANDLER HARRIS ('Uncle Remus') was scheduled to arrive from Atlanta at seven o'clock Sunday morning, so we got up early and went to meet him. We were able to identify him among the crowd of people arriving at the hotel front desk because he matched a description we had received from a reliable source. He was described as being short in stature, red-haired, and somewhat freckled. He was the only person in the group whose appearance matched these details. He was also said to be very shy. He is indeed a shy man. There is no question about this. It might not be immediately obvious, but the shyness is definitely there. Even after spending many days together, one is surprised to see that it remains just as strong as it was initially. There is a wonderful and beautiful character hidden beneath this shyness, as everyone who has read the Uncle Remus book knows; and there is also remarkable talent, as evidenced by the same work. I realize I am speaking quite openly about this acquaintance; but in speaking to the public I am simply speaking to his personal friends, and such candor is acceptable among friends.

He deeply let down many children who had rushed excitedly to Mr. Cable's house, hoping to catch a glimpse of the famous wise man and prophet of the country's nurseries. They said—

"Why, he's white!"

They felt disappointed about this. To comfort them, someone brought the book so they could listen to Uncle Remus's Tar-Baby story directly from Uncle Remus himself—or what remained of him in their upset opinion. However, it became clear that he had never read stories out loud to an audience before and felt too embarrassed to try it now. Mr. Cable and I took turns reading from our own books to demonstrate how simple it was, but his deep-rooted shyness couldn't be overcome even by this clever approach, so we ended up having to read the Brer Rabbit stories ourselves.

Mr. Harris should be able to read African American dialect better than anyone else, since he is the only master the country has produced when it comes to writing it. Mr. Cable is the only master in writing French dialects that the country has produced, and he reads them perfectly. It was a wonderful experience to hear him read about Jean-ah Poquelin, and about Innerarity and his famous 'pigshoo' representing 'Louisiana refusing to enter the Union,' along with passages of beautifully nuanced German dialect from a novel that was still in manuscript.

During a conversation, it emerged that Mr. Cable had encountered absurd difficulties on two separate occasions by including nearly impossible French names in his books that, despite their improbability, actually belonged to real and easily offended residents of New Orleans. His names were either made up or taken from the distant and forgotten past—I can't recall which now—but in either case, people who actually had those names came forward and were quite upset about having such intense public attention drawn to themselves and their personal matters.

Mr. Warner and I had a similar experience when we wrote the

book called 'The Gilded Age.' There's a character in it named 'Sellers.' I can't recall what his first name was originally, but Mr. Warner didn't like it and wanted to improve it. He asked me if I could imagine a person named 'Eschol Sellers.' Naturally, I told him I couldn't, not without some help. He explained that out West, he had once met, observed, and actually shaken hands with a man who had that incredible name—'Eschol Sellers.' He went on to say—

'That was twenty years ago; his name has likely taken him to his grave by now; and if it hasn't, he'll never see this book anyway. We'll take his name for ourselves. The name you're using is ordinary, and that makes it risky; there are probably a thousand people named Sellers out there, and the entire bunch will come after us; but Eschol Sellers is a secure name—it's solid as a rock.'

So we borrowed that name; and when the book had been published for about a week, one of the most dignified and handsome and aristocratic-looking white men who ever lived came by, carrying the most intimidating libel lawsuit in his pocket that ever—well, to put it simply, we got his permission to withdraw an edition of ten million[14] copies of the book and change that name to 'Mulberry Sellers' in future editions.

Chapter 48: Sugar and Postage

One day, while walking down the street, I ran into the man I most wanted to see—Horace Bixby, who had once been my pilot instructor, or more accurately, my superior, and was now captain of the magnificent steamer 'City of Baton Rouge,' the newest and

---

[14] Figures taken from memory, and probably incorrect. Think it was more.

fastest ship in the Anchor Line fleet. He had the same lean build, the same tight curls, the same energetic walk, the same sharp awareness, the same keen eye and quick hands to match, the same upright, military posture; he hadn't gained or lost a single inch around the waist, not a pound in weight, not a single gray hair. It's a strange thing to leave a man when he's thirty-five years old and return after twenty-one years to find him looking exactly thirty-five still. I don't think I've ever experienced anything quite like this before. There were a few wrinkles around his eyes, but they hardly mattered since you could barely notice them.

His boat had just arrived. I had been waiting several days for it, planning to return to St. Louis aboard it. The captain and I joined a group of ladies and gentlemen, who were guests of Major Wood, and traveled down the river fifty-four miles in a fast tugboat to ex-Governor Warmouth's sugar plantation. Stretched out below the city were numerous decayed, run-down, worn-out old steamboats, none of which I had ever seen before. They had all been constructed, used up, and discarded since my last visit here. This gives someone a clear understanding of how fragile a Mississippi boat is and how short its lifespan can be.

Six miles south of the city, a thick and weathered brick chimney rising above the magnolia trees and live oaks was identified as the memorial built by a grateful nation to commemorate the Battle of New Orleans—Jackson's triumph over the British on January 8, 1815. The war had already concluded, and the two countries were at peace, but this news had not yet arrived in New Orleans. Had we possessed cable telegraph technology during that era, this bloodshed would not have occurred, and those lives would not have been lost; even more significantly, Jackson would likely never have become president. We have recovered from the damage inflicted upon us by the War of 1812, but we have not yet overcome some of the harm caused by Jackson's time in office.

The Warmouth plantation spans an enormous area, and the hospitality at the Warmouth mansion matches that same grand scale. Here we witnessed steam-plows in operation for the first time. The traction engine moves around on its own wheels until it arrives at the designated location; then it stops and uses a wire rope to pull the massive plow toward itself across two or three hundred yards of field, threading between the rows of cane. This machine cuts into the black soil to a depth of a foot and a half. The plow resembles an inverted fore-and-aft brace from a Hudson River steamboat. When the Black operator sits on one end of it, that end tips down close to the ground while the opposite end points high into the air. This enormous seesaw rolls and rocks like a vessel on the ocean, and not every circus performer could maintain their balance on it.

The plantation covers two thousand six hundred acres, with six hundred and fifty acres dedicated to sugar cane cultivation, along with a productive orange grove containing five thousand trees. The sugar cane is grown using modern and sophisticated scientific techniques that are far too elaborate and complicated for me to try to explain, yet despite these methods, the operation lost $40,000 last year. I can't recall the other specific details. Nevertheless, this year's harvest is expected to produce ten to twelve hundred tons of sugar, which means last year's financial loss won't be significant. These demanding and costly scientific approaches produce a yield of one and a half to two tons per acre, which is three to four times greater than what an acre would yield back in my day.

The drainage ditches were teeming with small crabs called 'fiddlers.' You could see them scurrying sideways in all directions whenever they detected any disturbing sound. These crabs were costly pests because they burrowed into the levees and destroyed them.

The massive sugar factory was a maze of tubs, tanks, vats, and filters, along with pumps, pipes, and machinery everywhere. The sugar-making process is extremely fascinating. First, you throw your cane into the centrifugal machines and crush out the juice; then you run it through the evaporating pan to extract the fiber; then through the bone-filter to remove the alcohol; then through the clarifying tanks to discharge the molasses; then through the granulating pipe to condense it; then through the vacuum pan to extract the vacuum. At this point, it's ready for the market. I've written down these details from memory. The whole thing appears simple and straightforward. Don't fool yourself. Making sugar is actually one of the most challenging tasks in the world. And to make it correctly is nearly impossible. If you examine your own sugar supply from time to time over several years and record the results, you'll discover that fewer than two men out of twenty can make sugar without getting sand mixed into it.

We could have traveled down to where the river meets the sea and seen Captain Eads' impressive engineering project, the 'jetties,' where the river has been squeezed between walls, making it twenty-six feet deep; but everyone agreed it would be pointless to make the trip, since with the water at this level everything would be submerged and impossible to see.

We could have visited that ancient and unique town called 'Pilot-town,' which supposedly stands on stilts in the water; where almost all transportation happens by small boat and canoe, even when attending weddings and funerals; and where the smallest boys and girls handle oars as skillfully as land-dwelling children ride bicycles.

We could have done several other activities, but because of our limited time, we returned home. The journey up the breezy and sparkling river was a delightful experience, and it would have been perfectly sentimental and romantic if not for the constant interruptions from the tugboat's pet parrot, whose endless commentary on the scenery and passengers was always crude and often vulgar. He also possessed an excessive amount of that harsh, ear-piercing, metallic laugh typical of his species—an artificial laugh, a soulless Frankenstein laugh. He unleashed this laugh after every sentimental comment and every touching song. He cackled it out with terrible intensity after "Home again, home again from a foreign shore," and declared he "wouldn't give a damn for a tugboat full of such nonsense." Romance and sentiment cannot survive this kind of discouragement for long, so the singing and conversation eventually stopped, which pleased the parrot so much that he swore himself hoarse with joy.

Then the men in our group went to the front of the boat to smoke and chat. Several experienced steamboat workers were with us, and they told me a lot about what had happened to my old river friends while I'd been away for so long. I found out that a pilot I used to work under had become a spiritualist, and for over fifteen years he'd been getting a letter every week from a dead family member, delivered through a New York spiritualist medium called Manchester—with postage rates based on distance: from the local post office in Paradise to New York, five dollars; from New York to St. Louis, three cents. I remember Mr. Manchester quite well. I visited him once, ten years ago, with a couple of friends, one of whom wanted to contact a deceased uncle. This uncle had died in an extremely violent and strange way about six years earlier: a tornado had blown him roughly three miles and knocked down a tree with him that was four feet thick at the base and sixty-five feet tall. He didn't survive this ordeal. At the séance I'm talking about, my friend asked questions to his dead uncle through Mr. Manchester, and the dead uncle wrote back his answers, using Mr. Manchester's hand and pencil to do so. What follows is a good example of the kinds of questions that were asked, and also of the sloppy nonsense that passed for answers, provided by Manchester while pretending it came from the ghost. If this man isn't the most pathetic fraud alive, then I owe him an apology—

QUESTION. Where are you?

ANSWER. In the spirit world.

Q. Are you happy?

A. Very happy. Perfectly happy.

Q. How do you entertain yourself?

A. Conversation with friends, and other spirits.

Q. What else?

A. Nothing else. Nothing else is necessary.

Q. What do you talk about?

A. About how happy we are; and about friends left behind on earth, and how to influence them for their good.

Q. When all your friends on earth eventually reach the spirit world, what will you have to discuss with them then?—nothing except how happy you all are?

No response came. The explanation given was that spirits refuse to answer trivial questions.

How is it that spirits who are content to spend eternity engaged in trivial activities, and accept this as happiness, are so particular and demanding when it comes to trivial questions on the subject?

No reply.

Q. Would you like to come back?

A. No.

Q. Would you say that under oath?

A. Yes.

Q. What do you eat there?

A. We do not eat.

Q. What do you drink?

A. We do not drink.

Q. What do you smoke?

A. We do not smoke.

Q. What do you read?

We don't read.

Q. Do all the good people go to your place?

A. Yes.

You know how I'm living right now. Can you suggest any crimes I could add to my current lifestyle that would reasonably guarantee I'll end up somewhere else?

A. No reply.

Q. When did you die?

A. I didn't die, I passed away.

Q. Alright then, when did you die? How long have you been in the spirit world?

We don't have any way to measure time in this place.

Q. Even though you might feel indifferent and unsure about dates and times in your current state and surroundings, this doesn't change anything about your previous situation. You had specific dates back then. I'm asking for one of those dates. You passed away on a particular day in a particular year. Isn't this correct?

A. Yes.

Q. Then state what day of the month it is.

(The medium fumbled extensively with his pencil, his head and body jerking violently in spasmodic movements for quite some time. Eventually, an explanation was offered that spirits frequently forget dates, as such matters hold no significance for them.)

Q. So this spirit has actually forgotten when it passed over to the spirit world?

This was acknowledged to be true.

Q. This is very curious. Well, then, what year was it?

(More fumbling, jerking, and idiotic spasms from the medium. Finally, an explanation that the spirit has forgotten the year.)

Q. This is truly amazing. Let me ask you one more question, one final question, before we separate and never meet again— because even if I can't avoid ending up in your asylum, any meeting there won't count as a real meeting, since by then you will have easily forgotten me and my name: did you die naturally, or

323

were you killed in some disaster?

A. (After prolonged hesitation and numerous struggles and convulsions.) Natural death.

This brought the interview to a close. My friend explained to the medium that during his relative's time in this troubled world, the man had possessed remarkable intelligence and a completely flawless memory. It seemed unfortunate that he hadn't been permitted to retain even a small portion of these gifts for his own enjoyment in the realm of eternal happiness, and to inspire wonder and respect among the other inhabitants there.

This man had numerous clients—and still has many today. He gets letters from spirits situated throughout the spirit world, and delivers them across this country using the United States postal service. These letters are packed with guidance—guidance from 'spirits' who don't possess as much knowledge as a tadpole—and this guidance is faithfully followed by those who receive it. One of these clients was a man whom the spirits (if one can describe the clever Manchester in such plural terms) were instructing on how to design an enhanced railway car-wheel. It's crude work for a spirit, but it represents higher and more beneficial activity than constantly talking about 'how happy we are.'

Chapter 49: Episodes in Pilot Life

During conversations on the tugboat, I learned that out of every five former friends who had left the river, four had chosen farming as their profession. This wasn't because they possessed special agricultural talents that would make them more successful as farmers than in other fields—the reason for their choice had to come from somewhere else. They probably selected farming because that way of life offers privacy and isolation from unwanted visitors—much like the solitude of a pilot-house. They likely also chose it because during countless nights of fierce storms and perilous conditions, they had seen the flickering lights of remote farmhouses as their boat passed by, and imagined the peace, safety, and comfort of such havens during those dangerous moments, eventually coming to dream of that quiet and tranquil existence as the most desirable life to yearn for, look forward to, work toward, and finally experience.

But I never learned that any of these pilot-farmers had amazed anyone with their achievements. Their farms don't sustain them: they sustain their farms. The pilot-farmer vanishes from the river each year around the time spring arrives, and isn't seen again until the next frost. Then he reappears, wearing worn homespun clothing, brushes the hayseed from his hair, and takes a position in a pilot-house for the winter. This is how he pays off the debts that his farming has accumulated during the growing season. So his enslavement to the river is only partially broken; he remains the river's servant for the most difficult half of the year.

One of these men purchased a farm but didn't retire to live on it. He was too clever for that approach. He had no intention of ruining his farm by trying to work it himself without proper knowledge. Instead, he placed the farm under the management of an agricultural specialist who would operate it on a profit-sharing basis—for every three loads of corn produced, the specialist would receive two loads and the pilot would get one. However, when the season ended, the pilot didn't receive any corn. The specialist explained that the pilot's portion wasn't available. The farm had only produced two loads total.

Some of the pilots I had known had experienced adventures— sometimes with fortunate outcomes, but not always. Captain Montgomery, whom I had worked under when he was a pilot, commanded the Confederate fleet in the great battle before

Memphis; when his ship went down, he swam to shore, fought his way through a group of soldiers, and made a brave and narrow escape. He was always a calm man; nothing could upset his composure. Once when he was captain of the 'Crescent City,' I was bringing the boat into port at New Orleans, and constantly expecting orders from the hurricane deck, but received none. I had stopped the wheels, and there my authority and responsibility ended. It was evening—dim twilight—the captain's hat was sitting on the big bell, and I assumed the thinking part of the captain was inside it, but that wasn't the case. The captain was very strict; therefore I knew better than to touch a bell without orders. My job was to keep the boat steady on her dangerous course, and let the consequences handle themselves—which I did. So we went plowing past the backs of steamboats and getting closer and closer—the crash was certain to happen very soon—and still that hat never moved; for unfortunately, the captain was sleeping in the texas.... Things were becoming extremely tense and uncomfortable. It seemed to me that the captain wasn't going to show up in time to see the show. But he did. Just as we were about to collide with the stern of a steamboat, he stepped out on deck, and said, with perfect calm, 'Set her back on both'—which I did; but a little late, however, for the next moment we went crashing through that other boat's flimsy outer structures with a tremendous noise. The captain never said a word to me about the incident afterwards, except to mention that I had done right, and that he hoped I wouldn't hesitate to act the same way again in similar circumstances.

One of the pilots I had known during my time on the river died an extremely honorable death. His boat caught fire, and he stayed at the wheel until he brought her safely to shore. Then he climbed out over the front rail with his clothes on fire, and he was the last person to reach land. He died from his injuries within two or three hours, and his was the only life that was lost.

The history of Mississippi river piloting provides six or seven examples of this kind of heroic sacrifice, along with about fifty cases where pilots narrowly escaped a similar destiny by just a second or two before it would have been fatally too late; however, there is no recorded case of a pilot abandoning his position to save himself when staying at his post and giving up his life could protect others from death. This admirable truth deserves to be recorded, and it certainly deserves to be emphasized as well.

The trainee pilot is taught early on to look down on all dangers that come with a pilot's job, and to choose any kind of death over the terrible shame of abandoning his position while he might still be of use. These lessons are taught so well that even young and inexperienced pilots can be counted on to stay at the wheel and die there when the situation demands it. In a Memphis cemetery lies buried a young man who died at the wheel many years ago on the White River to save other men's lives. He told the captain that if the fire gave him enough time to reach a sandbar some distance away, everyone could be saved, but landing against the steep riverbank would certainly cost many lives. He made it to the bar and ran the boat aground in shallow water, but by then the flames had surrounded him, and while escaping through them he suffered fatal burns. Others had urged him to flee earlier, but he had answered as any pilot should answer—

'I will not go. If I go, nobody will be saved; if I stay, no one will be lost but me. I will stay.'

There were two hundred people on board, and no life was lost except the pilot's. There used to be a monument to this young man in that Memphis graveyard. While we stayed in Memphis on our downstream trip, I set out to look for it, but our time was so short that I was forced to turn back before I could accomplish my goal.

The tugboat crew's gossip brought me devastating news about old friends and colleagues. Dick Kennet was dead—killed in an explosion near Memphis. Several other people I had known well had died in the war, with one or two of them shot down while working at the wheel. Another close friend, someone I had steered many trips alongside, had left his house in New Orleans one evening years earlier to collect money in a distant part of the city and was never seen again. People believed he had been murdered and his body thrown into the river. Ben Thornburgh had also died long ago, along with his wild apprentice whom I used to argue with during every daylight shift. That young man was a careless, reckless person who constantly found himself in trouble and always causing problems. One day, a passenger from Arkansas brought an enormous bear on board and chained the animal to a lifeboat on the hurricane deck. Thornburgh's apprentice couldn't leave it alone until he had gone over there and freed the bear, wanting to see what would happen. He got his answer immediately. The bear chased him around and around the deck for what seemed like miles, with two hundred excited faces watching and grinning through the railings, until it finally tore off the young man's coat-tail and went into the texas to chew on it. The off-duty crew quickly emerged and left the bear in complete control of the area. Soon the bear grew lonely and decided to explore for entertainment. It roamed throughout the entire boat, visiting every section with a group of fleeing people running ahead of it and empty silence following behind. When the bear's owner finally captured it, those two were the only people visible anywhere on the vessel. Everyone else had found places to hide, leaving the boat completely deserted.

I learned that one of my pilot friends died suddenly at the wheel from heart disease in 1869. The captain was up on the roof when it happened. He noticed the boat heading toward the shore, called out, and received no response; he rushed over and discovered the pilot lying dead on the floor.

Mr. Bixby had been in an explosion at Madrid bend; he wasn't hurt, but the other pilot died.

George Ritchie had been caught in an explosion near Memphis—thrown from the pilot wheel into the river and badly injured. The water was freezing cold; he held onto a cotton bale—mostly gripping it with his teeth—and drifted along until he was nearly dead from exhaustion, when some crew members who were clinging to a piece of the wreckage rescued him. They ripped open the bale and wrapped him in the cotton, slowly warming him back to life, and managed to get him safely to Memphis. He now works as one of Bixby's pilots on the 'Baton Rouge.'

Into the life of a steamboat clerk, now dead, had fallen a touch of romance—somewhat strange romance, but romance all the same. When I knew him he was an aimless young man who spent money freely, loud and boisterous, kindhearted, full of thoughtless acts of generosity, and quite obviously likely to waste his potential early and amount to nothing. In a Western city there lived a wealthy and childless old immigrant and his wife; and in their household was a pretty young woman—part friend, part servant. The young clerk I've been talking about—whose real name wasn't George Johnson, but who I'll call George Johnson for this story—became acquainted with this young woman, and they had an affair; and the old immigrant discovered them, and scolded them. Feeling ashamed, they lied and claimed they were married; that they had been secretly wed. Then the old immigrant's pain was soothed, and he forgave and blessed them. After that, they were able to continue their affair openly. Eventually the immigrant's wife died; and soon after he passed away as well. Family friends gathered to grieve; and among those mourning sat the two young lovers. The will was opened and read aloud with ceremony. It left every cent of that old man's vast fortune to Mrs. George Johnson!

And there was no such person. The young sinners then fled and did something very foolish: they married themselves before an obscure Justice of the Peace and convinced him to backdate the ceremony. That didn't do any good at all. The distant relatives swarmed in and exposed the fraudulent date with remarkable speed and surprising ease, then carried off the fortune, leaving the Johnsons very legitimately, legally, and irrevocably bound together in honorable marriage, but without so much as a penny to their name. These are the actual facts; and not all novels have such a compelling situation as their foundation.

Chapter 50: The 'Original Jacobs'

WE had some conversation about Captain Isaiah Sellers, who had been dead for many years. He was an excellent man, a person of high principles, and deeply respected both on land and on the river. He was very tall, well-built, and good-looking; and in his later years—as I recall him—his hair was as black as a Native American's, and his vision and coordination were as strong and reliable and his composure and decision-making as solid and sharp as anyone's, whether young or old, among the community of pilots. He was the elder statesman of the profession; he had worked as a keelboat pilot before steamboats existed; and served as a steamboat pilot before any other steamboat pilot who was still alive during the period I'm discussing had ever operated a wheel. As a result, his fellow pilots regarded him with the kind of reverence that distinguished survivors of an earlier era always receive from their colleagues. He understood how others viewed him, and perhaps this awareness added a small measure of rigidity to his inherent dignity, which had already been quite formal to begin with.

He left behind a diary, but it apparently didn't go back to his first steamboat journey, which was reportedly in 1811, the same year the first steamboat disrupted the waters of the Mississippi River. When he died, a correspondent from the 'St. Louis Republican' gathered the following entries from the diary—

In February 1825, he boarded the steamboat "Rambler" at Florence, Alabama, and completed three round trips to New Orleans that year—these journeys were made on the "Gen. Carrol," traveling between Nashville and New Orleans. During his time working on this vessel, Captain Sellers introduced the practice of using a bell tap as a signal to take depth measurements, replacing the previous custom where the pilot would call down to the crew below when soundings were needed. The close distance between the crew quarters and the pilot house undoubtedly made this communication straightforward, but what a contrast this presents to the magnificent river vessels of today.

In 1827 we find him aboard the "President," a vessel with a capacity of two hundred and eighty-five tons, operating between Smithland and New Orleans. From there he joined the "Jubilee" in 1828, and on this vessel he performed his first piloting work in the St. Louis trade; his initial watch ran from Herculaneum to St. Genevieve. On May 26, 1836, he finished construction and departed Pittsburgh commanding the steamboat "Prairie," a vessel of four hundred tons, and the first steamboat featuring a stateroom cabin ever witnessed at St. Louis. In 1857 he established the signal system for encountering boats, which has, with minor modifications, remained the standard practice to this day; indeed, it has been made mandatory by congressional legislation.

"For general information about river history, we include the following notes written in the margins of his main logbook—

In March 1825, General Lafayette departed New Orleans bound for St. Louis aboard the low-pressure steamboat "Natchez."

In January 1828, twenty-one steamboats departed from the New Orleans wharf to commemorate General Jackson's visit to the city.

In 1830, the steamboat "North American" completed the journey from New Orleans to Memphis in six days, which was the fastest time ever recorded up to that point. Since then, the same trip has been accomplished in just two days and ten hours.

In 1831, the Red River cutoff was created.

In 1832, the steamboat "Hudson" completed the journey from White River to Helena, covering a distance of seventy-five miles in twelve hours. This achievement became the subject of considerable discussion and speculation among those who had a direct interest in the matter.

In 1839, the Great Horseshoe cut-off was formed.

Over the past thirty-five years, according to the diary records, he has completed four hundred and sixty round trips to New Orleans, covering a total distance of one million one hundred and four thousand miles, which averages out to eighty-six miles per day.

Whenever Captain Sellers walked up to a group of chattering pilots, an uncomfortable silence would fall over them, and all conversation would stop. Here's why: whenever six pilots gathered together, there would always be one or two newcomers among them, and the veteran pilots would constantly show off in front of these unfortunate fellows. They would make these new pilots painfully aware of how inexperienced they were, how recently they had earned their status, and how low their rank was by speaking grandly and pompously about their old experiences on the river. The veterans always made sure to date their stories as far back as possible, ensuring the newcomers felt their inexperience as sharply as possible while envying the old-timers to the same degree. And how these smug, balding men would puff themselves up, boast, exaggerate, and push their dates back ten, fifteen, even twenty years, and how much they relished the impact they had on the amazed and envious young pilots!

And perhaps right at this joyful moment in the conversation, the dignified figure of Captain Isaiah Sellers, that authentic and sole genuine Son of Antiquity, would drift majestically into their group. Picture the depth of the silence that would instantly follow.

And picture the emotions of those veteran pilots, and the triumph of their recent listeners when the elderly captain would start making casual and offhand comments of a nostalgic kind—about islands that had vanished, and shortcuts that had been created, a full generation before the most senior veteran pilot in the group had ever stepped foot in a pilot-house!

Time and time again, this old sailor would show up in exactly this manner, bringing chaos and embarrassment wherever he went. According to the pilots, he always traced his islands back to the earliest, most obscure periods of river history, and he never referenced the same island twice. He never mentioned an island that actually existed anymore, nor did he give one a name that anyone present would have been old enough to remember hearing before. If the pilots were to be believed, he was always meticulously careful about minor details. He would never simply say 'the State of Mississippi,' for example—instead, he would declare, 'When the State of Mississippi was located where Arkansas is today.' He would never speak about Louisiana or Missouri in broad terms that might leave you with the wrong idea—rather, he would specify, 'When Louisiana was situated further up the river,' or 'When Missouri was positioned on the Illinois side.'

The old gentleman wasn't particularly literary or gifted with words, but he would write down short paragraphs containing straightforward, practical information about the river, sign them 'Mark Twain,' and submit them to the 'New Orleans Picayune.' These pieces described the water level and current state of the river, and they were both accurate and useful; up to this point, they contained nothing harmful. However, when discussing the river's water level on any given day at a specific location, the captain had a tendency to slip in a small comment about how this was the first time he had witnessed the water so high or so low at that exact spot in forty-nine years; occasionally he would reference Island

Such-and-such, adding in parentheses an observation like 'vanished in 1807, if my memory serves me correctly.' These old-fashioned remarks contained venom and resentment for the other veteran pilots, and they would ridicule the 'Mark Twain' paragraphs with relentless scorn.

It happened that one of these paragraphs [15]—It reads as follows—

VICKSBURG May 4, 1859.

'My opinion for the benefit of the citizens of New Orleans: The water is higher this far up than it has been since 1808. My opinion is that the water will be several feet deep in Canal Street before the first of next June. Mrs. Turner's plantation at the head of Big Black Island is completely underwater, and it has not been flooded since 1815.

'I. Sellers.'

became the text for my first newspaper article. I exaggerated it wildly, extremely wildly, stretching my imaginative story to about eight hundred or a thousand words. I was a novice reporter at the time. I showed my work to some pilots, and they enthusiastically rushed it into print in the 'New Orleans True Delta.' It was a terrible mistake; it served no worthwhile purpose, and it caused deep pain to a good man's heart. There was no ill intent in my nonsense; but it mocked the captain. It ridiculed a man for whom such an experience was unfamiliar and frightening and awful. I didn't understand then, though I do now, that no pain compares to what a private individual feels when he is publicly humiliated in print for the first time.

Captain Sellers honored me by developing a deep hatred for me from that day forward. When I say he honored me, I'm not

---

[15] The original manuscript of it, written in the captain's own handwriting, was sent to me from New Orleans.

334

speaking carelessly. It was truly an honor to occupy the thoughts of such a remarkable man as Captain Sellers, and I was smart enough to recognize this and take pride in it. Being loved by such a man would have been special; but being hated by him was an even greater distinction, because he loved many people; however, he didn't lose sleep hating anyone except me.

He never published another paragraph during his lifetime, and he never again used the signature 'Mark Twain' on any of his work. When the telegraph delivered news of his death, I was on the Pacific coast. I was a young, inexperienced journalist who needed a pen name; so I took over the old sailor's abandoned pseudonym, and I have tried my best to maintain what it represented in his hands—a mark and emblem and guarantee that whatever appears alongside it can be trusted as the absolute truth; whether I have succeeded in this would be immodest for me to judge.

The captain took honorable pride in his profession and maintained a lasting love for it. He commissioned his monument before his death and kept it close to him until he passed away. It now stands over his grave in Bellefontaine cemetery, St. Louis. The marble sculpture depicts him standing at his post at the pilot wheel, and it deserves to stand there and face any criticism, because it represents a man who in life would have remained at his station until he was burned to ashes if duty demanded it.

The most magnificent sight we witnessed during our entire Mississippi journey appeared as we drew near New Orleans aboard the steam-tug. We beheld the curved waterfront of the crescent city illuminated by the brilliant white radiance of five miles of electric lights. The spectacle was extraordinary and breathtakingly beautiful.

Chapter 51: Memories

We departed for St. Louis aboard the 'City of Baton Rouge' on a wonderfully hot day, though the primary goal of my visit had been only partially achieved. I had intended to seek out and have conversations with a hundred steamboat workers, but I became so enjoyably caught up in the town's social activities that I managed nothing more than brief five-minute conversations with only a couple dozen people from that profession.

I was sitting on the bench in the pilot-house when we backed out and 'straightened up' for departure—the boat pausing for a 'good ready,' in the traditional manner, and the black smoke billowing out of the smokestacks just as it always had in the old days. Then we started to pick up speed, and soon we were properly underway and moving along at a good pace. Everything felt as natural and familiar—including the sights along the shore—as if there had been no interruption in my river life. There was a trainee pilot, and I figured he would take control of the wheel now; and sure enough, he did. Captain Bixby entered the pilot-house. Soon the trainee moved closer to the line of steamships. He made me anxious, because he left too much space between our boat and the other vessels. I knew perfectly well what was about to happen, because I could look back in my own experience and recall the same situation. The captain watched quietly for about thirty seconds, then took the wheel himself, and pushed the boat closer, until she was scraping along within inches of the ships. It was exactly the same lesson he had given me, about twenty-five years earlier, in that very same location, the first time I ever sailed out of the port of New Orleans. It gave me tremendous and genuine satisfaction to watch the scene play out again—with someone else as the target.

We reached Natchez (three hundred miles) in twenty-two and a half hours—the fastest trip I have ever made over that stretch of water.

The following morning I joined the four o'clock watch and witnessed Ritchie skillfully navigate half a dozen river crossings through thick fog, relying on the marked chart that he and Bixby had developed and patented together. This clearly demonstrated the tremendous value of their chart.

As time passed and the fog started to lift, I observed that the reflection of a tree in the calm water of a flooded riverbank, about six hundred yards in the distance, appeared more vivid and darker than the pale tree itself. The faint, ghostly trees that could barely be seen through the thinning fog created a beautiful sight to behold.

We experienced a powerful thunderstorm at Natchez, another one at Vicksburg, and yet another about fifty miles below Memphis. These storms possessed an old-fashioned intensity that I hadn't encountered in a long time. This third storm came with fierce winds. We secured the boat to the riverbank when we spotted the approaching tempest, and everyone abandoned the pilot-house except for me. The wind forced the young trees to bend low, revealing the pale undersides of their leaves; one gust after another swept through in rapid succession, violently whipping the branches up and down and from side to side, creating quick waves of alternating green and white depending on which side of the leaf was showing, and these waves chased one another just like those that race across a wind-blown field of oats. Every color visible had lost its natural appearance—all shades were tinted with a gray cast from the thick wall of clouds above. The river appeared gray; all distant views looked the same; and even the endless rows of foaming whitecaps were dimly colored by the dark, heavy atmosphere through which their countless masses moved forward. The thunder crashed continuously and deafeningly; one explosion followed another with only brief pauses in between, and the sounds became increasingly sharp and high-pitched, growing more painful to hear; the lightning worked as constantly as the thunder, creating spectacular displays that captivated the eye and sent electric thrills of combined wonder and fear racing through every nerve in the body without pause. The rain fell in incredible amounts; the ear-piercing thunder crashes came closer and closer; the wind grew more violent and started tearing off branches and treetops, hurling them through the air; the pilot-house began rocking and straining and creaking and heaving, and I went down into the hold to check what time it was.

People talk a lot about Alpine thunderstorms, but the storms I've been fortunate enough to witness in the Alps weren't as impressive as some I've experienced in the Mississippi Valley. Of course, I may not have seen the Alps at their most spectacular, and if they can outdo the Mississippi, I'd rather not find out.

On this upstream journey I observed a small towhead (a newly formed island) stretching about half a mile in length, which had developed over the past nineteen years. Given that there was apparently so much time available that nineteen years could be spent creating just a single towhead, what was the point of originally rushing the entire world to completion in only six days? It seems probable that if more time had been allocated from the beginning, the world would have been constructed properly, and this constant process of improvement and repair wouldn't be required today. However, when you rush the creation of a world or a house, you're almost certain to discover eventually that you've overlooked a towhead, or a broom closet, or some other small necessity here and there, which must be added later, regardless of how much cost and frustration it might involve.

We experienced a series of dark nights while traveling up the river, and we noticed that whenever we docked and suddenly flooded the trees with the brilliant burst of electric light, a particular fascinating phenomenon always occurred: hundreds of birds immediately flew out from the clusters of gleaming green leaves and went swooping back and forth through the bright beams, and frequently a songbird would start up and begin singing. We concluded that they mistook this magnificent artificial daylight for the real thing. We enjoyed a wonderful journey on that exceptionally well-managed steamboat and were sorry that it ended so quickly. Through persistence and effort, we succeeded in tracking down nearly all our old friends. One was absent, though; he went to his final rest, whatever that might have been, two years earlier. However, I discovered everything about him. His story helped me understand how enduring the impact of a very minor incident can be. When he worked as an apprentice blacksmith in our town, and I was a student, a pair of young Englishmen visited the community and stayed for a time; and one day they dressed themselves in inexpensive royal costumes and performed the Richard III sword battle with frenzied intensity and tremendous commotion, before the village children. This blacksmith apprentice was present, and the theatrical influence penetrated his very being. This enormous, clumsy, uneducated, slow-minded fellow became obsessed with the stage, and beyond recovery. He vanished and eventually appeared in St. Louis. I encountered him there later on. He stood contemplating on a street corner, with his left hand placed on his hip, his right thumb supporting his chin, head lowered and scowling, slouched hat pulled down over his brow—picturing himself as Othello or some similar character, and imagining that the people walking by noticed his dramatic posture and were filled with wonder.

I joined him and tried to bring him back down to earth, but I couldn't manage it. However, he casually mentioned to me that he was a member of the Walnut Street theater company—and he attempted to say it with indifference, but the indifference was shallow, and an enormous pride shone through it. He told me he was cast for a role in Julius Caesar that night, and if I came I would see him perform. If I came! I told him I wouldn't miss it even if I were dead.

I left completely stunned and amazed, thinking to myself, 'How incredible this is! We had always considered this person to be foolish; but the instant he arrives in a major city, where wisdom and recognition are plentiful, the ability hidden beneath this worn exterior is immediately recognized, and quickly embraced and celebrated.'

But I left the theater that night feeling disappointed and offended; I hadn't caught even a glimpse of my hero, and his name wasn't listed on the program. When I ran into him on the street the following morning, he spoke before I could say anything—

"Did you see me?"

"No, you weren't there."

He looked surprised and disappointed. He said—

"Yes, I was. Indeed I was. I was a Roman soldier."

'Which one?'

'Why didn't you see those Roman soldiers standing in formation back there, who sometimes marched in procession around the stage?'

'Are you talking about the Roman army?—those six sandal-wearing troublemakers in nightgowns, carrying tin shields and helmets, who marched around stepping on each other's feet, led by a skinny, sickly man dressed just like them?'

"That's it! That's it! I was one of those Roman soldiers. I was second to last in line. Six months ago, I was always the very last one, but I got promoted."

Well, they told me that this unfortunate man stayed a Roman soldier until the end—for about thirty-four years. Occasionally they gave him a 'speaking role,' but nothing too complex. He could be counted on to go and deliver lines like, 'My lord, the carriage waits,' but if they dared to give him an additional sentence or two beyond that, his memory would struggle and he was prone to stumble. Still, the poor soul had been diligently rehearsing the role of Hamlet for over thirty years, and he lived and died believing that someday he would be asked to perform it!

And this is what resulted from that brief visit of those young Englishmen to our village so many years ago! What excellent horseshoes this man could have crafted, if not for those Englishmen; and what a poor Roman soldier he turned out to be!

A day or two after we arrived in St. Louis, I was walking down Fourth Street when a gray-haired man seemed startled as he walked past me, then stopped, turned around, looked at me closely with a darkening expression, and finally spoke with sharp irritation—

"Listen, do you have that drink ready yet?"

A madman, I thought at first. But suddenly I recognized him. I forced myself to blush with such effort that it strained every muscle in my body, and I responded as sweetly and charmingly as I possibly could—

"I've been moving a bit slowly, but I'm just now getting close to the spot where they store it. Come inside and give me a hand."

He softened and said if I made it a bottle of champagne, he would agree. He told me he had seen my name in the newspapers and had set all his business aside to come out, determined to find me or die trying, and to make me answer that question properly or kill me, though most of his recent harshness had been more fake than real.

This meeting reminded me of the St. Louis riots from about thirty years ago. I was staying there for a week at that time, living in a boarding house, and this young man was my neighbor across the hall. We witnessed some of the fighting and violence; and eventually we went one evening to an armory where two hundred young men had gathered, responding to a call to be armed and march out against the rioters, under the leadership of a military officer. We trained until about ten o'clock that night; then word arrived that the mob had assembled in great numbers in the lower part of the city, and were destroying everything in their path. Our formation moved immediately. It was an extremely hot night, and my rifle was quite heavy. We marched and marched; and the closer we got to the center of the conflict, the hotter I became and the more thirsty I felt. I was walking behind my friend; so, eventually, I asked him to hold my rifle while I stepped out of line and found something to drink. Then I turned away and went home. I wasn't feeling any concern about him, naturally, because I knew he was so well equipped now that he could look after himself without any difficulty. If I had harbored any uncertainty about that, I would have taken another rifle for him. I departed the city quite early the following morning, and if this gray-haired man hadn't happened to come across my name in the newspapers the other day in St. Louis, and felt compelled to track me down, I would have taken to my grave a heart-wrenching doubt about whether he ever made it through the riots safely or not. I should have asked thirty years ago; I realize that. And I would have asked, if I had possessed the rifles; but, given the situation, he appeared better equipped to handle the investigation than I was.

One Monday, around the time we planned to visit St. Louis, the 'Globe-Democrat' published a couple of pages featuring Sunday attendance statistics, which showed that 119,448 St. Louis residents had attended morning and evening church services the previous day, while 23,102 children had gone to Sunday school. This meant that 142,550 people, from the city's total population of 400,000, had observed the day in a religious manner. I discovered these statistics in a condensed version within an Associated Press telegram and kept them for reference. The numbers suggested that St. Louis had achieved a higher level of spiritual devotion than it could have claimed during my earlier time there. However, now that I'm examining these figures more carefully, I believe the telegraph transmission may have corrupted them. There cannot possibly be more than 150,000 Catholics in the city; the remaining 250,000 residents must be categorized as Protestants. According to this dubious telegram, out of these 250,000 Protestants, only 26,362 attended church and Sunday school, whereas out of the 150,000 Catholics, 116,188 participated in church and Sunday school activities.

Chapter 52: A Burning Brand

All at once the thought came into my mind, 'I have not sought out Mr. Brown.'

Based on that passage, I want to step away from the main topic of my discussion and take a brief detour. I wish to share a secret that I have kept for nine years, and which has become a heavy burden to carry.

Nine years ago, on a particular occasion, I had declared with deep emotion, "If I ever return to St. Louis, I will find Mr. Brown, the prominent grain merchant, and request the honor of shaking his hand."

The situation and circumstances happened like this. A friend of mine, who was a clergyman, came by one evening and said—

'I have an extraordinary letter here that I want to read to you, if I can manage it without becoming emotional. However, I need to provide some background information first. The letter was written by a former thief and vagrant from the lowest social class and most degraded upbringing, a man completely tainted by criminal activity and immersed in ignorance; but, thank God, with a treasure of pure gold hidden within him, as you will discover. His letter is addressed to a burglar named Williams, who is serving a nine-year sentence in a state prison for burglary. Williams was an exceptionally bold burglar who practiced that criminal profession for several years; but he was finally caught and imprisoned, awaiting trial in a town where he had broken into a house at night, gun in hand, and forced the homeowner to give him $8,000 in government bonds. Williams was far from an ordinary criminal; he was a Harvard College graduate and came from respectable New England family. His father was a minister. While confined in jail, his health started to decline, and he faced the threat of tuberculosis. This circumstance, combined with the chance for contemplation provided by solitary confinement, produced its effect—its inevitable effect. He began to think deeply; his early moral education reasserted itself powerfully, and worked with strong influence on his mind and heart. He left his former life behind and became a devoted Christian. Some women in the town learned of this transformation, visited him, and through their encouraging words supported him in his good intentions and strengthened him to persist in his reformed life. The trial resulted in his conviction and sentencing to the state prison for nine years, as I mentioned earlier. In the prison he met the unfortunate man I referred to at the start of my story, Jack Hunt, the author of the letter I am about to read. You will see that this friendship proved beneficial for Hunt. When Hunt's sentence ended, he traveled to St. Louis; and from there he wrote his letter to Williams. The letter never went beyond the prison warden's office, naturally; inmates are rarely permitted to receive correspondence from the outside world. The prison officials read this letter, but they did not destroy it. They could not bring themselves to do so. They shared it with several people, and eventually it reached those women I mentioned earlier. Recently I encountered an old friend of mine—a minister—who had seen this letter and was deeply affected by it. The simple memory of it moved him so profoundly that he could not discuss it without his voice trembling. He promised to obtain a copy for me; and here it is—an exact reproduction, with all the flaws of the original maintained. It contains many slang terms—criminal jargon—but their meanings have been added in parentheses by the prison authorities'—

St. Louis, June 9, 1872.

Mr. W—— friend Charlie if I may call you that: I know you are surprised to get a letter from me, but I hope you won't be angry at my writing to you. I want to tell you my thanks for the way you talked to me when I was in prison—it has led me to try and be a better man; I guess you thought I did not care for what you said, and at first I didn't, but I knew you were a man who had done important work with good men and wanted no fool, nor wanted empty talk and all the boys knew it.

I used to think at night about what you said, and because of it I stopped swearing months before my time was up, because I saw it wasn't any good, no matter what—the day my time was up you told me that if I would give up the criminal life (quit stealing) and live honestly for months, it would be the best thing I ever did in my life. The state agent gave me a ticket to here, and on the train I thought more about what you said to me, but didn't make up my mind. When we got to Chicago on the trains from there to here, I stole an old woman's purse;

(Robbed her of her pocketbook) I had barely taken it when I wished I hadn't done it, because a while before that I had made up my mind to be an honest man, for months I swear, but I forgot about it when I saw the purse was easy to grab—but I stayed close to her and when she got off the train at a station I said, ma'am have you lost anything. And she discovered her purse was gone— is this it I said, giving it to her—well if you aren't honest, she said, but I didn't have enough nerve to stand that kind of talk, so I left her quickly. When I got here I had $1 and 25 cents left and I didn't get any work for 3 days since I'm not strong enough for rough work on a steamboat (as a deck hand)—The afternoon of the 3rd day I spent my last 10 cents on large round sea biscuits and cheese and I felt pretty bad and was thinking I would have to go back to picking pockets again, when I thought of what you once said about a person calling on the Lord when he was in trouble, and I thought I would try it once anyway, but when I tried it I got stuck at the beginning, and all I could get out was, Lord give a poor fellow a chance to make things right for 3 months for Christ's sake, amen; and I kept thinking about it over and over as I walked along— about an hour after that I was on 4th Street and this is what happened and is the reason I'm where I am now and which I will tell you about before I finish writing. As I was walking along I heard a loud noise and saw a horse running away with a carriage with 2 children in it, and I grabbed a piece of wooden box cover from the sidewalk and ran into the middle of the street, and when the horse came up I hit him over the head as hard as I could—the board split to pieces and the horse slowed down a little and I grabbed the reins and pulled his head down until he stopped—the gentleman who owned him came running up and as soon as he saw the children were all right, he shook hands with me and gave me a $50 bill, and my asking the Lord to help me came into my mind, and I was so amazed I couldn't let go of the reins or say anything—he saw something was wrong, and

coming back to me said, my boy are you hurt? & the thought came into my head just then to ask him for work; & I asked him to take back the bill and give me a job—he says, jump in here & let's talk about it, but keep the money—he asked me if I could take care of horses & I said yes, for I used to hang around livery stables & often would help clean & drive horses, he told me he wanted a man for that work, & would give me $16 a month & board me. You bet I took that chance at once. That night in my little room over the stable I sat a long time thinking over my past life & of what had just happened & I just got down on my knees & thanked the Lord for the job & to help me to make things right, & to bless you for putting me up to it, & the next morning I did it again & got me some new clothes & a bible for I made up my mind after what the Lord had done for me I would read the bible every night and morning, & ask him to keep an eye on me. When I had been there about a week Mr. Brown (that's his name) came in my room one night and saw me reading the bible—he asked me if I was a Christian & I told him no—he asked me how it was I read the bible instead of papers & books—Well Charlie I thought I had better give him a fair deal from the start, so I told him all about my being in prison & about you, & how I had almost given up looking for work & how the Lord got me the job when I asked him; & the only way I had to pay him back was to read the bible & make things right, & I asked him to give me a chance for 3 months—he talked to me like a father for a long time, & told me I could stay & then I felt better than ever I had in my life, for I had given Mr. Brown a fair start with me & now I didn't fear anyone exposing my past life & running me off the job—the next morning he called me into the library & gave me another honest talk, & advised me to study some every day, & he would help me one or 2 hours every night, & he gave me an Arithmetic, a spelling book, a Geography & a writing book, & he teaches me every night—he lets me come into the house for prayers every morning, & got me put in a bible class in the Sunday School which I like very much for it helps me to understand my bible better.

Now, Charlie, the 3 months on the square ended 2 months ago, and as you said, it is the best job I ever did in my life, and I started another of the same sort right away, only this one is to last a lifetime with God's help, Charlie—I wrote this letter to tell you I do think God has forgiven my sins and heard your prayers, for you told me you would pray for me—I know I love to read his word and tell him all my troubles and he helps me I know for I have plenty of chances to steal but I don't feel like it as I once did and now I take more pleasure in going to church than to the theater and that wasn't so once—our minister and others often talk with me and a month ago they wanted me to join the church, but I said no, not now, I may be mistaken in my feelings, I will wait awhile, but now I feel that God has called me and on the first Sunday in July I will join the church—dear friend I wish I could write to you as I feel, but I can't do it yet—you know I learned to read and write while in prison and I haven't gotten far enough along to write as I would talk; I know I haven't spelled all the words right in this and lots of other mistakes but you will excuse it I know, for you know I was brought up in a poor house until I ran away, and that I never knew who my father and mother were and I don't know my right name, and I hope you won't be mad at me, but I have as much right to one name as another and I have taken your name, for you won't use it when you get out I know, and you are the man I think most of in the world; so I hope you won't be mad—I am doing well, I put $10 a month in bank with $25 of the $50—if you ever want any or all of it let me know, and it is yours. I wish you would let me send you some now. I send you with this a receipt for a year of Little's Living Age, I didn't know what you would like and I told Mr. Brown and he said he thought you would like it—I wish I was near you so I could send you food on holidays; it would spoil in this weather from here, but I will send you a box next thanksgiving anyway—next week Mr. Brown takes me into his store as light porter and will advance me as soon as I know a little more—he keeps a big grocery store, wholesale—I forgot to tell you of my mission school, sunday school class—the school is in the sunday afternoon, I went out two sunday afternoons, and picked up seven kids (little boys) and got them to come in. Two of them knew as much as I did and I had them put in a class where they could learn something. I don't know much myself, but as these kids can't read I get on nicely with them. I make sure of them by going after them every Sunday an hour before school time, I also got 4 girls to come. Tell Mack and Harry about me, if they will come out here when their time is up I will get them jobs at once. I hope you will excuse this long letter and all mistakes, I wish I could see you for I can't write as I would talk—I hope the warm weather is doing your lungs good—I was afraid when you were bleeding you would die—give my respects to all the boys and tell them how I am doing—I am doing well and every one here treats me as kind as they can—Mr. Brown is going to write to you sometime—I hope some day you will write to me, this letter is from your very true friend

C—— W——

who you know as Jack Hunt.

I'm sending you Mr. Brown's business card. Please forward my letter to him.

Here was genuine eloquence; compelling eloquence; and without a single embellishment or decoration to enhance it. I have rarely been so profoundly moved by any piece of writing. The person reading it stumbled throughout, speaking with a faltering and broken voice; yet he had attempted to strengthen his composure through several private readings of the letter before bringing it before others. He was testing it on me to determine whether there was any possibility of his being able to read the document to his prayer meeting with some reasonable control over his emotions. The outcome was not encouraging. Nevertheless, he decided to take the chance; and he did. He managed to get through it reasonably well; but his audience broke down early, and remained in that state until the end.

The letter's reputation quickly spread throughout the town. A fellow minister came and borrowed the original document, incorporated it entirely into a sermon, delivered that sermon to twelve hundred people on a Sunday morning, and the letter moved them to tears. Then my friend included it in a sermon and presented it to his Sunday morning congregation. It achieved another victory. The entire congregation wept together as one.

My friend went on summer vacation to the fishing regions of our northern British neighbors, and he brought this sermon along with him, thinking he might possibly need to deliver a sermon. One day, he was asked to preach. The small church was packed. Among those in attendance were the late Dr. J. G. Holland, the late Mr. Seymour from the 'New York Times,' Mr. Page, the philanthropist and temperance advocate, and, I believe, Senator Frye from Maine. The remarkable letter performed its usual magic; everyone was deeply moved, everyone wept; tears streamed steadily down Dr. Holland's face, and much the same could be said about all who were present. Mr. Page was so filled with enthusiasm about the letter that he declared he wouldn't rest until he made a pilgrimage to that prison and spoke with the man who had been able to inspire a fellow prisoner to write such an invaluable piece.

Oh, that unfortunate messenger—and that other man! If they had only been in Jericho, that letter would have echoed throughout the world and moved the hearts of every nation for a thousand years to come, and no one might ever have discovered that it was the most outrageous, shameless, and cleverly crafted piece of deception and trickery that was ever devised to deceive poor trusting people!

The letter was nothing but a complete fraud, and that's the honest truth. When you look at it overall, it stood alone among all scams. It was flawless, it was well-crafted, balanced, thorough, and absolutely massive!

The reader discovers this information at this moment; however, we didn't find out until several miles and weeks after this point in the events. My friend returned from the forest, and he along with other ministers and lay missionaries started flooding audiences once again with their own tears and those of their listeners; I pleaded earnestly for authorization to publish the letter in a magazine and share the emotional account of its successes; many people received copies of the letter, with approval to distribute them in handwritten form, but not in printed format;

copies were mailed to the Sandwich Islands and other distant territories.

Charles Dudley Warner was attending church one day when the worn letter was read aloud and mourned over. Afterward, at the church door, he delivered a particularly cold blow to the clergyman with his question—

"Do you know if that letter is real?"

It was the first time anyone had ever expressed doubt; but it had that nauseating impact that initial suspicions about someone you admire always carry. Some conversation followed—

"Why—what would make you think it isn't real?"

'I don't know of anything specific, except that it's too polished, well-organized, and smoothly written, and too skillfully constructed for someone who lacks knowledge or experience. I believe it was created by an educated person.'

The writer had spotted the literary techniques being used. If you examine the letter now, you'll notice them yourself—they're visible in every single line.

Right away, the clergyman left with this growing suspicion taking root in his mind, and he wrote to a minister living in the town where Williams had been imprisoned and converted. He asked for clarification and also inquired whether someone in the literary profession (referring to me) might be permitted to publish the letter and share its story. He soon received this response—

Rev. —— ——

My dear friend, regarding that 'convict's letter,' there can be no question about whether it's authentic. 'Williams,' the person it was written to, was imprisoned in our jail and claimed to have been converted, and Reverend Mr. ——, the chaplain, had great confidence in the authenticity of this transformation—as much confidence as anyone can have in such circumstances.

The letter was sent to one of our ladies, who teaches Sunday school—sent either by Williams himself, or by the chaplain of the state prison, most likely. She has been very troubled by having so much public attention, worried that it might appear to be a violation of trust, or cause harm to Williams. Regarding its publication, I cannot give permission; however, if the names and locations were left out, and particularly if it were sent outside the country, I believe you could take responsibility and publish it.

This is a remarkable letter that no Christian intellectual, and certainly no unsaved person, could have ever written. By demonstrating how grace works within a human heart—particularly one that was deeply corrupted and sinful—it validates its own divine source and challenges our insufficient faith in grace's ability to overcome any type of evil.

"Mr. Brown" from St. Louis, someone mentioned, was originally from Hartford. Do all the people you send out from Hartford serve their Master with such dedication?

P.S.—Williams remains in the state prison, serving a lengthy sentence of nine years, I believe. He has been ill and at risk of developing tuberculosis, but I haven't checked on his condition recently. The woman I mentioned likely keeps in touch with him through letters and will certainly make sure he's looked after.

This letter showed up just a few days after it was written—and Mr. Williams's reputation shot right back up. Mr. Warner's underhanded suspicion was put to rest in the cold, cold ground, where it clearly belonged. It was a suspicion built on nothing but internal evidence anyway; and when it comes to internal evidence, it's a vast territory and a game that two people can play: as shown by this other internal evidence, found by the person who wrote the note mentioned above, that 'it is a remarkable letter—which no Christian genius, much less someone without divine blessing, could ever have written.'

I now had permission to publish—as long as I removed names and locations and sent my story outside the country. So I selected an Australian magazine as my outlet, since it was far enough away from the country, and began working on my article. Meanwhile, the ministers started the pumps running again, using the letter to operate the handles.

But in the meantime, Brother Page had been stirring up trouble. He hadn't visited the prison himself, but he had sent a copy of that famous letter to the prison chaplain, along with what appeared to be questions. He received a reply dated four days after that other Brother's comforting letter, and before I finished writing my article, it somehow made its way to me. I have the original document in front of me right now, and I'm including it here. It contains plenty of solid internal evidence—

STATE PRISON, CHAPLAIN'S OFFICE, July 11, 1873.

Dear Brother Page,—I'm returning the letter you kindly lent me. I'm afraid we cannot verify that it's genuine. The letter claims to be addressed to some prisoner here. No such letter was ever delivered to a prisoner at this facility. All incoming letters are thoroughly reviewed by prison officers before reaching the inmates, and such a letter would not have been overlooked. Furthermore, Charles Williams is not a Christian man, but rather a dissolute, cunning wastrel whose father serves as a minister of the gospel. The name he uses is false. I'm pleased to have made your acquaintance. I'm currently preparing a lecture about life as seen through prison bars, and I would like to present it in your area.

And so that little drama came to an end. My poor article was thrown into the fire; while the materials for it had become more abundant and infinitely richer than they had been before, there were people all around me who, despite having eagerly wanted the publication earlier, now stood united in wanting to suppress it at this stage and turn of events. They said: 'Wait—the wound is still too fresh.' All copies of the famous letter except mine vanished suddenly; and from that moment on, the same old silence returned to the churches as before. Generally, the town wore a broad grin for a while, but there were certain places where that grin didn't appear, and where it was dangerous to mention the ex-convict's letter.

A word of explanation. 'Jack Hunt,' the supposed author of the letter, was a fictional character. The burglar Williams—a Harvard graduate and the son of a minister—wrote the letter himself, addressing it to himself: he managed to smuggle it out of the prison and had it delivered to people who had supported and encouraged his conversion—knowing that two things would occur: no one would question or investigate whether the letter was genuine, and the main point of it would be recognized and would produce a valuable outcome—specifically, the result of launching a campaign to secure Mr. Williams's pardon and release from prison.

That crucial point is thrown in so cleverly and casually, then immediately left hanging at the end of the letter without any elaboration, that a casual reader would never realize it was the central message of the entire letter, assuming they even noticed it at all. This is the crucial point—

"I hope the warm weather is helping your lungs—I was worried when you were bleeding that you might die—give my respects," etc.

That's all there is to it—just a brief touch and then moving on—no lingering over it. Yet it was designed for an eye that would quickly notice it, and it was meant to stir a compassionate heart to attempt to bring about the freedom of a poor reformed and cleansed fellow trapped in the deadly grasp of tuberculosis.

When I first heard that letter read nine years ago, I felt it was the most extraordinary one I had ever come across. It warmed my heart so much toward Mr. Brown of St. Louis that I declared if I ever visited that city again, I would search for that wonderful man and kiss the hem of his garment if it was a new one. Well, I did visit St. Louis, but I didn't look for Mr. Brown; for sadly, investigations from long ago had revealed that the kind-hearted Brown, like 'Jack Hunt,' wasn't a real person at all, but simply a complete fabrication of that talented scoundrel, Williams—burglar, Harvard graduate, and son of a clergyman.

Chapter 53: My Childhood Home

We boarded one of the fast boats operated by the St. Louis and St. Paul Packet Company and began our journey up the river.

When I was a boy and first saw where the Missouri River flows into the Mississippi, it was located twenty-two or twenty-three miles upstream from St. Louis, based on what the river pilots estimated at the time; the constant erosion of the riverbanks has since shifted it downstream by eight miles; and those same pilots predict that within five years the river will carve through the land and move the mouth another five miles downstream, which would place it just ten miles from St. Louis.

About nightfall we passed the large and thriving town of Alton, Illinois; and before daylight the next morning we passed the town of Louisiana, Missouri, a quiet village in my day, but now a busy railway hub; however, all the towns out there are railway centers now. I couldn't clearly recognize the place. This struck me as strange, because when I left the rebel army in '61 I retreated to Louisiana in good order; at least in good enough order for someone who hadn't yet learned how to retreat according to military rules, and had to rely on natural instinct. It seemed to me that for a first attempt at a retreat it wasn't badly executed. I hadn't done any advancing in that entire campaign that came close to matching it.

There was a railway bridge spanning the river at this spot, dotted with bright, glowing lights, creating a truly beautiful sight.

At seven in the morning we arrived in Hannibal, Missouri, where I spent my childhood. I had caught a brief glimpse of it fifteen years earlier, and another quick look six years before that, but both visits were so short they barely mattered. The only impression of the town that stayed with me was how I remembered it when I first left twenty-nine years ago. That image remained as sharp and clear in my mind as a photograph. I stepped off the boat feeling like someone returning from a long-dead era. I experienced something like what the Bastille prisoners must have felt when they emerged to look at Paris after years of imprisonment, noticing how strangely the familiar and unfamiliar blended together before their eyes. I could see the new houses clearly enough, but they didn't disturb the older image in my memory, because through their solid brick and stone I could still see the vanished houses that had once stood in those same spots with perfect clarity.

It was Sunday morning, and everyone was still in bed. So I walked through the empty streets, still seeing the town as it used to be, not as it is now, and recognizing and mentally greeting a hundred familiar objects that no longer exist; and finally climbed Holiday's Hill to get a complete view. The entire town stretched out below me then, and I could identify and pinpoint every location, every detail. Naturally, I was quite moved. I said, 'Many of the people I once knew in this peaceful haven of my childhood are now in heaven; some, I hope, are in the other place.' The things around me and in front of me made me feel like a boy again— convinced me that I was a boy again, and that I had simply been having an unusually long dream; but my thoughts ruined all that; for they forced me to say, 'I see fifty old houses down there, into each of which I could walk and find either a man or a woman who was a baby or not yet born when I last noticed those houses, or a grandmother who was a young bride at that time.'

From this elevated position, the sweeping view stretching up and down the river and across the vast wooded landscapes of Illinois is truly magnificent—among the most stunning sights along the Mississippi, I believe; though this is a risky statement to make, since the eight hundred miles of waterway between St. Louis and St. Paul offer a continuous parade of breathtaking scenes. Perhaps my fondness for this particular vista clouds my judgment in its favor; I cannot be certain of that. Regardless, it was deeply satisfying in its beauty to me, and it possessed this benefit over all the other companions I was preparing to encounter once more: it had remained unchanged; it was as youthful and vibrant and attractive and elegant as it had always been; while the faces of the others would be aged, and marked by life's battles, and etched with their sorrows and failures, and would bring me no elevation of the soul.

An elderly man, out for an early morning walk, approached, and we talked about the weather before moving on to other topics. I couldn't recall his face. He mentioned he had been living here for twenty-eight years. So he had arrived after I left, and I had never encountered him before. I asked him several questions; first about a friend of mine from Sunday school—what had happened to him?

'He graduated with honors from a college in the East, drifted off somewhere into the world, failed at everything he tried, disappeared from people's knowledge and memory years ago, and is believed to have completely ruined his life.'

"He was intelligent and showed great potential when he was young."

"Yes, but what actually happened is what matters in the end."

I asked about another young man who had been by far the smartest student in our village school when I was a child.

'He also graduated with honors from an Eastern college, but life beat him in every fight from the very beginning, and he died years ago in one of the Territories as a broken man.'

I inquired about another one of the intelligent young men.

"He is a success, always has been, always will be, I think."

I asked about a young man who had come to town to study for one of the professions when I was a boy.

'He switched to something else before he finished—changed from medicine to law, or from law to medicine—then moved on to yet another new pursuit; left town for a year, returned with a young wife; started drinking, then gambling in secret; eventually took his wife and two small children to her father's house, and departed for Mexico; his situation deteriorated further and further, and he ultimately died there, without a penny to pay for a burial shroud, and without a single friend to come to the funeral.'

'It's a shame, because he was the kindest, most cheerful, and optimistic young man you could ever meet.'

I chose another boy.

"Oh, he's doing fine. He still lives here, has a wife and kids, and is doing well for himself."

Same verdict concerning other boys.

I named three schoolgirls.

"The first two live here, are married, and have children; the other died long ago and never married."

I mentioned, with deep feeling, one of my first loves.

"She's doing fine. She's been married three times—buried two husbands, divorced the third one, and I hear she's getting ready to marry some old guy out in Colorado. She's got children scattered all over the place, just about everywhere."

The response to several other questions was short and straightforward—

"Killed in the war."

I chose another boy.

"Well, his situation is really strange! There wasn't a single person in this town who didn't know that boy was a complete fool; a total idiot; just a stupid moron, you could say. Everyone knew it, and everyone said it. Well, if that same boy isn't the top lawyer in the State of Missouri today, then I'm a Democrat!"

'Is that so?'

"It's actually true. I'm telling you the truth."

"How do you explain it?"

'How do you explain it? There's no way to explain it, except that if you send a complete fool to St. Louis, and you don't tell them he's a complete fool, they'll never figure it out. One thing's for certain—if I had a complete fool, I'd know exactly what to do with him: send him to St. Louis—it's the finest market in the world for that kind of person. Well, when you really look at the whole situation, and think it through carefully, doesn't it just beat anything you've ever heard of?'

"Well, yes, it does seem that way. But don't you think perhaps the people from Hannibal were the ones who were wrong about the boy, rather than the people from St. Louis?"

"Oh, that's ridiculous! The people here have known him since he was a baby—they knew him a hundred times better than those St. Louis fools could have ever known him. No, if you've got any damn fools you want to make money off of, take my advice—send them to St. Louis."

I talked about many people I used to know. Some had died, some had moved away, some had done well for themselves, and some had failed completely. But when it came to about a dozen of them, the news was reassuring:

"Wealthy people still live here, and the town is filled with their children."

I asked about Miss ———.

Died in the mental hospital three or four years ago—never left from the time she was admitted; and she was always in pain, too; never recovered even a fragment of her sanity.

If what he said was true, this was indeed a terrible tragedy. Thirty-six years locked away in an asylum, all because some young people wanted to have a bit of fun! I was just a small child at the time, and I witnessed those foolish young women sneaking on their tiptoes into the room where Miss —— was sitting, reading by lamplight at midnight. The girl leading the group was dressed in a burial shroud and wore a pale mask. She crept up behind the unsuspecting woman, tapped her on the shoulder, and when she looked up, she let out a scream and immediately went into fits. She never recovered from the shock of that fright and lost her mind completely. Today it seems almost impossible to believe that people had such strong faith in ghosts just a short time ago. But they absolutely did.

After asking about all the other people I could think of, I finally asked about myself:

"Oh, he succeeded well enough—another case of damned fool. If they'd sent him to St. Louis, he'd have succeeded sooner."

I felt deeply satisfied that I had been wise enough to tell this honest gentleman from the start that my name was Smith.

Chapter 54: Past and Present

Being left alone up there, I continued identifying old houses in the distant town and summoning their former residents from the musty past. Among them I soon recognized the house belonging to Lem Hackett's father (fictitious name). It transported me back more than a generation in an instant, placing me in the middle of an era when life's events weren't the natural and logical outcomes of broad universal laws, but rather of specific commands, and were loaded with very precise and clear purposes—partly meant to punish, partly meant to warn; and typically limited to local circumstances.

When I was a small boy, Lem Hackett drowned on a Sunday. He fell out of an empty flatboat where he had been playing.

Weighed down by sin, he sank to the bottom like an anvil. He was the only boy in the village who slept that night. The rest of us lay awake, repenting. We didn't need the information delivered from the pulpit that evening telling us that Lem's death was a case of divine judgment—we already knew that. There was a fierce thunderstorm that night, and it raged continuously until nearly dawn. The winds howled, the windows rattled, the rain swept across the roof in driving sheets, and at the briefest intervals the pitch-black darkness of night disappeared, the houses across the way blazed out white and blinding for a trembling instant, then the solid darkness closed in again and a splitting clap of thunder followed, which seemed to tear everything in the neighborhood to pieces. I sat up in bed shaking and trembling, waiting for the end of the world and expecting it to come. To me there was nothing strange or out of place about heaven making such a commotion over Lem Hackett. It seemed like the right and proper thing to do. I had no doubt that all the angels were gathered together, discussing this boy's case and watching the terrible bombardment of our poor little village with satisfaction and approval. There was one thing that troubled me deeply: the thought that this focusing of heavenly attention on our village would surely draw the observers' notice to people among us who might otherwise have gone unnoticed for years. I felt that I was not only one of those people, but the very one most likely to be discovered. That discovery could only have one outcome: I would be burning in the fire with Lem before the chill of the river had even been warmed out of him. I knew this would be perfectly just and fair. I was making things worse for myself all the time by harboring a secret resentment against Lem for drawing this deadly attention to me, but I couldn't help it—this sinful thought kept invading my mind despite my efforts. Every time the lightning flashed I held my breath and thought I was finished. In my terror and misery, I shamefully began suggesting other boys and mentioning their acts that were more wicked than mine and especially deserved punishment—and I tried to convince myself that I was simply doing this casually, without any intention of redirecting heaven's attention to them in order to get it off myself. With cunning wisdom I disguised these mentions as sorrowful memories and backhanded fake prayers that these boys' sins might be overlooked—'Perhaps they may repent.' 'It's true that Jim Smith broke a window and lied about it—but maybe he didn't mean any harm. And although Tom Holmes uses more bad words than any other boy in the village, he probably plans to repent—though he's never said he would. And while it's a fact that John Jones did go fishing a little on Sunday once, he didn't really catch anything except one small worthless mudcat; and maybe that wouldn't have been so terrible if he had thrown it back—as he claims he did, but he didn't. Too bad they won't repent of these awful things—though maybe they still will.'

But while I was foolishly attempting to attract attention to these unfortunate men—who were undoubtedly drawing heavenly attention to me at that very moment, though I never once realized it—I had carelessly left my candle lit. This was not a time to overlook even minor safety measures. There was no need to provide any additional means for drawing notice to myself—so I extinguished the light.

It was a long night for me, and probably the most painful one I had ever experienced. I suffered terrible guilt for sins I knew I had committed, and for others I wasn't sure about, yet I was certain they had been recorded against me in a book by an angel who was wiser than I was and didn't rely on memory for such important matters. It occurred to me eventually that I had made a completely foolish and disastrous mistake in one way: no doubt I had not only guaranteed my own destruction by drawing attention to those other boys, but had already sealed their fate as well! Surely the lightning had struck them all dead in their beds by now! The agony and terror this thought brought me made my earlier suffering seem insignificant in comparison.

Things had gotten really serious. I decided to completely change my ways right away; I also decided to join the church the next day, if I lived to see the sun rise. I decided to stop sinning in every way possible, and to live a pure and perfect life from then on. I would always be on time for church and Sunday school; visit sick people; bring food baskets to the poor (just to meet the basic requirements, even though I knew we didn't have anyone so poor that they wouldn't hit me over the head with the basket for bothering them); I would teach other boys how to behave properly, and accept the beatings that would follow without complaint; I would live entirely on religious pamphlets; I would go into the bar and warn the drunks—and finally, if I avoided the fate of those who become too good for this world too young, I would become a missionary.

The storm calmed down as dawn approached, and I slowly drifted off to sleep feeling grateful to Lem Hackett for departing to eternal damnation so suddenly, thereby preventing a much more terrible catastrophe—my own destruction.

But when I woke up feeling refreshed after a while and discovered that those other boys were still alive, I had a vague feeling that maybe the whole thing had been a false alarm; that all the chaos had been about Lem and no one else. The world appeared so bright and secure that there didn't seem to be any genuine reason to change my ways. I felt somewhat subdued that day, and perhaps the following day as well; after that, my intention to reform gradually faded from my thoughts, and I enjoyed a peaceful, comfortable period once more, until the next crisis arrived.

That storm arrived about three weeks later, and it was the most bewildering one I had ever encountered, because that afternoon, 'Dutchy' drowned. Dutchy was part of our Sunday school. He was a German boy who lacked common sense, but he was irritatingly virtuous and possessed an extraordinary memory. One Sunday he became the envy of every young person and the subject of conversation throughout the admiring village by reciting three thousand verses of Scripture without making a single mistake; then he went out the very next day and drowned.

Circumstances made his death particularly striking. We were all swimming in a muddy creek that had a deep pool in it, and in this pool the barrel makers had submerged a stack of green hickory hoop poles to soak, about twelve feet underwater. We were diving and competing to see who could stay under the longest. We managed to stay down by gripping the hoop poles. Dutchy performed so poorly that he was met with laughter and mockery every time his head broke the surface. Finally he seemed wounded by the teasing, and pleaded with us to stand quietly on the bank and treat him fairly by giving him an honest count—'be friendly and kind just this once, and don't miscount just to have the pleasure of laughing at me.' Sneaky winks were shared among us, and everyone said 'Alright, Dutchy—go ahead, we'll play fair.'

Dutchy dove into the water, but instead of starting to count, the boys followed one of their group's lead and ran to a nearby cluster of blackberry bushes where they hid. They pictured Dutchy's embarrassment when he would surface after an incredible effort only to discover the area quiet and empty, with no one there to cheer for him. The thought delighted them so much that they kept bursting into stifled giggles. Time passed, and eventually one boy who was peeking through the thorny branches said with surprise—

"Why, he hasn't come up yet!"

The laughter came to an end.

"Boys, it's an amazing dive," said one.

"Don't worry about that," said another, "the joke on him is even better because of it."

There were a few more comments, and then silence fell. The conversation stopped, and everyone started looking through the vines. Soon, the boys' expressions began to show unease, then worry, then fear. The calm water remained completely still. Hearts started racing, and faces grew pale. We all quietly slipped out and gathered on the shore, our frightened eyes moving back and forth between each other's faces and the water.

"Someone has to go down there and check!"

Yes, that was obvious; but nobody wanted that gruesome job. "Draw straws!"

So we did—with hands that shook so violently we barely knew what we were doing. The lot fell to me, and I went down. The water was so murky I couldn't see anything, but I felt around among the hoop poles, and soon grasped a limp wrist that gave me no response—and even if it had, I wouldn't have known it, because I let it go with such frightened suddenness.

The boy had gotten trapped among the hoop poles and was stuck there, unable to free himself. I rushed to the surface and shared the terrible news. Some of us realized that if the boy was pulled out immediately he might have been saved, but we never considered that possibility. We couldn't think clearly; we didn't know what to do, so we did nothing—except the younger boys cried desperately, and we all frantically threw on our clothes, grabbing whatever we could find, and usually putting them on inside-out and backwards. Then we hurried away and raised the alarm, but none of us returned to witness the end of the tragedy. We had something more pressing to deal with: we all rushed home, wasting no time in preparing to live better lives.

The night soon fell. Then that incredible and completely inexplicable storm arrived. I was completely stunned; I couldn't make sense of it. It felt like there had to be some error. The forces of nature were unleashed, and they crashed and thundered and flashed wildly in the most chaotic and desperate way. All courage and optimism drained from me, and the grim thought kept drifting through my mind, 'If a boy who has memorized three thousand verses isn't good enough, what hope does anyone else have?'

Of course I never doubted for a moment that the storm had come because of Dutchy, or that he or any other insignificant creature deserved such a magnificent display from heaven; what bothered me was only the lesson it taught; because it convinced me that if Dutchy, with all his good qualities, wasn't pleasing to God, it would be pointless for me to try to change my ways, since I would certainly fall far short of that boy, no matter how hard I might try. Still, I did try to change—an overwhelming fear forced me to do so—but the following days of happiness and bright weather kept interfering, and within a month I had slipped back so far that once again I was as lost and comfortable as I had ever been.

Breakfast time was approaching while I pondered these thoughts and recalled these ancient events; so I returned to the present and walked down the hill.

On my way through town to the hotel, I noticed the house where I lived as a child. Based on today's standards, the people who live there now have the same worth as I do; but back in my day, they would have been valued at no less than five hundred dollars each. They are Black people.

After breakfast, I went out by myself again, planning to find some of the Sunday schools and see how today's students might compare with their predecessors who had sat beside me in those same places and had likely looked up to me as an example— though I can't really recall that clearly now. Near the public square, there had been in my time a run-down little brick church called the 'Old Ship of Zion,' where I had gone as a Sunday school student; and I found the location easily enough, but the old church was nowhere to be found; it had been torn down, and a neat and rather cheerful new building stood in its place. The students were better dressed and more attractive than those from my era; as a result, they bore no resemblance to their forebears; and therefore there was nothing recognizable to me in their faces. Nevertheless, I watched them with profound interest and a longing sadness, and if I had been a girl I would have wept; for they were the children of, and represented, and filled the seats of, boys and girls some of whom I had cherished loving, and some of whom I had enjoyed disliking, but all of whom were precious to me for one reason or another, from so many years past—and, Lord, where are they now!

I was deeply moved and would have been thankful to be permitted to stay undisturbed and observe to my heart's content; but a bald-headed supervisor who had been a blonde-haired Sunday school classmate of mine in that same place during our childhood years recognized me, and I spoke a stream of excited gibberish to those children to conceal the emotions that were within me, and which could not have been expressed without revealing feelings that would have been seen as inconsistent with my usual character.

Making speeches without any preparation isn't one of my talents, and I had decided to avoid any new opportunities to do so. However, in the next and larger Sunday school, I found myself standing at the back of the gathering, which made me quite willing to step onto the platform for a moment just to get a better view of the students. In that spontaneous moment, I couldn't remember any of the old foolish speeches that visitors used to subject me to when I was a student there myself. I regretted this because it would have provided me with both time and an excuse to linger there and take a long, satisfying look at what I feel free to describe as a display of fresh young beauty that couldn't be matched in any other Sunday school of the same size. Since I was speaking merely to get an opportunity to observe, and since I was stretching out this random nonsense solely to extend my observation time, I thought it only proper to admit these selfish motives, and I did exactly that.

If the Model Boy attended either of these Sunday schools, I didn't notice him there. The Model Boy from my era—we only ever had one—was flawless: flawless in his manners, flawless in his appearance, flawless in his behavior, flawless in his devotion to his parents, flawless in his outward display of religious devotion; but deep down he was self-righteous; and as for what was inside his head, it could have been swapped with the filling of a pie and no one would have suffered except the pie. This boy's faultless behavior served as a constant reminder of inadequacy to every other boy in town. All the mothers admired him, while all their sons despised him. I learned what happened to him later, but since it disappointed me, I won't go into the specifics. He became successful in life.

Chapter 55: A Vendetta and Other Things

During my three-day visit to the town, I woke up each morning feeling like a young boy again—because in my dreams, all the faces appeared youthful once more, looking exactly as they had in those earlier days—but each night I went to sleep feeling like I was a hundred years old, since throughout the day I had been seeing those same faces as they appear now.

Of course I experienced some surprises at first, before I had gotten used to how things had changed. I encountered young women who appeared not to have changed at all; but it turned out they were the daughters of the young women I was thinking of— sometimes their granddaughters. When someone tells you that a fifty-year-old stranger is a grandmother, there's nothing surprising about that; but if, instead, she's someone you knew as a little girl, it seems impossible. You tell yourself, 'How can a little girl be a grandmother.' It takes some time to accept and understand the reality that while you've been aging, your friends haven't been frozen in time.

I observed that the most significant changes I could see were in the women, not the men. I encountered men who had barely changed after thirty years; however, their wives had aged considerably. These were virtuous women; being virtuous takes a heavy toll.

There was a saddler I wanted to visit, but he was no longer there. He had been dead for many years, they told me. Once or twice each day, the saddler would come rushing down the street, pulling on his coat as he ran, and then everyone knew a steamboat was approaching. Everyone also understood that John Stavely wasn't actually expecting anyone on that boat—or any cargo, for that matter; and Stavely must have realized that everyone understood this, yet it didn't matter to him at all; he enjoyed pretending to himself that he was waiting for a hundred thousand tons of saddles on this boat, and so he continued this way throughout his entire life, taking pleasure in being dutifully present to receive and sign for those saddles, just in case they might miraculously arrive. A spiteful Quincy newspaper always used to mock this town by calling it 'Stavely's Landing.' Stavely was one of my earliest heroes; I was jealous of his rush of make-believe business, and the show he managed to put on for strangers as he went racing down the street wrestling with his billowing coat.

But there was a carpenter who became my greatest hero. He was an enormous liar, though I didn't realize that at the time; I believed every word he spoke. He was a romantic, sentimental, melodramatic fake, and his presence filled me with wonder. I can clearly recall the first time he shared his secrets with me. He was smoothing a board with his plane, and every so often he would stop and let out a heavy sigh; sometimes he would mumble broken phrases—jumbled and impossible to understand—but from these fragments an exclamation would occasionally slip out that made

369

me tremble with excitement: one was, 'O God, it is his blood!' I sat on the tool chest and humbly and fearfully admired him; I was convinced he was steeped in criminal deeds. Finally he spoke in a quiet voice—

'My little friend, can you keep a secret?'

I enthusiastically said I was able to.

"A dark and dreadful one?"

I reassured him about that matter.

"Then I'll share some parts of my story with you; I absolutely must unburden my troubled soul, or I'll die!"

He warned me again to be 'as silent as the grave;' then he told me he was a 'red-handed murderer.' He set down his plane, held his hands out in front of him, looked at them with sadness, and said—

"Look—with these hands I have taken the lives of thirty human beings!"

The impact this had on me inspired him, and he threw himself into his topic with enthusiasm and vigor. He stopped speaking in broad terms and got specific—starting with his first killing; he described it in detail, explained what steps he had taken to avoid suspicion; then moved on to his second murder, his third, his fourth, and continued from there. He had always committed his killings with a bowie-knife, and he made all my hair stand on end by suddenly pulling it out and displaying it to me.

At the end of this first session I went home carrying six of his terrifying secrets with me, and discovered they greatly helped my dreams, which had been dull for some time. I sought him out again and again during my Saturday breaks; in fact, I spent the entire summer with him—all the time that mattered to me. His appeal never faded, because he brought something new and exciting, in terms of horror, to each following murder. He always provided names, dates, locations—everything. This eventually allowed me to notice two things: that he had killed his victims in every corner of the world, and that these victims were always named Lynch. The elimination of the Lynches continued peacefully, Saturday after Saturday, until the original thirty had grown to sixty—with more still to come; then my curiosity overcame my fear, and I asked how it came to be that these rightfully punished people all shared the same name.

My hero told me he had never revealed that dark secret to anyone alive, but he felt he could trust me, so he would share the story of his tragic and ruined life. He had loved someone "too beautiful for this world," and she had returned his feelings "with all the tender love of her pure and noble heart." However, he had a rival, a "lowly mercenary" named Archibald Lynch, who declared the girl would be his, or he would "stain his hands with her heart's precious blood." The carpenter, "innocent and joyful in love's youthful dream," paid no attention to the threat, but brought his "golden-haired beloved to the altar," and there, the two became husband and wife; there also, just as the minister's hands were raised in blessing over their heads, the terrible act was committed—with a knife—and the bride collapsed dead at her husband's feet. And what did the husband do? He pulled out that knife, and kneeling beside the body of his beloved, vowed to "dedicate his life to destroying all the human filth that carry the despised name of Lynch."

That was it. He had been tracking down the Lynches and killing them, from that day until now—twenty years. He had always used that same blessed knife; with it he had murdered his long line of Lynches, and with it he had carved upon the forehead of each victim a distinctive mark—a cross, deeply cut. He said—

'The cross of the Mysterious Avenger is recognized across Europe, America, China, Siam, the Tropics, the Polar Seas, the deserts of Asia—throughout the entire world. Wherever a Lynch has traveled to the most remote corners of the globe, the Mysterious Cross has appeared, and those who witnessed it have

trembled and declared, "This is his symbol—he has been here."
You have heard tales of the Mysterious Avenger—now look upon
him, for you stand before that very person! But take warning—
speak not a single word to anyone. Remain silent and wait. One
morning this town will gather in horror to discover a bloodied
corpse; upon its forehead will appear the terrible sign, and people
will shake with fear and whisper, "He has been here—this is the
Mysterious Avenger's mark!" You will return to this place, but I
will have disappeared; you will never see me again.'

This fool had obviously been reading the 'Jibbenainosay' and
had gotten his poor romantic mind completely twisted by it; but
since I hadn't read the book yet at that time, I believed his made-
up stories were true and didn't realize he was stealing someone
else's ideas.

However, we had a Lynch living in the town; and the more I
thought about his approaching fate, the more I couldn't sleep. It
felt like my clear responsibility to save him, and an even clearer
and more pressing responsibility to get some rest for myself, so
finally I decided to go to Mr. Lynch and tell him what was going
to happen to him—in complete confidence. I urged him to
'escape,' and definitely expected him to do so. But he laughed at
me; and he didn't stop there; he took me down to the carpenter's
shop, delivered a mocking and contemptuous speech to the
carpenter about his foolish claims, struck his face, forced him to
get down on his knees and plead—then walked away and left me
to witness the pathetic and miserable destruction of what, in my
view, had so recently been a magnificent and unmatched hero.

The carpenter blustered, waved his knife around, and
condemned this Lynch in his typical explosive manner, his
dramatic words just as powerful as ever; but none of it affected me
anymore; he was no longer a hero in my eyes, but simply a pitiful,
foolish, exposed fraud. I felt embarrassed by him and embarrassed

by myself; I lost all interest in him and never visited his shop again. His loss hit me hard, since he had been the greatest hero I had ever known. The man must have possessed some real skill; some of his made-up murders were described so vividly and dramatically that I still remember every detail of them today.

The people of Hannibal have changed just as much as the town itself. It's no longer a village; it's become a city, complete with a mayor, a city council, water systems, and probably municipal debt. The population has grown to fifteen thousand people, making it a thriving and energetic place that's paved like the rest of the western and southern regions—where well-paved streets and good sidewalks are so rarely seen that you question their reality when you actually encounter them. The typical half-dozen railroad lines now converge in Hannibal, and there's a new train station that cost one hundred thousand dollars to build. Back in my day, the town had no particular specialty or commercial importance; the daily steamboat would typically drop off one passenger and purchase a catfish, then pick up another passenger and a small amount of cargo before departing; but now a massive lumber trade has developed, along with a large and diverse commercial business as one of the outcomes. A considerable amount of money changes hands there these days.

Bear Creek—probably named that way because it was always especially lacking in bears—is now hidden from view beneath massive piles of stacked lumber, and only an expert could locate it today. Every summer I would regularly end up drowning in it, then get pulled out, revived, and sent on my way again by some random passerby who happened to be around; but there isn't enough open water left now to drown anyone in. Back in its time, it was well-known for causing chills and fever. I recall one summer when everyone in town came down with this illness all at the same time. Numerous chimneys collapsed, and all the buildings were damaged so badly that the entire town had to be reconstructed.

Scientists believe that the gap or canyon between Lover's Leap and the hill to the west was formed by glacial movement. This theory is wrong.

There's a fascinating cave located a mile or two downstream from Hannibal, nestled among the cliffs. I wished I could have visited it again, but I didn't have enough time. During my era, the man who owned the cave at that time converted it into a tomb for his fourteen-year-old daughter. The body of this unfortunate girl was placed inside a copper container filled with alcohol, which was then hung in one of the cave's gloomy passages. The container had a removable lid, and it was reportedly common for the more vulgar tourists to pull the deceased child's face into sight, examine it, and make remarks about it.

Chapter 56: A Question of Law

The slaughterhouse has disappeared from the mouth of Bear Creek, and so has the small jail (or 'calaboose') that once stood nearby. A citizen asked, 'Do you remember when Jimmy Finn, the town drunkard, was burned to death in the calaboose?'

Look at how history gets corrupted over time, helped along by people's faulty memories. Jimmy Finn wasn't burned to death in the jail, but died naturally in a tanning vat from a combination of delirium tremens and spontaneous combustion. When I say natural death, I mean it was natural for Jimmy Finn to die that way. The jail victim wasn't a local citizen; he was a poor stranger, a harmless drunk vagrant. I know more about his case than anyone else; I knew too much about it back then to enjoy talking about it. That vagrant was wandering the streets one cold evening with a pipe in his mouth, asking people for a match; he got neither matches nor kindness; instead, a group of cruel little boys followed him around and entertained themselves by harassing and bothering him. I joined in; but finally, some plea the wanderer made for mercy, along with a heartbreaking mention of his lonely and friendless situation, touched whatever sense of shame and decent feeling I had left, and I walked away and got him some matches, then hurried home to bed, my conscience heavy and my spirits low. An hour or two later, the man was arrested and locked up in the jail by the marshal—a grand title for a constable, but that's what he was called. At two in the morning, the church bells rang out for fire, and everyone rushed out, naturally—me included. The vagrant had used his matches catastrophically: he had set his straw mattress on fire, and the wooden walls of the room had caught flame. When I got there, two hundred men, women, and children stood crowded together, frozen with horror, staring at the barred windows of the jail. Behind the iron bars, pulling desperately at them and screaming for help, stood the vagrant; he looked like a dark silhouette against the sun, so bright and fierce was the light behind him. That marshal couldn't be found, and he had the only key. A battering ram was quickly put together, and the thundering of its strikes against the door sounded so promising that the crowd burst into wild cheering, believing the rescue was assured. But it wasn't. The wooden beams were too strong; they wouldn't break. It was said that the man's death grip still clung to the bars even after he died; and that in this position the flames surrounded him and burned him up. As for this, I don't know. What happened after I recognized the face that was begging through the bars was witnessed by others, not by me.

I saw that face in that exact position every night for a long time after that incident, and I felt just as responsible for the man's death as if I had deliberately given him the matches so he could burn himself alive. I had no doubt whatsoever that I would be executed if anyone discovered my involvement in this tragedy. The events and feelings from that period are burned into my memory, and examining them now fascinates me just as much as they tormented me back then. Whenever anyone mentioned that horrific incident, I immediately became completely focused and alert to catch every word that might be spoken, because I was constantly afraid and anticipating that I would discover I was under suspicion. My guilty conscience was so sharp and sensitive that it frequently detected suspicion in the most innocent comments, and in expressions, movements, and glances that meant nothing at all, yet still sent me trembling away in terrified panic just the same. And how nauseated it made me feel whenever someone casually dropped the comment, no matter how thoughtlessly and without any particular meaning, that 'murder will out!' For a ten-year-old boy, I was carrying an incredibly heavy burden.

All this time I was fortunately forgetting one thing—the fact that I was a habitual sleep talker. But one night I woke up and found my bed-mate—my younger brother—sitting up in bed and looking at me in the moonlight. I said—

"What's wrong?"

"You talk so much I can't sleep."

I shot up to a sitting position immediately, my heart pounding in my throat and my hair standing on end.

"What did I say? Quick—tell me—what did I say?"

"Nothing much."

"That's not true—you know everything."

"Everything about what?"

"You know perfectly well what I'm talking about. About that."

"About what? I don't know what you're talking about. I think you're sick or crazy or something. But anyway, you're awake, and I'll get some sleep while I have the chance."

He fell asleep while I lay there in a cold sweat, turning this new fear over and over in the chaotic mess that served as my mind. The weight of my thoughts centered on: How much had I revealed? How much does he know?—what agony this uncertainty brought! But gradually I came up with an idea—I would wake my brother and test him with a hypothetical situation. I shook him awake and said—

"Imagine if someone came to you while drunk—"

"This is ridiculous—I never get drunk."

'I don't mean you, you fool—I mean the man. Let's say a man comes to you drunk and wants to borrow a knife, or a hatchet, or a gun, and you forget to tell him it's loaded, and—'

"How could you load a tomahawk?"

"I'm not talking about the tomahawk, and I never mentioned the tomahawk; I was referring to the pistol. Stop interrupting me like that, because this is a serious matter. Someone has been murdered."

"What! In this town?"

"Yes, in this town."

"Well, go ahead—I won't say a single word."

"Well, then, let's say you forgot to warn him to handle it carefully because it was loaded, and he left and ended up shooting himself with that gun—messing around with it, you know, and likely doing it accidentally while he was drunk. Well, would that be murder?"

'No—suicide.'

"No, no. I don't mean his actions, I mean yours: would you be a murderer for allowing him to have that gun?"

After careful consideration, this answer emerged—

"Well, I suppose I must be guilty of something—perhaps murder—yes, most likely murder, but I'm not entirely sure."

This made me extremely uneasy. Nevertheless, it wasn't a final judgment. I would need to present the actual situation—there appeared to be no alternative. But I would proceed carefully and stay alert for any troubling consequences. I said—

"I was just imagining a scenario, but now I'm getting to what actually happened. Do you know how that man ended up being burned to death in the jail?"

'No.'

"Don't you have even the slightest clue?"

"Not at all."

"I hope you drop dead right where you stand if you have!"

"Yes, I swear on my life."

'Well, here's what happened. The man needed some matches to light his pipe. A boy brought him some. The man used those exact matches to set the jail on fire, and burned himself to death.'

'Is that so?'

"Yes, it is. Now, do you think that boy is a murderer?"

"Let me see. The man was drunk?"

"Yes, he was drunk."

'Very drunk?'

'Yes.'

"And the boy knew it?"

"Yes, he knew it."

There was a long pause. Then came this heavy verdict—

"If the man was drunk, and the boy knew it, the boy murdered that man. This is certain."

Weak, nauseating feelings spread through every fiber of my body, and I felt like I understood how someone feels when they hear their death sentence announced from the judge's bench. I waited to hear what my brother would say next. I thought I knew what it would be, and I was correct. He said—

"I know the boy."

I had nothing to say, so I remained silent. I simply shuddered. Then he added—

"Yes, before you were even halfway through describing what happened, I knew exactly who the boy was; it was Ben Coontz!"

I emerged from my breakdown like someone rising from the dead. I said, with admiration—

"Why, how on earth did you ever figure it out?"

"You said it while you were sleeping."

I told myself, "How wonderful that is! This is a habit that needs to be developed."

My brother continued talking innocently—

'While you were talking in your sleep, you kept mumbling something about "matches," which I couldn't understand; but just now, when you started telling me about the man and the jail and the matches, I remembered that in your sleep you mentioned Ben Coontz two or three times; so I put this and that together, you see, and right away I knew it was Ben who burned that man up.'

I praised his wisdom enthusiastically. Soon he asked—

"Are you going to turn him over to the authorities?"

"No," I said. "I think this will teach him a lesson. I'll certainly keep watching him, because that's only fair, but if he stays put and changes his ways, no one will ever say I gave him away."

"How good you are!"

"Well, I try to be. It's all a person can do in a world like this."

Now that my burden had been transferred to someone else, my fears quickly disappeared.

The day before we left Hannibal, something curious caught my attention—the remarkable way that time seems to stretch out there. I discovered this from one of the most modest men I've ever met—the Black coachman who worked for a friend of mine living three miles outside of town. He was supposed to pick me up at the Park Hotel at 7:30 P.M. and drive me out there. However, he was quite late—he didn't show up until ten o'clock. He apologized by explaining—

"The time is about an hour and a half slower in the country than what it is in the town; you'll be in plenty of time, boss. Sometimes we leave early for church on Sunday, and end up there right in the middle of the sermon. It's the difference in time. A person can't make any calculations about it."

I had lost two and a half hours, but I had learned something worth four times that amount.

Chapter 57: An Archangel

From St. Louis heading north, you can see all the encouraging signs that active, energetic, intelligent, prosperous, and practical nineteenth-century communities are thriving there. The people don't spend time dreaming—they work. The positive outcome is clearly visible everywhere in the solid, substantial appearance of everything around you, and the signs of healthy living and comfort that you notice wherever you look.

Quincy serves as an excellent example—a vibrant, attractive, well-organized city that remains, as it has always been, deeply engaged with art, literature, and other cultural pursuits.

But Marion City is an exception. Marion City has moved backward in the most puzzling way. This metropolis showed such promise that the developers added 'city' to its name right from the start, with complete confidence; but it turned out to be a poor prediction. When I first visited Marion City thirty-five years ago, it had one street and nearly six houses. Now it contains only one house, and this single structure, falling apart, is preparing to join the other five that have already tumbled into the river. Without doubt, Marion City was located too close to Quincy. It faced another drawback: it was built on flat, muddy ground below the high-water line, while Quincy sits elevated on a hillside.

In the beginning, Quincy had the appearance and character of a model New England town, and it still maintains these qualities today: wide, clean streets, well-maintained, tidy homes and lawns, beautiful mansions, and impressive blocks of commercial buildings. The city also features spacious fairgrounds, a well-maintained park, and numerous scenic drives, along with a library, reading rooms, a few colleges, several handsome and expensive churches, and a magnificent courthouse with grounds that take up an entire square. The city's population is thirty thousand. There are several large factories located here, and manufacturing of various kinds is conducted on a massive scale.

La Grange and Canton are expanding towns, but I didn't make it to Alexandria; I was informed it was flooded, but would emerge to catch its breath during the summer months.

Keokuk was easy to recognize. I had lived there in 1857—a remarkable year for real estate in that area. The boom was absolutely incredible. Everyone was buying, everyone was selling—except for widows and ministers; they always hang onto their property; and when the market crashes, they're the ones left behind. Any piece of land that even remotely resembled a town lot, regardless of its location, could be sold, and for a price that would have seemed expensive even if the ground had been covered with dollar bills.

The town now has a population of fifteen thousand and is experiencing steady, healthy growth. It was nighttime, and we couldn't make out the details, which disappointed us because Keokuk has a reputation for being a beautiful city. It was a pleasant place to live many years ago, and it has undoubtedly improved rather than declined in that regard.

A massive construction project that was underway during my time there has now been completed. This is the canal that bypasses the Rapids. It stretches eight miles in length, spans three hundred feet in width, and maintains a depth of at least six feet throughout. The stonework is built in the grand style that the War Department typically employs, and it will last as long as a Roman aqueduct. The project cost four or five million dollars.

After spending an hour or two with old friends, we resumed our journey up the river. Keokuk had once been a place where that unpredictable genius, Henry Clay Dean, would occasionally spend his idle time. I think I only saw him once, but people talked about him frequently when I lived there. This is what they used to say about him—

He started life in poverty without any formal education. However, he taught himself—right there on the street corners of Keokuk. He would settle down on a curbstone with his book, paying no attention to the noise of business activity and the footsteps of crowds walking by, and immerse himself completely in his studies for hours at a time, only shifting his position occasionally to pull his knees closer when a cart needed to pass through; and once he finished reading a book, its contents, no matter how complex or difficult, had been burned into his memory and became his forever. Through this method, he accumulated an enormous collection of knowledge on all kinds of subjects, and had it organized in his mind where he could access any piece of information whenever he needed it.

His clothing was no different from that of a dock worker, except that it was more tattered, mismatched, and clashing (which made it even more dramatically colorful), and covered with several more layers of dirt. No one could have guessed at the brilliant mind housed within that physical structure simply by looking at the structure itself.

He was a natural-born speaker who later refined his abilities through experience and practice. During his campaign tours, his reputation acted like a magnet, drawing farmers from fifty miles in every direction to hear him speak. Politics was always his subject. He never used notes because a volcano doesn't need them. In 1862, the son of Keokuk's late distinguished citizen, Mr. Claggett, shared this story about Dean with me—

The war fever was running high in Keokuk in 1861, and a large mass meeting was scheduled to be held on a particular day in the new Athenaeum. A distinguished visitor was supposed to address the audience. After the building had been filled to its maximum capacity with perspiring people of both genders, the stage remained empty—the distinguished visitor had failed to appear. The crowd became impatient, and eventually angry and rebellious. Around this time a frantic manager found Dean sitting on a curb, explained the situation to him, took his book from him, hurried him into the building through the back entrance, and instructed him to get to the stage and save his country.

Suddenly, a hush fell over the grumbling crowd, and everyone's gaze turned to a single spot—the wide, empty, bare stage. A figure emerged whose appearance was recognizable to barely a dozen people in the audience. It was the shabby Dean—wearing worn brown shoes with run-down heels; mismatched socks, also falling down; damaged pants that were relics from another era and far too short, revealing several inches of bare ankle; an unbuttoned vest that was also too short, exposing a strip of dirty and wrinkled shirt between the vest and his waistband; his shirt front hanging open; a long black handkerchief wrapped around and around his neck like a bandage; a short blue coat that only reached the small of his back, with sleeves that left four inches of his forearms exposed; a small, stiff-brimmed military cap perched on one side of his head. This figure walked solemnly onto the stage and, with calm and deliberate steps, moved down to the front, where he stopped and thoughtfully examined the audience without saying a word. The stunned silence lasted for a moment, then was interrupted by a barely audible ripple of amusement that swept across the sea of faces like a gentle wave. The figure remained as before, pensively observing. Another wave began—laughter this time. It was followed by another, then a third—this last one loud and unrestrained.

The stranger then stepped back one pace, removed his soldier's cap, threw it into the wing, and began to speak deliberately, with no one listening and everyone laughing and whispering. The speaker continued talking without embarrassment, and soon delivered a remark that hit its mark, resulting in silence and attention. He followed it quickly with other powerful statements; he warmed to his task and began pouring out his words instead of letting them drip; he grew more and more passionate, and started unleashing lightning and thunder—and now the audience began to break into applause, which the speaker ignored, continuing to hammer straight ahead; he unwound his black bandage and threw it away, still thundering; soon he discarded the bob-tailed coat and flung it aside, becoming more fired up all the time; finally he threw the vest after the coat; and then for an unmeasured period he stood there, like another Vesuvius, spewing smoke and flame, lava and ashes, raining pumice stone and cinders, shaking the moral earth with intellectual crash upon crash, explosion upon explosion, while the frenzied crowd stood on their feet as one body, responding with an endless hurricane of cheers, through a thrashing snowstorm of waving handkerchiefs.

'When Dean arrived,' Claggett said, 'people believed he was a lunatic who had broken free from an asylum; but when he left, they were convinced he was an archangel who had escaped from heaven.'

Burlington, home to the sparkling Burdette, is another city built on hills, and it's undeniably beautiful. It's a thriving and prosperous city with a population of twenty-five thousand people, surrounded by bustling factories that produce almost every type of product you can imagine. At the time, it was also a very serious city—temporarily—because a very sobering piece of legislation was under consideration. This bill would ban the manufacturing, exporting, importing, buying, selling, borrowing, lending, stealing, drinking, smelling, or possessing—whether through conquest, inheritance, intention, accident, or any other means—every harmful beverage known to humanity within the State of Iowa, with the exception of water. All the reasonable people in the state supported this measure, but the judges did not.

Burlington has all the modern equipment and systems that a progressive contemporary city needs for proper and smart governance, including a paid fire department—something that the major city of New Orleans lacks, as it still relies on that outdated relic, the volunteer system.

In Burlington, like all these Upper River towns, you can feel an ambitious, forward-moving energy that's invigorating to experience. A new opera house has recently been constructed there that stands in sharp contrast to the run-down venues that typically serve as theaters in cities the size of Burlington.

We didn't have time to go ashore in Muscatine, but we got a good look at it during daylight from the boat. I lived there for a while many years ago, but the place looked rather unfamiliar now; I suppose it has completely outgrown the town I used to know. In fact, I know it has, because I remember it as a small place—which it certainly isn't anymore. But what I remember most about it is a madman who cornered me out in the fields one Sunday and pulled a butcher knife from his boot, threatening to carve me up with it unless I admitted he was the Devil's only son. I tried to reach a compromise by acknowledging that he was the only member of that family I had ever encountered, but that didn't satisfy him; he wouldn't accept any half-measures; I had to say he was the one and only son of the Devil—and he sharpened his knife on his boot to make his point. It didn't seem worthwhile to cause trouble over such a small matter, so I came around to his way of thinking and kept my skin intact. Not long after that, he went to visit his father, and since he hasn't shown up since then, I trust he's still there.

And I remember Muscatine—even more fondly—for its summer sunsets. I have never witnessed any, on either side of the ocean, that matched them. They transformed the wide, calm river into their canvas, painting across it every conceivable vision of color, from the speckled subtleties and refinements of the opal, all the way through building intensities, to blazing purple and crimson fires that captivated the eye, yet severely tested it simultaneously. The entire Upper Mississippi region displays these remarkable sunsets as a common sight. It is the genuine Sunset Land: I am certain no other region can demonstrate such a strong claim to that title. The sunrises are also reported to be exceptionally beautiful. I cannot say.

Chapter 58: On the Upper River

The large cities appear frequently now, one after another, and between them stretch long lines of prosperous farms rather than empty wilderness. Hour after hour, the boat pushes deeper and deeper into the vast and densely populated Northwest; and with each new section that comes into view, one's amazement and admiration grow stronger and more intense. Such people, and such accomplishments as they have achieved, demand respect. This is a self-reliant population who think independently, and who are capable of doing so, because they are educated and informed; they read, they stay current with the finest and most recent ideas, they strengthen every vulnerable area in their territory with a school, a college, a library, and a newspaper; and they live under the rule of law. Worry about the future of a people like this is unnecessary.

This area is new; so new that you could say it's still in its infancy. Based on what it has achieved while still cutting its teeth, you can predict what wonders it will accomplish when it reaches full maturity. It's so new that foreign tourists haven't heard about it yet and haven't come to visit. For sixty years, foreign tourists have traveled by steamboat up and down the river between St. Louis and New Orleans, then returned home to write their books, thinking they had seen everything worth seeing on the river or anything there was to see. Not even six of all these books mention these Upper River towns—because the five or six tourists who explored this region did so before these towns were even planned. The most recent tourist among them all (1878) took the same old standard trip—he hadn't heard that there was anything north of St. Louis.

Yet there was. There was this incredible region, filled with major cities that seemed to be planned just the day before yesterday and constructed the very next morning. About twenty of these towns have populations ranging from fifteen hundred to five thousand residents. Beyond those, we find Muscatine with ten thousand people; Winona with ten thousand; Moline with ten thousand; Rock Island with twelve thousand; La Crosse with twelve thousand; Burlington with twenty-five thousand; Dubuque with twenty-five thousand; Davenport with thirty thousand; St. Paul with fifty-eight thousand, and Minneapolis with sixty thousand and growing.

The foreign tourist has never heard of these places; there's no mention of them in his guidebooks. They've appeared overnight, while he was sleeping. This region is so new that I, despite being relatively young, am still older than it is. When I was born, St. Paul had a population of three people, while Minneapolis had exactly one-third of that number. The entire population of Minneapolis at that time died two years ago; and when he passed away, he had witnessed his own multiplication over forty years by fifty-nine thousand nine hundred and ninety-nine additional people. He possessed the reproductive capacity of a frog.

I should clarify that the population figures I provided earlier for St. Paul and Minneapolis are now several months out of date. Both cities have grown significantly larger since then. Actually, I recently came across a newspaper report that estimates St. Paul's current population at seventy-one thousand and Minneapolis at seventy-eight thousand. Since this book won't be published for another six or seven months, none of these numbers will have much value by the time readers see them.

We caught sight of Davenport, another stunning city perched on a hilltop—a description that fits all these communities; they're all attractive, well-constructed, spotless, organized, pleasing to look at, and uplifting to the soul; and they're all positioned on elevated ground. So we'll retire that description for now. Local Native Americans have a legend that Marquette and Joliet made camp where Davenport currently sits, back in 1673. The following white settler who established camp there did so roughly one hundred and seventy years afterward—in 1834. Davenport has assembled its thirty thousand residents over the last thirty years. The city now enrolls more students in its schools than its entire population counted twenty-three years earlier. The community boasts the typical Upper River collection of manufacturing plants, publications, and educational establishments; it features telephone service, local telegraph systems, an electric warning system, and an excellent professional fire department, made up of six hook and ladder units, four steam-powered fire engines, and thirty churches. Davenport serves as the official home for two bishops—Episcopal and Catholic.

Across from Davenport sits the thriving town of Rock Island, positioned at the base of the Upper Rapids. A massive railroad bridge links these two communities—one of thirteen bridges that trouble both the Mississippi River and its pilots along the stretch between St. Louis and St. Paul.

The beautiful island of Rock Island, stretching three miles in length and half a mile in width, is owned by the United States, and the Government has transformed it into a magnificent park, improving its natural beauty through artistic design, and weaving numerous miles of roadways throughout its splendid forests. Close to the island's center, visitors can spot through the trees ten enormous stone buildings, each standing four stories tall and covering an acre of land. These structures house the Government workshops, as the Rock Island facility serves as a national armory and arsenal.

We travel up the river—always through captivating landscapes, since there's no other type of scenery along the Upper Mississippi—and pass Moline, a hub of enormous manufacturing industries; and Clinton and Lyons, major lumber centers; and soon arrive at Dubuque, which sits in a wealthy mineral region. The lead mines are highly productive and cover a vast area. Dubuque has numerous manufacturing facilities; among them a plow factory that serves customers throughout all of Christendom. At least that's what a company representative who was on the boat told me. He said—

'Show me any country in the world where they truly understand how to plow, and if I can't point out our trademark on the plow they're using, I'll eat that plow; and I won't even ask for any Worcestershire sauce to make it taste better, either.'

This entire stretch of the river is steeped in Native American history and legends. Black Hawk's name once carried great power in these parts, as did Keokuk's name further downstream. A few miles south of Dubuque stands the Tete de Mort—Death's-head rock, or bluff—where French forces once drove a group of Indians to the summit in earlier times, trapping them there with certain death as their only fate, leaving them to choose only how they would die—whether by starvation or by leaping to their deaths. Black Hawk embraced the customs of white society during his final years, and when he passed away, he was laid to rest near Des Moines in Christian tradition, though modified by Native American practices; specifically, he was dressed in a Christian military uniform and held a Christian walking stick in his hand, but was placed in the grave in a seated position. In the past, a horse had always been interred alongside a chief. The replacement of the horse with a walking stick demonstrates that Black Hawk's proud spirit had truly been humbled, and he anticipated having to walk on foot in the afterlife.

We observed that upstream from Dubuque, the Mississippi River's water appeared olive-green—rich, beautiful, and somewhat transparent when the sunlight hit it. Naturally, the water wasn't as clear or as attractive as it becomes during other times of the year, since it was currently at flood level and had become cloudy and murky from the mud created by collapsing riverbanks.

The magnificent cliffs that rise above the river throughout this area captivate visitors with the elegance and diversity of their shapes, and the gentle beauty of their decoration. The steep green hillside, which begins at the water's edge, is crowned by a towering wall of jagged, castle-like rocks that display wonderfully rich and warm colors—primarily deep browns and muted greens, but accented with other shades. And then there's the gleaming river, curving this way and that, its flow broken occasionally by groups of tree-covered islands connected by shimmering waterways; and you catch sight of far-off towns, resting peacefully on headlands; and of quiet rafts drifting silently in the shadow of the wooded banks; and of white steamboats disappearing around distant bends. And everything is as peaceful and restful as a dream, with nothing earthly about it—nothing to cause anxiety or concern.

Until that unholy train comes roaring along—which it soon does, tearing the sacred peace apart with its devilish whistle and the thunderous rumble of its speeding wheels—and suddenly you're thrust back into this world, with one of its worries immediately at hand to occupy your thoughts: you recall that this is the very railroad whose stock price always drops right after you purchase it, and always climbs back up the moment you sell it. It still makes me shudder today to think that I once nearly failed to get rid of my stock entirely. It must be a terrible thing to be stuck with a railroad investment you can't unload.

The locomotive can be seen from the steamboat's deck for almost the entire journey from St. Louis to St. Paul—a distance of eight hundred miles. These railroads have devastated the steamboat industry. Our boat's clerk had worked on steamboats before these railroad lines were constructed. Back then, the population growth was so massive and the cargo business so intense that the boats couldn't meet the demands placed on their transportation capacity; as a result, the captains were very independent and arrogant—quite 'uppity,' as Uncle Remus would put it. The clerk summarized the difference between the earlier era and today in this way—

The boat they used for landing—the captain standing on the hurricane deck—extremely rigid and upright—with a steel rod for a backbone—wearing kid gloves, a top hat, hair parted in the back—a man on the shore removes his hat and says—

"I've got twenty-eight tons of wheat, captain—it would be a great favor if you could take them."

"The Captain says—"

"I'll take two of them"—and don't even bother to look at him.

'But nowadays the captain removes his old slouch hat, and smiles so broadly it reaches all the way to the back of his ears, and delivers a bow that isn't hindered by any ramrod, and says—

"Great to see you, Smith, great to see you—you're looking good—haven't seen you looking this good in years—what do you have for us?"

"Nothing," says Smith; and keeps his hat on, and just turns his back and goes to talking with somebody else.

'Oh, yes, eight years ago, the captain was in charge; but it's Smith's turn now. Eight years ago a boat would travel up the river with every cabin completely full, and people crowded five and six deep on the cabin floor; plus a packed deck full of immigrants and harvest workers down below, on top of everything else. To get a first-class cabin, you had to prove sixteen generations of noble blood and four hundred years of family lineage, or be personally friends with the Black man who polished the captain's boots. But everything has changed now; plenty of cabins available above, no harvest workers below—there's a mechanical harvesting machine now, and they don't need harvest workers anymore; they've disappeared into history—and they didn't travel by steamboat, either; they went by train.'

In this area we encountered vast expanses of lumber rafts heading downstream—but they weren't drifting casually along in the traditional manner, operated by cheerful and carefree crews of fiddle-playing, song-belting, whiskey-guzzling, dance-loving rascals; instead, the entire operation was pushed rapidly forward by a powerful steamboat at the rear, in the modern style, and the small crews consisted of calm, well-behaved men with a serious business demeanor, without even a hint of adventure or excitement about them.

Along this stretch, somewhere in the darkness of night, we navigated through some extremely narrow and complex channels between islands using electric lighting. Behind us lay complete darkness—an unbroken wall of black; ahead stretched a tight bend of water, winding between thick walls of vegetation that nearly brushed our bow on either side; and here each separate leaf, and each separate ripple appeared in its true color, bathed in light as bright as an intensified midday sun. The result was unusual, beautiful, and remarkably impressive.

We passed Prairie du Chien, another one of Father Marquette's camping spots, and after several hours of traveling through diverse and stunning landscapes, we arrived at La Crosse. This is a city with a population of twelve or thirteen thousand people, featuring electrically lit streets and impressive building complexes that are both grand and architecturally beautiful enough to earn admiration in any major city. It's an excellent town, and we made good use of the hour we were given to explore it thoroughly, even though the weather was rainier than we would have liked.

Chapter 59: Legends and Scenery

We picked up several new passengers at La Crosse, including an elderly gentleman who had arrived in this northwestern region with the early settlers and knew every part of it well. He was understandably proud of it, too. He said—

'You'll discover scenery between here and St. Paul that can outshine the Hudson River. You'll see Queen's Bluff—seven hundred feet tall, and as magnificent a sight as you can find anywhere; and Trempeleau Island, which isn't like any other island in America, I believe, because it's a massive mountain with steep sides, filled with Native American legends, and once crawling with rattlesnakes; if you catch the sunlight just right there, you'll witness a scene that will remain with you forever. And beyond Winona you'll encounter beautiful prairies; and then you'll reach the Thousand Islands, too stunning for words; green? you've never seen leaves so vibrant, or packed so densely; it's like a thousand velvet cushions floating on a mirror—when the water is calm; and then the enormous bluffs on both sides of the river—jagged, rough, dark-featured—exactly the border that's needed; you always need a bold frame, you know, to highlight the finer details of a delicate scene and make them pop.'

The elderly gentleman also shared a couple of moving Native American legends with us—though they weren't particularly compelling ones.

After this historical detour, he returned to describing the landscape, painting it detail by detail from the Thousand Islands to St. Paul. He rattled off place names with remarkable ease, moving through his subject with quick and confident grace, dropping in a massive word here and there with the smug attitude of "it's nothing—I can do this whenever I feel like it," and unleashing impressive bursts of vivid eloquence at perfectly timed moments, which made me start to suspect—

But regardless, I started to have my doubts. Listen to him—

Ten miles upstream from Winona, we reach Fountain City, nestled beautifully at the base of towering cliffs that rise majestically, like something godlike, toward the deep blue sky, surrounded by pure air that seems untouched by anything except the wings of angels.

We then drift through shimmering waters, surrounded by beautiful and magnificent natural scenery that fills our hearts with reverent wonder, traveling about twelve miles until we reach Mount Vernon, rising six hundred feet high, with the romantic ruins of what was once a first-rate hotel positioned high among the shifting cloud shadows that dapple its dizzying peaks—the only remaining trace of the once-thriving town of Mount Vernon from earlier times, now abandoned and completely empty.

And so we continue our journey. We pass Chimney Rock, flying by this magnificent six-hundred-foot tower; then just before we reach Minnieska, our attention is drawn to a remarkable cliff rising more than five hundred feet—a perfect mountain pyramid. Its cone-like form, with thick forests wrapping around its slopes and its pointed peak resembling that of a cone, makes observers marvel at nature's handiwork. From its dizzying heights, spectacular views of the woodlands, rivers, cliffs, hills and valleys below and stretching for miles come into view. What more magnificent river scenery could one imagine, as we look out over this captivating landscape from the highest point of these bluffs down into the valleys? The untouched wilderness and profound solitude of these majestic works of nature and nature's Creator stir feelings of limitless wonder, creating memories that can never be erased from the mind, no matter which direction we look.

Next we have the Lion's Head and the Lioness's Head, carved by nature's hand, to decorate and overlook the beautiful stream; and then soon the river widens, and a most delightful and magnificent view of the valley ahead suddenly appears before our eyes; rough hills, covered with green forests from top to bottom, flat prairie lands, cradling the beautiful Wabasha, City of the Healing Waters, powerful enemy of Bright's disease, and that greatest creation of nature's works, unmatched Lake Pepin—these form a picture that the tourist's eye may look upon for countless hours, with joy unsatisfied and impossible to satisfy.

And so we drift along, eventually coming upon those magnificent domes, the massive Sugar Loaf, and the awe-inspiring Maiden's Rock—which romantic legend has given a voice; and often as the birch canoe passes by at dusk, the shadowy paddler imagines he hears the gentle, sweet melody of the long-gone Winona, beloved of Native American song and legend.

'Then Frontenac appears before us, a delightful destination for weary summer vacationers; then progressive Red Wing; and Diamond Bluff, striking and imposing in its solitary grandeur; then Prescott and the St. Croix; and soon we witness the domes and spires of St. Paul bursting into view, the mighty young leader of the North, advancing with giant strides at the forefront of progress, carrying the flag of the most advanced and modern civilization, cutting his beneficial path with the hatchet of business enterprise, calling out the battle cry of Christian culture, stripping away the foul scalp of laziness and ignorance to establish there the steam-powered plow and the schoolhouse—always ahead of him stretch barren lawlessness, ignorance, crime, and despair; always behind him flourish the prison, the gallows, and the church; and always'

"Have you ever traveled with a panorama?"

"I have previously served in that role."

My suspicion was confirmed.

"Do you still travel with it?"

"No, she's docked until the fall season begins. I'm currently helping to develop the materials for a Tourist's Guide that the St. Louis and St. Paul Packet Company plans to publish this summer for travelers who use that route."

"When you mentioned Maiden's Rock, you talked about the long-gone Winona, beloved figure of Native American songs and stories. Is she the maiden of the rock?—and are the two linked by legend?"

"Yes, and it's an extremely tragic and heartbreaking story. It's probably the most famous legend of the Mississippi River, and also the most deeply moving one."

We asked him to share the story. He effortlessly shifted away from his casual conversation and slipped back into his formal speaking style, then continued as follows—

A short distance above Lake City stands a famous landmark called Maiden's Rock, which is not only a beautiful scenic location but also holds deep romantic significance due to the tragic event that gave it its name. Not many years ago, this area served as a popular gathering place for the Sioux Indians because of the excellent fishing and hunting opportunities available there, and large groups of them could always be found in this region. Among the families that regularly came to this place was one from the Wabasha tribe. We-no-na, meaning "first-born," was the name of a young woman who had promised herself to a lover from the same band. However, her strict parents had already promised her hand in marriage to another man, a renowned warrior, and they demanded that she marry him instead. Her parents set the wedding date, causing her tremendous sorrow. She seemed to accept their decision and agreed to go with them to the rock to gather flowers for the wedding celebration. When they reached the rock, We-no-na rushed to its highest point and stood at its edge, where she scolded her parents below for their heartless treatment of her, then sang a funeral song and threw herself from the cliff, shattering her body on the rocks below.

"Completely destroyed—her parents?"

'Yes.'

"Well, it definitely was a tragic situation, as you mentioned. And what's more, there's a shocking kind of dramatic twist to it that I wasn't expecting. It's a clear improvement over the worn-out style of Indian legend. There are fifty Lover's Leaps along the Mississippi from which heartbroken Indian girls have jumped, but this is the only jump among all of them that ended up working out properly and satisfactorily. What happened to Winona?"

'She was badly shaken and traumatized, but she pulled herself together and vanished before the coroner arrived at the scene of death. It's said that she found and married her true love, and traveled with him to some faraway land, where she lived happily ever after. Her gentle spirit had been softened and refined by the tragic event that had so early taken away the loving guidance of her mother and the protective strength of her father, leaving her completely alone and dependent on the harsh mercy of a judgmental world.'

I was happy to listen to the lecturer describe the landscape, as it helped me better appreciate what I could see and allowed me to picture the parts we missed because darkness had fallen.

As the lecturer pointed out, this entire region is filled with Indian tales and traditions. However, I reminded him that people typically just mention this fact—doing so in a way that makes one's mouth water—and wisely stop there. Why? Because the impression left was that these tales were packed with incident and imagination—a pleasant impression that would be quickly destroyed if the tales were actually told. I showed him a large amount of this type of literature that I had been collecting, and he admitted that it was poor material, extremely sorry rubbish; and I dared to add that the legends he had told us were of this same character, with the single exception of the excellent story of

Winona. He acknowledged these facts, but said that if I would look up Mr. Schoolcraft's book, published nearly fifty years ago, and now undoubtedly out of print, I would find some Indian stories in it that were very far from being lacking in incident and imagination; that the tales in Hiawatha were of this type, and they came from Schoolcraft's book; and that there were others in the same book which Mr. Longfellow could have turned into verse with good results. For example, there was the legend of 'The Undying Head.' He could not tell it, because many of the details had become dim in his memory; but he would recommend that I find it and increase my respect for the Indian imagination. He said that this tale, and most of the others in the book, were popular among the Indians along this part of the Mississippi when he first arrived here; and that the contributors to Schoolcraft's book had obtained them directly from Indian lips, and had written them down with complete accuracy, and without embellishments of their own.

I have found the book. The lecturer was correct. It contains several legends that support what he stated. I will present two of them—'The Undying Head,' and 'Peboan and Seegwun, an Allegory of the Seasons.' The second one appears in Hiawatha; however, it is valuable to read in its original form, if only to see how powerful an authentic poem can be without the assistance and elegance of poetic meter and rhythm—

PEBOAN AND SEEGWUN.

An elderly man sat by himself in his cabin beside a frozen stream. Winter was coming to an end, and his fire had nearly died out. He looked extremely old and utterly alone. His hair had turned white with age, and his whole body shook with tremors. One day followed another in complete isolation, and the only sound he heard was the roar of the storm as it swept the freshly fallen snow across the landscape.

One day, as his fire was beginning to fade, a handsome young man came near and walked into his home. His cheeks glowed red with youthful vitality, his eyes shone brightly with life, and a smile danced across his lips. He moved with a light and swift stride. His forehead was adorned with a crown of fragrant grass instead of a warrior's headband, and he held a bouquet of flowers in his hand.

"Ah, my son," the old man said, "I'm so glad to see you. Come in. Come and tell me about your adventures and the strange lands you've visited. Let's spend the night together. I'll tell you about my skills and accomplishments, and what I'm capable of doing. You can do the same, and we'll entertain ourselves."

He then pulled from his bag an intricately crafted antique pipe, and after filling it with tobacco that had been made mild by mixing in certain leaves, he passed it to his guest. Once this ritual was finished, they started to talk.

"I breathe out," the old man said, "and the stream stops flowing. The water turns solid and hard like transparent stone."

"I breathe," said the young man, "and flowers bloom across the meadow."

"I shake my hair," the old man replied, "and snow blankets the earth. The leaves drop from the trees when I tell them to, and my breath sweeps them away. The birds rise up from the water and fly to faraway places. The animals hide from my breath, and the ground itself becomes as hard as stone."

"I toss my curls," the young man replied, "and gentle showers of warm rain cascade down to the earth. Plants raise their heads from the soil, like children's eyes sparkling with joy. My voice calls the birds back. The heat of my breath frees the flowing streams. Music echoes through the woods wherever I go, and all of nature celebrates."

Eventually the sun started to come up. A mild warmth spread across the area. The old man's voice fell quiet. The robin and bluebird started singing from the top of the lodge. The stream started babbling beside the door, and the sweet scent of sprouting herbs and flowers drifted gently on the spring breeze.

When daylight fully appeared, the young man could clearly see what his host truly looked like. As he gazed upon him, he saw the frozen face of Peboan.[16] Water began streaming from his eyes. As the sun grew stronger, his body became smaller and smaller, until he had completely melted away. All that remained where his lodge fire had been was the miskodeed,[17] a small white flower with pink edges, which is among the first plants to bloom in the northern regions.

'The Undying Head' is quite a lengthy story, but it compensates for its lack of brevity with strange imaginative concepts, fairy-tale wonders, diverse incidents, and dynamic pacing.[18]

Chapter 60: Speculations and Conclusions

We arrived at St. Paul, located at the uppermost navigable point of the Mississippi River, where our two-thousand-mile journey from New Orleans came to an end. The trip takes approximately ten days by steamboat. It could likely be completed faster by railroad. I believe this because I'm aware that one can travel by train from St. Louis to Hannibal—a distance of no less than one hundred and twenty miles—in seven hours. This beats walking, unless someone is in a rush.

The season was well into its course when we found ourselves in New Orleans, where the roses and magnolia blossoms were

---

[16] Winter.

[17] The trailing arbutus.

[18] See appendix D.

dropping from their branches; but here in St. Paul it was the snow that was falling. In New Orleans we had occasionally felt a scorching breath that seemed to come from over a crater; here in St. Paul we frequently felt a numbing one that seemed to come from over a glacier.

But I'm getting off track from my main point. St. Paul is a remarkable city. It's constructed with solid blocks of genuine brick and stone, giving it the appearance of a place that plans to endure. The post office was established thirty-six years ago, and according to legend, when the postmaster first received a letter, he rode on horseback all the way to Washington to ask what he should do with it. That same year, two wooden frame houses were constructed, and several people were added to the town's population. A recent issue of St. Paul's leading newspaper, the 'Pioneer Press,' provides statistics that create a striking contrast to those early days: the population in the fall of this year (1882) reached 71,000; during the first six months of the year, 1,209,387 letters were processed; in the first nine months of the year, 989 houses were constructed at a cost of $3,186,000. The number of letters increased by fifty percent compared to the same six-month period the previous year. Last year, new buildings added to the city cost more than $4,500,000. St. Paul's power comes from its commerce—I should say his commerce. He is certainly a manufacturing city, as are all cities in that area, but he is especially strong when it comes to commerce. Last year his wholesale trade totaled more than $52,000,000.

He has a custom house and is constructing an expensive capitol building to replace the one that recently burned down—since he serves as the state capital. He has countless churches, and not the inexpensive, modest type, but the kind that wealthy Protestants build, the kind that poor Irish housemaids take pleasure in constructing. What a remarkable passion for building magnificent churches the Irish housemaid possesses. This benefits our architecture greatly, but too often we appreciate her grand temples without offering her a single grateful thought. In reality, rather than considering that 'every brick and every stone in this beautiful building represents pain and suffering, along with countless drops of sweat, and hours of exhausting labor, contributed by the backs and foreheads and bones of the impoverished,' we tend to forget these things completely, and simply admire the impressive temple itself, without granting one appreciative thought to its humble creator, whose generous heart and empty wallet it represents.

This is a place filled with libraries and schools. St. Paul has three public libraries that together hold around forty thousand books. The city has one hundred and sixteen school buildings and spends more than seventy thousand dollars annually on teachers' salaries.

There is an exceptionally impressive railway station; it's so large that it initially seemed somewhat excessive in terms of size; however, after a few months it became clear that the mistake was definitely in the opposite direction. The error will be corrected.

The town sits on elevated terrain, rising approximately seven hundred feet above sea level. Its height provides expansive views of the river and surrounding lowlands from its streets.

It's truly a remarkable town, and construction is still ongoing. Every street is blocked with building materials, which are being assembled into houses as quickly as possible to clear space for more construction—since other people are eager to start building as soon as they can use the streets to stack their bricks and supplies.

How profound and striking is the idea that the first pioneer of civilization, the advance guard of progress, is never the steamboat, never the railroad, never the newspaper, never the Sunday school, never the missionary—but always whiskey! This is indeed the case. Examine history carefully; you will observe this pattern. The missionary arrives after the whiskey—I mean he shows up after the whiskey has already arrived; then comes the struggling immigrant, carrying ax and hoe and rifle; then, the merchant; then, the chaotic influx of people; then, the gambler, the outlaw, the bandit, and all their partners in vice of both genders; and then, the clever fellow who has purchased an old land grant that encompasses all the territory; this attracts the legal profession; the vigilance committee summons the undertaker. All these various interests establish the newspaper; the newspaper launches politics and a railroad; everyone joins together to construct a church and a jail—and suddenly, civilization is permanently established in the region. But whiskey, you understand, served as the advance guard in this beneficial endeavor. It invariably does. It was characteristic of a foreigner—and forgivable in a foreigner—to be unaware of this fundamental truth, and drift away into astronomy to find a metaphor. But if he had been familiar with the facts, he would have said—

Westward the Jug of Empire takes its way.

This remarkable pioneer leader reached the area where St. Paul now stands in June 1837. Indeed, on that date, Pierre Parrant, a Canadian, constructed the first cabin, opened his jug, and started selling whiskey to the Indians. The outcome lies before us.

Everything I've described about St. Paul—its freshness, vitality, rapid growth, prosperity, intelligence, impressive and solid architecture, and overall dynamism and energy—applies equally to its close neighbor, Minneapolis, with the added distinction that Minneapolis is the larger of the two cities.

These remarkable towns were located ten miles apart just a few months ago, but they were expanding so rapidly that they might already be connected now, operating under a single mayor. In any case, within the next five years there will certainly be such a solid chain of buildings extending between them and linking them together that a visitor won't be able to determine where one Siamese twin ends and the other begins. When combined, they will have a population of two hundred and fifty thousand people, assuming they maintain their current rate of growth. Therefore, this population center at the head of Mississippi navigation will begin competing in terms of size with that population center at its mouth—New Orleans.

Minneapolis is located at St. Anthony Falls, which extends across the river for fifteen hundred feet and drops eighty-two feet—a source of water power that has been developed through engineering into something of immeasurable commercial value, though this development has somewhat diminished the Falls as a scenic attraction or as a picturesque backdrop for taking photographs.

Thirty flour mills produce two million barrels of the finest flour each year; twenty sawmills generate two hundred million feet of lumber annually; additionally, there are woolen mills, cotton mills, paper and oil mills; along with sash, nail, furniture, barrel, and countless other factories. The major flour mills here and at St. Paul employ the 'new process' and crush the wheat by rolling it, rather than grinding it.

Sixteen railroads converge in Minneapolis, with sixty-five passenger trains arriving and departing each day. In this city, just as in St. Paul, journalism flourishes. The area supports three major daily newspapers, ten weekly publications, and three monthly magazines.

There is a university with four hundred students, and even better, its valuable work isn't limited to educating just one gender. The city has sixteen public schools housed in buildings that cost $500,000 to construct, serving six thousand students with one hundred and twenty-eight teachers. Additionally, there are seventy churches currently operating, with many more planned for the future. The banks have a combined capital of $3,000,000, and the town's wholesale trading business reaches $50,000,000 annually.

Near St. Paul and Minneapolis, you'll find several interesting attractions—Fort Snelling, a fortress perched on a river bluff one hundred feet above the water; Minnehaha Falls, White Bear Lake, and other notable sites. The stunning Minnehaha Falls are already famous enough—they don't need any promotion from me. White Bear Lake is less well-known. It's a gorgeous body of water that has become a summer destination for the state's wealthy and fashionable residents. The lake features a clubhouse and hotel equipped with modern amenities and conveniences, elegant summer homes, and excellent opportunities for fishing, hunting, and scenic drives. While there are about a dozen smaller summer retreats scattered around St. Paul and Minneapolis, White Bear Lake stands out as the premier destination. Associated with White Bear Lake is an absolutely ridiculous Indian legend. I wish I could resist the urge to include it here, but I simply don't have the willpower. The guidebook identifies who preserved this legend and praises his 'skillful writing.' So without any additional commentary or hesitation, let me unleash this so-called skillful writer upon you, the reader—

A LEGEND OF WHITE-BEAR LAKE.

Every spring, for perhaps a century, or as long as there has been a nation of Native Americans, an island in the middle of White-bear Lake has been visited by a band of Indigenous people for the purpose of making maple sugar.

Tradition tells us that many springs ago, while on this island, a young warrior fell in love with and courted the daughter of his chief, and it is also said that the maiden loved the warrior in return. He had repeatedly been denied her hand in marriage by her parents, with the old chief claiming that he was not brave, and his elderly wife calling him a woman!

The sun had set once again over the sugar-bush, and the bright moon climbed high into the clear blue sky, when the young warrior took down his flute and ventured out alone, ready to sing the story of his love once more. The gentle breeze softly stirred the two colorful feathers in his headdress, and as he climbed onto the trunk of a slanted tree, wet snow dropped heavily from his feet. When he lifted his flute to his lips, his blanket slipped from his well-built shoulders and fell partially onto the snow below. He started his haunting, passionate love song, but soon realized he was getting cold, and as he reached back for his blanket, an invisible hand gently placed it on his shoulders—it was the hand of his beloved, his guardian angel. She sat down beside him, and for now they were content, because the Indian possesses a heart capable of love, and in this dignity he shows the same nobility as in his natural freedom, which makes him a child of the wilderness. According to the legend, a large white bear, perhaps believing that arctic snows and harsh winter conditions existed everywhere, began traveling south. Eventually he reached the northern shore of the lake that now carries his name, walked down the bank, and made his way silently through the deep, heavy snow toward the island. It was during the following spring that the lovers came together. They had abandoned their original hiding place and were now sitting among the branches of a massive elm tree that stretched far out over the lake. (This same tree still stands today and draws widespread curiosity and fascination.) Afraid of being discovered, they spoke in barely audible whispers, and now, wanting to return to camp at a reasonable hour to avoid raising suspicion, they were just getting up to leave when the young woman let out a scream that echoed to the camp. Leaping toward the young brave, she grabbed for his blanket but lost her footing and tumbled, pulling the blanket with her into the massive arms of the fierce beast. Immediately every man, woman, and child from the group rushed to the bank, though none carried weapons. Screams and cries rose from every throat. What could be done? Meanwhile, this white and savage creature held the terrified maiden in his enormous grip, playing with his valuable prize as though he was accustomed to such situations. One thunderous cry from the warrior lover rang out above the screams of hundreds from his tribe, and racing to his tepee he seized his trusted knife, returned in what seemed like a single leap to the scene of terror and panic, charged out along the leaning tree to where his beloved had fallen, and jumping with the rage of an enraged panther, attacked his target. The beast turned, and with one swipe of his massive paw brought the lovers face to face, but the next instant the warrior, with one thrust of his knife blade, opened the red channels of death, and the dying bear loosened his grip.

That night, neither the group nor the lovers could sleep, and as both young and old danced around the dead monster's body, the brave warrior received another feather, and before the next moon had appeared, he had gained a living treasure for his heart. For many years afterward, their children played on the white bear's hide —which is how the lake got its name—and both the maiden and the warrior long remembered the terrifying scene and rescue that united them, because Kis-se-me-pa and Ka-go-ka could never forget their frightening encounter with the enormous beast that came so close to sending them to the happy hunting-ground.

It's a confusing story. First, she tumbled down from the tree— both she and the blanket; and the bear caught her and held her close—her and the blanket; then she fell back up into the tree— leaving the blanket behind; meanwhile the lover goes whooping and hollering home and returns armed, climbs the tree, leaps down onto the bear, the girl jumps down after him—apparently, since she was up in the tree—takes her place back in the bear's arms along with the blanket, the lover plunges his knife into the bear, and saves—what, the blanket? No—nothing like that. You get all worked up and excited about that blanket, and then suddenly, just when a satisfying ending seems about to happen, you're completely disappointed—nothing gets saved except the girl. But nobody cares about the girl; she's not the main focus of the legend. Still, there you are stuck, and there you have to stay; because even if you lived a thousand years you'll never find out who ended up with the blanket. A dead person could come up with a better legend than this one. I don't mean someone recently dead either; I mean someone who's been dead for weeks and weeks.

We hit the trail home, and within a few hours found ourselves in that incredible Chicago—a city where they're constantly rubbing the magic lamp, summoning genies, and devising and accomplishing new impossibilities. It's futile for the occasional visitor to attempt keeping pace with Chicago—she outpaces his predictions faster than he can form them. She remains perpetually fresh; because she's never the same Chicago you witnessed when you traveled through previously. The Pennsylvania railroad whisked us to New York without falling behind schedule by even ten minutes anywhere along the route; and there concluded one of the most delightful five-thousand-mile trips I have ever been fortunate enough to experience.

Appendix

Appendix A

(FROM THE NEW ORLEANS TIMES DEMOCRAT OF MARCH 29, 1882.)

JOURNEY OF THE TIMES-DEMOCRAT'S RELIEF BOAT THROUGH THE FLOODED AREAS

It was nine o'clock on Thursday morning when the 'Susie'

departed the Mississippi and entered Old River, which is now known as the mouth of the Red. Moving upstream on the left side, floodwater was rushing through and over the levees at the Chandler plantation, the northernmost location in Pointe Coupee parish. The water had completely submerged the property, even though the levees had failed only a short time earlier. The livestock had been collected on a large flat-boat, where the animals were crowded together without food as we passed by, waiting for a boat to pull them to safety. On the right side of the river lies Turnbull's Island, which contains a large plantation that was once considered among the most productive in the State. The water had previously spared it during typical floods, but now vast expanses of water marked the only evidence of where fields once existed. Portions of the protective levee's top remained visible in places, but almost all of it lay underwater.

The trees have taken on greener leaves since the water flooded in, and the forest appears bright and fresh, but this pleasing sight is offset by the endless expanse of water. We travel mile after mile, seeing nothing but trees standing with water reaching up to their branches. A water-turkey occasionally rises and flies ahead into the long corridor of silence. A canoe sometimes emerges from the bushes and crosses the Red River on its journey to the Mississippi, but the somber-faced paddlers never turn their heads to glance at our boat. The chugging of the boat provides music in this gloom, which affects a person in the most unusual way. It is not the darkness of dense forests or deep caves, but a distinctive kind of solemn quiet and striking reverence that compels one to acknowledge it. We passed two Black families on a raft moored among the willows this morning. They were clearly from the prosperous class, as they had a store of grain and three or four pigs with them. Their rafts measured about twenty feet square, and in front of a makeshift shelter, soil had been laid down where they built their fire.

The current flowing down the Atchafalaya was extremely fast, with the Mississippi displaying a clear preference for that direction, which only needs to be witnessed to confirm the belief that the river is desperately trying to find a shorter route to the Gulf. Small watercraft like boats, skiffs, and pirogues are in high demand, and many have been stolen by criminal groups who take them to wherever they can get the best price. According to what Mr. C. P. Ferguson told me—a plantation owner near Red River Landing whose property has just been flooded—there is considerable hardship behind that location. The local residents had abandoned all expectations of a levee break there, since the upper levee had held for such a long time, and when it finally happened they were completely helpless. On Thursday several people were rescued from trees and cabin rooftops and brought to safety, with many others still waiting to be saved.

One doesn't truly value the sight of dry land until they've journeyed through a flood. When you're out at sea, you don't expect or search for it, but here, with leaves rustling in the breeze, dark forest pathways, and rooftops barely peeking through, you expect to see it. In truth, even a cemetery would be welcomed, as long as the burial mounds rose above the water. The river's presence here can only be detected by a gap in the trees, and that's the only indication. The width stretches from Fort Adams on the Mississippi's left bank to the shore of Rapides Parish, covering roughly sixty miles. Much of this area had been farmed, especially along the Mississippi and behind the Red River. When we reached the Red River itself, a powerful current was flowing straight across it, moving in the same direction as the Mississippi.

After traveling for several hours, they reached Black River. As soon as they entered the area, evidence of devastation became apparent. All the willow trees lining the riverbanks had been completely stripped of their foliage. One local resident that your correspondent interviewed explained that he had owned one hundred and fifty cattle and one hundred pigs. When the floodwaters first appeared, he had attempted to drive his livestock to the higher ground in Avoyelles, thirty-five miles away, but he ended up losing fifty of his cattle and sixty of his pigs. Black River maintains its scenic beauty, even with its banks submerged underwater. A thick forest of ash, oak, gum, and hickory trees creates an almost impenetrable barrier along the shoreline, and when you can catch a glimpse through the tree-lined pathways, only the faint silhouettes of far-off tree trunks are barely visible in the darkness.

A few miles upstream, the water along the banks reached a full eight feet in depth, and on every side, the tops of cabins could be seen still standing firm against the powerful current. Scattered throughout the area, an overturned cabin was encircled by driftwood, creating what might become the foundation of a future island.

To conserve coal, since it was impossible to obtain that fuel at any location that would be reached during the expedition, they kept watch for a wood supply. When they rounded a point, a canoe, expertly paddled by a young man, darted out, and in its front sat a fifteen-year-old girl with a lovely face, striking black eyes, and modest behavior. The boy requested a paper, which was tossed to him, and the pair steered their small vessel out into the wake of the boat.

Soon a young girl, no more than twelve years old, paddled out in the tiniest canoe and maneuvered it with all the skill of an experienced river traveler. The child looked more like a Native American than a white youngster, and she laughed when someone asked if she was scared. She had grown up in a small boat and could navigate anywhere. She was heading out to gather willow leaves for the livestock, and she gestured toward a nearby house that had three inches of water covering its floors. Behind the house, a raft roughly thirty feet square was tied up, with a makeshift fence constructed on top of it, and within this enclosure stood about sixteen cattle and twenty pigs. The family wasn't complaining much, except about the potential loss of their animals, and they quickly brought over a load of firewood on a flatboat.

From this point to the Mississippi River, fifteen miles away, there isn't a single spot of dry land above water, and stretching westward for thirty-five miles there's nothing but the river's floodwaters. Black River had risen during Thursday, the 23rd, by one and three-quarters inches, and was still climbing at nightfall. As we travel upstream, homes appear more often, though they're still miles apart from each other. Nearly all of them stand empty, with their outbuildings swept away by the flood. Adding to the somber atmosphere, almost every living creature seems to have fled, and you can't hear a single bird's song or squirrel's chatter in this desolate landscape. Occasionally a sullen gar fish will slap its tail above the surface before vanishing back into the river, but aside from this, everything remains silent—the silence of destruction. Drifting downstream comes a freshly whitewashed chicken coop, followed by a bundle of carefully split fence rails, or a door alongside a swollen animal carcass, solemnly watched over by a pair of buzzards, the only birds visible, which feed on the remains as the current carries them along. A picture frame containing a cheap print of a mounted soldier, floating past, told the story of some home invaded by the waters and stripped of this simple decoration.

At nightfall, since it wasn't safe to continue traveling, they searched for a spot near the woods and secured the boat to a tall gum tree for the night.

A beautiful crescent moon cast gentle light across the forest and river, creating a scene that would make a wonderful landscape painting if an artist could somehow capture it on canvas. The engine noise had stopped, the hissing of released steam had quieted, and complete silence surrounded us—what incredible silence it was! Typically in a nighttime forest you can hear frogs calling, insects buzzing, or branches falling, but here nature was completely quiet. The shadowy depths, like aisles in a great cathedral, produced no sound at all, and even the gentle splashing of the flowing water faded away.

At dawn on Friday morning, everyone was awake and ready, and we began our journey up the Black River. The morning was beautiful, and the river, which runs remarkably straight, displayed its most stunning appearance. The hawthorn blossoms filled the air with their delightful fragrance, and several birds sang cheerfully along the riverbanks. The trees were larger here, and the forest appeared much older than what we had seen downstream. We passed more fields than we had encountered closer to the river's mouth, but the same scene repeated itself—smokehouses floating out in the pastures, slave quarters clustered haphazardly around oak trees, and modest homes with only their rooflines visible above the water. The sun rose in magnificent shades of deep red, and the trees glowed brilliantly in their various tones of green. Not a single patch of dry ground could be seen anywhere, and the water seemed to be rising deeper and deeper, as it now reached up into the branches of the tallest trees. Throughout the area, the willow trees along the banks had been stripped of their leaves, showing how long the residents had been working to gather this feed for their livestock. We asked an elderly man in a small boat how the willow leaves were working out for his cattle. He paused in his work and shook his head gravely as he answered: 'Well, sir, it's enough to keep them alive and that's all we can hope for, but it's hard on the pigs, especially the young ones. They're dying off at an alarming rate. But what choice do we have? It's all we have left.'

At thirty miles above where Black River meets the Mississippi, floodwater stretches from Natchez on the Mississippi all the way to Louisiana's pine hills—a span of seventy-three miles—and virtually every spot lies under at least ten feet of water. The current flowing up the Black River moves toward the west. This westward flow has become so pronounced that Red River waters have been pushed down toward the Calcasieu region, while Black River waters now flow into the Red River about fifteen miles above the Black's mouth—something even the most experienced steamboat captains have never witnessed before. All the water we can see comes entirely from the Mississippi.

Up to Trinity, or more precisely Troy, which lies just a short distance downstream, nearly all the residents have evacuated, with those who stayed behind having sufficient supplies for their immediate personal requirements. However, their livestock are experiencing hardship and dying at an alarming rate, since being confined on rafts and the feed they receive creates conditions that lead to disease.

After a brief stop, we continued on and soon reached an area filled with open fields and cabins scattered densely throughout the landscape. Here we witnessed even more scenes of suffering. Inside their homes, the residents had constructed makeshift platforms using boxes as supports, placing their furniture on top of these elevated surfaces. The bedposts had been cut down at the top since the ceiling hung no more than four feet above this improvised floor. The structures appeared extremely unstable and seemed ready to float away at any moment. Near these dwellings, cattle stood with water reaching up to their chests, completely motionless. They remained fixed in their positions, standing patiently as they waited for rescue to arrive. The scene was heartbreaking, and these unfortunate animals would certainly perish unless they were quickly saved. Cattle behave differently from horses in this particular way. When a horse realizes that no help is coming, it will swim away to search for food, while cattle will remain exactly where they are until exhaustion overtakes them and they collapse into the water and drown.

At twelve-thirty, someone called out from a flatboat

positioned inside the bank's edge. We turned around and pulled up alongside, and General York climbed aboard. He was currently working on evacuating livestock and gave the Times-Democrat boat a warm welcome, explaining that there was an urgent need for assistance. He confirmed that the reports of suffering were not overstated in any way. People were living in conditions that were almost impossible to comprehend. The water had risen so high that their homes were in serious danger of being washed away. The flood had already climbed so high that it was nearing the rooflines, and once water reaches this level, houses face immediate risk of being swept away. Should this happen, many lives will be lost. The General praised the brave efforts of numerous residents who were trying to rescue their livestock, though he estimated that a full twenty-five percent had already died. Twenty-five hundred people had already been given food supplies from Troy on Black River, and he had managed to tow many cattle to safety, but a vast number still remained in desperate need of help. The water level was now eighteen inches higher than it had been in 1874, and no dry land existed between Vidalia and the Catahoula hills.

At two o'clock, the 'Susie' arrived at Troy, located sixty-five miles upstream from where Black River meets its mouth. On the left bank, Little River flows into the main waterway; just past that point, the Ouachita joins in, while the Tensas enters from the right side. These three waterways come together to create Black River. Troy, or at least part of the town, sits on and around three massive Indian burial mounds that are round in shape and rise approximately twelve feet above the current water level. Each mound measures roughly one hundred and fifty feet across, and they stand about two hundred yards from one another. All the houses have been constructed in the spaces between these ancient mounds, which means every building experiences flooding that reaches eighteen inches deep on the ground floors.

These elevated areas, constructed by native peoples hundreds of years ago, serve as the only places of safety for miles around. When we reached them, we discovered they were packed with livestock, all of which appeared emaciated and could barely remain standing. The animals were all mixed together—sheep, pigs, horses, mules, and cattle. One of these mounds has served as a cemetery for many years, and today we observed gaunt cows resting against the marble headstones, peacefully chewing their cud after eating corn provided by General York. Here, just as in the areas below, we noticed the extraordinary expertise of the women and girls in handling the smaller canoes. Children were navigating these extremely unstable boats with the casual confidence of experts.

General York has implemented a comprehensive system for providing relief assistance. He personally inspects each location where help is requested, assesses what needs to be accomplished, and then charters two boats with flat-bottomed vessels to send them quickly to the area, where livestock are loaded and transported to the pine hills and higher ground of Catahoula. He has established Troy as his base of operations, and boats arrive at this location to obtain their supply of feed for the cattle. On the far side of Little River, which splits off to the left from Black River, and positioned between it and the Ouachita, lies the town of Trinity, which faces the constant threat of complete destruction. It sits at a much lower elevation than Troy, and the water reaches eight to nine feet deep inside the buildings. A powerful current flows through the town, and it's surprising that all of the structures haven't been swept away already. The people living in both Troy and Trinity have received care, though some of their livestock still require food supplies.

As soon as the 'Susie' arrived at Troy, she was handed over to General York and placed under his command to carry out relief work more efficiently. Almost all of her supplies were unloaded onto one of the elevated areas to make her lighter, and she was directed downstream to help those below. At Tom Hooper's property, several miles from Troy, a large flatboat carrying approximately fifty head of livestock was taken under tow. The animals were given food and soon recovered some of their strength. Today we continue to Little River, where the suffering is most severe.

DOWN BLACK RIVER

Saturday Evening, March 25.

We began our journey down Black River quite early in the morning, guided by General York, with the goal of rescuing whatever livestock we could reach. As we traveled downstream, a flat-bottomed boat being towed was positioned in a central location, and from there men used poles to navigate it behind the plantations, gathering animals wherever they could be found. In the upper level of a cotton gin building, seventeen animals were discovered, and after constructing a walkway, they were led down onto the flat without any trouble. Taking a small boat with the General, your reporter was rowed up to a modest two-room house where water stood two feet deep on the floors. In one of the larger rooms, the horses and cattle of the property were crowded together, while in the other room, Widow Taylor and her son sat on a platform they had built above the floor. One or two dugout canoes floated around in the room, ready to be used whenever needed. When the flat was brought up to the house, the wall had to be cut away as the only way to get the animals out, and the cattle were herded onto the boat. General York, as he did in every situation, asked if the family wanted to leave, telling them that Major Burke from 'The Times-Democrat' had sent the 'Susie' upriver for exactly that purpose. Mrs. Taylor expressed her gratitude to Major Burke but said she would try to hold on. The extraordinary attachment these people have to their homes is completely beyond understanding. Just downstream, at a location sixteen miles from Troy, we received word that Mr. Tom Ellis's house was in danger, with his entire family inside. We immediately steamed to that location, and a heartbreaking scene awaited us. Looking out from the portion of a window that remained above water was Mrs. Ellis, who was in poor health, while at the doorway stood her seven children, the eldest not yet fourteen years old. One side of the house had been given over to the work animals, about twelve head, along with pigs. The family lived in the adjacent room, where the water came within two inches of the bed frame. The stove was submerged, so cooking was being done over a fire built on top of it. The house seemed ready to collapse at any moment: one end was sinking, and the entire structure looked like nothing more than a fragile shell. As our boat came around, Mr. Ellis emerged in a dugout canoe, and General York informed him that he had come to help; that 'The Times-Democrat' boat was available to him and would immediately transport his family to higher ground, and that on Monday a flat would come for his livestock, as they would be occupied until then. Despite the terrible situation he and his family faced, Mr. Ellis was reluctant to leave. He said he thought he would wait until Monday and take the chance that his house might collapse. The children gathered around the doorway appeared perfectly calm, seeming to care little about the danger surrounding them. These are just two examples among many others. After weeks of hardship and suffering, people still hold fast to their homes and only leave when there isn't enough space between the water and the ceiling to build a platform to stand on. It seemed impossible to understand, yet their love for their old home was stronger than their desire for safety.

After departing from the Ellis property, the next location they reached was the Oswald property. At this site, the flat was pulled up next to the gin-house where fifteen animals were standing in floodwater; even though they were positioned on raised platforms, their heads extended above the top of the doorway. It proved impossible to remove them without cutting away part of the front wall; therefore, axes were put to use and an opening was created. Following considerable effort, the horses and mules were safely loaded onto the flat.

At every location where we stop, there are consistently three, four, or even more dugout boats arriving, carrying reports about livestock in other areas that require assistance. Despite the reality that many people had already moved portions of their animals to higher ground some time earlier, a substantial number of livestock still remains, which General York, who is working with relentless determination, will successfully transport to the pine-covered hills by Tuesday.

Throughout the Black River region, the steamboat 'Susie' has been visited by numerous plantation owners, whose stories echo the same tales of hardship and devastation that have already been shared. An elderly planter who has lived along the river since 1844 stated that he had never witnessed such a severe flood, and he was convinced that more than a quarter of all livestock had perished. Fortunately, the residents prioritized saving their work animals first, and whenever they could locate horses and mules, these animals were moved to secure locations. The flooding, which continues to rise and increased by two inches just last night, forces them to relocate the animals to higher ground in the hills; this is precisely why General York's efforts are so tremendously valuable. From dawn until well into the evening, he travels back and forth throughout the area, offering encouragement through his compassionate words and providing clear-headed guidance on what actions need to be taken. One disturbing account about a particular merchant in New Orleans is being shared all along the river. It seems that for several years, the planters had been conducting business with this person, and many of them maintained credit balances with him. When the flooding occurred, they sent letters requesting coffee, meal, and other basic necessities that were desperately needed. No replies to these letters arrived, so additional letters were sent, yet these longtime customers, whose plantations were completely submerged, were denied even the essential supplies needed to survive. It goes without saying that this merchant is now extremely unpopular along Black River.

The hills mentioned as the refuge location for the people and livestock on Black River are located in Catahoula parish, twenty-four miles from Black River.

After loading the barge with cattle, we brought aboard the family of T. S. Hooper, consisting of seven people, who could no longer stay in their home, and we are now transporting them up Little River to the hills.

THE FLOOD STILL RISING

Troy: March 27, 1882, noon.

The flood here is rising approximately three and a half inches every twenty-four hours, and rains have begun which will make this worse. General York now believes that our efforts should focus on saving lives, since the rising water has put many houses in danger. We plan to head up the Tensas in a few minutes, and then we will come back and go down Black River to rescue families. There isn't enough steam transportation here to handle this emergency. The General has chartered three boats, with barges being towed behind them, but the need for these vessels to move livestock to safety is greater than they can handle quickly. Everyone is working around the clock, and the 'Susie' barely stops for more than an hour anywhere. The rising water has put Trinity in a dangerous situation, and people expect that some of the houses might float away at any moment. Troy sits a little higher, but all the buildings are still in the water. Reports have come in that a woman and child have been swept away downstream from here, and two cabins have floated off. The people living in them are the same ones who refused to leave the day before yesterday.

You wouldn't believe how completely passive these people are.

No news has yet been received about the steamboat 'Delia,' which is believed to be the vessel that sank in yesterday's storm on Lake Catahoula. She should have arrived here by now, but she hasn't shown up. Even the mail service here is extremely unreliable, so I'm sending this letter by small boat to Natchez to make sure it reaches you. It's impossible to obtain accurate information about previous harvests and other matters, since the people who knew much about these subjects have left, and those who stayed behind don't have much knowledge about this area's agricultural production.

General York wants me to tell you that the amount of food supplies previously sent needs to be doubled and delivered immediately. It's impossible to make any accurate assessment because people are escaping to the hills due to how quickly the water is rising. The local residents are in such a state of panic that you can only truly understand it by witnessing it firsthand, and total chaos has taken hold.

If supplies are allocated for any specific area around here, there's no guarantee they would actually be distributed, so everything should be sent to Troy as a central hub, and the General will ensure proper distribution. He has requested one hundred tents, and if everyone currently moving heads to the hills, two hundred tents will be needed.

Appendix B

THE MISSISSIPPI RIVER COMMISSION

The situation in this wealthy valley of the Lower Mississippi, right after the war and in the years that followed, represented one of the most devastating and regrettable consequences of the conflict. The artificial wealth tied up in enslaved people was not only justly eliminated, but much of the infrastructure that had relied on slave labor was also destroyed or severely damaged, particularly the levee system.

It might have been expected by those who haven't studied the matter that such crucial improvements as building and maintaining the levees would have been taken on immediately by the various states. But what can a state accomplish when its people are subjected to interest rates ranging from 18 to 30 percent, and are also forced to pledge their crops in advance of even planting them, at these same rates, just for the privilege of buying all their supplies at 100 percent profit?

The control of the Mississippi River requires only a brief examination to make it completely clear that if such an undertaking is to be attempted at all, it must be handled by the federal government and cannot be accomplished by individual states. The river must be managed as a single entity; its control cannot be achieved through a fragmented or divided system of administration.

The states that have a particular interest in this matter are not capable of working together effectively to carry out the necessary operations. The work must start far upstream, at least as far as Cairo if not even further upriver, and must be executed according to a unified overall plan that covers the entire length of the river.

You don't need technical or scientific expertise to understand the basic facts of this situation if you're willing to spend some time and attention on the matter. When a Mississippi River commission has been formed, like the current one, made up of highly capable individuals from various professions and backgrounds, shouldn't we consider accepting their judgment as definitive, at least as far as any theoretical approach to construction or management can be considered final?

It's important to remember that this board includes General Gilmore, General Comstock, and General Suter from the United

States Engineers; Professor Henry Mitchell, who is the most qualified expert on hydrography matters, from the United States Coast Survey; B. B. Harrod, Louisiana's State Engineer; James B. Eads, whose successful work with the jetties at New Orleans demonstrates his expertise, and Judge Taylor from Indiana.

It would be arrogant for any individual, no matter how skilled, to challenge the decision of such a distinguished panel.

The improvement method recommended by the commission aligns perfectly with both engineering experience and natural observations of how nature meets our needs. Just as trees grow naturally and tend to fall across slopes when their foundations are weakened, thereby supporting riverbanks and creating adequate channel depth with some stability, the engineer's plan similarly relies on timber, brush, and encouraging forest growth as its primary elements. The proposal involves narrowing excessively wide areas using brushwood dikes that start low but gradually rise higher as river sediment accumulates beneath their protection, eventually sloping them back at an angle that allows willows to flourish. This work includes numerous technical details regarding the design of these protective dikes and their arrangement to create a sequence of settling pools, but describing these would unnecessarily complicate the overall concept. Throughout most of the river, narrowing structures won't be necessary, but nearly all banks on the inner curves must be protected against stream erosion, while many opposite banks need defense at vulnerable locations. The construction aimed at this protective purpose can be broadly called revetment work, which will also primarily use brushwood woven into continuous mats or twisted into wire mesh. This surface treatment has proven successful on the Missouri River, and in several cases, these installations have accumulated so much sediment and become so densely covered with willows that they can be considered permanent fixtures. To secure these mats, small amounts of rubble stone will be used, and in certain situations, the graded slope between high and low water levels will need partial or complete stone paving.

Anyone who has traveled along the Rhine will have noticed operations similar to those we just mentioned; in fact, most European rivers that flow through their own sediment deposits have needed comparable treatment to support navigation and farming.

The levee represents the ultimate achievement in riverbank protection, though it doesn't always need to be directly connected to the bank. It can be positioned a short distance back from the protected riverbank, but it essentially serves as the necessary protective barrier. The river during flood season and the river during low water periods cannot be aligned and forced to work together in creating a single lasting channel without complete management of all water levels. Even unusually high water levels must be planned for, since these would put the levee at risk, and once flooding gets behind the protective structures, it would destroy them as well.

Based on the general principle that a river's local slope results from and measures the resistance of its riverbed, it's clear that a narrow and deep stream should have less slope because it has less frictional surface relative to its capacity—meaning less perimeter relative to the cross-sectional area. The ultimate effect of levees and revetments that confine floods and bring all river stages into alignment is to deepen the channel and reduce the slope. The initial effect of levees is to raise the water surface, but this increases flow velocity, which inevitably causes the channel to enlarge. If this enlargement cannot occur at the banks' expense, the bottom must erode, and the waterway's shape must improve to allow this flow with less water level rise. The actual experience with levees on the Mississippi River, without attempting to stabilize the banks, has been positive. No one can doubt, based on the evidence provided in the commission's reports, that if the earliest levees had been built with bank revetments and made complete, we would have today a river navigable during low water periods and surrounding land protected from flooding.

Naturally, it would be unreasonable to assume that a controlled river could ever reduce its flood gradient enough to eliminate the need for levees entirely, but experts believe that through this sideways containment, the river as a waterway can be enhanced in its structure so that even those unusual floods caused by multiple tributaries rising simultaneously will be able to flow through without breaking levees of standard height. The fact that the true capacity of a channel cutting through sedimentary deposits relies on its performance during flood conditions has been demonstrated repeatedly, though this capacity doesn't account for extraordinary yet recurring flood events.

It's hardly worthwhile to consider the plans for reducing Mississippi River floods by creating new outlets, since these dramatic proposals have only appealed to people who haven't thought them through, and they receive no support from engineers. If the riverbed were made of cast iron, using openings for excess water might be necessary; but since the bottom is flexible, and the best type of outlet is a single deep channel, which achieves the smallest ratio of perimeter to cross-sectional area, there couldn't be a more impractical treatment method than multiplying escape routes.

In the previous statement, we have tried to summarize in as brief a space as the significance of the topic would allow, the basic elements of the problem and the main characteristics of the proposed improvement method that the Mississippi River Commission has adopted.

The author feels it may be somewhat presumptuous to try to present the facts about an undertaking that requires the highest level of scientific expertise; however, this is a matter that concerns every citizen of the United States, and it represents one of the reconstruction methods that should be supported. This is a war claim that involves no private profit, and no compensation except for one of the instances of destruction caused by war, which the people of the entire country may rightfully repair.

EDWARD ATKINSON.
Boston: April 14, 1882.

Appendix C

RECEPTION OF CAPTAIN BASIL HALL'S BOOK IN THE UNITED STATES

As we near the end of our journey, I feel compelled to discuss once more what I believe to be one of the most striking characteristics of the American national character: their extraordinary sensitivity and defensiveness regarding anything said or written about them. Perhaps the most notable example I can offer is the reaction that Captain Basil Hall's 'Travels in North America' provoked among nearly every type of reader. The book's publication created what could only be described as a moral earthquake, and the tremors it sent through the nation's consciousness, from one end of the Union to the other, had not yet subsided when I departed the country in July 1831, a full two years after the initial impact.

I was in Cincinnati when these volumes were published, but I didn't get a copy until July 1830. One bookseller I approached told me he had stocked a few copies before he realized what kind of book it was, but once he understood its content, nothing could convince him to sell another copy. Other booksellers must have been less concerned about such matters, though, because the book was being read everywhere—in cities, towns, villages, and small communities, on steamboats and stagecoaches—and it created an uproar unlike anything I had ever witnessed before.

A passionate craving for approval and a tender sensitivity to criticism have always been viewed, I believe, as endearing qualities of character; however, the state into which the publication of Captain Hall's work plunged the republic clearly demonstrates that these emotions, when taken to extremes, create a weakness that borders on helplessness.

It was absolutely amazing to hear men who showed reasonable judgment on other topics express their opinions on this matter. I had never encountered any situation where the common sense typically found in national criticism was so completely overwhelmed by emotion. I'm not referring to the lack of justice or fair and generous interpretation—these qualities were probably too much to hope for anyway. Other nations have been described as overly sensitive, but the citizens of the Union seem to have no protective layer at all; they flinch at the slightest criticism unless it's sweetened with praise. It wasn't particularly shocking, then, that they would react irritably to the sharp and powerful observations of a traveler whose words they knew people would pay attention to. What made this situation truly remarkable were two things: first, the extreme intensity of the fury they worked themselves into, and second, the childish nature of the explanations they invented to justify what they imagined was harsh treatment they had received.

Not satisfied with simply claiming that the books contained absolutely no truth from start to finish (a statement I heard made almost every time they were discussed), the entire nation began working to uncover the reasons why Captain Hall had come to the United States and why he had published his book.

I've heard people say with complete certainty and seriousness, as if they were quoting from an official government document, that Captain Hall had been deliberately sent by the British Government specifically to counter England's increasing respect for the United States Government—that he had come on a mission funded by the treasury, and that he was simply following orders when he criticized anything about America.

I'm not sharing this as mere gossip from a small social circle; I'm convinced that a very large portion of the country holds this belief. This remarkable people are so deeply convinced that they cannot be observed without being admired, that they refuse to accept the possibility that anyone could honestly and sincerely find anything to criticize about them or their nation.

Many of the American reviews are, I believe, well known in England, so I don't need to quote them here. However, I sometimes found it surprising that none of them ever considered translating Obadiah's curse into classic American English. If they had done so, by putting (he, Basil Hall) in brackets instead of (he, Obadiah), it would have saved them a great deal of trouble.

I can barely express the intense curiosity I felt when I finally sat down to read through these massive volumes; even less can I adequately convey my astonishment at what they contained. To say that I discovered not a single exaggerated claim throughout the entire work doesn't even begin to capture it. Anyone familiar with the country cannot help but recognize that Captain Hall actively searched for things to praise and appreciate. When he offers compliments, he does so with clear enjoyment; and when he criticizes, he does so with obvious hesitation and restraint, except when purely patriotic motives compel him to speak frankly about what his country needs to understand for its own good.

In reality, Captain Hall experienced the country under the most favorable circumstances possible. Armed with letters of introduction to the most prominent figures, and carrying the even more powerful endorsement of his own distinguished reputation, he was welcomed with full ceremonial honors and formal reception from coast to coast throughout the Union. He witnessed the nation at its finest, dressed up for company, and had little to no chance of seeing it in its natural, unpolished state, with all its flaws and shortcomings exposed, as my family and I frequently did.

Captain Hall certainly had excellent opportunities to familiarize himself with the structure of the government and its laws, while also receiving the finest oral commentary on these matters through conversations with the most prominent citizens. He made excellent use of these opportunities; nothing significant escaped his notice without receiving the kind of analytical attention that only an experienced and philosophical traveler can provide. This approach has made his volumes highly interesting and valuable; however, I am deeply convinced that if a person of equal insight were to visit the United States with no other means of understanding the national character than the ordinary everyday interactions of life, he would form an infinitely lower opinion of the country's moral atmosphere than Captain Hall appears to have developed; and I am strongly convinced that if Captain Hall had not exercised firm self-restraint, he would have expressed far deeper indignation than any he has voiced against many aspects of the American character, which he clearly understood well based on other evidence. His approach seems to have been to present just enough of the truth to leave his readers with an accurate impression, while causing the least amount of pain to the sensitive people he was writing about. He presents his own opinions and feelings, and allows readers to infer that he has solid reasons for holding them; but he spares the Americans the harsh criticism that a detailed account of the circumstances would have produced.

If someone decides to claim that some evil hatred toward twelve million strangers is the source of my viewpoint, I will have to endure it; and if this were simply a matter of pointless theorizing, I certainly wouldn't invite the criticism I'm bound to face for expressing it. But that's not the case.

. . . .

The honesty he shows and clearly feels, they misinterpret as

429

sarcasm or completely doubt; his reluctance to hurt people who have been kind to him, they contemptuously dismiss as pretense, and even though they must know perfectly well, deep down in their hearts, how much more he could have exposed about them than he actually chose to reveal; they convince themselves, and even pretend to believe, that he has overstated the flaws in their character and systems; when in reality, he has treated them with a level of gentleness that may be appropriate for him to show, regardless of whether they deserve it; while at the same time, he has worked very hard to highlight their good qualities whenever he could possibly find something positive to say.

Appendix D

THE UNDYING HEAD

In a remote part of the North lived a man and his sister, who had never seen another human being. The man rarely, if ever, had any reason to leave home; whenever he needed food, he would simply walk a short distance from their lodge and place his arrows in a specific spot with their points stuck in the ground. After telling his sister where he had put them, she would go out every morning to search and would always find each arrow piercing the heart of a deer. All she had to do then was drag the deer back to the lodge and prepare their meals. She lived this way until she reached womanhood, when one day her brother, whose name was Iamo, spoke to her: "Sister, the time is approaching when you will become ill. Listen carefully to what I'm telling you. If you don't follow my advice, it will likely cause my death. Take the tools we use to start our fires. Go some distance away from our lodge and build a separate fire there. When you need food, I will tell you where to find it. You must cook your own meals, and I will cook mine. When you become ill, don't try to come near the lodge, and

430

don't bring any of the tools you're using. Make sure you always keep the implements you need attached to your belt, because you never know when the time will arrive. As for me, I must manage as best I can." His sister promised to follow everything he had told her.

Shortly after, her brother needed to leave home. She was alone in her lodge, combing her hair. She had just untied the belt that held her tools, when suddenly the event her brother had warned her about happened. She rushed out of the lodge, but in her hurry she forgot the belt. Too frightened to go back, she stood outside for some time thinking. Finally, she decided to enter the lodge and retrieve it. She reasoned that her brother wasn't home, and she would only stay a moment to grab it. She went back inside. Rushing in quickly, she seized the belt and was heading out when her brother appeared. He understood what had happened. "Oh," he said, "didn't I tell you to be careful? But now you have killed me." She was about to continue on her way, but her brother said to her, "What can you do out there now? The accident has happened. Go inside, and stay where you have always stayed. And what will become of you? You have killed me."

He then removed his hunting clothes and equipment, and shortly afterward both of his feet began to turn black, making it impossible for him to move. Despite this, he continued to guide his sister on where to position the arrows so she would always have food available. The swelling kept getting worse and had now spread to his first rib, prompting him to say: "Sister, my time is coming to an end. You need to follow my instructions exactly. Look at my medicine bag with my war club attached to it. Inside are all my healing remedies, my war feathers, and my paints in every color. Once the swelling reaches my chest, you must take my war club. It has a sharp tip, and you will use it to cut off my head. After you separate it from my body, take the head and put its neck into the bag, which you need to open at one end. Then hang it back in its usual spot. Don't forget about my bow and arrows. Use one of the arrows to hunt for food. Bundle up the rest and tie them in my bag, then hang everything up so I can face toward the door. I'll talk to you from time to time, but not very often." His sister promised once more that she would do as he asked.

Soon his chest began to suffer. "Now," he said, "take the club and strike off my head." She felt frightened, but he urged her to find her courage. "Strike," he said, and a smile crossed his face. Gathering all her courage, she delivered the blow and severed the head. "Now," said the head, "place me where I instructed you." And with fear she followed all its instructions. Still alive, it gazed around the lodge as it always had, and it would direct its sister to visit certain places where it believed she could obtain the meat of various animals she required. One day the head spoke: "The time is approaching when I shall be released from this condition, and I will have to endure many terrible hardships. This is what the great spirit has ordained, and I must accept everything with patience." In this state we must leave the head.

In a certain part of the country was a village inhabited by a large and warlike band of Indians. In this village lived a family of ten young men who were brothers. It was in the spring of the year when the youngest of these brothers blackened his face and fasted. His dreams were favorable. After ending his fast, he went secretly to gather his brothers at night, so that no one in the village could overhear or discover the direction they planned to go. Though their drum could be heard, this was a common occurrence. After completing the usual ceremonies, he told them how encouraging his dreams had been, and that he had called them together to see if they would join him on a war expedition. They all answered that they would. The third brother from the eldest, known for his strange behavior, came forward with his war-club when his brother had finished speaking, and jumped up. "Yes," he said, "I will go, and this is how I will treat those I am going to fight," and he struck the post in the center of the lodge and let out a yell. The others spoke to him, saying: "Calm down, calm down, Mudjikewis, when you are in other people's lodges." So he sat down. Then, taking turns, they took the drum and sang their songs, and finished with a feast. The youngest told them not to whisper their plans to their wives, but to secretly prepare for their journey. They all promised to obey, and Mudjikewis was the first to agree.

The time for their departure was approaching. They received word to gather on a specific night, when they would leave right away. Mudjikewis spoke loudly, demanding his moccasins. His wife asked him several times why he needed them. "Besides," she said, "you're already wearing a good pair." "Hurry, hurry," he replied, "since you insist on knowing, we're going on a war expedition; so move quickly." In this way, he revealed the secret. That night they assembled and set out. Snow covered the ground, and they traveled through the entire night to prevent others from following them. When daylight came, the leader gathered snow and formed it into a ball, then threw it up into the air, saying: "This is how I saw snow falling in a dream, so that my tracks could not be followed." He instructed them to stay close together to avoid getting separated, as the snow began falling in very large flakes. Even walking near each other, they could barely see one another. The snow kept falling throughout that entire day and the night that followed, making it impossible for anyone to track them.

They had been walking for several days now, with Mudjikewis always staying at the back of the group. One day, he suddenly rushed forward and let out the saw-saw-quan, then struck a tree with his war-club, shattering it into pieces as if lightning had hit it. "Brothers," he said, "this is how I'll deal with those we're going to fight." The leader replied, "Easy, easy, Mudjikewis. The one I'm taking you to shouldn't be taken so lightly." Once again, he dropped back and thought to himself: "What! What! Who could this be that he's leading us to?" He felt afraid and remained quiet.

They traveled day after day until they reached a vast plain where human bones lay bleaching in the sun along its edges. The leader spoke: "These are the bones of those who came before us. No one has ever returned to tell the tragic story of what happened to them." Mudjikewis grew restless again and ran forward, letting out his usual yell. He approached a large rock that jutted up from the ground, struck it, and it crumbled to pieces. "Look, brothers," he said, "this is how I'll handle those we're going to fight." "Calm down, calm down," the leader said once more. "The one I'm leading you to cannot be compared to that rock."

Mudjikewis stepped back, lost in thought, wondering to himself: 'I wonder who this could be that he plans to attack,' and fear crept over him. They kept encountering the remains of warriors from the past who had ventured to the same destination they were heading toward, some of whom had managed to retreat only as far as the spot where they first discovered the bones—no one had ever made it back alive beyond that point. Eventually they reached a hill that rose above the surrounding land, and from there they could clearly see, resting on a far-off mountain, an enormous bear fast asleep.

The distance between them was enormous, but the creature's massive size made it clearly visible. "There," the leader said, "that's who I'm taking you to see. This is where our real troubles begin, because he's a mishemokwa and a manito. He possesses what we value most highly—the wampum—and to get it, the warriors whose bones we passed gave their lives. Don't be afraid. Be brave. We'll find him sleeping." The leader then moved forward and touched the belt around the animal's neck. "This is what we need to take," he explained. "It holds the wampum." They asked the eldest brother to try slipping the belt over the bear's head. The creature seemed to be sound asleep, showing no sign of being disturbed by their attempt to remove the belt. All their efforts failed until it was the second youngest's turn. He tried, and the belt moved almost completely over the monster's head, but he couldn't get it any further. Then the youngest brother, who was also the leader, made his attempt and succeeded. Placing the belt on the oldest brother's back, he said, "Now we have to run," and they took off. When one grew tired from carrying its weight, another would take over. They ran this way until they had passed all the bones of the previous warriors and were some distance beyond them. Looking back, they saw the monster slowly getting up. He stood there for a while before he noticed his wampum was missing. Soon they heard his thunderous howl, like distant thunder, slowly filling the entire sky. Then they heard him speak: "Who could have dared to steal my wampum? The earth isn't so big that I can't find them." He came down from the hill in pursuit. The earth shook violently with every leap he made, as if it were having convulsions. Very quickly he caught up to the group. However, they kept the belt, passing it from one to another and encouraging each other, but he was gaining on them rapidly. "Brothers," the leader said, "hasn't any of you ever dreamed during fasting of some friendly spirit who would help you as a guardian?" Complete silence followed. "Well," he continued, "while fasting, I dreamed of being in mortal danger when I saw a small lodge with smoke rising from its top. An old man lived there, and I dreamed he helped me. May that dream come true soon." He ran forward, giving a distinctive yell and a howl that seemed to come from deep in his stomach— what's called checaudum. Climbing onto higher ground, they saw it: a lodge with smoke curling from its top. This gave them all renewed strength, and they ran forward and entered it. The leader spoke to the old man sitting in the lodge: "Nemesho, help us. We ask for your protection because the great bear will kill us." "Sit down and eat, my grandchildren," the old man said. "Who is a great manito?" he asked. "There's no one but me. But let me look." He opened the lodge door and saw the furious animal approaching with slow but powerful leaps. He closed the door. "Yes," he said, "he truly is a great manito. My grandchildren, you're going to cost me my life. You asked for my protection, and I granted it, so whatever happens, I will protect you. When the bear reaches the door, you must run out through the other door of the lodge." Then, reaching to the side of the lodge where he sat, he brought out a bag and opened it. Taking out two small black dogs, he placed them in front of him. "These are what I use when I fight," he said. He began patting the sides of one of them with both hands, and it started to swell until it soon filled the lodge with its bulk and had enormous, strong teeth. When it reached full size, it growled, and instinctively jumped out the door to meet the bear, who would have reached the lodge in one more leap. A terrible battle began. The skies echoed with the howls of the fierce monsters. The remaining dog soon joined the fight. Following the old man's advice, the brothers escaped through the opposite side of the lodge as soon as the battle started. They hadn't gone far when they heard the dying cry of one dog, and soon after, the other. "Well," the leader said, "the old man will meet the same fate, so run—he'll be after us soon." They started running with renewed energy because they had eaten the old man's food, but very soon the bear came into sight and was rapidly gaining on them again. Once more the leader asked his brothers if they could do anything for their safety. Everyone remained silent. The leader ran forward and did as before. "I dreamed," he called out, "that when I was in great trouble, an old man who was a manito helped me. We'll see his lodge soon." Taking courage, they continued on. After traveling a short distance, they saw the lodge of the old manito. They entered immediately and asked for his protection, telling him a manito was chasing them. The old man set meat before them and said, "Eat! Who is a manito? There's no manito but me. There's no one I fear." The earth trembled as the monster approached. The old man opened the door and saw him coming. He closed it slowly and said, "Yes, my grandchildren, you've brought trouble upon me."

Getting his medicine bag, he took out his small war clubs made of black stone and told the young men to run through the other side of the lodge. As he handled the clubs, they grew very large, and the old man stepped outside just as the bear reached the door. Striking him with one of the clubs, it shattered into pieces, and the bear stumbled. Trying again with the other war club, that one also broke, but the bear fell unconscious. Each blow the old man delivered sounded like a thunderclap, and the bear's howls echoed until they filled the heavens.

The young men had been running for quite some time when they decided to look back. They could see the bear starting to recover from the beating he had received. First, he began moving his paws, and before long they watched him get back on his feet. The old man met the same terrible end as the first victim, as they could now hear his screams while he was being torn apart. Once again, the beast was chasing after them, rapidly closing the distance between them. Still not giving up hope, the young men continued their escape, but the bear had gotten so close that the leader turned to his brothers for help once more, though they were powerless to assist. "Well," he said, "my dreams are almost used up; I only have one left after this one." He stepped forward, calling upon his guardian spirit for assistance. "Once," he explained, "I had a dream where I was desperately fleeing and came upon a large lake. On its shore sat a canoe that was partially pulled out of the water, with ten paddles all ready for use. Don't be afraid," he called out, "we'll reach it soon." And everything happened exactly as he had described. When they arrived at the lake, they found the canoe with its ten paddles and quickly climbed aboard. They had barely made it to the middle of the lake when they spotted the bear reaching the water's edge. Standing up on his back legs, he surveyed the area in all directions. Then he waded into the water, but when he lost his balance, he turned around and began walking around the lake's perimeter. Meanwhile, the group stayed in the center, keeping still while they observed his actions. He walked the entire way around until he eventually returned to his starting point. Then he began drinking the lake water, and they could see the current flowing rapidly toward his open jaws. The leader urged everyone to paddle as hard as they could toward the far shore. When they were just a short distance from reaching land, the current had become so powerful that it pulled them backward, making all their attempts to reach safety completely futile.

Then the leader spoke again, instructing them to face their destiny with courage. "Now is the moment, Mudjikewis," he said, "to demonstrate your strength. Be brave and take your position at the front of the canoe; and when we get close to his mouth, see what damage your club can do to his head." Mudjikewis followed the command and prepared himself to strike; meanwhile, the leader, who was steering, guided the canoe straight toward the gaping mouth of the beast.

Moving quickly forward, they were about to enter his mouth when Mudjikewis delivered a powerful blow to the head and let out the saw-saw-quan. The bear's legs buckled beneath him, and he collapsed, dazed from the strike. However, before Mudjikewis could strike again, the creature expelled all the water it had consumed with such tremendous force that it launched the canoe at great speed toward the far shore. Immediately abandoning the canoe, they ran once more, continuing until they were completely worn out. The ground shook again, and soon they spotted the monster pursuing them relentlessly. Their courage faltered, and despair crept in. The leader pushed himself to lift their spirits through both his actions and encouraging words, and once again he asked if they could think of anything or do something to save themselves; and, just like before, everyone remained quiet. 'Then,' he declared, 'this is the final time I can call upon my guardian spirit. Now, if we fail, our destiny is sealed.' He rushed ahead, calling to his spirit with intense urgency, and released the yell. 'We will soon reach,' he told his brothers, 'the place where my final guardian spirit lives. I have tremendous faith in him. Do not, do not be frightened, or fear will paralyze your body. We will soon arrive at his lodge. Run, run,' he shouted.

Returning now to Iamo, he had remained in the same condition we had left him in, with his head instructing his sister on where to place the magic arrows in order to obtain food, and speaking only occasionally. One day his sister noticed the eyes of the head brighten, as though filled with joy. Finally it spoke. "Oh, sister," it said, "what a terrible situation you have caused me to be in! Soon, very soon, a group of young men will come and ask me for help; but unfortunately! How can I provide what I would have given so willingly? Still, take two arrows, and put them where you have always put the others, and have meat prepared and cooked before they get here. When you hear them approaching and calling my name, go outside and say, 'Unfortunately! it was long ago that an accident happened to him. I was responsible for it.' If they still come closer, invite them in, and serve meat to them. And now you must follow my instructions exactly. When the bear gets near, go outside and face him. You will take my medicine-sack, bows and arrows, and my head. You must then open the sack, and lay out in front of you my paints of every color, my war-eagle feathers, my bundles of dried hair, and everything else it holds. As the bear comes closer, you will take all these items, one after another, and tell him, 'This is my dead brother's paint,' and continue this way with all the other items, throwing each of them as far as you possibly can. The power within them will make him stumble; and, to finish destroying him, you will take my head, and you will also throw that as far away as you can, shouting loudly, 'Look, this is my dead brother's head.' He will then collapse unconscious By this time the young men will have finished eating, and you will call them to help you. You must then cut the body into pieces, yes, into tiny pieces, and scatter them to the four winds; because, unless you do this, he will come back to life again." She promised that everything would be done exactly as he instructed. She had just enough time to prepare the meat, when the voice of the leader was heard calling upon Iamo for help. The woman went outside and spoke as her brother had told her to. But the war party, being chased closely, arrived at the lodge. She welcomed them in, and served the meat to them. While they were eating, they heard the bear getting closer. Opening the medicine-sack and taking the head, she had everything ready for his arrival. When he appeared she did exactly as she had been instructed; and, before she had used up all the paints and feathers, the bear started to stumble, but, still moving forward, came right up to the woman. Speaking as she was told, she then grabbed the head, and threw it as far away from herself as she could. As it rolled across the ground, the blood, stirred by the emotions of the head during this horrific scene, poured from the nose and mouth. The bear, staggering, soon collapsed with a thunderous crash. Then she called for help, and the young men came running out, having somewhat recovered their strength and courage.

Mudjikewis stepped forward, let out a yell, and struck the creature with a powerful blow to the head. He continued this assault repeatedly until the head appeared to be nothing but a mass of crushed brains, while his companions worked as quickly as they could to cut the body into very small pieces, which they then scattered in all directions. While they were busy with this task, they happened to glance around at the places where they had thrown the flesh, and to their amazement, they witnessed an incredible sight: small black bears were springing to life and running off in every direction, bears just like the ones we see today. The entire countryside was quickly filled with these black creatures. It was from this enormous monster that the current race of bears first came into existence.

Having defeated their pursuer, they made their way back to the lodge. Meanwhile, the woman collected the tools she had been using along with the head and put them back into the sack. However, the head remained silent, likely exhausted from the tremendous effort it had taken to defeat the monster.

Having spent so much time and traveled across such a vast country during their escape, the young men abandoned any hope of ever returning to their homeland, and since game was abundant, they decided to stay where they were now. One day they moved some distance away from the lodge to hunt, leaving the wampum with the woman. They were very successful, and entertained themselves, as all young men do when alone, by talking and joking with each other. One of them spoke up and said, 'We have all this fun to ourselves; let us go and ask our sister if she will let us bring the head to this place, since it is still alive. It might be pleased to hear us talk and be in our company. In the meantime, take food to our sister.' They went and asked for the head. She told them to take it, and they brought it to their hunting grounds, and tried to entertain it, but only occasionally did they see its eyes shine with pleasure. One day, while busy in their camp, they were suddenly attacked by unknown Indians. The battle was long and bloody; many of their enemies were killed, but still they were outnumbered thirty to one. The young men fought desperately until they were all killed. The attacking party then retreated to higher ground, to gather their men, and to count the number of missing and dead. One of their young men had fallen behind, and, in trying to catch up with them, came to the place where the head was hanging. Seeing that it alone remained alive, he stared at it for some time with fear and surprise. However, he took it down and opened the sack, and was very pleased to see the beautiful feathers, one of which he placed on his head.

Starting out, it waved gracefully above him until he reached his group, where he threw down the head and sack, telling them how he had discovered it and that the sack was filled with paints and feathers. Everyone looked at the head and made fun of it. Many of the young men took the paint and painted themselves, and one member of the group grabbed the head by the hair and said—

"Look at yourself, you hideous creature, and see your war paint on the faces of the warriors."

But the feathers were so stunning that many of them also put them on their heads. Then they subjected the head to all sorts of disrespectful treatment, which resulted in the death of those who had worn the feathers. Then the chief ordered them to discard everything except the head. "We'll see," he said, "when we return home, what we can accomplish with it. We'll attempt to make it close its eyes."

When they arrived at their homes, they brought it to the council lodge and suspended it in front of the fire, securing it with soaked rawhide that would contract and tighten as the fire's heat dried it. "We'll see then," they declared, "whether we can make it close its eyes."

Meanwhile, for several days, the sister had been waiting for the young men to return with the head; finally, growing impatient, she went out to search for it. She discovered the young men lying within short distances of each other, dead and covered with wounds. Various other bodies were scattered in different directions around them. She looked for the head and sack, but they were nowhere to be found. She raised her voice and wept, and blackened her face. Then she walked in different directions until she came to the place where the head had been taken. There she found the magic bow and arrows, which the young men, unaware of their powers, had left behind. She thought to herself that she would find her brother's head, and came to a piece of rising ground, where she saw some of his paints and feathers. These she carefully gathered up and hung upon the branch of a tree until her return.

At dusk she reached the first lodge of a very large village. Here she used a charm that was common among Indians when they wanted to receive a kind welcome. When she approached the old man and woman of the lodge, they received her kindly. She explained her mission. The old man promised to help her, and told her the head was hanging in front of the council-fire, and that the chiefs of the village, along with their young men, watched over it constantly. The former were considered as manitoes. She said she only wanted to see it, and would be satisfied if she could just get to the door of the lodge. She knew she didn't have enough power to take it by force. 'Come with me,' said the Indian, 'I will take you there.' They went, and they sat down near the door. The council-lodge was filled with warriors, entertaining themselves with games, and constantly maintaining a fire to smoke the head, as they said, to make dry meat. They saw the head move, and not knowing what to think of it, one spoke and said: 'Ha! ha! It is starting to feel the effects of the smoke.' The sister looked up from the door, and her eyes met those of her brother, and tears rolled down the cheeks of the head. 'Well,' said the chief, 'I thought we would make you do something at last. Look! look at it—shedding tears,' said he to those around him; and they all laughed and made their jokes about it. The chief, looking around, and noticing the woman, after some time said to the man who came with her: 'Who do you have there? I have never seen that woman before in our village.' 'Yes,' replied the man, 'you have seen her; she is a relative of mine, and rarely goes out. She stays at my lodge, and asked me to let her come with me to this place.' In the center of the lodge sat one of those young men who are always eager, and fond of boasting and showing off before others. 'Why,' said he, 'I have seen her often, and it is to this lodge I go almost every night to court her.' All the others laughed and continued their games. The young man didn't know he was telling a lie to the woman's advantage, who by that means escaped.

She went back to the man's lodge and immediately began her

journey home to her own country. When she reached the place where the bodies of her adopted brothers were lying, she arranged them side by side with their feet pointing toward the east. She then took an ax that she had brought with her and threw it high up into the air, calling out, 'Brothers, get up from under it, or it will fall on you.' She did this three times, and on the third attempt, all the brothers came back to life and stood up on their feet.

Mudjikewis began rubbing his eyes and stretching himself. "Why," he said, "I have overslept myself." "No, indeed," said one of the others, "don't you know we were all killed, and that it is our sister who has brought us back to life?" The young men took the bodies of their enemies and burned them. Shortly after, the woman went to find wives for them in a distant country, though they didn't know where; but she returned with ten young women, whom she gave to the ten young men, starting with the eldest. Mudjikewis paced back and forth, worried that he might not get the one he liked. But he wasn't disappointed, for she was assigned to him. And they were well matched, for she was a female magician. They then all moved into a very large lodge, and their sister told them that the women must now take turns going to her brother's head every night, trying to untie it. They all said they would do so with pleasure. The eldest made the first attempt, and with a rushing noise she flew through the air.

As dawn approached, she came back. Her mission had failed, as she had only managed to untie a single knot. Everyone took their turn in order, and each person was able to undo just one knot during their attempt. However, when the youngest sister's turn came, she began working immediately upon reaching the lodge; even though the place had always been inhabited, the Indians were never able to see anyone there. For ten nights straight, the smoke had stopped rising properly and instead filled the entire lodge, forcing the occupants to flee outside. On this final night, they were all driven out completely, and the young woman successfully took the head with her.

The young people and the sister heard the young woman approaching high through the air, and they heard her calling out: 'Prepare our brother's body.' As soon as they heard this, they went to a small lodge where Iamo's blackened body lay. His sister began cutting the neck area where the head had been severed. She cut deep enough to make it bleed, while the others present rubbed the body and applied medicines to drive out the blackness. Meanwhile, the one who had brought the head cut the neck portion of it, causing that to bleed as well.

As soon as she arrived, they positioned it close to the body, and with the help of medicines and various other methods, they managed to restore Iamo to all his previous beauty and strength. Everyone celebrated the joyful end of their hardships, and after they had spent some time happily together, Iamo announced: 'Now I will distribute the wampum,' and taking the belt that held it, he began with the oldest, dividing it into equal shares. However, the youngest received the most magnificent and beautiful portion, since the bottom of the belt contained the most valuable and precious beads.

They were told that since they had all died once and been brought back to life, they were no longer mortal beings but had become spirits, and each was given different positions in the unseen world. However, only Mudjikewis's position was specifically identified. He was assigned to control the west wind, which is why he's commonly known as Kebeyun, and he would stay there forever. They were instructed to use their abilities to help the people living on earth, and to put aside the pain they had endured while obtaining the wampum and give generously to all. They were also told that the wampum should remain sacred to them; the light-colored beads or shells would represent peace, while the darker ones would bring about evil and war.

The spirits then, singing and shouting, flew away to their

homes in the heavens above; meanwhile, Iamo and his sister Iamoqua went down into the deep places below.

Thank You For Reading

You've Just Read a Piece of the Greatest Library Ever Rebuilt

Thank you for reading.

This book is one of thousands we're restoring, reimagining, and translating as part of the **Modern Library of Alexandria** — a global movement to preserve and share humanity's most important ideas.

What was once lost to fire and time is now rising again — not just as memory, but as living, breathing knowledge, freely accessible to all.

What You Can Do Next:

- **Keep Reading.**

  Discover more legendary works — in beautiful print, audiobook, or digital form — at LibraryofAlexandria.com.

- **Build Your Own Library.**

  Every title is available as a paperback, hardcover, or collectible boxset — at true printing cost. Craft a personal library worthy of display.

- **Spread the Light.**

  Share this book. Tell others about the movement. Help us translate every timeless work into every language, so no reader is ever left behind.

By finishing this book, you've already taken part in something extraordinary.

Join us at LibraryofAlexandria.com

Together, we're rebuilding the greatest library the world has ever known.

With appreciation,

The Modern Library of Alexandria Team

Visit:
www.libraryofalexandria.com
Or scan the code below:

www.ingramcontent.com/pod-product-compliance
Lightning Source LLC
Chambersburg PA
CBHW011401010726
47495CB00009B/2722